Evolving Dynamics of
Nuclear South Asia

Air Commodore **Tariq Mahmud Ashraf** (Retd)
Pakistan Air Force

KW
KNOWLEDGE WORLD

KW Publishers Pvt Ltd
New Delhi

ISBN 978-93-83649-10-5

Published in India by Kalpana Shukla

KW KNOWLEDGE WORLD

KW Publishers Pvt Ltd
4676/21, First Floor, Ansari Road, Daryaganj, New Delhi 110002
Phone: +91 11 23263498/43528107
Email: knowledgeworld@vsnl.net • www.kwpub.com

Printed and Bound in India

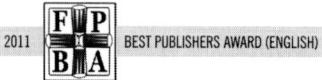

2011 F P B A BEST PUBLISHERS AWARD (ENGLISH)

Dedicated

To my late parents:

Honorary Lieutenant Colonel (Retired) Muhammad Ashraf
and Mrs. Fatima Ashraf

To my beloved wife of over 34 years: Afshan "Kitty" Tariq
To our eldest son Zomir Tariq who left us in his infancy,
our remaining three sons

Sheraz Tariq

Hassam Tariq and

Zaid Tariq

their lovely wives

Camilla "Noor" Sheraz and Taha Hassam

and above all,
to our beloved eldest grand-daughter

Aroob Lillian Afshan Ashraf

Contents

Introduction

    vii

Section I: South Asia on the Road to the Bomb

1. Regional Imperatives for the Nuclearisation of South Asia   2
2. US Ambivalence and South Asian Nuclear Programmes   10
3. Pakistan, China and the Bomb   32
4. Chinese Assistance to Pakistan's Nuclear Weapon Design   46

Section II: Pakistan's Nuclear Weapons Control System

5. Pakistan's Nuclear Weapons Control System (NWCS)   60
6. Overcoming the Weaknesses of Pakistan's NWCS   72

Section III: Pakistan's Doctrinal Thinking

7. A Nuclear Policy for Pakistan   92
8. Nuclear Weapons Development and Employment Options for Pakistan   100
9. Essential Elements of Pakistan's Nuclear Doctrine   122
10. "Minimality" and "Credibility" in the South Asian Nuclear Milieu   144
11. The Impact of Nuclearisation on Pakistan's Military System   156
12. Assessing Pakistan's Nuclear First Use Option   188

Section IV: Indian Doctrinal Thinking

13. Transformation in Doctrinal Rethinking of the Indian Armed Forces   196
14. Indian Army's "Cold Start" Doctrine   208
15. Indian Navy's "Maritime" Doctrine   218
16. Indian Air Force's "Aerospace" Doctrine   224
17. Draft Indian Nuclear Doctrine   236
18. The Indian Ballistic Missile Programme   242

Section V: Employment Considerations & Impact

19. Divergence in South Asian Nuclear Doctrinal Thinking   252

20. Nuclearisation and South Asian Strategic Stability   262

21. Will Nuclear SSMs ever be used in South Asia?   280

22. Simulating a South Asian Holocaust   290

23. Air Power Imbalance: Pakistan's Achilles Heel   304

24. Nuclear CBMs in South Asia   314

25. Accepting South Asian Nuclearisation   322

26. The Nuclear Transparency Ladder   328

27. The South Asian Nuclear Military Balance   334

28. Nuclear Terrorism and Pakistan   344

29. Security of Pakistan's Nuclear Arsenal   360

Annexes and References   372

Reference A   Agreement between India & Pakistan on Prohibition of Attack Against Nuclear Installations and Facilities

Reference B   The Lahore Declaration

Reference C   Joint statement

Reference D   Memorandum of Understanding

Reference E   Statement issued after meeting of Pakistan NSC on 05 September, 2013

Reference F   Amended draft Indian Nuclear Doctrine 2003

Introduction

This book is a collection of my writings on the Nuclearisation of South Asia and its continuing impact on the regional politics of this volatile region.

Right at the outset, I must mention that these ramblings of mine that constitute the contents of this volume are purely my own personal thoughts and ideas. These must not be construed in any way to represent the views of any Government agency or organisation, including those that I have had the honour and privilege of being associated with during my lifetime of service.

Despite having been in the military for over three decades, the exposure to higher education in the UK at this late a stage of my life has convinced me of the fact that the resolution of international disputes lies in negotiated settlement and not through resort to the employment of the military instrument, particularly the nuclear one.

For the betterment of our future generations in South Asia, I hope and pray that we are able to amicably resolve our mutual disputes and continue to exist with amity, peace, honour, mutual respect and dignity.

Islamabad
January 10, 2014

Tariq Mahmud Ashraf
Air Commodore (Retired)
Pakistan Air Force

Section I

South Asia on the Road to the Bomb

01 Regional Imperatives for the Nuclearisation of South Asia[1]

Introduction

Ever since the first nuclear weapon was dropped over Hiroshima in 1945 to bring the Second World War to an end, the spread of nuclear weapons has been at the forefront of international relations and affairs. The political and military clout enjoyed by the five declared nuclear powers and the restraints imposed by them on other countries going nuclear have made the acquisition of this capability even more desirable and lucrative for the rest of the world. In 2001, the US Secretary of Defence reported to the Congress that eight Third World countries, "either have or may be near to acquiring nuclear weapons."[2] The nations who have seriously attempted to join the nuclear bandwagon have been motivated by a variety of disparate factors; the desire to achieve military superiority in their geographical region, to enhance their status in the world, to ensure national survival or to balance the conventional superiority of hostile nations in the region.

The aspect of nuclear proliferation which is most destabilising for the world is that even though nuclear capability is being aspired to by a host of nations for regional reasons, the achievement of this capability is of significance to the entire world and carries with it enormous global implications. The development of ballistic missiles and the dangers of nuclear fallout have made nuclear proliferation the concern of the entire world. While advocating the Star Wars missile defence plan during his 1992 State of the Union address, President Bush said, "We must have this protection because too many people in too many countries have access to nuclear arms."[3] The adverse impact on the influence and clout of the erstwhile nuclear states is also a major issue because the emergence of a new nuclear power would inexorably alter the existing global balance of power. Nuclear proliferation, therefore, even at the regional level, is a global issue which needs to be addressed at the international level.

This chapter aims to suggest measures which must be taken to contain the spread of nuclear weapons in South Asia. It presents an analysis of why the major nations in the region felt it necessary to go nuclear, how did they go about attaining nuclear capability, what threat does a nuclear capable South Asia pose to world peace and what can the rest of the world do about it? This chapter generally touches upon global nuclear non-proliferation issues, while specifically addressing nuclear weapon proliferation in the South Asian region with emphasis on suggesting ways and means to arrest this trend.

Regional Imperatives for Nuclearisation of South Asia

Ever since the British left India in 1947, the subcontinent has been one of the principal trouble spots of the world. In recent years, few regions have seen more violent conflict than South Asia.[4] In their relatively short independent history, India and Pakistan have fought three major wars and the recent disturbances in Kashmir have brought them to the brink of yet another conflict. The irreconcilable differences between India and Pakistan stem as much from their religious differences as from their ideological antipathy. Their rivalry has been further exacerbated by the inequality that exists between the two countries in terms of territorial expanse, population and resources. While India is a huge country with a population of over a billion, Pakistan is only 1/4 its size in area and has only 1/6 of its population. This imbalance has emboldened Indian leaders and made them overtly aggressive and belligerent while forcing Pakistan to embark upon a road of militarisation to ensure her security and territorial integrity in the face of the Indian threat. Because of their differing threat perceptions, both the countries have starkly different reasons for developing nuclear weapons.

India was prompted by a range of motives in her quest to achieve nuclear weapons capability. "These have included concerns over the nuclear threat from the People's Republic of China, aspirations for regional pre-eminence and international recognition, and, during the 1980s, the desire to maintain a clear edge over Pakistan's growing nuclear potential."[5] India has always sought global status as a major world power[6] and most Indians think that their country has never been accorded the respect which its size and power deserve. In their opinion, achieving nuclear weapons capability would herald the emergence of India on the world power stage as a force to be reckoned with, and would contribute greatly to India attaining her rightful position in the world. In Nehru's words, "Leaving the three big powers, the USA, the Soviet Union and China aside for the moment, look at the world. There are many advanced and highly cultured countries. But if you peep into the future, the obvious fourth power in the world is India."[7]

Though India considers Pakistan to be her foremost and most implacable threat in the region, her primary aim in going nuclear was to counter the Chinese threat. Coming in the immediate aftermath of their 1962 military defeat at the hands of China, the explosion of a nuclear device by China in 1964 put enormous pressure on the Indian government. This internal pressure was instrumental in the Indian government's decision to embark on the development of a nuclear weapons capability. According to B. K. Nehru, the then Indian Ambassador to the USA, "There is a great pressure on the Indian government to explode a nuclear bomb. This pressure has come after the Chinese nuclear explosion ... ."[8] Added to this internal pressure, was the visualised threat of an emerging Sino-Pak coalition against India.[9]

The Indian desire to go nuclear had regional as well as global connotations. It expected to balance China as a force in the region, dominate Pakistan and attain a place of importance in the international community. With the threat from China and Pakistan balanced or removed, India would be well on its way to becoming a world power since there is no other significant force in South Asia which could hinder this process. India's regional ambitions have been more than amply demonstrated by its recent military interventions in Sri Lanka and the Maldives as well as the imposition of an economic blockade on Nepal when the small Himalayan state ventured to display a slight element of independence in its foreign policy.

From the Pakistani perspective, the development of a nuclear capability has been necessitated by Pakistan's "motivation to acquire a nuclear deterrent to provide a sense of immunity from potential military aggression by India."[10] The unfavourable imbalance in conventional weaponry forced Pakistan to believe that "the only safeguard against major aggression is the deterrent power of the nuclear weapon."[11] It is no surprise, therefore, that Pakistan's nuclear weapons development programme gained impetus immediately after the Indian peaceful nuclear explosion (PNE) of 1974.

Pakistan feels that being nuclear weapons capable would make it a significant contender for the leadership of the Islamic world and also serve to unite the divided Islamic nations. Pakistan's late Prime Minister, Bhutto lent further credence to this widely publicised view of an Islamic bomb when he stated, "The Christian, Jewish and Hindu civilisations have this (nuclear) capability. The Communist powers also possess it. Only the Islamic civilisation is without it, but this position is about to change."[12]

Suffering from an almost psychotic and myopic fear of India, the Pakistani populace has been led to believe by the ruling elite that it is only by developing a viable nuclear capability that Pakistan can thwart Indian hegemonic designs. It is not surprising, therefore, that "Pakistan's capacity to defend itself against India is also a domestic political issue, which any national leader can shy away from only at his own peril."[13] This domestic pressure is so strong that any political government which even contemplates cancelling the nuclear programme is likely to find itself out of office the next day.

The enormous burden of attempting to match Indian conventional military might over the last several decades has not been easy for Pakistan. Moreover, "Conventional defence not only has proven inadequate for Pakistan, it has also proved to be a heavy financial burden. Despite modernisation of equipment, conventional military doctrines cannot in themselves provide the visible deterrence ... ."[14] It is thought that the availability of a credible nuclear deterrent will permit Pakistan to reduce its expenditure on conventional defence and as such contribute to the strengthening of the beleaguered Pakistani economy.

Indian Nuclear Development Programme

Though India embarked immediately after independence on a peaceful nuclear research programme, its public stance was one of unequivocally rejecting the development of nuclear arms. In the words of Prime Minister Nehru, "... whatever might happen, whatever the circumstances, we shall never use this atomic energy for evil purposes ... ."[15] Three major events, however, were to have a significant impact on Indian nuclear policy: "the Chinese nuclear test in October 1964; Nehru's death; and international negotiations on a nuclear non-proliferation treaty."[16] The pressure on post-Nehru governments to respond to Chinese nuclear weapons became too intense to be neglected since none of the succeeding Prime Ministers enjoyed Nehru's political stature. Shastri, Nehru's immediate successor, "is believed to have launched a programme to reduce the lead time needed to build nuclear arms to six months."[17] In a major departure from past official statements, he stated that he supported the development of nuclear explosives, provided they were for peaceful purposes. Considering that peaceful nuclear explosives are essentially indistinguishable from nuclear weapons, Shastri thus gave official sanction for the development of an Indian nuclear weapon.

Indira Gandhi, who took over power from Shastri in 1966 also declared India's desire to develop peaceful nuclear explosives. Moreover, by refusing to sign the Non-Proliferation Treaty in 1968, India retained the option to build nuclear weapons. In its efforts to develop this peaceful nuclear explosive, India was at an advantage since its peaceful nuclear programme was fairly advanced at that time and it also had a pool of highly trained scientists and engineers available to it. In spite of all this, the Indian PNE of 1974 came as a shock not only to Pakistan but also to the Western countries who had exported nuclear expertise to India.

Though by calling it a PNE, India managed to emerge relatively unscathed after the 1974 explosion, its nuclear programme suffered a major setback. "The test brought some short-lived prestige to India but it also moved her into the category of those non-nuclear weapon states (NNWS) whose nuclear programmes were deeply suspect."[18] The reluctance of the Western nations from providing any further assistance in the nuclear field forced India to go it alone. In these efforts at indigenous nuclear development, India was helped by the USSR which provided two reactors to it free from any safeguards. An important aspect of going it alone was that none of India's subsequent indigenous ventures in the nuclear field were subject to any international safeguards. Though India has not conducted any further nuclear tests, "its nuclear potential has increased significantly in comparison to its ability to produce one bomb per year in 1974."[19] In 1985, with the commissioning of the Dhruva research reactor, India gained the ability to produce weapons grade plutonium free from all safeguards. In the same year, it started to separate unsafeguarded plutonium at the Tarapur reprocessing plant. Most of the Indian nuclear installations are free from any safeguards and "taken together, the capabilities of these installations could permit India to manufacture enough plutonium for more than 40 weapons each year."[20] According to unofficial estimates, India probably had enough plutonium for 40-60 weapons by mid-1990.[21]

India's successful testing of an intermediate range ballistic missile (IRBM) in May 1989 added further to the international concern about her long-term nuclear ambitions. Christened Agni, the IRBM can deliver a payload of 2,200 pounds (1,000 kg) over 1,550 miles (2,500 km). Strategically speaking, this missile could reach even the main cities on the Chinese East coast. For shorter range tactical usage, the indigenously developed nuclear capable Prithvi missile (150 miles range) has already been ordered by the Indian army, albeit with a conventional warhead. Additionally, India "is also reported to have acquired beryllium, to have produced tritium, and to be working on a hydrogen bomb."[22]

Pakistan's Nuclear Development Programme

Pakistan was a late starter in the nuclear field and has always lagged behind India by almost 15-20 years. At the time of its military defeat in 1971, Pakistan had only one Canadian supplied nuclear reactor and a small research reactor, both of which were under International Atomic Energy Agency (IAEA) safeguards. There is no evidence to indicate that any Pakistani government prior to 1971, had any serious nuclear ambitions.

After losing the conventional war against India in 1971, Pakistani leaders realised that their country could never match India's conventional might. They also realised that no other country including the superpowers was ever likely to intercede on their behalf against India.[23] These two factors contributed greatly to Pakistan's decision to embark on a nuclear weapons development programme. This programme gained impetus after India's PNE in 1974 and in the same year Pakistan signed a deal with France for a nuclear re-processing plant. The nuclear climate in the world, however, had soured quite a bit after the Indian explosion and fearing that Pakistan would also follow India on the proliferation path, USA prevailed upon France to renege on this deal. Having failed to obtain nuclear expertise through legitimate means, Pakistan embarked upon a programme to procure it clandestinely. Even though it abandoned the easier route to the bomb through plutonium usage and embarked upon the more difficult uranium enrichment process, Pakistan proved almost unstoppable. Pakistan's nuclear weapons development efforts got a significant boost when a Pakistani scientist working on a nuclear enrichment project in Holland returned to Pakistan bringing with him not only the plans of the plant but also a list of the major equipment suppliers. In early 1984, it was announced that Pakistan had the capability to produce enriched uranium. In February 1992, Pakistan's Foreign Ministry issued the first formal acknowledgement that Pakistan has "the elements which, if put together, would become a device."[24] According to unofficial estimates, Pakistan now has the capability to assemble 5-10 nuclear weapons.[25]

Unlike India which has a significant civilian nuclear power infrastructure, Pakistan's only achievement in the nuclear arena has been the development of the bomb. Considering the acute power shortage that it suffers from, it is likely that having created the minimum military deterrent, Pakistan will embark on a programme to harness nuclear power for civilian purposes. Additionally, though not as advanced in its ballistic missile development programme as India, Pakistan has already tested its first indigenous 180 miles range surface-to-surface missile in February 1989.

Nuclear Proliferation in South Asia and the Threat to World Peace

Given the instability which has been an essential ingredient of South Asian geopolitics since 1947 and the deep-rooted hatred and mistrust which characterises the bilateral relations between India and Pakistan, another conventional conflict in the region in the near future cannot be ruled out. What is going to be different, however, is that being outnumbered conventionally, Pakistan may be forced to use the nuclear option as a weapon of last resort forcing India to retaliate in kind. Such an eventuality would have grave regional and global consequences.

Having seen the successful development of nuclear weapons in South Asia, several other third world countries may be lured to follow suit. This could not only spark off regional nuclear arms races but would also have an extremely adverse effect on global security and peace. The eventuality which scares the West most, is the possible though highly unlikely prospect of Pakistan exporting its nuclear expertise to other Islamic countries.

With both India and Pakistan actively pursuing the development of ballistic missiles, there exists a distinct possibility of their nuclear assets being employed in extra-regional contingencies. This is more applicable to India which is going to actively pursue its goal of becoming a regional power wielding global influence. In these endeavours to achieve regional primacy, India is bound to be challenged by China.

Notes

1.   The contents of this chapter have been extracted from an essay titled "Controlling

Nuclear Proliferation in South Asia" that the author wrote while undergoing the Advanced Staff Course at the Royal Air Force Staff College, Bracknell, UK in 1992. This essay went on to be declared the best research essay written by a non-British officer on the course and the author was awarded the coveted "Andover Prize" for it. Since this essay predates South Asia's overt nuclearisation by almost six years, it must be read from that perspective. Readers might find statements such as "The eventuality which scares the West most, is the possible though highly unlikely prospect of Pakistan exporting its nuclear expertise to other Islamic countries" might sound very perceptive and almost visionary when viewed against the backdrop of the recent unearthing of incidents of nuclear proliferation involving Dr. Abdul Qadeer Khan, Pakistan and Libya.

2. *Defence Monitor*, "Stopping the Spread of Nuclear Weapons," p. 2.

3. *Defence Monitor*, p. 1.

4. *Time Magazine*, January 27, 1992, p. 18.

5. *Spector*, "Nuclear Ambitions," p. 63.

6. Dunbar, *India in Transition*, p. 55.

7. As quoted by Aliuddin in *Pakistan's Nuclear Dilemma*, p. 7.

8. As quoted by Ziba Moshaver in *Nuclear Weapons Proliferation in the Indian Subcontinent*, p. 37.

9. Ispahani, Pakistan: *Dimensions of Insecurity*, p. 60.

10. Jones, *Small Nuclear Forces*, p. 41.

11. Fischer, *Stopping the Spread of Nuclear Weapons*, p. 209.

12. As quoted by Moshaver, op. cit., p. 71.

13. Jones, op cit., p. 41.

14. Mazari, *The Nuclear Issue—Options for Pakistan*, p. 45.

15. As quoted in Moshaver, op. cit., p. 28.

16. Ibid., p. 33.

17. Spector, op. cit., p. 64.

18. Fischer, op. cit., p. 93.

19. Spector, op. cit., p. 45.

20. Ibid., p. 72.

21. *Defence Monitor*, p. 3.

22. *Defence Monitor*, p. 3.

23. Ispahani, op cit., p. 37.

24. *Defence Monitor*, p. 3.

25. Ibid., p. 3.

02 US Ambivalence and South Asian Nuclear Programmes[1]

Introduction[2]

The South Asian region is an area of the world with growing economic and strategic significance. India, in particular, offers a market of over one billion people, a well-developed high technology sector, and a large pool of skilled labour. It is also the world's largest democracy and is viewed by US and Western officials as a potentially valuable counterweight to China, which the US administration considers to be a "strategic competitor." Pakistan, the other main country in South Asia, is plagued by political uncertainty and economic turmoil that could undermine stability in both South Asia and the Middle East.

The South Asian region is also fraught with the danger of a nuclear war. Both India and Pakistan maintain active nuclear and missile programmes, and both are producing fissile materials for nuclear weapons. Neither of the countries has signed either the Non-Proliferation Treaty (NPT) or the Comprehensive Test Ban Treaty (CTBT), although they adhere to self-imposed moratoriums on nuclear tests. Indo-Pakistan tensions over the disputed territory of Kashmir remain high, and in May 2001, the Indian military conducted large-scale war game that included nuclear attack scenarios. Given this combination of nuclear build-ups, security tensions, and mistrust, the possibility that an armed skirmish over a territory such as Kashmir could escalate to the nuclear level—either intentionally or by accident—remains dangerously high.

Twenty-two previously classified US Government documents that have been made public recently have been analysed in this chapter due to their relevance to the nuclear weapons programmes of India and Pakistan. The salient conclusion that emerges from the contents of these documents is that the US has always maintained an ambivalent stance towards nuclear proliferation in South Asia. It has looked the other way and ignored all the goings-on when it has suited her interests and has victimised India and Pakistan when it suited her.

Document 1: State Department Instruction: "Indian Capability and Likelihood to Produce Atomic Energy," June 29, 1961 (Secret)[3]

The oldest document in the archive dates back to 1961. In an instruction issued to its various embassies that are relevant to and concerned with the events of the South Asian region, the State Department asks that these offices should collect and despatch information about India's nuclear energy programme and its intentions regarding the development of nuclear weapons. In 1961, Prime Minister Jawaharlal Nehru was strongly opposed to nuclear warfare, although India had a very active civilian nuclear energy programme. However, many foreign policy analysts considered it likely that India would eventually choose to develop a nuclear weapons capability. The US used various means to monitor India's nuclear plans and activities. The importance accorded to these reports is obvious when one considers the sentence wherein the State Department stipulates that this is a continuing requirement. The message says, "Posts should consider this as a continuing requirement to be reported upon as pertinent information becomes available."[4]

Document 2: Memorandum for the Secretary of Defence: "The Indian Nuclear Problem: Proposed Course of Action," October 23, 1964, attached to Letter from Robert McNamara to Dean Rusk, October 28, 1964 (Secret)[5]

This document, which has been declassified in response to a Freedom of Information Act (FOIA) request, is a memorandum from the Secretary of Defence Robert McNamara to the Secretary of State Dean Rusk in which the former encloses the comments received from the Joint Chiefs of Staff (JCS) regarding Indian nuclear issues. This document is significant in that this is the first such document related to South Asian nuclear development that is from the period in the immediate aftermath of China's first nuclear weapons test. The JCS support earlier US official statements providing assurances for non-nuclear states against nuclear attack, but oppose any measures on behalf of India that could alienate Pakistan by saying, "The JCS consider that it is most important that no actions be taken which could alienate US allies, especially Pakistan."[6] This is understandable since at that time Pakistan was a vital member not only of the CENTO but also the SEATO pact with India being a notable omission from both. In fact the two wings of Pakistan were at that time serving as a sort of a link between CENTO and SEATO Pact countries. The memo notes that additional assurances under discussion are *general in nature* and permit US *flexibility of response*. The Joint Chiefs argue that the US should not support Soviet guarantees, because they feared that such a move could lead to increased Soviet influence within India's armed forces. It is significant that this document pertains to the period after the Sino-Indian war of 1962 which led to a significant flow of US military aid to India and possibly contributed to the progressive alienation of Pakistan and its ultimate withdrawal from the US sponsored security alliances in the region. Despite the fact that the US Government was involved in militarily supporting India at that time, the US military did not desire the complete alienation of Pakistan whom they considered as a key ally in the region. All this, however, was to change in the aftermath of the September 1965 India-Pakistan war during which the US, being forced in a position to choose sides, opted to remain detached.

Document 3: Letter from John G. Palfrey, Atomic Energy Commission, to Ambassador Llewellyn E. Thompson, November 23, 1964, with attached report: "Discussion Paper on Prospects for Intensifying Peaceful Atomic Cooperation with India (Confidential)[7]

This letter gives an indication that the relationship between the US Atomic Energy Commission and its Indian counterpart had been established a long time back. Mr. Palfrey, in the opening remarks of his letter, refers to the close relationship that Dr. Homi Bhabha, the "Father of the Indian Nuclear Programme" had developed with them. Mr. Palfrey writes, "As you know, the Commission has developed a rather close relationship with Dr. Bhabha over the years and we believe this relationship and channel of communication can serve a useful purpose in our becoming more aware and perhaps influencing Indian plans in nuclear energy."

Two significant events contributed to the US Government wooing India and providing it with nuclear wherewithal for peaceful purposes; firstly, the fact that Communist China had successfully tested her nuclear weapons and secondly, the fact that India and China had been involved in a military conflict. Mr. Palfrey alludes to the "China" factor in his letter when he says, "the commission has considered possible forms of cooperation with India in peaceful uses of atomic energy which might serve to offset the propaganda effects of the Chinese nuclear device by increasing the stature of India in the eyes of the less developed countries." Interestingly, even in the days of the CENTO/SEATO alliances when Pakistan was an acknowledged and confirmed ally, this statement indicates an underlying desire on the part of the Americans to develop and strengthen India as a counter to China— something that we are seeing happening nowadays.

Although the purported reason for providing India with nuclear technology was "peaceful" some of the proposals included in this document definitely went far beyond the peaceful use of nuclear energy. This document proposes the following main areas of Indo-US nuclear cooperation:
- Cooperative programme on the recycling of Plutonium
- Thorium Recycle
- Joint Nuclear Desalting Project
- Project Plowshare
- Construction of Commercial Nuclear Power Stations

- Cooperation on an Advanced Prototype Reactor to be located in India
- Radioisotopes
- Fostering Trombay as a Regional Centre
- International Scientific Conference to be held at Trombay
- Possible Assignment of US AEC Scientific Representative to India

The commissioner of the Atomic Energy Commission sends the State Department proposals for US cooperation with India on peaceful uses of nuclear energy, in the belief that enhancing India's scientific prestige might dissuade it from developing its own nuclear weapons in response to China's first nuclear test. Among the collaborative projects suggested are the recycling of plutonium as fuel for India's nuclear reactors, cooperative "Plowshare" projects (nuclear explosions for civil uses), and reactor construction.

Interestingly, the proposal document states, "As of late, there has been a great deal of speculation (due to remarks made by Dr. Bhabha) that India might elect to embark on Plowshare device development programme as a 'cover' and rationalisation for a nuclear weapons programme. This appears to be a highly remote possibility due to technical and economic considerations as well as the recent statements made by Mr. Shastri disavowing any intention on the part of the Indian Government to embark on a nuclear weapons programme." As if the recommendations contained in his proposed agenda for nuclear cooperation with India were not enough in themselves to ensure India's embarking on a nuclear weapons programme, Mr. Palfrey, exhibiting the typical tone of naiveté that Americans adopt when it suits them, goes on to write, "If, however, there is any truth to this rumour (of India wanting to develop nuclear weapons) then it is believed an aggressive programme of US assistance to India in this area would deter, rather than encourage, India from embarking on such a programme."

Document 4: State Department Telegram, November 25, 1964 (Secret)[8]

India has always been ready and eager to exploit any opportunity for its advantage and the Chinese nuclear test provided it with a God-sent opportunity. In a telegram to the new Commissioner of the US Atomic Energy Commission (Glenn T. Seaborg), Dr. Bhabha writes, "We would greatly appreciate an arrangement with you to exchange full information on a daily or regular basis regarding fallout and other physical measurements on present and future Chinese tests. No fresh fallout has been detected by our monitoring stations in India but Indian aircraft which returned from

New York on October 21, showed fresh fallout but aircraft from London which returned via Moscow yesterday showed no fallout."[9]

Atomic Energy Commission Chairman Glenn Seaborg responds to this telegram in a non-committal manner and suggests that the US Embassy in New Delhi should coordinate exchanges of information between India and the US regarding Chinese nuclear tests.

Document 5: Memorandum from the State Department, Ambassador at Large: "New Delhi's 1862 of December 31, 1964," December 31, 1964 (Secret)[10]

Ambassador Llewellyn E. Thompson, a principal participant in the formulation of Johnson Administration's non-proliferation policy, criticises any suggestions to the Indians by the American ambassador to India that the US would provide specific security guarantees to a non-aligned country. He says that policy regarding the issue has not yet been established. This letter was sent as a consequence to one by the US Ambassador in India which suggested that he had probably indicated to the Indians the willingness of the US to provide nuclear guarantees against any Chinese nuclear attack against India. Taking a serious note of the suggestion given by the US Ambassador to India, Thompson writes, "I believe we previously sent a message to the Ambassador warning him about this problem, but it does not seem to have had any effect. I suggest that a very specific instruction be sent to him."

Document 6: Memorandum from the State Department, Ambassador at Large: "Indian Nuclear Weapons Capability," January 30, 1965 (Secret)[11]

In this message, Ambassador Thompson asserts that US security assurances against any nuclear attacks on India by a third country (insinuating China) will be a definite factor in dissuading India from developing nuclear weapons. In his view, however, India's overtly neutral stance precluded the acceptance of a formal US guarantee. As a means of getting around this predicament, he suggests a statement from India indicating that it was confident that the major nuclear powers would react if it were the target of nuclear attack and as such, it does not intend to develop nuclear weapons. In his view, the adoption of this stratagem would be acceptable to both, India and the US while leaving the US retaining the freedom to determine how it would respond if there were an actual crisis.

Document 7: State Department Telegram for Governor Harriman from the Secretary, February 27, 1965 (Secret)[12]

With information indicating that China will soon conduct a second nuclear weapons test, Secretary of State Dean Rusk asks Averall Harriman, on an official Asian tour, to sound out Indian officials on nuclear issues. He says that although Prime Minister Shastri has discussed security guarantees with British Prime Minister Harold Wilson, Indian representatives have yet to raise the subject directly with the US. He says that the US does not want to go beyond general public assurances issued by President Lyndon Johnson in October 1964. However, he asks Harriman to review with Indian officials some evidence that demonstrates the US's capacity and intent to respond in the event of a Chinese nuclear attack. The detailed telegram also asks Harriman to inquire from the Indians whether Harold Wilson gave any suggestion of involving the Commonwealth in any nuclear security guarantees for India, during his meeting with Prime Minister Shastri.

Document 8: State Department Cable: "Possible Indian Nuclear Weapons Development," March 29, 1966 (Secret)[13]

In the first indication of how far advanced the Indian Nuclear programme was, this cable asserts that though the Indians have not as yet embarked on a nuclear weapons development programme, they could develop one within a year if they decided to go ahead. Worried that in the aftermath of her indecisive 1965 war against Pakistan, India might opt for the nuclear option, the State Department asks the Embassy in New Delhi to gather information providing "even tenuous indications of nuclear weapons activity." The State Department also mentions its apprehensions about the possibility that India might be stockpiling plutonium from its CIRUS nuclear reactor in order to conduct a test.[14]

In a clear evidence that the Indians were up to some clandestine activity, the report says, "The fuel (from the safeguarded Canada-India reactor) has reportedly been removed from the reactor after an average burn-up of only 450-600 MWD/t, which is significantly lower than the 900 MWD/t for which the reactor is designed." The cable goes on to say, "while this circumstance alone does not necessarily indicate that a decision has been made to develop nuclear weapons, it hints strongly that suitable material is being produced to permit the rapid implementation of such a decision." Knowing that the Canada-India reactor was capable of producing enough plutonium for 1–2 nominal yield nuclear weapons on an annual basis, the removal of the fuel from this reactor before it had achieved its complete burn-up should have raised at least some eye-brows in Washington but the US Government preferred to stay quiet about the entire issue and rather than upbraiding India, preferred to demonstrate its ambivalence once again.

The cable also mentions that most of the other components required to fabricate a nuclear weapon, such as electronic neutron generators and high-quality detonators, were readily available to the Indians from open market sources in Western Europe.

As a guideline to the US Embassy in New Delhi, the cable asks that any information that becomes available on the following subjects should be reported:

- Signs of activity in remote areas which might portend the construction of a nuclear test site.
- Indications that nuclear-assisted research facilities are being established surreptitiously or that security is being tightened at existing facilities.
- Evidence of continued operation of the Canada-India reactor at Trombay to produce relatively "clean" plutonium.
- Procurement or development by India of small electronic neutron generators and high-quality, electrically-initiated, high-explosive detonators.
- Testing of highly instrumented high-explosive shapes or sections.

All these questions indicate that the US State Department had realised as early as March 1966 that the Indian nuclear programme had reached a stage where they stood on the verge of becoming a nuclear power. Despite this knowledge, however, no pressure was put on India to refrain from this course of action. This act of ignoring the visible and confirmed signs ultimately led to India's so-called Peaceful Nuclear Explosion (PNE) at Pokharan in 1974, more than eight years after this cable was sent.

In fact, the complete disregard of this knowledge by the US Government could even lead one to the conclusion that probably the Americans wanted India to develop nuclear weapons in the first place (again an insinuation that India had to be brought up to counter China) without appearing to be publicly helping them out in their efforts.

Document 9: State Department Telegram Regarding Estimated Cost of Indian Nuclear Weapon Programme, May 24, 1966 (Secret)[15]

Having realised that the Indians were on the verge of going nuclear, we see this gambit of the US Government sharing classified information about the costs of the US and French Nuclear programmes with India in an effort to dissuade it from embarking on the nuclear path. This was done on a suggestion from the US Embassy in New Delhi. Though this effort was carried out, it was probably too late for it to have any effect on the Indian Government.

Another significant aspect that gets highlighted from this message is that the Indians had probably managed to convince the Americans about China and not Pakistan being their adversary. This telegram goes to great lengths to provide compelling evidence of the exorbitant cost that a nuclear arsenal would entail for the weak and developing Indian economy by citing what a similar endeavour had cost the US and what it was costing France. Considering the fact that national security has no determinable price for any nation's government or people, I believe it was foolhardy on the part of the US to expect that the contents of this message would have any real impact on India, especially when the contents graphically elaborate on what the Chinese could do in any future nuclear conflict against India.

In my opinion this attempt of the US State Department to try and influence the nuclear debate in India had no impact in dissuading the Indians from the path of nuclear weapons development that they were steadily embarked upon. Innocuously and with traditional American naiveté, the cable concludes by saying that while testing of the first nuclear device and possessing a small nuclear arsenal would be "well within India's financial capabilities," it is actually increasing the size of this arsenal and its maintenance that would be prohibitive.

This amounts to saying that it would be all right for India to have just one test and a handful of nuclear weapons as long as she does not desire becoming a major nuclear power. The overall tone of this telegram indicates that the US had already reconciled itself to the fact of India having become a nuclear capable country.

Interestingly, as regards the potential size of the Indian nuclear arsenal, this document cites the Chief of the Indian Atomic Energy Establishment, Mr. Sethna as having mentioned that *India would need at least 250 atomic bombs for establishing a credible deterrence against Communist China.*[16]

Document 10: State Department Memorandum for the President: "NSC Meeting, June 9, 1966," June 7, 1966 (Secret)[17]

In preparation for a meeting of the US National Security Council, the Acting Secretary of State (George W. Ball) forwards a paper to the US President, titled "The Indian Nuclear Weapons Problem: Current Issues."

Just the title of the paper itself appears to confirm the US knowledge of India having achieved nuclear weapons capability.

The paper begins by highlighting that "in the wake of the third Chinese Communist nuclear test, domestic pressures for India to embark on a nuclear weapons effort have mounted sharply. Government leaders are continuing to hold the line against such a course. But a decision point is likely to be reached within a few years and, unless there is some new development, India almost certainly will go nuclear."

In the preamble to the paper, Ball highlights the following key issues that the paper aims to address:

- What would be the effects of an Indian national nuclear programme on US interests? While attempting to elaborate on this issue, the paper says, "Should India go down this line (the path of nuclear weapons development), the Paks (Pakistanis) would be critically concerned about their own security and would probably turn to the US, Communist China, or the Soviet Union either for assistance in acquiring nuclear weapons or for support in deterring India."
- Is there anything more that we (the US) can and should do to acquaint India with the costs and difficulties of a nuclear programme?
- Should we (the US) be prepared to go further than we have so far in using economic leverage to deter such a programme?
- How effective would a non-proliferation treaty, a comprehensive test ban, and/or a threshold test ban be in deterring an Indian nuclear programme?
- What price should we (the US) be prepared to pay for such (non-proliferation) agreements?
- Is there any dramatic new approach which would have greater effect on Indian nuclear intentions than the courses of action discussed in the attached paper?
- Should the US National Security Council (NSC) direct State, the DoD, and the ACDA to undertake a study, in greater depth, of the issues raised above?

Acting Secretary of State George Ball while reporting that India is almost certain to develop nuclear weapons, argues that efforts to influence India's decision, including arms control proposals and a US campaign emphasising that a nuclear weapons programme would be costly, are not likely to achieve more than a short-term delay in that outcome.

The paper suggests other options to deter India from going nuclear, such as using US economic leverage, or finding alternative ways to meet India's security concerns and stresses that India will only seek security guarantees that are consistent with its non-aligned status, because it depends on good relations with the Soviet Union for aid and support against China, and because it wants to maintain its stature among Afro-Asian nations. It also argues that the US should be willing to defend India if it were the subject of Chinese nuclear attack, but should not agree to a possibly entangling commitment. It recommends further discussions regarding a joint guarantee with the Soviets, although they oppose the idea at present. The paper goes so far as to recommend consideration of a resolution calling for UN members to support any non-nuclear state subjected to nuclear aggression. The passage of this sort of a resolution would then enable the US to offer the Indians private assurances of nuclear guarantee in case of a Chinese nuclear attack against India.

One of the options considered in the paper relates to a formal Indo-US military alliance, the advantages of which are negated on the premise that, "If such a US-Indian alliance were concluded, it might result in a complete US break with Pakistan and in a Pakistan-Chinese Communist alliance."

The seriousness with which the US Government was viewing the Indian nuclear weapons programme is obvious when one sees that paper also consider two such extreme options as *Nuclear Sharing* and the *Plowshare Loophole*. While the first proposal suggests that "the US might offer to assist India in acquiring the capability to deter or retaliate against Communist Chinese nuclear attack with its own delivery means, using American warheads" the second one considers the possibility of an Indian PNE but advises against the latter.

While admitting that the US Government was already pursuing some of the suggested courses of action, it admits that "each of these approaches has potentialities, limitations and costs" and also that "these courses of action are likely to secure delay for only a relatively limited period." The paper cites the following initiatives as being already implemented:

- We are already seeking to impress the Indians with the cost and difficulty of acquiring a nuclear deterrent.[18]
- We are trying to make clear to India the interrelation between external aid and levels of Indian military expenditure.
- We are seeking to negotiate arms control proposals, including a non-proliferation agreement, and we are examining new proposals, notably a threshold test ban.

- We are exploring the problem of general security assurances, particularly action that can be taken in the UN.

Document 11: State Department Cable Regarding Efforts to Influence Indian Nuclear Decision Making, July 28, 1966 (Secret)[19]
Having embarked on what appears to be an *appeasing* rather than a *coercive* campaign to rein in India's nuclear weapons programme, this telegram encloses an unclassified document dealing with "Cost Factors in Nuclear Weapons Development" with the hope that "discreet dissemination of data contained in study can reinforce support within India for the Government of India's no-bomb policy."

The letter depicts the US Government almost adopting an apologetic stance by advising the US Embassy in New Delhi to be very discreet in disseminating the information contained in this document lest it invite a backlash by appearing to apply pressure on the Indian Government. It cites two Americans as having reported that when they and other US scientists from the AAAS Arms Control Group discussed the subject with Sarabhai and other Indian leaders, the Indians drew a sharp distinction between an independent Indian decision to refrain from developing nuclear weapons and a decision that appeared to have been made under US influence.

The State Department also informs the Embassy that the following initiatives were being considered by various US Government agencies to dissuade India from developing nuclear weapons and seeks its advice regarding the efficacy of adopting either of these:

- Pass data on private, non-attributable basis to carefully selected Indian leaders considered trustworthy and basically opposed to India going nuclear.
- Encourage, without public display of US Government interest, replay of data and related information in India that may appear or be caused to appear in a reputable third country (e.g., West Germany or Japan).
- Encouraging reputable private US scholars and authorities to publish articles which could be replayed for Indian audiences.

Document 12: State Department Cable Regarding US Public Stance towards Nuclear Proliferation, October 27, 1966 (Secret)[20]
In an effort to formally make all US diplomats aware of the US Government's official stance on nuclear proliferation, this cable includes a public policy document that US diplomats can refer to when required

to speak on nuclear proliferation issues since this document enunciates the official position of the US Government. This document recommends abandoning rhetoric suggesting that nuclear powers have special prestige. Instead, it urges that the US representatives abroad should emphasise the wisdom of a national decision to forgo nuclear weapons, and that instead, stress the benefits of civilian nuclear energy use. In order to mitigate India's concern about China's nuclear weapons capabilities, this policy document recommends accentuating the US's capacity for retaliation. The guidelines also call for stressing the position that a comprehensive nuclear weapons programme, including a delivery system, would be prohibitively costly.

Essentially, this document is a compilation of all the previous measures that the US had already tried with India and offers nothing substantially new. It does, however, cite that some countries like Canada, India, Israel, Italy, Japan and Sweden could develop nuclear weapons capability in a very short time if their governments were inclined to do so. This policy document endeavours to divide nuclear capable countries into civil nuclear powers and military nuclear powers and discourages use of the terms like "five nuclear states" and "nuclear weapon states," etc.

In yet another attempt to dissuade potential nuclear weapon states from developing nuclear weapons, this policy document asks US diplomats to emphasise the following aspects:

- Building and testing a single nuclear device is only the beginning of a nuclear weapons programme. Relatively weak national nuclear forces with enemy cities as their targets are not likely to be sufficient to perform even the function of deterrence.
- Once the decision to acquire nuclear military force has been taken, a nation embarks on rising scale of costs and risks.
- Developing a small nuclear force is a costly, difficult, and uncertain undertaking because of the following factors:
  o Modern delivery systems tend to be far more expensive than nuclear weapons costs and necessitate large-scale, time-consuming, and industrially advanced effort.
  o In addition to the investment costs, operating, maintenance and obsolescence costs must also be borne.
  o Critical manpower and material dislocations as well as direct costs would be incurred.
  o Much of technology involved in developing military nuclear force is of no value for civilian applications and economic advancement.

Document 13: Memorandum for the Secretary of Defence: "The Indian Nuclear Weapons Problem: Security Aspects," January 4, 1967, attached to a Letter from Morton H. Halperin, Special Assistant to the Secretary of Defence, to Douglas Heck of the State Department (Secret)[21]

The Joint Chiefs respond to a study from the State Department on Indian security problems. They reaffirm their view that the US can do little to influence any nation's decision to seek nuclear status. They continue to oppose any security assurances for India that could alienate Pakistan, as they did in 1964 (see Document 1). They do not believe that the US should provide private assurances, except in response to an initiative from India, suggesting that refraining might lead Indian leaders to reconsider opposition to "certain US policies" (they are presumably referring to the Vietnam War). The memorandum indicates that the intelligence community expects that India will probably test a nuclear device "within the next few years."

In the opinion of the Joint Chiefs of Staff, the following recommendations that they had made earlier still remained valid:

- No nuclear assurances be made to India other than those made by the President in 1964.
- No action be taken in regard to India that could alienate US allies, especially Pakistan.
- United States should avoid creating an impression that it is willing to broaden its commitments to India.
- US retain maximum flexibility for future US action in response to CHICOM nuclear attack or blackmail.

Interestingly, the Joint Chiefs of Staff response concludes by saying that regardless of what sort of guarantees were provided to India, the US National Intelligence Community was convinced that she would not refrain from developing nuclear weapons and at best, all that could be achieved by any US overtures or assurances would be a delay in the Indians going nuclear.

Document 14: Memorandum from the State Department: "Security Assurances for India," April 20, 1967, with attached Memorandum of Conversation; "Rough Translation of the Revised Russian Draft"; and Memorandum for the President (Secret)[22]

L. K. Jha, who has been referred to at one place as a Secretary to Indian Prime Minister Indira Gandhi and at another as the Secretary to the Indian Cabinet, embarked on a visit to the major countries of the world in an effort to elicit nuclear assurances of security as the price for India's accession to the Non-proliferation Treaty (NPT). Interestingly, he visits Moscow before coming to Washington with London being his next step.

In what appears to be a diplomatic coup, he brings with him a draft proposal that according to him has the approval of the Soviet Government regarding nuclear safeguards for non-nuclear states such as India. So impressed and excited are the US Government officials at this change in the Soviet policy that they arrange for Mr. Jha to not only meet Robert McNamara, the Secretary of Defence but also President Lyndon Johnson.

A memo from Deputy Under Secretary Foy D. Kohler shows that the US State Department supports the idea of parallel US and Soviet guarantees associated with acceptance of the nuclear non-proliferation treaty, and indicates that a Soviet draft on the subject is considered promising. During their meeting, Johnson tells Jha that India's proposal regarding guarantees is "very interesting." Signalling his principal foreign policy preoccupation, Johnson then suggests that India support US policy in Vietnam.

Document 15: Memorandum of Conversation from the Office of the Assistant Secretary of Defence: "Meeting Between the Secretary of Defence and Mr. L. K. Jha, Tuesday, April 18 at 10 a.m.," April 25, 1967 (Secret)[23]

At a meeting with Secretary L. K. Jha, Secretary of Defence Robert S. McNamara says that the US appreciates the importance of assurances against nuclear attacks, but warns India against overreaction to a perceived threat from China. He supports parallel assurances from the nuclear powers for non-nuclear states, in conjunction with their acceptance of the nuclear non-proliferation treaty (NPT). He comments that although signing the treaty might entail some risks for India, refraining from doing so would be even more dangerous. Dr. Vikram Sarabhai, Director of the Indian Atomic Energy Commission, indicates that India is concerned about new US sales of military spare parts to Pakistan. He says that his country is reluctant to give up the option of nuclear weapons if the NPT is not a step toward total nuclear disarmament by all nations. McNamara downplays the significance of US providing some essential military spare parts to Pakistan and even suggests that in his opinion, India needs to cut her defence budget by at least 25% and reduce military manpower by 200,000 personnel.

While the US leaders evince a keen interest in the draft Soviet nuclear guarantees proposal for non-nuclear states, they do not give any commitment to Jha and confine their response to saying that they would study it seriously.

Interestingly, L. K. Jha's meeting with Secretary McNamara was also attended by Dr. Sarabhai, the Director of the Indian Atomic Energy Authority.

In what appears to be almost a "blackmail" or "threat," Sarabhai tells McNamara that unless the nuclear states also think of eventual disarmament, it would be extremely difficult for India to restrain herself from going nuclear.

Document 16: Memorandum of Conversation from the State Department: "Non-Proliferation Treaty; Assurances to Non Nuclear Powers; Latin American Nuclear Free Zone," June 23, 1967 (Secret)[24]

During discussions of the nuclear non-proliferation treaty with Soviet Foreign Minister Andrei Gromyko, Secretary of State Dean Rusk says that a few problems remain, including security assurances for India. Rusk says that the US wants any assurances to be provided via a Security Council resolution, and Gromyko says the Soviet position is also based on a UN role. The dialogue focuses on France and Italy being the two main European countries that had serious reservations regarding the NPT and also alludes to the possibility of the Latin American states agreeing to a nuclear non-proliferation agreement on a regional basis.

Rusk, Gromyko and Secretary of Defence Robert McNamara agree that a final treaty may be completed by October. (In the end, India abandoned its efforts to obtain assurances, having concluded that they would not necessarily be honoured during a crisis. It also did not, and still has not, signed the Nuclear Non-Proliferation Treaty.)

Document 17: Embassy, New Delhi Telegram: "Conversation with Senior GOI Nuclear Official," May 7, 1968 (Secret)[25]

Homi Sethna, Member of the Indian Atomic Energy Commission and the Director of India's Bhabha Atomic Research Centre, dismisses as useless an Indo-Soviet nuclear agreement, and says that the Soviets are not honest with India in nuclear matters. He believes that they want to collaborate with India in order to obtain information on China's nuclear tests. He does not expect India to sign the Nuclear Non-Proliferation Treaty "unless Mrs. [Indira] Gandhi wants to commit political suicide." (There was strong public opposition to signing because many Indians shared the view, widespread within the Indian leadership that the treaty was discriminatory, and that India needed to reserve the option of developing nuclear weapons.)

The following salient aspects regarding Indo-Soviet nuclear cooperation can be gleaned from Mr. Sethna's conversation:

- Russians are excessively secretive in nuclear matters and are reluctant to reveal any information of significance.
- The Indians perceived the main motivation underlying Soviet nuclear overtures as being the need for them to tap into the wealth of information that the Indians had amassed through various sources on the nuclear tests conducted by China.
- In an insinuation that India was well advanced in nuclear research, Sethna tells the Americans that even the top Soviet nuclear scientists who visit India are impressed by the advances that have been made in nuclear issues, especially in the realm of fabrication of nuclear fuel.

Document 18: Mission to NATO: "Assessment of Indian Nuclear Test," June 5, 1974 (Secret)[26]

This is a significant document since it is one of the first US Government communications regarding South Asian nuclear programmes to emerge after the Indian conduct of the so-called Peaceful Nuclear Explosion (PNE) at Pokharan on May 18, 1974.

The report says that India might view even a rudimentary nuclear system as a deterrent to China, and suggests that domestic problems might have contributed to the timing of the explosion. It estimates that India could easily afford to conduct additional tests, but a sophisticated weapons programme would require a large-scale diversion of resources. The State Department notes that the test has alarmed Pakistan and set back efforts toward regional reconciliation.

The report estimates that India has spent almost US$ 1 billion on nuclear research with her annual nuclear development allocation having reached a figure of US$ 130 million. It also asserts that the current US$ 2.6 billion defence budget of India would permit the development of a rudimentary nuclear device without any significant additional financial burden.

Alluding to the impact on South Asian stability, the report singles out Pakistan as being the most seriously affected country. It says, "Pakistan's fears have intensified and immediate prospects in South Asia for normalisation are likely to receive a setback." The report cites the US fear that India's example might lead other countries down the nuclear path. "The Indian example, however, could make it easier for others to follow suit, claiming that they too are following the path of 'peaceful' accession to nuclear status."

Citing Argentina as one of the "near-nuclear" countries, the report also alludes to a nuclear cooperation agreement that Argentina and India have signed.

Document 19: Bureau of Intelligence and Research Intelligence Note: "India: Uncertainty over Nuclear Policy," June 13, 1974 (Confidential)[27]

A month after India's first nuclear test on May 18, 1974, the State Department assesses internal reaction in India. The Department reports that most Indians welcomed the test at first, but some now doubt their government's claim that its nuclear intentions are strictly peaceful. Some journalists say that foreign pressure regarding nuclear issues could strengthen Hindu nationalist factions. Others worry that the test will induce Pakistan to seek nuclear weapons, which would in turn increase sentiment for a full-scale Indian military programme.

Document 20: State Department Background Paper: "Pakistan and the Non-Proliferation Issue," January 22, 1975 (Secret)[28]

This is the first of the documents in this collection that makes any mention of Pakistan's nuclear development programme. The State Department reports that Pakistan is negotiating for facilities that will give it an independent nuclear fuel cycle and the opportunity to produce enough plutonium for a nuclear bomb. It says that Pakistan may already have decided to produce nuclear weapons. The paper adds that India's test gave Pakistan the incentive to produce a nuclear weapon, and that because of the Indian explosion, Pakistan could now do so "with less world condemnation than might otherwise be expected."

The paper asserts that with Arab finance and Chinese technical assistance, Pakistan could be expected to achieve nuclear weapons capability as early as 1980 if she persists with the nuclear development programme with earnestness and continued effort.

Attempting to address some of the issues that Pakistan's Prime Minister Zulfiqar Ali Bhutto might raise with the US Government officials, this background paper highlights that Bhutto might raise the following questions:

- US position on Pakistan's recent proposal for a South Asian Nuclear Weapons Free Zone.
- US position on the Pakistani assertion that the latter's decision whether to go nuclear or not would depend primarily on the US provision of adequate conventional military weaponry.

The paper suggests that the US viewpoint on international safeguards being mandatory for all nuclear power plants must be impressed upon the Pakistani Prime Minister. This probably was included because according to the paper, Pakistan is already in negotiation with China, Belgium, Canada and France for the provision of nuclear power plants, heavy water and fuel reprocessing installations.

Document 21: State Department Memorandum: "Demarche to Pakistan on Nuclear Fuel Reprocessing," January 30, 1976 (Secret)[29]

According to the State Department, intelligence reports indicate that Pakistan has undertaken "a crash programme to develop nuclear weapons." It is trying to obtain a uranium reprocessing facility to produce plutonium, presumably for weapons use, since it does not need the plutonium for its civil nuclear energy programme.

The document specifically refers to the ongoing negotiations between Pakistan and France for the acquisition of a reprocessing plant and asserts that since the only existing nuclear power plant that Pakistan has employs unenriched Uranium as fuel, there does not exist any justification for Pakistan to acquire a reprocessing facility that enables it to produce plutonium, since it has no possible use for the latter except to divert the plutonium for nuclear weapons development programme that Pakistan has embarked upon.

Document 22: State Department Briefing Paper: "The Pakistani Nuclear Programme," June 23, 1983 (Secret)[30]

Having started with the first document dated June 1961, this collection of 22 documents ends with this detailed overview of the Pakistani nuclear weapons development programme and is dated almost exactly 22 years later.

Reiterating that there is "unambiguous evidence that Pakistan is actively pursuing a nuclear weapons development programme," this paper says that the US has information indicating that Pakistan began to develop a nuclear explosive device "soon after the 1974 Indian nuclear test." Pakistan has obtained technology for its research in Europe, using procurement agents and front organisations to undertake these clandestine operations. It refers to a Pakistani national having obtained the know-how from Europe and also mentions the facilities that have cropped up around Islamabad, specifically alluding to Kahuta. According to this detailed briefing paper, Pakistan initially opted to pursue both the routes to nuclear weapons capability—the enriched Uranium method and the Plutonium method but subsequently elected to pursue only the latter. The US has also concluded that China is assisting Pakistan's nuclear programme: it believes that they have cooperated in the production of fissile material, and possibly also in "nuclear device design."

The paper also indicates that the US Government had also approached the Pakistan Government regarding its concerns about the way that Pakistan's nuclear weapons programme was shaping up.

Conclusion

The declassified US Government documents placed on the National Security Archive website serve to provide a good insight into how the US vacillated while both India and Pakistan were pursuing their respective nuclear weapons development programmes. Unfortunately, some of the relevant documents still remain classified for a variety of reasons and as such, it is difficult to visualise the complete picture.

What is obvious, however, is that the US Government has only attempted to deter India or Pakistan from their journey along the nuclear path whenever it has suited its interests. At other moments, such as, during the Soviet invasion of Afghanistan and the ongoing US War against Terror, when the US needed to court Pakistan, the entire matter of Pakistan's nuclear programme was conveniently forgotten. However, as soon as the US interest in the region waned, it again reimposed sanctions on Pakistan.

As regards India, the US policy has not been as erratic as the policy towards Pakistan. Probably for the reason of building up India as a counter to China, the US has seldom ever imposed sanctions on India like it did to Pakistan. This goes to indicate that although against nuclear proliferation in policy, the US did not really do all that it could to stem proliferation in South Asia.

For instance, during the 1980s, the US was criticised for providing massive levels of aid to Pakistan, its military ally, despite laws barring assistance to any country that imported certain technology related to nuclear weapons. President Ronald Reagan conveniently waived the legislation, arguing that cutting off aid would harm US national interests.

Notes

1. The George Washington University's National Security Archive has launched a programme focusing on the US policy towards nuclear proliferation in South Asia. This project is creating a comprehensive history of nuclear developments in South Asia, including weapons programmes in India and Pakistan, as well as international efforts to curtail proliferation in the region. The analyst for the South Asia nuclear project is Joyce Battle, who compiled the Electronic Briefing Book No. 6 on the subject. She is also the analyst for the Archive's documentation projects on the Persian Gulf and US policy toward Iraq. Current archive documents number a total

of 22 and relate to the period between 1961 and 1983. Information is being collected from the National Archives and the presidential libraries, and through Freedom of Information Act (FOIA) and Mandatory Review requests, used to obtain the declassification of previously classified documents and materials. A selective and focused collection of documents will be made available to researchers. This article is based on the contents of the 22 declassified US government documents which pertain to US Policy towards nuclear proliferation in South Asia. The electronic briefing book on the South Asian nuclear programmes prepared by the George Washington University's National Security Archives Project can be accessed on the internet at http://www.gwu.edu/~nsarchiv/NSAEBB/NSAEBB6/index.html.

2. This introductory text has been downloaded from http://64.177.207.201/pages/16_128.html and its unrestricted usage is permitted by the authors.
3. http://www.gwu.edu/~nsarchiv/NSAEBB/NSAEBB6/docs/doc01.pdf.
4. Quoted sentence extracted from ibid., p. 1.
5. http://www.gwu.edu/~nsarchiv/NSAEBB/NSAEBB6/docs/doc02.pdf.
6. Ibid.
7. Mandatory Review declassification by the Lyndon Baines Johnson Presidential Library. http://www.gwu.edu/~nsarchiv/NSAEBB/NSAEBB6/docs/doc03.pdf.
8. http://www.gwu.edu/~nsarchiv/NSAEBB/NSAEBB6/docs/doc04.pdf.
9. This is a masterpiece of drafting and appears to have been done by an astute diplomat rather than by a scientist. The report implies that because of Indian capability to monitor fallout, it would be beneficial for the US to share information with India. Although it cannot be said with any certainty but it appears highly improbable that normal Indian aircraft (presumably the reference is to airliners) could have been equipped with equipment that could detect radioactive fallout as far back as 1964.
10. http://www.gwu.edu/~nsarchiv/NSAEBB/NSAEBB6/docs/doc05.pdf.
11. http://www.gwu.edu/~nsarchiv/NSAEBB/NSAEBB6/docs/doc06.pdf.
12. http://www.gwu.edu/~nsarchiv/NSAEBB/NSAEBB6/docs/doc07.pdf.
13. http://www.gwu.edu/~nsarchiv/NSAEBB/NSAEBB6/docs/doc08.pdf.
14. This situation is an example of the US ambivalence towards the Indian Nuclear Programme. Even though it suspects that India is secretly moving towards weaponisation of her nuclear capability, it opts to remain quiet about it and does not take any initiative whatsoever to preclude the same.
15. http://www.gwu.edu/~nsarchiv/NSAEBB/NSAEBB6/docs/doc09.pdf.
16. This figure of 150 nuclear weapons to offer a credible deterrence against China should be studied in today's *perspective* to arrive at what could possibly be the figure that India would consider necessary to establish a credible level of nuclear deterrence against Pakistan.
17. http://www.gwu.edu/~nsarchiv/NSAEBB/NSAEBB6/docs/doc10.pdf.
18. Please refer to Document 9 and the elaboration for it. Also, please monitor that this paper does not refer to India acquiring a nuclear capability for offensive purposes—rather it assumes that (due to the possible Chinese threat), the Indian nuclear weapons would primarily be an element of deterrence.
19. http://www.gwu.edu/~nsarchiv/NSAEBB/NSAEBB6/docs/doc11.pdf.
20. http://www.gwu.edu/~nsarchiv/NSAEBB/NSAEBB6/docs/doc12.pdf.

21. http://www.gwu.edu/~nsarchiv/NSAEBB/NSAEBB6/docs/doc13.pdf
22. http://www.gwu.edu/~nsarchiv/NSAEBB/NSAEBB6/docs/doc14.pdf.
23. http://www.gwu.edu/~nsarchiv/NSAEBB/NSAEBB6/docs/doc15.pdf. Declassified in response to a Freedom of Information Act request.
24. http://www.gwu.edu/~nsarchiv/NSAEBB/NSAEBB6/docs/doc16.pdf.
25. http://www.gwu.edu/~nsarchiv/NSAEBB/NSAEBB6/docs/doc17.pdf.
26. http://www.gwu.edu/~nsarchiv/NSAEBB/NSAEBB6/docs/doc18.pdf. Declassified in response to a Freedom of Information Act request.
27. http://www.gwu.edu/~nsarchiv/NSAEBB/NSAEBB6/docs/doc19.pdf.
28. http://www.gwu.edu/~nsarchiv/NSAEBB/NSAEBB6/docs/doc20.pdf.
29. http://www.gwu.edu/~nsarchiv/NSAEBB/NSAEBB6/docs/doc21.pdf.
30. http://www.gwu.edu/~nsarchiv/NSAEBB/NSAEBB6/docs/doc22.pdf.

03 Pakistan, China and the Bomb[1]

This Chapter is based on an analysis of 25 relevant and previously classified US Government documents pertaining to China-Pakistan cooperation in the nuclear domain.

Document 2:[2] George C. Denney, Deputy Director of Intelligence and Research, US Department of State, to Secretary Rusk, "Pakistan and Communist China Strengthen Cooperation," December 4, 1968, Secret. Source: US National Archives, Record Group 59, Records of the Department of State, Subject-Numeric Files, 1967-1969, POL 1 Chicom-Pak

One of the major consequences of the 1965 Indo-Pak war was Pakistan's break-up of the US-Pakistan alliances. The power vacuum created by this afforded China and Pakistan to develop military links. This document highlights the growing Sino-Pakistan military relations that involved the provision of Chinese combat aircraft and other weapon systems for the Pakistan military.

This document also mentions the case of Pakistan providing access to China to examine military hardware that had been provided by the US, including several components of the Lockheed F-104 Starfighter supersonic combat aircraft.[3]

Document 3:[4] "Proposed Cable to Tehran on Pakistani Nuclear Processing," May 12, 1976, Secret. Source: National Archives, Records of the State Department, Record Group 59, Office of the Counsellor, 1955-1977, box 3, Chron-Official April-June 1976

This proposal never saw the light of day primarily because it was based on a fallacy that Pakistan and Iran would ever agree to establishing a joint nuclear re-processing facility. Needless to say, both the countries would want this facility to be located inside their own geographic bounds and would even be desirous of controlling the operational functioning of such a facility.

Document 4:[5] Secretary of State Cyrus Vance to National Security Assistant Zbigniew Brzezinski, "Nuclear Safeguards—Pakistan, South Africa, China," July 14, 1977, Secret. Source: State Department Freedom of Information Act (FOIA) Release

China is not yet involved in foreign nuclear transfers though it has reportedly told Pakistan that it will provide her with fuel services if all other sources are cut off. The Chinese have visited KANUPP heavy water reactor to familiarise themselves with the technique of fabricating fuel for it. Pakistani access to fuel fabrication services is of more concern than the safeguards on the country's raw uranium imports.

Document 5:[6] State Department cable to US Embassy, Austria, "Pakistan Nuclear Issue: Briefing of IAEA Director General Eklund," July 9, 1979, Secret. Source: State Department FOIA Release

During this meeting, Ambassador Smith shocked Dr Eklund who was then the Director of the IAEA by informing him of the Pakistani weapon development plans. Dr. Eklund wanted the news to be made public but the Ambassador convinced him to remain quiet. Ambassador Smith confided to Dr. Eklund that he expected Pakistan to take at least 2-3 years before being able to develop a nuclear weapon.

Document 6:[7] Friday Morning Session, September 14, 1979, General Advisory Committee on Arms Control and Disarmament, Secret. Excised Copy, Excerpt. Source: State Department FOIA Release

When asked who was helping Pakistan in developing nuclear weapons, the response was China. The Chinese neither want to appear being in favour of stopping Pakistan from going nuclear nor do they want to appear to be helping them. In fact, they want the US to provide Pakistan with more conventional weapons to counter the USSR.

Document 7:[8] "Secretary's Talking Points: US-China Relations," June 1981, Secret. Source: State Department FOIA Release

A Pakistan nuclear test could prompt Indian response by a resumption of testing and produce nuclear weapons. As such going nuclear would not be in Pakistan's interest but would be detrimental. The Soviets could also increase military co-operation with India and deploy forces along Pak-Afghan border.

Document 8:[9] US embassy China cable 17090 to State Department, "Arms Control and Disarmament," December 17, 1982, Secret. Source: State Department FOIA Release

While continuing to reject the NPT, the Chinese are willing to concede in private that they have not, and will not assist any country in developing nuclear weapons. While apparently becoming more willing to discuss non-proliferation issues, the Chinese have refused to give an unequivocal answer that they are not assisting Pakistan's nuclear weapons development programme. The US should warn the Chinese to inform Pakistan of the sanctions that they could possibly face.

Document 9:[10] US embassy China cable 17168 to State Department, "US-PRC Nuclear Cooperation—Or the Lack of It," December 18, 1982, Secret. Source: State Department FOIA Release

The Chinese have also sold sensitive technology through private companies after merely asking them to provide assurances that these were intended for peaceful purposes. There are also suspicions that Chinese nuclear cooperation with Pakistan may have facilitated Islamabad's acquisition of weapons related know-how.

Document 10:[11] State Department cable 348835 to US Embassy Pakistan, "Newsweek Article on Chinese Nuclear Cooperation with Pakistan," December 18, 1982, Confidential. Source: State Department FOIA Release

This report talks of a Pakistani scientist allegedly stealing uranium enrichment technology from a facility in Netherlands (Dr. Abdul Qadeer Khan). It also refers to recent reports that China has provided raw uranium as well as the blueprints for building a nuclear weapons to Pakistan. There are also reports of Pakistan having attempted to acquire nuclear weapons technology from the UK as well as Argentina.

Document 11:[12] US State Department, "The Pakistani Nuclear Programme," June 22, 1983, Secret, excised copy. Source: State Department FOIA Release (Note 14)

The US believed that the Pakistanis were experiencing difficulties in making the enrichment machines work and as such had been unable to produce significant quantities of enriched uranium. Although these operational problems had earlier led to the Pakistanis seeking help from China, the current status of this cooperation remained unknown.

This document affirms the conclusion that China has provided assistance to Pakistan's programme to develop a nuclear weapons capability. Commencing with co-op at KANUPP, this cooperation is believed to have taken place in the area of fissile material prod and possibly also nuclear device design.

Document 12:[13] Memorandum from Assistant Secretary of State for East Asian and Pacific Affairs Paul Wolfowitz to Deputy Secretary of State Kenneth Dam,

"The Secretary's Meeting with Premier Zhao—Nuclear Cooperation," January 10, 1984, with attachments, Secret. Source: State Department FOIA Release

During this meeting, Sino-US leaders agreed to cooperate in stopping nuclear proliferation.

Document 13:[14] US Embassy China cable 00644 to State Department, "Premier Zhao's Statement on Non-Proliferation Published in Beijing," January 12, 1984, Confidential. Source: State Department FOIA Release

Chinese Premier's statement on nuclear proliferation is reproduced below:

> "China has always opposed the arms race, particularly the nuclear arms race, and stands for the complete prohibition and thorough destruction of nuclear weapons. We have long declared that China will never be the first to use nuclear weapons. We are critical of the discriminatory 'Treaty on Non-Proliferation of Nuclear Weapons,' but we do not advocate or encourage nuclear proliferation. We do not engage in nuclear proliferation ourselves, nor do we help other countries develop nuclear weapons. We actively support all proposals that are truly helpful to realising nuclear disarmament, terminating the nuclear arms race and eliminating the threat of nuclear war."

Document 14:[15] US Embassy India cable 14048 to State Department, "News Reports of Pakistan Nuclear Capabilities," June 22, 1984, Unclassified. Source: State Department FOIA Release

The US Embassy in New Delhi sent this cable based on Senator Cranston's disclosure in the Senate in which he elaborated that according to a US Government document, Pakistan had, with Chinese assistance, already acquired the capability to make nuclear weapons. Other significant aspects that the Senator highlighted, included the following:

- The US State Department had been hiding these details from the Senate for fear that its disclosure would jeopardise the passage of the US$ 3.2 billion aid package for Pakistan.
- According to Senator Cranston, it was estimated that Pakistan could manufacture ten nuclear weapons during the next three to five years.
- He said that the possibility of extremist elements employing nuclear weapons against India, Israel or other countries would place the US on a weak footing in the world.

- The Reagan Administration had failed to keep the Senate fully informed of these developments.
- The Senator got this information from a classified 15-page document that had been prepared by 90 experts.
- Pakistan had been working on nuclear warhead design for the past four years and had received assistance from China during the past 10-12 years.
- Based on blueprints provided by the Chinese, Pakistan had already manufactured a rudimentary nuclear explosive device and was currently engaged in manufacturing a casing for this weapon.
- Since this crude Pakistani weapon could not be delivered by a combat aircraft such as the F-16, the Pakistan Air Force was likely to use the US-provided C-130 transport aircraft for delivering these weapons onto the desired target.

Document 15:[16] US Embassy China cable 24244 to State Department, "Pakistan Foreign Minister Visits PRC: Nuclear Cooperation and Afghanistan," September 29, 1986, Confidential, excised copy. Source: State Department FOIA Release

Pakistan and China signed an agreement for peaceful nuclear cooperation stipulating that they would both register this agreement with the IAEA and the sale of nuclear equipment and material between the two countries would be under IAEA supervision "wherever necessary." It was obvious that this agreement which had been under discussion for several years, had been signed primarily to satisfy all those who were complaining that China and Pakistan were involved in the trade of nuclear material and equipment. Originally, this agreement was supposed to have been signed by the Chairman of the Pakistan Atomic Energy Commission (PAEC) but considering its enormous importance and significance, the Foreign Minister of Pakistan himself paid a one-day visit to Peking to sign the agreement. In reciprocity, the Chinese Premier accompanied by the State Councillor, and the Foreign Minister and the Deputy Foreign Minister were all present at the occasion of the signing of the agreement.

Document 16:[17] US State Department Briefing Papers, "The President's Meeting with President Yang Shangkun," February 8, 1989, Secret. Source: State Department FOIA Release.

Salient extracts:

- The US is concerned over the dangers posed by the possibility of an Indo-Pak nuclear arms race.
- Chinese assistance to Pakistan's nuclear programme could become a severe burden on Sino-US relationship.
- The US hopes that China will work it in an effort to curb the proliferation of ballistic missiles with a range greater than 300 kilometres.
- Although Sino-US approaches towards arms control have differed, their interests and goals are similar.
- In the nuclear domain, the US is concerned over continuing reports of Chinese assistance to Pakistan's nuclear programme.

Document 17:[18] US Embassy China Cable 14868 to State Department, "Ranking MFA Official on PRC Nuclear Matters: No Proliferation or Subs for Pakistan; Zip for Pyongyang," May 30, 1989, Secret, excised copy. Source: State Department FOIA Release

China neither encourages, not advocates, nor participates in nuclear proliferation. Specifically, in connection with the accusations that China had assisted Pakistan in the latter's nuclear weapons programme, China had the following explanation to offer:

- Although China has serious reservations regarding the NPT it did not and would not indulge in proliferation.
- China refuted Indian assertion that the latter could not enter into regional nuclear arms control agreements because of the former.

How did the threshold states (India, South Africa and Israel) reach where they have? Some of the advanced states must have been involved and they must accept this responsibility

There have been unfounded rumours that China assisted Pakistan's development of nuclear weapons and even the Sino-Pak bilateral agreement specifically includes a provision for acceptance of safeguards.

There is no possibility of China providing Pakistan with a nuclear submarine since Chinese technology in this realm is lagging behind the modern world.

There is no truth in the Indian rumour that China has deployed nuclear warheads on intermediate range ballistic missiles in Xinjiang or Tibet. Moreover, there is no truth in the Indian spread news that chemical weapons are being used in Tibet.

Document 18:[19] US Department of State, Office of Non-Proliferation and Export Technology, "US Interaction with the PRC Concerning the PRC's Nuclear Relationship with Pakistan," November 28, 1989, Secret, excised copy. Source: State Department FOIA release

It was in the early 1980s that the US started becoming increasingly concerned about the Sino-Pak nuclear relationship. The significant events that took place in the ensuing years are listed below:

Time frame	Event
February 1982	US Secretary of State visits Beijing and invites Chinese to send their team to the US to discuss non-proliferation policy and nuclear cooperation issues
July 1983-April 1984	Five rounds of Sino-US talks are held on the Sino-US Nuclear Cooperation Agreement
January 1984	While the above talks were being held, the Chinese PM visits the White House and makes several important clarifications regarding China's non-proliferation policy
April 1984	President Reagan visits China and the US-China Nuclear Cooperation Agreement is signed
June 1985	Sino-US talks are held in Beijing to discuss their respective non-proliferation policies. The report of these discussions is presented to the Congress for approval
July 23, 1985	US-China Agreement for Nuclear Cooperation is signed
December 30, 1985	The Agreement is ratified by both, China and the United States.

Document 19:[20] US Embassy China Cable 1884, "Proliferation Issues: The View from Beijing Looks Grim," April 16, 1991, Confidential, excised copy. Source: State Department FOIA Release

Chinese attitude towards South Asian nuclear proliferation

Despite the fact that it kept opposing the NPT and did not sign it for so many years, China has repeatedly mentioned that it supports the following three goals of the Treaty:

- Preventing the spread of nuclear weapons to non-nuclear states
- Reducing nuclear weapons arsenals worldwide
- Promoting the peaceful use of nuclear energy

Based on these three objectives, the Chinese have formulated the following three principles that will govern their nuclear cooperation with other countries:

- They will only cooperate on projects that fall under the IAEA safeguards
- They will not cooperate on projects that are geared towards weapons development
- They will not cooperate on projects that are geared towards transfer of technology to third countries.

Beijing's "principles" regarding nuclear non-proliferation have not translated into a willingness to take concrete actions to address specific nuclear proliferation concerns. South Asia is a case in point. The Chinese have rejected the persistent reports that they are assisting the Pakistani nuclear weapons programme and US contacts in China further clarified that they see little role for China to play in trying to arrest the spread of nuclear weapons in South Asia.

The Chinese do not see the Pakistani nuclear programme to be provoking a full-scale nuclear arms race with New Delhi. Rather, they view it primarily as being defensive in nature and merely a logical response to India's 1974 explosion of a "peaceful nuclear device" and perhaps a check to what the Chinese perceive to be Indian "hegemonism" in South Asia. At the same time, the Chinese dismiss Indian insinuations that the PRC's nuclear arsenal prevents New Delhi from addressing nuclear proliferation issues with Islamabad on a bilateral basis. The Chinese argue that their guarantee that the Chinese nuclear weapons will never be used to attack a non-nuclear state should suffice to assuage New Delhi's concerns over Beijing's intentions.

Chinese officials and researchers have made it clear to the United States that China believes resolving the South Asian nuclear programme issue on a multilateral basis is a task primarily for the superpowers. Only Moscow and Washington, the Chinese maintain, have the necessary influence in the subcontinent to broker an agreement. Moreover, Beijing emphasises that her nuclear arsenal should not be made a topic for discussion in talks aimed at defusing the South Asian nuclear proliferation problem.

In Beijing, Chinese officials have been unresponsive to US attempts to engage them on South Asian nuclear proliferation. They have offered no suggestions regarding any multilateral solutions to the problem and have admitted that they have not raised the issue of nuclear proliferation with the Indians. Several officials have stated that China would be willing to "consider" any suggestions the US might advance for a multilateral approach to the issue; we take these statements as a polite dig at US for not having advanced a concrete formulation which would interest the Indians without affecting in any way China's nuclear arsenal, rather than a serious offer to get involved in multilateral negotiations over South Asian nuclear proliferation. In a recent conversation, the Chinese attitude towards South Asian nuclear proliferation was summed up "the key lies with India," and India is reluctant to give up its right to possess nuclear weapons.

This document ends by describing the Chinese track record as regards sale of nuclear material and strategic weapons to be based on "aggressive pragmatism" and cites the examples of Saudi Arabia, Iran, Iraq and Pakistan.

Document 20:[21] Department of State cable 09394 to US Embassy China, "China's Nuclear Reactor Deal with Pakistan; Chinese Steps toward joining NPT," January 10, 1992, Confidential. Source: State Department FOIA Release

This report refers to an announcement by Pakistan and China regarding the planned sale of a 300 MW nuclear power plant by China to Pakistan. The US is fairly is upset over this news which highlights the following positive and negative aspects:

Positive	Negative
The reactor will apparently be subject to IAEA safeguards	Terms of the deal do not apparently contain the full-scope safeguards export conditions suggested by the US to China
The Chinese have been significantly more transparent regarding this deal as compared with their other similar deals with other countries.	Goes against the recent general policy of nuclear suppliers to make full-scope safeguards an essential requirement for all transactions involving non-nuclear states.

Considering these aspects, the US Department of State recommends to the US Embassy in Beijing to convey the following to the Chinese:
- The US welcomes the Chinese decision to join the NPT and hopes that China will move quickly to start adhering to the treaty.
- The US is disappointed with the Chinese decision to provide a nuclear reactor to Pakistan.
- While the US appreciates the fact that this deal would be in accordance

with the IAEA requirements, the lack of imposition of full-scope safeguards is a worrying aspect.

• Other nuclear suppliers have already agreed to make the imposition of full-scope safeguards an essential requirement for all nuclear deals, specially to countries of proliferation concern such as Pakistan, and would encourage and expect China to do the same.

Document 21:[22] US Embassy China cable 01109 to State Department, "China's Nuclear Deal with Pakistan—Demarche Delivered," January 14, 1992, Confidential. Source: State Department FOIA Release

When the US Embassy in Beijing delivered a demarche to the Chinese Ministry of Foreign Affairs, they were informed that while China was familiar with the US policy of nuclear safeguards, China had not yet implemented any such policy. Moreover, the Chinese were about to ratify the NPT which also did not make the imposition of such safeguards mandatory. The Chinese also reiterated that Pakistan was a long-time friend and ally of China and its economic requirements necessitated the provision of a nuclear power plant.

Document 22:[23] US Embassy China cable 02139 to State Department, "Recent Nuclear Developments in China," January 24, 1992 [incomplete document], Confidential. Source: State Department FOIA Release

This report cites a source at the German Embassy as saying that the Chinese had approached a German firm for an estimate of the reactor cooling equipment for the Pakistani reactor. When the German firm refused citing the need for safeguards being in place, the Chinese asked them to provide the same information for one of their own planned reactors and the German firm obliged.

Document 23:[24] US Embassy China cable 025699, "ACDA Director Lehman's Beijing Consultations: Non-CWC Topics," August 19, 1992, Secret, excised copy. Source: State Department FOIA Release

Mentioning about the talks that Ambassador Lehman had with the Chinese regarding nuclear proliferation in South Asia, this report highlights that Ambassador Lehman had expressed an appreciation for China's willingness to attend the five power talks on nuclear proliferation in South Asia and asked China to consider what steps might be taken to bring these talks about. He also repeated the US concerns over reports of Chinese involvement in Pakistan's nuclear weapons development programme.

Document 24:[25] US Embassy China cable 037741, "Chinese Views on NPT Extension," November 25, 1992, Confidential. Source: State Department FOIA Release

This document talks of the Chinese belief that just as US-Soviet nuclear arms race had "produced a de facto political stability that prevented direct conflict," could it not be possible to imagine that the same formula would work in the other troubled regions such as the Middle East and South Asia.

Document 25:[26] US State Department Briefing Paper, "China," circa December 1992, Secret, excised copy. Source: State Department FOIA Release

This briefing paper reiterates the ongoing and continuous US effort to convince the Chinese at the highest level of government to follow the internationally accepted forms of nuclear non-proliferation including the imperative of applying all necessary safeguards.

Despite all these efforts, and some improvements having been made, Chinese non-proliferation policies still fall well short of the minimum desirable standards, particularly as regards support to the Pakistan Nuclear Weapons programme. This document suggests that since mere talks and negotiations have failed to develop any result, the US might need to adopt a more harsh stance in attempting to convince China to adhere to non-proliferation.

Document 26:[27] "Classified Report to Congress on the Non-Proliferation and Practices of the People's Republic of China," 1997, Secret, excised copy. Source: State Department FOIA Release

This report to the Congress highlights that since the Chinese commitment of May 1996 regarding nuclear non-proliferation, the US has had no basis to conclude that they have reneged on their pledge. The Chinese are, however, continuing to provide assistance to some of Pakistan's unsafeguarded nuclear facilities such as the 300 MW Chasma power reactor that China is building.

In their negotiation with the Chinese, the Americans have continued to emphasise the importance of ensuring that Pakistan is not allowed to divert equipment and information from her safeguarded nuclear facilities to her unsafeguarded nuclear installations.

Notes

1. This article is based on, and replicates, a collection of documents on "China, Pakistan, and the Bomb" edited by William Burr and published by the National Security Archive at George Washington University, Washington, DC, USA, on March 5, 2004. The author thanks the National Security Archive for authorisation to use its work. Founded in 1985 by journalists and scholars to check rising government secrecy, the National Security Archive combines a unique range of functions: investigative journalism centre, research institute on international affairs, library and archive of declassified US documents ("the world's largest nongovernmental collection" according to the *Los Angeles Times*), leading non-profit user of the US Freedom of Information Act, public interest law firm defending and expanding public access to government information, global advocate of open government, and indexer and publisher of former secrets. Based at George Washington University's Gelman Library, the Archive relies for its 3 million yearly budget on publication revenues, grants from individuals and grants from foundations such as the Carnegie Corporation of New York, the Ford Foundation, the William and Flora Hewlett Foundation, the John S. and James L. Knight Foundation, the John D. and Catherine T. MacArthur Foundation, and the Open Society Foundations. The National Security Archive receives no government funding. Incorporated as an independent Washington, DC non-profit organisation, the Archive is recognised by the Internal Revenue Service as a tax-exempt public charity.

2. http://www.gwu.edu/~nsarchiv/NSAEBB/NSAEBB114/chipak-2.pdf.

3. For more details of the Chinese contribution in building up the Pakistan Air Force, please refer to the author's article titled, "All Weather Friends" that was published in *Force India*, in March 2013.

4. http://www.gwu.edu/~nsarchiv/NSAEBB/NSAEBB114/chipak-3.pdf.

5. http://www.gwu.edu/~nsarchiv/NSAEBB/NSAEBB114/chipak-4.pdf.

6. http://www.gwu.edu/~nsarchiv/NSAEBB/NSAEBB114/chipak-5.pdf.

7. http://www.gwu.edu/~nsarchiv/NSAEBB/NSAEBB114/chipak-6.pdf.

8. http://www.gwu.edu/~nsarchiv/NSAEBB/NSAEBB114/chipak-7.pdf.

9. http://www.gwu.edu/~nsarchiv/NSAEBB/NSAEBB114/chipak-8.pdf.

10. http://www.gwu.edu/~nsarchiv/NSAEBB/NSAEBB114/chipak-9.pdf.

11. http://www.gwu.edu/~nsarchiv/NSAEBB/NSAEBB114/chipak-10.pdf.

12. http://www.gwu.edu/~nsarchiv/NSAEBB/NSAEBB114/chipak-11.pdf.

13. http://www.gwu.edu/~nsarchiv/NSAEBB/NSAEBB114/chipak-12.pdf.

14. http://www.gwu.edu/~nsarchiv/NSAEBB/NSAEBB114/chipak-13.pdf.

15. http://www.gwu.edu/~nsarchiv/NSAEBB/NSAEBB114/chipak-14.pdf.

16. http://www.gwu.edu/~nsarchiv/NSAEBB/NSAEBB114/chipak-15.pdf.

17. http://www.gwu.edu/~nsarchiv/NSAEBB/NSAEBB114/chipak-16.pdf.

18. http://www.gwu.edu/~nsarchiv/NSAEBB/NSAEBB114/chipak-17.pdf.

19. http://www.gwu.edu/~nsarchiv/NSAEBB/NSAEBB114/chipak-18.pdf.

20. http://www.gwu.edu/~nsarchiv/NSAEBB/NSAEBB114/chipak-19.pdf.

21. http://www.gwu.edu/~nsarchiv/NSAEBB/NSAEBB114/chipak-20.pdf.

22. http://www.gwu.edu/~nsarchiv/NSAEBB/NSAEBB114/chipak-21.pdf.

23. http://www.gwu.edu/~nsarchiv/NSAEBB/NSAEBB114/chipak-22.pdf.
24. http://www.gwu.edu/~nsarchiv/NSAEBB/NSAEBB114/chipak-23.pdf.
25. http://www.gwu.edu/~nsarchiv/NSAEBB/NSAEBB114/chipak-24.pdf.
26. http://www.gwu.edu/~nsarchiv/NSAEBB/NSAEBB114/chipak-25.pdf.
27. http://www.gwu.edu/~nsarchiv/NSAEBB/NSAEBB114/chipak-26.pdf.
     Note: complete text of the scanned documents is accessible at the hyperlink provided
     in each respective footnote.

04 Chinese Assistance to Pakistan's Nuclear Weapon Design[1]

This Chapter is based on an analysis of relevant and previously classified US Government documents pertaining to China-Pakistan cooperation in the domain of nuclear weapon design and development.

Document 1:[2] "Covert Programmes." National Intelligence Estimate, "The Likelihood of Further Nuclear Proliferation," NIE 4-66, January 20, 1966, Secret, Excised copy, released on appeal by Interagency Security Classifications Appeal Panel

This NIE was aimed at estimating the capabilities of other countries to acquire nuclear weapons, and the likelihood that such countries would do so. Its salient conclusions included the following:

- Other than the five accepted nuclear power states, only India is considered capable of undertaking a nuclear weapons development programme in the next several years with the possibility of Israel and Sweden also following suit.

- Germany and Japan, although technologically capable of doing so, are not expected to embark on a nuclear weapons development programme even if India, Israel and Sweden develop nuclear weapons. This clearly indicates that in the reckoning of US Intelligence, the three countries considered most capable of and likely to be able to successfully develop nuclear weapons, are India, Israel and Sweden.

- In the second category of countries that could possibly develop nuclear weapons in the long term, this NIE lists Pakistan, United Arab Republic (Union of Egypt and Syria) and South Africa. As events would actually unfold, two of these second tier countries (Pakistan and South Africa) were able to develop nuclear weapons as were two of the first tier countries (India and Israel).

This document lists Japan, West Germany, Switzerland, Australia, Taiwan and South Africa as the third tier of countries that could possibly be also expected to develop nuclear weapons. Basically, this NIE categorised the nations that could aspire for nuclear weapons on two broad determinants: technological prowess (capability) and security imperative (need).

Tier 1	India	Expected to be technically capable and justifiable because of perceived security threat
	Israel	
	Sweden	Technically capable but no perceived security threat
Tier 2	United Arab Republic	Technically incapable at present but need justified if Israel achieves nuclear weapons capability
	Pakistan	Technically incapable at present but need justified if India achieves nuclear weapons capability
	Indonesia	Neither technically capable nor justifiable security threat but expressed intent of Government
	South Africa	Technically incapable at present but no justifiable security threat other than adverse international image due to then prevalent apartheid
Tier 3	Japan	Technically capable but no security threat due to presence of US security umbrella through alliances and security arrangements
	Australia	
	West Germany	
	Switzerland	
	Taiwan	

Although this NIE indicated that India possessed the capability to produce nuclear weapons and test her first device within a year of a decision to go nuclear, she would have to violate the current safeguards agreed to with Canada and the US. Additionally, the US was fairly satisfied that since several key leaders of the Congress Party supported Prime Minister Shastri's publicly announced policy of not producing nuclear weapons, they believed that irrespective of who was the next Prime Minister, this policy would not be reversed in the future.

As regards the erstwhile UAR and Pakistan, the NIE believed that the development of nuclear weapons by these countries was linked to the fact whether the countries posing the maximum security threat to them, i.e., Israel and India respectively, ventured into the domain of development of nuclear weapons successfully or not.

The NIE expected that each of these countries would need substantial aid in virtually all phases and aspects of nuclear weapons development which was not likely to be forthcoming from the five existing nuclear powers. As regards the People's Republic of China, however, which had become the fifth entrant into the nuclear weapons club barely three months prior to the issuance of this intelligence estimate, the document expressed some doubts regarding its adherence to the established tenets of nuclear non-proliferation as agreed to by the established nuclear powers. The

NIE concluded that since the Chinese were still novices in the domain of nuclear weapons, they would be unable to become nuclear proliferators for several years. In future, however, the possibility of China becoming a proliferator of nuclear weapons technology could not be excluded.

Document 3A:[3] Deputy Director for National Foreign Assessment, Central Intelligence Agency, to Christine Dodson, National Security Council, December 7, 1979, enclosing report, "A Review of the Evidence of Chinese Involvement in Pakistan's Nuclear Weapons Programme," November 7, 1979, Top Secret, Excised Copy

Titled, "A Review of the Evidence of Chinese Involvement in Pakistan's Nuclear Weapons Programme," this assessment opens by affirming that although the precise nature of the nuclear cooperation between China and Pakistan is uncertain, the CIA is convinced that China is involved in some mutually beneficial cooperation with Pakistan, particularly in connection with nuclear power. The report mentions several unsubstantiated reports of actual instances or mere promises of Chinese assistance to Pakistan in the realm of nuclear weapons technology, including nuclear weapon delivery systems and nuclear test preparations. Notwithstanding Chinese denials, therefore, the CIA, considering the lack of concrete evidence, was not in a position to flatly rule out that some weapons related aid had been provided by China to Pakistan.

The report then goes on to describe the nuclear cooperation that took place during the period 1974-1978:

Time frame	Salient Events
1974-1976	Pakistan's interest in seeking Chinese assistance in the domain of nuclear weapons development was a direct consequence of the Indian Peaceful Nuclear Explosion in May 1974 and started during the same year as Pakistan launched her nuclear weapon development programme to counter the Indian edge in this area.
	During a subsequent visit to China, Pakistan's Prime Minister Zulfiqar Ali Bhutto raised the issue of nuclear cooperation between the two countries.
	In December 1976, after it had become certain that the Canadians would not be providing nuclear fuel for the Karachi Nuclear Power Plant (KANUPP) which they had provided, Pakistan reportedly approached China once again for the provision of fuel as well as spare parts for that facility.

	Since this was the time when France, presumably under US pressure, had started to reconsider the provision of a nuclear fuel processing plant to Pakistan, it is possible that the latter approached China for the provision of a replacement for the French reprocessing facility. The Chinese expressed their inability to provide a reprocessing plant and asked Pakistan to seek assistance elsewhere while pledging that they would continue to support Pakistan's nuclear programme.
	All this while, there was no evidence whatsoever that China actually followed through with its repeated assurances of nuclear assistance to Pakistan.
1977	China and Pakistan signed a scientific and technical cooperation agreement on January 21, 1977.
	An 11-member Chinese delegation visited KANUPP during the summer and observed the power plant during operation as well as when it was inoperative.
1978	During the summer, the French, bowing to immense pressure from the United States, formally cancelled the supply of a nuclear reprocessing plant to Pakistan.
	Several regional newspapers speculated that China would now step in and provide a similar plant to Pakistan but the Chinese continuously denied the veracity of these reports.

Other than the numerous instances where the Chinese have denied that they were involved in assisting Pakistan in the development of nuclear weapons, there also have been several incidents where a number of Chinese diplomats have conveyed to US diplomats their displeasure over Pakistan's nuclear weapons programme.

There has also been an odd incident in May 1979 of a Chinese diplomat based in Islamabad strongly defending Pakistan's right to develop nuclear weapons during a conversation with a US Embassy political officer. Specially after the Soviet invasion of Afghanistan, the threat posed by the Russian arrival in the region has led to several Chinese diplomats suggesting to the US not to pressurise Pakistan over its nuclear programme and also to restore its weapons supply. Senior Chinese Government officials have also approached the US in this context.

In this effort to assist Pakistan's nuclear weapons development, the Chinese have been possibly motivated by the following:

• China views Pakistan as a key ally and has been compelled to further strengthen the political ties in the wake of a pro-Soviet regime assuming power in Afghanistan.

- The Chinese overture could have been based on the assessment that Pakistan was so well advanced along the nuclear weapons path that it could conceivably develop nuclear weapons sooner or later with or without Chinese assistance.
- Enable China to stay abreast of the latest developments taking place in Pakistan's nuclear weapons development programme.
- To prevent Pakistan from drifting into the Soviet orbit of influence.
- To extract benefit for Chinese nuclear weapons development efforts by learning from the Pakistani experience with those nuclear technologies that the Chinese have not been exposed to earlier.

4. Document 3B:[4] Special National Intelligence Estimate, "Chinese Policy and Practices Regarding Sensitive Nuclear Transfers," SNIE 13/32-83, January 20, 1983, Top Secret, Excised Copy

According to Dr. Burr, these two documents pertaining to the Indian Nuclear Weapons Programmes have been "massively excised" which he construes to be indicative of the CIA's extreme inexplicable sensitivity to releasing information about the Indian nuclear weapon programme even after the lapse of several decades. He makes a special mention of the fact that some of these documents were classified "Top Secret Umbra" which could possibly mean that the information contained therein could have been collected through extremely sensitive "communication intelligence intercepts."

Key Judgements. Having been involved in the following incidents of exporting unsafeguarded nuclear materials, China has been an exporter of these since 1981:

Argentina	Heavy Water and Low enriched Uranium
South Africa	Low enriched Uranium
Pakistan	Provision of technical assistance to Pakistan's nuclear programme including consultations on the operation of an enrichment plant and probably some assistance in nuclear weapon design and development.

These incidents having been in violation of the established global non-proliferation regimes and Chinese refusal to place controls on the export of unsafeguarded nuclear material have compromised and weakened nuclear proliferation efforts, created obstacles in the way of provision of US civilian nuclear power plants to China and have also been a source of worry for Pakistan's regional adversary—India. The report categorises

Chinese nuclear assistance for Pakistan as a consequence of their close and growing strategic relationship and as such, does not consider this to be a part of any global/widespread Chinese proliferation design. Commencing with helping out Pakistan when it was confronted with a nuclear materials embargo, this cooperation subsequently expanded to include assistance in weapons design with the Chinese also benefiting from their access to Pakistan's civilian nuclear plants as well as modern western military equipment.

The report predicts that the Chinese assistance to Pakistan will continue at the existing level since China cannot afford to endanger its strategic relationship with Pakistan. Alleging that China ventured into the sale of nuclear material apparently due to expected financial returns, the report mentions that the sale of nuclear technology and the sale of Chinese conventional military weaponry in the international market both started at the same time. On an encouraging note the report mentions an increasing awareness at the senior levels of the Chinese Government regarding the seriousness of nuclear proliferation that did not exist earlier. Moreover, encouragingly, the Chinese have agreed to hold talks with the US on a bilateral nuclear cooperation agreement, they have ceased their earlier practice of selling Uranium through commercial channels and have repeatedly asserted that they would neither "encourage nor advocate" the spread of nuclear weapons.

China-Pakistan Nuclear Relations
This SNIE views the Sino-Pak nuclear relation as an outgrowth of their lasting ties and common strategic interests. Whereas China is apprehensive about being encircled by unfriendly states, Pakistan needs China as a counterbalance to India. The Sino-Pak relationship outdates the Indian and Pakistan nuclear programmes and dates back to 1963 and is based essentially on geostrategic factors and considerations. As mentioned earlier, the Sino-Pak nuclear relations date back to the India PNE of 1974 when the Chinese accorded a "verbal consent to help Pakistan develop a nuclear blast capability." Although what this verbal arrangement signified was not clear, it was essentially an agreement in principle that was designed to assure Pakistan that China would aid it in countering the new Indian threat.

Although this unwritten and non-formalised bilateral arrangement stayed in existence, China exercised caution and apparently turned down a Pakistani request for four kilograms of plutonium, implying that Pakistan would need to seek other sources for such supplies. In May 1976, Prime Minister Bhutto asked for a more specific commitment which was partially acceded to by the Chinese who agreed to provide the necessary technology required to produce a nuclear weapon but cited their own limitations and said that Pakistan should solicit Chinese help in this realm only as a last resort.

In the aftermath of Bhutto's visit to China, a spate of Chinese nuclear scientists and technicians visited Pakistan including a group that accompanied a military delegation in 1976 and another group that visited KANUPP in 1977. The Chinese involvement in Pakistan's uranium enrichment programme that began in 1979 has continued unabated ever since.

Although Chinese assistance to Pakistan's nascent nuclear weapons programme has been fairly regular and substantial, this SNIE makes it a point to mention that even though Pakistan could have developed a nuclear weapon without Chinese assistance, the access to Chinese weapons design and test data might have proved to be of crucial significance in establishing Islamabad's confidence in its untested weapon's capability.

Document 4:[5] A "Greater Threat to US Interests." US National Intelligence Estimate, "Nuclear Proliferation Trends through 1987." NIE-4082, July 1982, Secret, Excised copy, under appeal

Extracts/Quotes relating to Sino-Pakistan Nuclear relations

In the more volatile areas of the world such as South Asia and the Middle East, nuclear proliferation will threaten US efforts to enhance stability and to improve US security relationships:

- Stability in South Asia will be seriously weakened as Pakistan approaches a nuclear weapons capability threatening to India.
- The potential for a preventive military strike by India, the consequence of which could well be a fourth Indo-Pakistani war, will increase.
- The likely alternative is that India will establish its own nuclear force, thus making India and Pakistan the first pair of nuclear armed adversaries in the Third World.
- When Pakistan achieves the capability to test a nuclear device, the value it places on its security ties with the United States may slow Pakistan's nuclear efforts, including the deferral of a nuclear test. In the meantime, Pakistani efforts to amass plutonium *could* jeopardise the US-Pakistani relationship.

China's recent entry into the nuclear export business warrants special attention. Although not strictly representative of the above trend in new supplier states, recent Chinese sales of unsafeguarded heavy water and enriched uranium to Argentina either through direct sales or through intermediaries illustrate the potential for unbridled nuclear exporters to undermine international non-proliferation efforts.

China has exported enriched uranium to South Africa through West European intermediaries and has considered sales to several other developing states as well.

Although China appears to be in the nuclear market to stay, concern about its image and a desire for foreign nuclear technology may induce Beijing to accommodate some Western views on proliferation. China does not appear ready to cooperate formally, however, with the international non-proliferation regime. It is doubtful that Beijing in the near term will require international, IAEA safeguards as a condition of export.

India's nuclear test in 1974 was largely unrelated to the concerns about China that originally prompted the necessary research. The potential for miscalculations further multiplies the number of possible developments.

Over the past year, for example, Indian advisers have been informing Prime Minister Gandhi on a regular basis that Pakistan could explode a nuclear device on short notice—a judgment that appears one-to-two years premature. Even President Zia of Pakistan believed mistakenly in 1979 that his country would be ready to explode a device in that year.

Document 7A:[6] Central Intelligence Agency, Directorate of Intelligence, Intelligence Assessment, "India's Nuclear Programme: Energy and Weapons," July 20, 1982, Top Secret, Excised copy, under appeal

This document is focused purely on the Indian Nuclear Programme and significant portions of this have been excised, especially the estimate of Israel's nuclear arsenal and its impact in the Middle East. Nevertheless, much information remains on the countries of greatest concern: Iraq and Libya in the Near East, India and Pakistan in South Asia, Brazil and Argentina in Latin America, and the Republic of South Africa, as well as those of lesser concern: Iran, Egypt, Taiwan and the two Koreas.

As regards the India PNE of 1974, this document mentions the Indian claim that this test was aimed at studying cratering and cracking effects on rocks and although it used plutonium recovered from a reactor that had been provided by Canada, India managed to avoid any sanctions or restrictions by describing it as a scientific experiment.

The report goes on to elaborate on the problems that the Indian nuclear research programme has been plagued with and also explains that the Indians have adequately mastered most of the fuel cycle technology that is supporting its nuclear power programme. India has ample uranium reserves and is capable of fabricating natural and enriched uranium into reactor fuel. Although India is currently operating a small reprocessing plant, a much larger plant has become functional while yet another one is planned. India has also established India Rare Earths Ltd., a public sector enterprise aimed to exploit the Thorium deposits that India possesses in plenty.

Document 7B:[7] Central Intelligence Agency, Directorate of Intelligence, "India's Nuclear Procurement Strategy: Implications for the United States," December 1982, Secret, Excised copy. Source: CREST National Archives

Once again, the level to which this document has been excised reveals the reluctance of the US intelligence community towards exposing and making public any details of the Indian nuclear weapons development programme despite the lapse of several decades. In all fairness, however, this particular document has not been censored to the extent that the previous one was.

This document provides details of how the Indians have continued to pursue their nuclear power and nuclear weapons programmes by circumventing international controls through purchase of sensitive technology on the "grey markets." Highlighting the presence of a growing crisis in the Indian civilian nuclear programme and the difficulties in meeting nuclear weapons development goals, the report indicates that India is being forced to seek more external foreign assistance for the development of her nuclear weapon. However, due to the implementation of tighter nuclear export controls having been implemented by the advanced nuclear countries, the availability of unsafeguarded nuclear material was becoming increasingly difficult.

The high degree of Indian activity and involvement in nuclear development becomes obvious when one sees that from 1961 when India signed her first bilateral nuclear-related agreement, the number of such pacts mushroomed to 27 over the next eleven years.

Another extremely interesting piece of information contained in this document is the fact that India approached China for a heavy water nuclear reactor in the 1980s but this could not materialise due to Chinese refusal to provide one. The main suppliers of nuclear equipment and supplies to India have included Japan, the United Kingdom, West Germany and the Netherlands.

Document 8:[8] Central Intelligence Agency, Directorate of Intelligence, Research Paper, "Pakistan's Nuclear Weapons Programme: Personnel and Organisations," November 1985, Top Secret, Excised copy, under appeal

Just like they are overly secretive regarding the Indian nuclear developments, the US intelligence community appears to be equally tightlipped about Pakistan's nuclear programme. Although some structural information about the Pakistan Atomic Energy Commission and its Directorate of Nuclear Fuels and Materials (DNFM) has been included in the document, all information concerning the Khan Research Laboratories and the gas centrifuge programme has been withheld.

The information about the DNFM also includes details regarding the Kundian (Chasma) Reprocessing plant and the Khushab Chemical plant. Interestingly, both these establishments have been constructed with Chinese assistance.

The report talks of the New Laboratories that contain a pilot-scale fuel reprocessing plant that is potentially capable of giving Pakistani scientists experience in reprocessing nuclear fuel. The New Laboratories contain laboratories for dual handling, waste management and plutonium metallurgy and it is thought that by late 1983, this installation was ready to commence reprocessing but political and safety considerations precluded the initiation of reprocessing activity.

In order to ensure that suitably trained manpower is readily available for the management of Pakistan's nuclear programme, the PAEC has established a Centre for Nuclear Studies at PINSTECH (Pakistan Institute for Nuclear Technology) near Islamabad.

8. Document 10:[9] Central Intelligence Agency, Directorate of Intelligence, "The Libyan Nuclear Programme: A Technical Perspective," February 1985, Top Secret, excised copy

This document tells the tale of Libya's crude effort at developing nuclear weapons which was so rudimentary that even the Americans never really took it seriously. The report mentions both India and Pakistan having been approached by the Libyans for obtaining assistance in the nuclear domain but this cooperation was never really taken seriously by any of the countries that Libya approached. This report alludes to Pakistan's assistance by citing the incident of the discovery of the shipment of nuclear material from the A. Q. Khan network destined for Libya in 2003. Elsewhere, it was also reported that some of the cartons/crates in this shipment bore markings in Chinese language.

Document 119:[10] Special weapons Proliferation. Director of Central Intelligence, National Intelligence Estimate, "Prospects for Special weapons Proliferation and Control," NIE 5-91C, Volume 1: The Estimate and Volume 2: Annexes A (Country Studies), B (Weapons and Technologies) and C (Control Regimes), July 1991, Top Secret, excised copy, under appeal

Since the term "weapons of mass destruction—WMD" had not yet become common usage, this NIE used the term "special weapons" to describe nuclear, chemical and biological weapons. This NIE estimates that both Pakistan and India have the ability to develop "nuclear weapons" quickly and regrets that both, "Western European reluctance or inability to enforce controls as well as China's role as a supplier of nuclear technology" served to weaken the global non-proliferation effort.

The following relevant and interesting extracts from this document that pertain to China and the two main South Asian rivals are given below:

- China is a principal supplier of weapons and related technology and materials. China is a full-fledged member of the nuclear club, with wide range of ballistic missiles and a panoply of other special weapons. China sells to others to fund its own programmes and to enhance its political influence worldwide.

- China has provided Pakistan with enriched uranium, the design of a 10 kiloton (kt) nuclear device, and assistance developing the high-explosive components of a nuclear device. Beijing has since maintained high-level exchanges of nuclear scientists with Islamabad.

- China has sold the 300 km range M-11 SRBM to Pakistan. Although both systems have encountered delays, we anticipate the M-11 will be exported this year and the M-9 by 1992. China is also selling technological assistance to missile programmes in Third World countries. For example, Chinese engineers have been assisting Pakistan in the testing and production of its Hatf I and Hatf II missiles, and Beijing has negotiated to provide Iran with production technology to indigenously produce rocket motors, nozzles and propellants.

Notes

1. This article is based on, and replicates, a collection of documents from "China May Have Helped Pakistan Nuclear Weapons Design" edited by William Burr and published by the National Security Archive at George Washington University, Washington, DC, USA, on April 23, 2013. The author thanks the National Security Archive for authorisation to use its work. Founded in 1985 by journalists and scholars to check rising government secrecy, the National Security Archive combines a unique range of functions: investigative journalism centre, research institute on international affairs, library and archive of declassified US documents ("the world's largest nongovernmental collection" according to the *Los Angeles Times*), leading non-profit user of the US Freedom of Information Act, public interest law firm defending and expanding public access to government information, global advocate of open government, and indexer and publisher of former secrets. Based at George Washington University's Gelman Library, the Archive relies for its 3 million yearly budget on publication revenues, grants from individuals and grants from foundations such as the Carnegie Corporation of New York, the Ford Foundation, the William and Flora Hewlett Foundation, the John S. and James L. Knight Foundation, the John D. and Catherine T. MacArthur Foundation, and the Open Society Foundations. The National Security Archive receives no government funding. Incorporated as an independent Washington, DC non-profit organisation, the Archive is recognised by the Internal Revenue Service as a tax-exempt public charity.
2. http://www.gwu.edu/~nsarchiv/nukevault/ebb423/docs/1.1966NIE.pdf.
3. http://www.gwu.edu/~nsarchiv/nukevault/ebb423/docs/3a.Chinese involvement in Pakistan nuke program 1979.pdf.
4. http://www.gwu.edu/~nsarchiv/nukevault/ebb423/docs/3b.PRC transfer policy.pdf.
5. http://www.gwu.edu/~nsarchiv/nukevault/ebb423/docs/4.nuke prolif trends thru 87.pdf.
6. http://www.gwu.edu/~nsarchiv/nukevault/ebb423/docs/7A.India 1982.pdf.
7. http://www.gwu.edu/~nsarchiv/nukevault/ebb423/docs/7B.India   procurement strategy.pdf.
8. http://www.gwu.edu/~nsarchiv/nukevault/ebb423/docs/8.pakistan 1985.pdf.
9. http://www.gwu.edu/~nsarchiv/nukevault/ebb423/docs/8.pakistan 1985.pdf.
10. http://www.gwu.edu/~nsarchiv/nukevault/ebb423/docs/10.libya 1985.
    Note: complete text of the scanned documents is accessible at the hyperlink provided in each respective footnote.

Section II

Pakistan's Nuclear Weapons Control System

05 Pakistan's Nuclear Weapons Control System (NWCS)

Introduction

Nuclear weapons bestow the ability of massive destruction being caused by the country that develops these weapons, and makes this country the focus of international concern especially if it happens to be located in a region that is already plagued by instability. This was precisely the case when both Pakistan and India unmasked their erstwhile clandestine nuclear weapons development programmes in May 1998. Since South Asia had already witnessed three major wars and the volatile issue of Kashmir still remained unresolved, the prospects of these lingering differences leading to an undesirable and catastrophic exchange of nuclear weapons presented a truly frightening possibility.

In order to demonstrate that they were both responsible countries capable of behaving in a manner required of declared nuclear powers, India and Pakistan immediately embarked on establishing the requisite organisational and structural mechanisms for the efficient, secure, fail-safe and foolproof management of their respective nuclear arsenals.

While India went the theoretical way of first coming out with her nuclear doctrine, Pakistan adopted the more practical option of first setting-up a Nuclear Weapons Control System (NWCS). On February 3, 2000, less than two years after the nuclear tests, Pakistan announced the establishment of her NWCS[1] which can essentially be split into three distinct tiers, as will be explained later.

Essential Requirements for a NWCS

Being a new entrant into the nuclear-club, Pakistan was understandably inexperienced about nuclear matters. This lack of knowledge and experience necessitated the establishment of a basic structural organisation which could not only act as the focal point of contact for all matters pertaining to nuclear capability development, employment and management but would also function as a "think tank." Some of the essential aspects that figured out as prominent considerations in designing Pakistan's NWCS were:

- *Hierarchical structure.* Like most military structures, the NWCS is also required to possess a clear and distinct hierarchal structure which would embody a suitable mix of civilian–military control with the pyramid of the structure being based on unitary control and unambiguous distribution of responsibilities at all levels. Since most affairs of state in Pakistan have generally been dominated by the military, the requirement of including enough members from the civilian political hierarchy in the strategic command chain was an imperative that could not be lost sight of. This is all the more important since one of the prime objectives of establishing a strategic command organisation was to indicate to the world how responsible a country Pakistan is.

- *Clear and Distinct Compartmentalisation.* Considering the importance of information security and secretiveness, the various organs of the NWCS were to be established in distinct and separate compartments. Based on the essential principle of "Need to Know" basis of dissemination of information being followed, horizontal linkages within the various organs were to be minimised while ensuring that robust and effective vertical linkages were put in place. Such compartmentalisation would also contribute to the requirement of maintaining a high degree of security of information about Pakistan's nuclear programme and potential.

- *Secure Communications.* Secure, non-tamperable, uninterruptible and continuous means of communication are a critical requirement for any strategic command and control organisation and these have to be put in place before any strategic organisation can be expected to function satisfactorily. In order to ensure round-the-clock and uninterrupted communications, an adequate degree of redundancy would also be required to be built into the communication system that would support the NWCS.

- *Availability of Accurate and Timely Strategic Intelligence.* The availability of real-time and accurate strategic intelligence is an essential prerequisite for the efficient functioning of a strategic command organisation. The strategic intelligence collected through all possible and available means would not only facilitate the selection of targets for a nuclear strike but would also ensure the availability of updated information on the potential enemy's nuclear posture and assets disposition. During peacetime, the intelligence so gathered and collated would help in the selection of targets and also in the suitable reorientation of own nuclear weapons development programme based on what the potential adversary is doing.

- *Affordability.* Due to the financial constraints that most military programmes in Pakistan are experiencing, the factor of affordability figures very prominently in the establishment of any new military infrastructure. The extent to which this aspect was accorded priority is obvious when one considers that the newly set-up SPD was housed entirely in an existing building that had fallen vacant rather than being housed in a new and expensive structure that has been erected specifically for it. Logically speaking, the induction of nuclear weapons should reduce the defence expenditure on the conventional military systems but whether Pakistan is able to get this benefit or not remains to be seen.

- *Security.* One of the biggest issues of concern for the world is the security of Pakistan's nuclear arsenal. Essentially, the West is worried about the chances of Pakistan's nuclear weapons falling into the hands of fundamentalist groups which could precipitate their undesirable and unwanted use. This aspect, therefore, had to be built into the strategic command structure so as to obviate the chances of any unauthorised access to this capability.

- *Responsiveness.* All credible instruments of deterrence are required to be responsive and readily available. Both these attributes essentially flow from the manner in which the strategic command and control structure of a nuclear weapons state is designed. Pakistan's NWCS, therefore, must be structured in a manner that it contributes to enhancing the credibility of her nuclear deterrence potential. This would imply that all the essential attributes discussed above have been adequately built into it. The NWCS must enable the nuclear potential to be brought into action in a short time so as to respond in the time of need. This element of responsiveness must, therefore, be also built into the entire structure of the NWCS since such responsiveness is integral to nuclear deterrence.

All of these and a number of other considerations must have been taken into account by Pakistan's strategic military planners immediately after May 1998 since they realised the urgency with which Pakistan needed to establish her NWCS. The realisation of this requirement led to the establishment of the Strategic Plans Division as an adjunct to the existing Joint Staff Headquarters. Though located within the environs of the JSHQ, the SPD is independent of this organisation and only relies on the former merely for administrative support. Functionally, the SPD comes directly under the NCA and also acts as its Secretariat.

Structure of Pakistan's Nuclear Command and Control System
In the post-nuclear environment, establishment of an effective Command and Control Organisation had become a strategic imperative for achieving three main objectives:
- Establishment of a harmonised command and control mechanism

- Formalisation of an operational policy and development strategy
- Provision of credible stability for the country's strategic deterrence

Furthermore, its formal announcement has transmitted the right signals at the regional and international levels that Pakistan's nuclear and strategic capability is being handled in a professional and responsible manner under an effective command and control system. Pakistan's NWCS is structurally grouped under three constituent tiers as alluded to earlier:

The Three Tiers of Pakistan's NWCS
- Top Tier (Executive Decision level)—*National Command Authority* (NCA)
- Middle Tier (Staff/Secretarial level)—*Strategic Plans Division* (SPD JSHQ)
- Bottom Tier (Field/Implementation level)—Services *Strategic Force Commands* (SFC)

National Command Authority

President (Chairman)
Prime Minister (Vice Chairman)

Strategic Plans Division

Employment Control Committee
- *Deputy Chair,* Foreign Minister
- Minister for Defence
- Minister for Interior
- Minister for Finance
- Chairman JCSC
- COAS/VCOAS
- CNS
- CAS
- *Secretary:* DG SPS
- *Others*: as required

Development Control Committee
- *Deputy Chair* CJCSC
- COAS/VCOAS
- CNS
- CAS
- Head of concerned strategic orgs.
- *Secretary:* DG SPD

Services Strategic Forces
(Operation Control - NCA)

Army   Navy   PAF

(Technical, Training & Administration Control)

Graphic 1 Pakistan National Command Authority

Organisational Structure of Pakistan's National Command Authority (NCA)

Top Tier: National Command Authority
This is designed to be the apex executive level decision-making body

overseeing the management of Pakistan's strategic nuclear potential. Chaired by the Prime Minister,[2] this body and its subordinate organs embody a suitable mix of civilian–military membership. The primary functions of the NCA are:

- Policy Formulation regarding Pakistan's Nuclear Potential
- Planning the Employment of Strategic Weapon Systems
- Development of Strategic Weapon Systems

Functional Organs of the NCA

For the accomplishment of the second and the third function, the NCA has the following two dedicated committees which are both placed under the Prime Minister's control who oversees their functioning:

- Nuclear Weapons Employment Control Committee
- Nuclear Weapons Development Control Committee

Composition of Nuclear Weapons Control Employment Committee[3]

• **Deputy Chairman:** Foreign Minister
• Members: Ministers for Defence, Interior and Finance, Chairman JCSC and the three Services Chiefs
• **Secretary:** DG SPD
• **By Invitation:** Others as required.

Functions of Nuclear Weapons Employment Control Committee

During wartime or period of emergency, the Employment Control Committee of the NCA will function from the National Command Centre or the Alternative National Command Centre. Its functions will include the following:

- Conducting a continuous review of the latest intelligence information regarding the nuclear/strategic weapons programme of the potential adversary or adversaries, and the deployment of these assets.
- Providing policy directions for the nuclear potential during peacetime and exercising authority over the employment of strategic elements of each of the concerned Armed Services during war.
- Based on a factual assessment of the threat and an analysis of own technological prowess vis-à-vis the adversary, provide policy directions and guidance for the evolution of doctrines and employment policies for own nuclear forces.
- Establishing of a clear, distinct and well-defined hierarchy of command for the management of strategic assets and stipulating unambiguous

guidelines for the delegation of authority for the employment of nuclear weapons.
- Laying down of guidelines for an effective strategic command and control system that minimises the chances of accidental or unauthorised use of strategic weapons and obviates the possibility of a faulty strategic decision being taken on the basis of inaccurate and unconfirmed/unverified intelligence information.

Composition of Nuclear Weapons Development Control Committee

- **Deputy Chairman:** CJCSC
- Members: COAS/VCOAS, CNS, CAS and heads/representatives of Strategic Industrial Organisations (Scientists/Engineers)
- **Secretary:** DG SPD

Functions of Nuclear Weapons Development Control Committee

Headed by the Prime Minister through the Chairman, Joint Chiefs of Staff Committee, the prime responsibility of this organ is to exercise control over the strategic weapons development programme. In doing this, the committee will aim to harmonise and integrate the efforts of strategic industrial organisations and optimise their efficiency. Its specific functions would include the following:
- Exercising technical, financial and essential administrative control over the entire spectrum of strategic weapons organisations involved in the research, development and production of strategic weapon systems.
- Overseeing the systematic development of strategic weapons programmes according to the approved Developmental Strategy.
- Establishment of new facilities/organisations for the research/production of strategic weapon systems.
- Integration of the activities of existing strategic weapons research and production facilities.

Middle Tier: Strategic Plans Division (SPD)

This was the first organ of Pakistan's strategic command and control structure to become functional. Its essential roles are to act as an agency of secretarial support for the NCA and to be the focal point of contact for all matters pertaining to Pakistan's nuclear weapons programme and potential. Functioning directly under the Chief Executive (Prime Minister) and through the Chairman of the Joint Chiefs of Staff Committee, the SPD has until now been headed by a two/three star General (Serving/Retired) from the Army.

Recently, a fresh slot for an additional Major General from the Pakistan Army has been created to command a newly created force of 10,000 troops in order to provide security and protection for the entire NWCS. This organisation also falls within the ambit of the SPD.

As per the existing organisational layout, the SPD has nothing to do whatsoever with the operational employment of the nuclear weapons other than its Director General functioning as the Secretary of the NCA and its Employment and Development Committees.

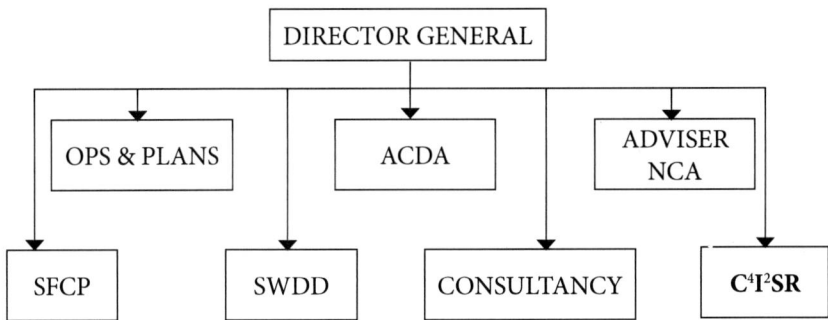

```
                    ┌─────────────────────┐
                    │  DIRECTOR GENERAL   │
                    └─────────────────────┘

┌──────────────┐      ┌──────────────┐      ┌──────────────┐
│ OPS & PLANS  │      │     ACDA     │      │   ADVISER    │
│              │      │              │      │     NCA      │
└──────────────┘      └──────────────┘      └──────────────┘

┌────────┐    ┌──────────┐    ┌──────────────┐    ┌──────────┐
│  SFCP  │    │   SWDD   │    │ CONSULTANCY  │    │  C⁴I²SR  │
└────────┘    └──────────┘    └──────────────┘    └──────────┘
```

Organisational Structure of SPD[4]

SPD is currently sub-divided into seven distinct Directorates, each dealing with a specific and well-defined area of responsibility. These Directorates are headed by an officer of one-star rank (Brigadier/Commodore/Air Commodore) from the armed forces. Usually, these Directors have been taken from the Army with very little representation of the PAF and the PN.

Functions of SPD

In its capacity of comprehensively handling all the aspects of Pakistan's nuclear programme, SPD while acting as the Secretariat for the NCA, is also responsible for performing the following functions on behalf of the NCA. In most cases, its recommendations regarding these aspects have to be approved by the NCA before implementation:

- The SPD, on the guidance of the NCA, is responsible for formulating Pakistan's nuclear policy, nuclear strategy and nuclear doctrine. The recommendations in this regard require to be approved by the NCA before subsequent dissemination and implementation.

- Under the functional umbrella of the NCA, the SPD is required to prepare the short and long-term goals for Pakistan's strategic weapons development strategy. While formulating these development plans, the SPD will ensure that it stays within the ambit of national power potential, national nuclear doctrine, and arms control regimes, nuclear doctrine and development plans of the potential adversary nation or nations. Having obtained the approval of the NCA and depending upon the availability of financial resources, SPD would subsequently also oversee the implementation of the Strategic weapons development programme.

- Considering that the Services Forces Commands of the three Services fall directly under the administrative command and control of the SPD, it will be the responsibility of this organisation to prepare the strategic and operational plans for the strategic assets available with the three Services as regards the movement, deployment and employment of these strategic assets.

- Being the national-level focal point of contact for all issues relating to the development, deployment and employment of all strategic military assets, the SPD must also oversee the clear definition of the entire chain of command involved in the strategic nuclear process including the aspects of command, authority and the delegation of these powers by those in whom these are vested. SPD will prepare and implement the necessary plans that ensure the safety and security of Pakistan's strategic assets against any threat, whether external or internal. These arrangements must be absolutely foolproof and fail-safe so as to also assuage the apprehensions of the other countries about the chances of undesirable elements gaining any unauthorised access to Pakistan's nuclear weapons.

- Being the Secretariat of the NCA, SPD will assist the President, the Prime Minister and the Chairman of the Joint Chiefs of Staff Committee in the exercise of control over all strategic organisations, and will also coordinate their financial, technical, developmental, and essential administrative aspects.

- SPD will be responsible through its Arms Control and Disarmament Directorate (ACDA) to provide military inputs on international/regional arms control regimes, disarmament and related strategic issues, to the Pakistan Foreign Office and our representatives/delegates to the Conference on Disarmament in Geneva.

- Since the collection, collation, analysis and dissemination of strategic intelligence inputs from the various agencies is an issue of the utmost importance, this activity would be overseen by the SPD at the national level. These responsibilities will include coordination of all C^4I^2SR activities and ensuring the establishment of strategic C^4I^2SR system so that the NCA can exercise effective command and control over this sphere of strategic activity. The entire C^4I^2SR network thus established must also embody real-time linkages to the Services C^4I^2SR networks as well as that of the Strategic Forces.

Tier 3: Strategic Forces Command of the Three Services

At the field/implementation level of the strategic command hierarchy, separate Strategic Force Commands have been created or are planned to be raised in all the three Services. These service-specific strategic force commands (SFCs) will have the authority over and responsibility for overseeing the training, technical and administrative activities of their respective Strategic Forces. However, operational planning and control will rest with the National Command Authority under the overall direction of the Prime Minister. The Strategic Plans Division will coordinate on behalf of the NCA with the three Services Headquarters on all nuclear weapons related aspects. The Army Strategic Force Command (ASFC) headed by a three-star General and Air Force Strategic Command (AFSC) that is headed by an Air Marshal/Air Vice Marshal, have already been established while the Pakistan Navy is in the process of establishing the Naval Strategic Force Command (NSFC).

Conclusion

The aim of this chapter was to highlight how seriously Pakistan has taken its status as a responsible, rational and pragmatic nuclear weapons state. A lot of thought went into the creation of the entire edifice of strategic weapons command and control with due importance being accorded to all the imperatives that such an organisation is required to fulfil. It is a measure of the seriousness with which the Government of Pakistan views this subject that the outlines of the country's strategic command structure were announced less than two years after the nuclear tests were conducted in May 1998.

Being a dynamic organisation that is prone to being required to be modified in the event of a significant change in adversary policies or capabilities, Pakistan's strategic command organisation must adapt with time to the changing requirements so that it retains its relevance as well as its effectiveness.

One of the negative aspects of the current strategic command organisation is the high percentage of personnel from the military that are involved in it in various capacities. A continuation or perpetuation of this state of affairs could well lead to one single organisation (in this case the Pakistan Army) exercising an inordinate percentage of control over the nuclear potential. Such an eventuality is unacceptable and must not be allowed to materialise. One solution could be the inclusion of more personnel from the Pakistan Navy, the Pakistan Air Force and civilian departments in the strategic command and control infrastructure. Some of the visible weaknesses in the Pakistan strategic weapons command and control system and the remedies to rectify these are discussed in Chapter 6.

As regards the Americans, they appear fairly satisfied with the safety and security of Pakistan's nuclear arsenal as was obvious from the statement of a US State Department spokeswoman, expressing general satisfaction with Pakistan's command and control system of nuclear assets in these words:[5]

> *"Pakistan's nuclear weapons are in safe hands and the United States is satisfied with the measures Islamabad has taken to secure them ... Our overall assessment is that Pakistan has control of its nuclear arsenal and there is very little doubt about the fact that they have got it under wraps. ... Talking about security concerns within the country against seizure, diversion, accidents, or theft she said: we are always concerned with circumstances like this ... our overall assessment is that their nukes are controlled ..."*
>
> — US State Department Spokesperson, February 22, 2003

Notes

1. http://www.fas.org/pakistan/2000000203-pak-app1htm.
2. According to the Constitution, the control of the NCA should lie with the elected Prime Minister of the country but as has happened so often, whenever the Chief of the Army Staff takes over power, he usually assumes all control of the Pakistan NCA.
3. http://www.fas.org/nuke/guide/pakistan/agency/nca.htm.
4. Currently the SPD is headed by Lieutenant General (Retired) Khalid Kidwai who was appointed to this assignment while he was a Major General and has the distinction of being the first individual to head this organisation. He continued in this assignment even after his retirement from active service. Abbreviations have been used in the above organogram to indicate the nomenclature of the various

directorates. The complete titles of these directorates is as follows:

OPS & PLANS	Operations and Plans Directorate
ACDA	Arms Control and Disarmament Affairs Directorate
ADVISER	Adviser NCA Security
SWDD	Strategic Weapons Development Directorate
CONSULTANCY	Consultancy
C4I2SR	Command, Control, Computers, Communications, Intelligence, Information, Surveillance and Reconnaissance Directorate
SFCP	Strategic Forces Command Directorate

5. *Dawn*, February 24, 2003.

06

Overcoming the Weaknesses of Pakistan's NWCS

This Chapter is aimed at analysing Pakistan's existing strategic command and control structure, highlighting the problem areas that it suffers from, and offering suggestions to suitably modify it so that the highlighted deficiencies can be overcome. For analytical purposes, Pakistan's entire strategic command and control structure will be divided into the following three subject areas which will then be dealt with separately in this chapter:

Part I: Policy Level Strategic Nuclear Control Organisation
Part II: Operational Level Strategic Nuclear Control Organisation
Part III: Reducing Military Control over Pakistan's Nuclear Arsenal

Part I: Policy Level Strategic Nuclear Control Organisation

Analysis of Pakistan's Nuclear Command and Control System

An analysis of the envisaged structure reveals that Pakistan's NWCS, while meeting most of the requirements that such a strategic command and control organisation is required to embody within its functioning, does suffer from the following weaknesses that need to be addressed to so as to further improve its functioning:

- **Lack of Civilian Involvement in Nuclear Control Authority**. Though the planned structure does place the Chief Executive (Prime Minister) at the top of Tier 1 and also includes several of the key cabinet members at Tier 2 in the Employment and the Development Committees, none of these political entities can be expected to overrule the military hierarchy, who though outnumbered by the civilian elected cabinet members, wields substantially greater power. In a country like Pakistan where the military has taken over the reins of power several times, it is conceivable that the Army Chief could concurrently also be the President of the country. If such a political dispensation is permitted to exist, then the top tier of the NWCS, which will be responsible for the final decision as regards the employment of nuclear weapons, could well end up being entirely dominated by the Pakistan military.

- **Lower Two Tiers of Nuclear Control Completely Dominated by Military**. The second issue of concern is the fact that the lower two tiers are also manned solely by military personnel with hardly any meaningful civilian bureaucratic and political representation. This could create a problem since with all the three tiers being controlled by the military and more importantly, within the military by the Pakistan Army, then the imperative of shared civilian control over the NWCS cannot be met.

- **Dilemma Faced during Army Rule.** Theoretically speaking, under circumstances when the Army is ruling Pakistan and the Army Chief is also the President/Chief Executive of the country, he could direct the SPD which is also headed by an Army three-star General and through him, or directly order the Commander of the Army Strategic Force Command (ASFC) to launch nuclear weapons. Although the possibility of such an eventuality occurring is extremely remote, it must be guarded against. It is imperative to ensure, therefore that no single institution or organisation, whether military or civilian, be ever permitted to exercise control over all three tiers of the Pakistan NWCS. In order to preclude such an eventuality, either of the following measures could be adopted whenever the Army is ruling Pakistan:

  ○ If the elected Prime Minister is ousted, the civilian elected President could assume authority as the Head of the NCA. This would only be permissible in the case of a civilian who has been elected as President of Pakistan jointly by the National and the four Provincial Assemblies and not any military officer who assumes power through a coup.

  or

  ○ The elected Speakers of the Senate and the National Assembly are constitutionally mandated to retain their positions till such time that a new elected Government takes office. Through a constitutional amendment, the Chairmanship of the NCC could be transferred to the Speaker of the National Assembly.

  or

  ○ A minimum quorum of the NSC/DCC members could continue to remain in office even in case of the Government having been overthrown so that the NWCS remains functional. In this case, these individuals and their positions must be made secure through constitutional provisions.

The Table below graphically elaborates how the Pakistan Army could possibly be controlling each and every tier of the Nuclear Weapons command and control chain during periods when the COAS has assumed power following a coup. In these circumstances, it would be possible for the Pakistan Army leadership to completely circumvent everyone else and not only decide to use nuclear weapons unilaterally but also, and more worryingly, be able to actually launch these weapons without referring in the least to any other governmental agency, whether civilian or military.

Level/ Tier of Control	Role/Function in Nuclear Command Chain	Person empowered to take decisions and linkage with Pakistan Army	Institutional Control
Tier 1	Executive Decision regarding Nuclear Weapons Employment	Prime Minister of Pakistan	PM **(COAS when Army is in power)**
Tier 2	Staff/Secretarial Support	SPD (headed by a serving/retired 3-star General and staffed mainly by Army officers)	Pakistan Army
Tier 3	Implementation	ASFC (headed by a serving Army Lt. Gen. and manned by Army personnel)	Pakistan Army/ Pakistan Air Force

The spectre of such an eventuality occurring is strengthened even more when one studies the example of the Kargil crisis where the Pakistan Army virtually brought Pakistan to the verge of a full-scale war with India without even having informed or consulted their comrades-in-arms in the Pakistan Navy and the Pakistan Air Force, what to talk of civilian government officials and politicians. While a controversy still exists whether the then Prime Minister Mr. Nawaz Sharif was taken into confidence by the Army about its plans or not, just the possibility of such a unilateral move by the Army, is too scary an eventuality even to contemplate. Kamran Khan, the noted investigative reporter of the Daily News International, published a front page story titled "Army Overhauls Nuclear Command and Control Structure" which further highlighted how the Pakistan Army has virtually assumed total control of Pakistan's Nuclear Command and Control Structure.[1]

Nuclear weapons, at least for the time being and even in the foreseeable future, are expected to remain confined to being employed in the strategic role only within the South Asian regional scenario. Even if Pakistan and India do develop tactical nuclear weapons in the future, the control of these tactical weapons will presumably still continue to be exercised at the strategic level. Since effective military leadership essentially revolves around the principle of Unity of Command, the control of the country's nuclear arsenal must also rest with one organisation. In the case of Pakistan, either Ministry of Defence, or the Joint Staff Headquarters should be tasked to perform this function under the command and control of the country's elected Chief Executive (Prime Minister).

Measures to Address Highlighted Deficiencies
Restructuring/Redesigning of the Top Tier. In Pakistan's chequered political and constitutional history since 1947, several situations have arisen where a serving Army Chief has concurrently been appointed the President of the country. This is why there is some merit in taking the President out of the NWCS Command loop and replacing him with the elected Prime Minister. Half way during his current tenure, President Asif Ali Zardari relinquished his control over the NCA and handed it over to the Prime Minister. The problem is neither fully solved by entrusting the control of the NCA to the Prime Minister nor by removing the President from the nuclear command loop since if a coup does occur, the Prime Minister would be one of the first ones to be thrown out of office. How to handle this eventuality is one of the major issues that Pakistan must resolve.

Since leaving such critical decision making to just one individual is not considered feasible, the Prime Minister would be required to seek the approval of the majority of the members of the Defence Committee of the Cabinet or the proposed National Security Council, in case the latter is established and replaces the DCC.

Consequent to the approval by the NSC/DCC, the Prime Minister could initiate the preparations for the launch of nuclear weapons. Since he is in direct command of the Strategic Force Commands of all the three Services, he could subsequently convey the orders directly to them.

Restructuring of the Strategic Plans Division. An analysis of the current organisational structure of the SPD highlights several areas that warrant a review or an improvement in order to make this set-up more effective and participatory.

Revised Set-up of Directorates. It is proposed that the existing seven directorates of the SPD be revised and replaced with the following six directorates each headed by a military officer of 2-star rank or a civilian officer of BPS-21 grade. The upgradation of the Directors to Director Generals would warrant the existing DG SPD to be designated as Chairman SPD.

- Directorate General Strategic Weapons Development (Pakistan Navy)
- Directorate General Strategic Operations and Weapons Employment (Pakistan Army)

- Directorate General Strategic Intelligence (Pakistan Air Force)
- Directorate General Strategic Research and Production (Nuclear Scientist)
- Directorate General Strategic Arms Control, CBMs and Disarmament (Diplomat)
- Directorate General Strategic Security and Protection (Police)

Inclusion of Civilian Bureaucrats/Nuclear Scientists in SPD Directorates
Currently, the SPD is almost a purely military organisation with this second tier of the nuclear command and control organisation having no meaningful representation from the civilian sector. The new proposal bases itself on reducing the number of military directors excluding the Chairman, to just three with the remaining three Directors being from the civilian sector. This would put the relative ratio of civilian directors to military directors at 50:50 and this ratio must never be allowed to change in favour of the military participation in the SPD. It is proposed that civilian officials of BPS-21 grade be inducted to head the following directorates of the SPD:

- **Strategic Research and Production Directorate**. This directorate should be headed by an officer who is essentially a nuclear scientist and is serving in one of the nuclear scientific organisations of the country, e.g., Pakistan Atomic Energy Commission, SUPARCO, NESCOM, etc. This directorate could include staff officers from each of the three Services as well as from the Engineering and Scientific Organisations.
- **Strategic Arms Control, CBMs and Disarmament Directorate**. This directorate should be headed by an officer from the Foreign Service of Pakistan who must have had prior experience of attending international arms control moots and conferences. The primary functions of this directorate would include monitoring all international agreements, meetings and conventions related to arms control. This directorate could include staff officers from each of the three Services as well as from the Pakistan Foreign Service.
- **Strategic Security and Protection Directorate**. This directorate should be headed by an officer from the Pakistan Police/civilian Intelligence Bureau. He would be responsible for the provision of security and protection to all components of the Pakistan Nuclear Weapons System. This directorate could include staff officers from each of the three Services as well as from the Pakistan Police and Intelligence Organisations.

Equal representation of all three Services at higher levels of SPD. Consequent to the inclusion of civilian officers as mentioned above, the following three key slots would be left open for the military in the SPD:

Chairman SPD	Lieutenant General/Air Marshal/ Vice Admiral in strict rotation[2]
DG Strategic Weapons Development	Rear Admiral from Pakistan Navy
DG Strategic Operations and Weapons Employment	Major General from Pakistan Army
DG Strategic Intelligence	Air Vice Marshal from Pakistan Air Force

The structure of the SPD as well as the appointment of the Chairman of the SPD, after being approved will be afforded constitutional protection through a legislative amendment in the Constitution of Pakistan. In case of the Chairman SPD not being available the senior most military DG out of the three would officiate for him.

SPD to be excluded from Executive Command Chain of Nuclear Weapons Employment. Though designed to act purely as a staff/secretarial organisation functioning as an adjunct to the NCA, the SPD over the years has assumed significant executive authority. This is contrary to its charter and needs to be corrected. This proposed reorganisation will completely exclude the SPD from the executive/decision cycle.

SPD to continue functioning as a staff/secretariat organisation for NCA but under the executive authority of the Defence Minister. With its revised composition and charter, the SPD would move to the Ministry of Defence from the Joint Staff Headquarters and function directly under the control of the Defence Minister.

Services Strategic Force Commands to be under direct executive control of Prime Minister. With the SPD having been completely excluded from the executive/decision command chain, the Strategic Force Commands (SFCs) of the Army, the Navy and the Air Force will take direct orders from the Prime Minister. These SFCs will continue to be commanded by two/three star officers from their respective Service.

Additional Task for Chairman SPD. Chairman SPD would, in addition to his primary assignment, also act as the Secretary for all NSC/DCC meetings that are called for discussing issues pertaining to the employment of nuclear weapons and record the minutes and decisions of these meetings.

Involvement of the NSC/DCC. As mentioned above, a majority of the members of either the NSC or the DCC, depending on which of the two is in place and functional, must accord assent to the Prime Minister before the latter can order the launch of nuclear weapons. The decision to launch nuclear weapons must stipulate the following in very clear and unambiguous terms:

Type of weapon to be launched. This should be based on the type of target planned to be engaged and the degree of damage desired to be inflicted. Essentially, the yield of the weapon to be selected would depend on these considerations.

Type of platform/platforms to be employed for weapons launch. Currently Pakistan can only deliver nuclear weapons through aircraft or surface-to-surface missiles. The selection of the delivery means to be adopted would also be dictated by the required yield of the weapon and the depth of the target inside India (essentially, the range that the delivery mechanism adopted would need to traverse from launch to impact). It may also happen that in order to ensure that the weapon reaches the target, both the means of delivery are employed simultaneously against the same target. Subsequent to Pakistan's development of a submarine launched nuclear weapon capability, this choice would also become available.

Specific enemy target against which the nuclear weapon is to be launched. While the aspect of counter-value or counter-force target selection should have been addressed during the process of nuclear doctrine development, the vital decision regarding the specific target that is to be attacked must be taken at the highest level. This decision must take into account all the consequences including enemy response, implications and fallout of taking out the selected target. Accurate photographs and intelligence information about all the possible targets must be obtained during peacetime and disseminated amongst all concerned.

Date and timing of the weapon launch. After a detailed review of the current military situation and how it is expected to develop over the subsequent days, a precise determination of the date and time of the nuclear attack must be arrived at during the deliberations.

Recording/Authentication of Decision. The total proceedings of the meeting and specifically all the decisions listed above must be recorded and the signatures of all those in attendance be taken to authenticate their agreement and concurrence. This would be the responsibility of the Chairman SPD who would act as the Secretary for all such meetings during war.

Constitutional Provisions. The significance of Pakistan's NWCS and the need to ensure that it is permitted to operate without any hindrance or snag necessitates the promulgation and enactment of constitutional amendments that would allow this system to function exactly as planned.

In view of the serious, and likely to be permanent nature of their functions, the specific roles, the authority that they would wield, their organisation hierarchy and the institutional affiliations of individuals involved at each of the three tiers of nuclear command and control must be made a formal part of the Constitution of the Islamic Republic of Pakistan through an Act of Parliament.

At the national level, the necessary mechanism to deal with the nuclear weapons issue already exists in the form of the Defence Committee of the Cabinet (DCC) which could possibly now be replaced by the National Security Council (NSC). The need is to formalise the existing structure and allocate it the required responsibilities. The decision of opting for the employment of nuclear weapons would vest directly in the Chief Executive of the country—this in Pakistan's case should be the elected Prime Minister of the country. Regardless of whether the NSC or the DCC is functional, what must be ensured is that the composition of this body is numerically in favour of the civilian ruling hierarchy. Even if the Chairman JCSC and the three Services Chiefs are included as members, they would be outnumbered by the Prime Minister, the Ministers for Defence, Foreign Affairs, Finance and Interior. The acceptable quorum for such a meeting must always be based on full attendance with no abstention being allowed whatsoever. Provisions will have to be made to cater for the non-availability of some of the members of the DCC/NSC provided that the aspect of civilian leadership being in a majority is never be allowed to be violated under any circumstances. Another option that could be explored in the long term could be to strengthen the post of CJCSC, make it strictly rotational and allow him alone to represent the military at the NCA, with the other Services Chiefs being invited to attend whenever considered necessary.

In terms of nuclear command authority, the channel would flow directly from the Chief Executive (elected Prime Minister) to the respective Commander of the Army Strategic Force Command or the Pakistan Air

Force Strategic Command (subsequent to the development of a sub-launched nuclear weapon capability, the spectrum of this authority would also span to include the Naval Strategic Force Command.) This chain, unlike the existing one, would not include the Director General (Chairman) of the Strategic Plans Division (SPD) in the executive chain of command in any capacity whatsoever. The following are some of the aspects that would need to be addressed by and included in this piece of legislation that stipulates the Constitutional provisions:

Issues Concerning NSC/DCC
- Composition of NSC/DCC
- Authority of decision-making of NSC/DCC regarding the employment of nuclear weapons
- Rules of business of the NSC/DCC/SPD
- According of permanence to NCC if Government is removed

Issues Concerning SPD
- Establishment of the SPD as an adjunct to the Ministry of Defence
- Composition of the SPD to be modified as per recommendations
- Functions of the SPD and its rules of business
- Procedure for selection of personnel for the SPD
- Tenure of personnel deputed to the SPD

Any other issue pertaining to the foolproof functioning of the NSC/DCC/SPD that might be considered necessary.

Impact of Proposed Modifications on Structure of NWCS
As is apparent from the details of the reorganisation that are required to be implemented within the SPD so that the weaknesses existing in the nuclear command and control apparatus are removed, a complete reorganisation of the SPD is in order so as to ensure that an adequate representation of civilian officials involved in the process is made possible. Additionally, the proposed organisation must also cater for the following two aspects:
- None of the Government organisations/institutions or any individual should have a decisive role in the structure at all three tiers that would permit it to employ nuclear weapons on its own without any reference to the other elements of the nuclear command organisation. Checks and balances and multi-organisational presence needs to be ensured at each

and every tier of the nuclear command and control structure with the SPD being no exception to this rule.

- A balanced and equitable presence of the three military Services must be ensured in the system so as to make sure that none has a dominant role to play. Not only must the three Services be equally represented but also the inclusion of an adequate civilian presence within the command and control hierarchy must be ensured.

Part II: Operational Level Strategic Nuclear Control Organisation

Although the plan envisages the establishment of service-specific strategic force commands in all the three Services, currently only the Army Strategic Force Command (ASFC) and the Air Force Strategic Command (AFSC) have been established. The third such organisation—the Pakistan Navy Strategic Command will only be established after the triad-based nuclear weapons potential has been developed and is in place,

This organisational chain of control would also be divided into three tiers on the same lines as the Strategic Policy Organisation with the three tiers being structured as follows:

Command Tier

Each of the three service-specific strategic force commands will be headed by a 2-star officer from that particular service (Major General/Rear Admiral/Air Vice Marshal). Administratively, these force commands will remain in coordination and liaison with the SPD. Manpower for these set-ups will be provided by the respective Services Headquarters and DG SPD/Force Commanders would be fully involved in the process of selection of these officers and personnel. All these personnel would be required to possess the highest security clearance with no exceptions being made in this regard. Functionally and operationally, however, the respective Force Commanders would only take direct orders from the Chief Executive (Prime Minister of Pakistan).

Implementation Tier

The Force Commanders would be responsible for overseeing the storage, preparedness and employment of nuclear weapons by the personnel of their own services. These officers would directly control the Nuclear Weapons Control Units (NWCUs) which, though being manned entirely by personnel from their services, would be deployed with one of the other two services. The primary purpose of this arrangement is not to leave the possibility of independent nuclear weapons usage open to any single service and to obviate any accidental or unplanned use of these weapons. In order to elaborate on the role of the NWCUs, it needs to be mentioned that these units, commanded by officers of the rank of Lieutenant Colonels or equivalent, would be responsible for the security of the nuclear warheads placed in their custody. The NWCUs would also be responsible for insertion of the requisite code that would be a necessary prerequisite for the usage of these weapons. Any particular NWCU would be manned entirely by the personnel from one particular service but would be deployed with one of the other two services. For example, the nuclear bombs available at any PAF base could be with a Pakistan Navy NWCU while the sea-launched missiles of the PN could be with the Pakistan Army NWCU and land-based strategic weapons, though the responsibility of the Pakistan Army, could be under the control of a PAF NWCU.

Execution Tier

This level will consist of those personnel who would be actually responsible for the launching/dropping of the nuclear weapon. In case of nuclear-tipped SSMs, this tier would represent the Officer Commanding the specific Pakistan Army SSM Battery that is tasked to launch the SSM while in the case of the weapons that are to be dropped from aircraft this task would be handled by the Squadron Commander of the concerned Pakistan Air Force Squadron. In the case of the Pakistan Navy, it could be the Captain on the ship or the submarine.

The proposed system would offer quadruple levels of safety and security. Each nuclear weapon would need a set of code in order to be activated and made ready for usage. The first four digits of the code would be communicated by the Chief Executive (Prime Minister of Pakistan) to the concerned Strategic Force Commander who would add his own 4-digit code and transmit the 8-digit code to the Commander of the concerned NWCU. After the Commander of the NWCU adds his own 4-digit code to the 8-digit code that he has received from the Strategic Force Commander, the weapon would be released to the personnel who would be launching the nuclear-tipped SSM or dropping the air-delivered nuclear bomb. The Commander of the SSM battery and/or the Squadron Commander of the relevant attack Squadron of the PAF would add their own 4-digit code to the twelve digits that they have received and the feeding of the resultant 16-digit figure will arm the weapon that has to be launched or dropped. In order to make this system further foolproof, the codes could be random arrangements of numerals and alphabet characters.

The Chief Executive (Prime Minister) would convey his instructions along with the code to the Strategic Force Commander of the Service that has to be tasked for the employment of nuclear weapons. The concerned Strategic Force Commander would transmit the message further in the following manner:

- He would add his own 4-digit code and forward the same to the Officer Commanding the relevant concerned NWCU.
- He would simultaneously inform the Strategic Force Commander of the Service that is required to launch the weapon regarding the fact that he will be authorising the issue of weapons to his personnel. This would act as a readiness warning for the personnel of the Service that will be launching/dropping the nuclear weapon.

Since the NWCUs would be under the control of personnel from a different Service, the command from the Prime Minister (Chief Executive) would have to be conveyed according to the following chart:

Service to Launch Weapon	Strategic Force Commander to be informed	Remarks
Pakistan Air Force	Commander Naval Strategic Command	All PAF nuclear weapons would be in the custody of PN personnel manning the NWCUs located at or near PAF bases
Pakistan Army	Commander Air Force Strategic Command	Pakistan Army nuclear weapons would be in custody of PAF personnel manning the NWCUs located at or near the Pakistan Army strategic missile sites
Pakistan Navy	Commander Army Strategic Force Command	All PN nuclear weapons would be in the custody of Pakistan Army personnel manning the NWCUs on board nuclear capable submarines or ashore

In order to enhance the element of security, these four digit codes would be changed at random intervals. Moreover, DG SPD would plan, arrange and conduct regular dry exercises to ensure that the entire system works smoothly and without a glitch.

In order for this system to be able to spring into action at a short notice, all those in the chain of command would have to remain available all the time so that they can be reached whenever required. The status of alert as regards the weapons themselves, however, would be regulated according to the prevalent level of tensions and could be lowered or raised by the DG SPD in consultation with the Chief Executive (Prime Minister of Pakistan). The importance of a reliable and adequately redundant, tamper-proof and efficient communication system, therefore, cannot be overstressed.

In order to ensure the quick and timely availability of Pakistan's nuclear response potential, the NCA must stipulate the status of alert that the various components of Pakistan's nuclear potential would be required to maintain. The determination of this alert status must be based on the prevailing situation in the region and also cater to its rapidly changing dynamics. The proposed operational-level nuclear command structure depicted below caters for most, if not all of the requirements elaborated upon in the preceding text:

Proposed Operational-Level Strategic Command Structure

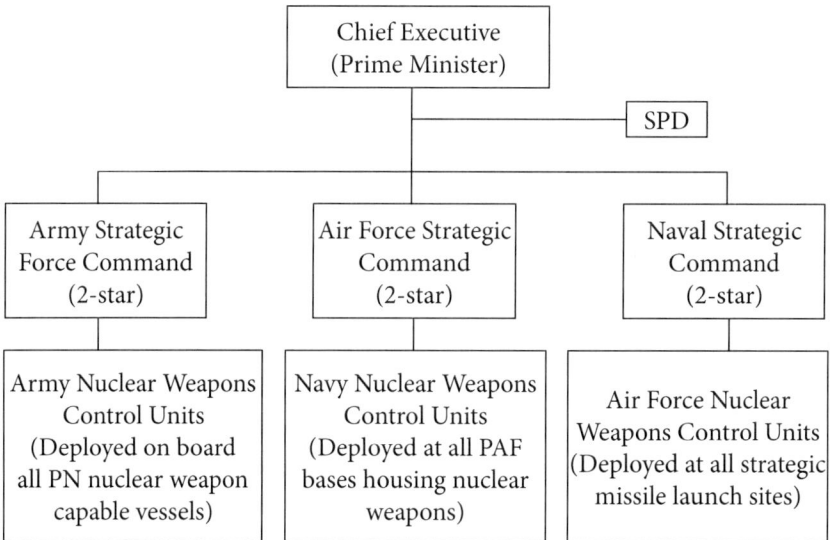

This system would ensure adequate safety against any single organisation or individual deciding to go nuclear since even a single break in the chain would not permit the weapon being configured and made ready for employment. This entire set-up would operate independently of the three service headquarters.

It is mandatory that the selection of the officers and personnel involved in the various NWCUs be accomplished very carefully after a detailed scrutiny of their background for capability, professional acumen, psychological stability and loyalty to their country. This must be considered as a prime assignment in the career pattern of the individuals and be accorded due importance.

Part III: Reducing Military Control over Pakistan's Nuclear Arsenal

The year 2007 was of great significance from the perspective of terrorism in Pakistan. Starting off as a fairly normal year with four incidents of terrorism being experienced during the first half of the year, the situation altered radically in the immediate aftermath of the storming of the Lal Masjid and Jamia Hafsa religious seminary (Madrassa) complex in Islamabad by the security forces. The retaliation for the military's involvement in this episode was so strong that the last six months of 2007 witnessed 52 incidents of suicide terrorism. These included the tragic assassination of Benazir Bhutto outside Rawalpindi's Liaquat Bagh during the last week of 2007.[3]

More significantly, most of these incidents were directed against the security personnel, including the regular armed forces, and rather than being confined to the already troubled region of the Federally Administered Tribal Areas (FATA) on the Pakistan–Afghanistan border, these occurred in the heart of the major urban centres all over the country, from Karachi to Rawalpindi, Islamabad, Lahore, Sargodha and Peshawar.

While the change in targeting indicated the anger against the security apparatus and the emboldened posture of the terrorists, the countrywide spread of these incidents illustrated the extent of their reach all over Pakistan. Three significant events appear to have precipitated this increased spate of acts of terrorism and the altered targeting strategy: the operation against the Lal Masjid which culminated in its storming; the sudden increase in the intensity of military operations in the Swat Valley; and the death by suicide of Abdullah Mehsud, a former Guantanamo Bay inmate, after he was surrounded by the Pakistani security forces in Baluchistan.

Ever since Pakistan went overtly nuclear in May 1998, the West has continuously voiced its concerns over the security of its nuclear arsenal and the danger of this falling into the hands of the extremist Islamic elements. It was understandable, therefore, that in the wake of the increased terrorist activity in Pakistan during 2007, observers and officials of concerned

Governments all over the world started to voice their concerns regarding the safety of Pakistan's nuclear weapons.

Having been associated with the Pakistan military for over three decades and having followed nuclear developments in the country closely,[4] I am also concerned about the security of Pakistan's nuclear arsenal but a detailed analysis of the situation has led me to conclude that while there was a negligible amount of chance of the nuclear weapons falling into the hands of the radical Islamic militants because of adequate and effective safeguards having been built into Pakistan's NWCS, most of the analysts were incorrect in assuming that the threat to Pakistan's nuclear weapons was posed by the Islamic extremists.[5]

At the time of independence, Pakistan inherited a well-trained Army with an officer clique well-versed in classical British military traditions. Being a remnant of the British colonial era, the officers of this Army had been brought up in an artificial atmosphere of superiority vis-à-vis the common inhabitants of British India and considered themselves to be the most suitable successors to the British rulers.

Since the British colonial rulers had not really allowed local political institutions and leaders to develop, Pakistan was also faced with a vacuum in the political domain which was initially filled up by the larger-than-life figures like Quaid-i-Azam Muhammad Ali Jinnah and Nawabzada Liaquat Ali Khan but the early demise of both these stalwarts of the freedom movement created an environment of political instability which afforded the Pakistan Army an opportunity of usurping the weak and ineffective political government and gaining control of the country through the imposition of Martial Law in 1958. Since that fateful day, the Army has effectively engineered coups and ensured that it ruled the country for almost half its life since independence.

Over time, the power and authority of the Army started being considered as a fact of life in Pakistan. Apart from derailing democracy and inhibiting the creation of sound political institutions, these periods of military rule have resulted in critical national issues such as Pakistan's policy towards Afghanistan, the Taliban and also Kashmir being managed by the Inter-Services Intelligence (ISI) and the Pakistan Army's General Headquarters (GHQ), rather than being formulated by the political government and the Pakistan Foreign Office.

Right from the outset, the Pakistan Armed Forces have played a major role in the development of the country's nuclear weapons. Partly, this can be attributed to the stable existence of the military as an institution of state in Pakistan where the civilian governments have always been characterised by instability.

Over the years, the military developed an ownership of the nuclear weapons programme to an extent that it eventually developed an dominant influence which has persisted ever since. While it is easy to blame the military for its excessive control over matters nuclear, it must be understood that Pakistan owes the successful development of its nuclear weapons to the continuous and unabated involvement of its military.

Conclusion

Developing nuclear weapons is the first step while learning to live and exist with these weapons in today's world is quite another. While Pakistan has successfully surmounted the numerous obstacles and achieved nuclear weapons capability, it still has to overcome some hurdles as regards its NWCS.

In summary, the following aspects of Pakistan's NWCS need to be modified and improved:

- Balance between civil and military control is to be constitutionally ensured with the elected Prime Minister to head the NCA.
- SPD to be placed under the Ministry of Defence.
- Manpower composition changes warranted in SPD to be completed:
  - DG SPD to be re-designated as Chairman SPD
  - Chairman SPD position to be rotated among the three Services
  - Inclusion of three civilian DGs in SPD
  - Upgradation of three military Directors to Director Generals
  - Balance between manpower from all three armed services
- All activities/functional aspects of SPD to be afforded Constitutional approval
- Legislation to ensure that NSC/DCC always remain functional even if the Government is removed due to any reason.

Notes

1. Kamran Khan, "Army Overhauls Nuclear Command and Control Structure," *The News International*, December 24, 2003, pp. 1, 9.
2. In order to ensure that the assignment of Chairman SPD is regularly rotated between the three Services, the details of the eligibility of the key manpower for SPD should

also be clearly spelled out in the relevant legislation. If this is not done then it might not be possible to implement this system of rotation. The appointment of Chairman Joint Chiefs of Staff Committee is a typical example.

3. B. Raman, "Suicide Terrorism In Pakistan." Accessible on internet at http://www.outlookindia.com/full.asp?sid=1&fodname=20080114&fname=raman.   There were 56 acts of suicide terrorism in Pakistan during 2007, resulting in the death of 419 members of the security forces—the majority of them from the police and paramilitary forces—and 217 civilians. The most important civilian killed was Mrs. Benazir Bhutto, former Prime Minister. As against this, there were only six incidents in 2006 in which 46 members of the security forces and 91 civilians were killed. Of the 56 incidents of 2007, there were only four during the first six months of the year. The remaining 52 took place after the Pakistani commando action in the Lal Masjid of Islamabad between July 10 and 13, 2007.

4. The author is now working on the current volume which presents a detailed discussion of South Asia's nuclear options. His first writing on the subject was a research essay titled "Controlling Nuclear Proliferation in South Asia" which he wrote while attending the No. 84 Advanced Staff Course at the Royal Air Force Staff College in Bracknell, UK in 1991-1992. This research essay was adjudged to be the best among all those submitted and won him the coveted "Andover Prize" which is awarded for the best research essay submitted by an overseas officer attending the course. His individual research paper titled "The Impact of Nuclearisation on Pakistan's Military System" that he wrote while attending the Pakistan National Defence Course during 1999-2000 was adjudged as one of the best research papers during that year and was selected for publication in the Pakistan National Defence College Journal.

5. Please refer to the author's article titled, "Myths and Realities: The Security of Pakistan's Nuclear Arsenal." *Force India*, January 2013.

Section III

Pakistan's Doctrinal Thinking

07   A Nuclear Policy for Pakistan

Introduction

Having commenced her nuclear weapons development programme as a response to the Indian Peaceful Nuclear Explosion of 1974, Pakistan's hand was once again forced by Indian conduct of nuclear tests in 1998 that prompted Pakistan to respond in kind within a few days with tests of her own. These nuclear tests radically altered the security paradigm of South Asia and necessitated the formulation of nuclear doctrines and policies by both India and Pakistan. While India did come out with a draft nuclear doctrine, Pakistan, probably trying to maintain an element of vagueness regarding her nuclear intentions, has not done so till now. Since Pakistan has not yet issued her nuclear doctrine, it may appear premature that this chapter on Nuclear Policy has been written since "Policy" essentially flows out from the established doctrinal precepts and as such, the former could only be finalised after the latter has been definitised.[1]

While the first nuclear weapon dropped on Hiroshima on August 6, 1945 and the second on Nagasaki on August 9, 1945 did manage to bring the Japanese Empire to its knees and marked the end of the Second World War, the development of these weapons of mass destruction ushered in a new dimension of war—that of mutual deterrence. This formed the basis of the Cold War between the US and the erstwhile USSR of over four decades and also influenced the rapid proliferation of nuclear weapons capability. The importance of nuclear weapons in the current and emerging nuclear paradigm has led to eight countries possessing nuclear weapons today including the original five who hold the monopoly or self-professed "legitimacy" and the three non-accepted nuclear weapons capable states of India, Pakistan and Israel.

Although a lot of material has been written on the Cold War and the analysis of this tumultuous period of human existence continues unabated, I feel that the most essential aspect of the Cold War was the emergence of nuclear deterrence as a major player in defining the security landscape of the world. The massive nuclear arsenals and long-range nuclear delivery mechanisms developed and fielded by the US and the erstwhile USSR shaped the global dynamics for almost 44 years and ultimately resulted in the dismemberment of the mighty Soviet Union, to be replaced by a host of relatively smaller countries located in a virtual geographic necklace around Russia.

The demise of the Soviet Union despite her massive nuclear wherewithal left one very important lesson which cannot be lost sight of. What the end of the Cold War highlighted was that "While nuclear deterrence might succeed in preventing a conflict or war between two nuclear weapons capable countries, the possession of nuclear capability, howsoever mighty it might be, is by itself incapable of preventing a comprehensive defeat." The demise of the Soviet Union is an example of this.

As newer nuclear weapons capable countries like Pakistan and India emerge on the scene, it is imperative that they remain mindful of this important lesson and build it into their evolving nuclear doctrines, policy and strategy.

Objectives of Pakistan's Nuclear Policy

Objectives of a country's nuclear policy should specify what she wants to achieve from her nuclear potential whether through the expressed or implied threat of its use or the actual employment of these weapons against any potential adversary. As such, the objectives form the first rung or the foundation of any country's nuclear policy and must be finalised before the rest of the nuclear policy is evolved. Pakistan's nuclear policy in my opinion, should focus on the following objectives:

- Pakistan's nuclear policy would be based on deterrence and would be designed to ensure that all possible forms of external aggression that can endanger Pakistan's national security, are successfully deterred. By the implied resolve of a nuclear response, this policy of deterrence should be able to deter all potential aggressors from harbouring any hostile intentions and as such contribute to an era of peace centred on stability of deterrence.
- Working within the resource constraints that Pakistan is currently facing, the country must endeavour to build up adequate levels of conventional and nuclear deterrence, which when combined, will provide the requisite deterrence against any aggressive intent and designs of the possible adversaries. The requirement to review the level of both, conventional and nuclear deterrence potentials, is necessary due to the rapid pace at which India is strengthening her military capability.
- Pakistan's nuclear policy would ensure that her own nuclear arsenal is so sited and located inside protective environment that the possibility of the enemy successfully launching a first strike against her nuclear potential is minimised. This directly implies that Pakistan's nuclear potential must be survivable enough to survive an enemy first strike and still remain available as a potent, viable and credible second strike potential. The options available in this context are to place these assets inside NBC proof shelters which are not easily identifiable or discernible by air and space surveillance assets, or to place these assets on a mobile platform such as a train so that their location is continuously changing. The requirement for taking such extreme and expensive steps flows from the following:

o Pakistan's north-east south-west geographical orientation and limited depth place virtually the whole of the country within easy reach of Indian nuclear delivery aircraft and nuclear warhead fitted ballistic missiles.

o The long contiguity of the India–Pakistan border enables India to virtually threaten the entire expanse of Pakistan with her available nuclear delivery potential.

o The lack of early warning due to non-availability of any suitable surveillance system with Pakistan and the virtually non-existent early warning of any Indian nuclear launch.

o India's preponderance in conventional military potential in general, and air power potential, in specific puts Pakistan on the backfoot and is likely to cause a lowering of Pakistan's nuclear employment threshold.

o The maintenance of an effective environment of deterrence is a dynamic process and Pakistan's nuclear potential and capability would have to take the enemy's similar capabilities into active consideration at all times. This would ensure that the atmosphere of deterrence created in the region is stable and lasting than being temporary and would usher in a period of stabilisation of strategic deterrence in South Asia.

o In the face of a looming conventional imbalance vis-à-vis India, Pakistan's nuclear policy will have to be dynamic and must adapt to the changing dimensions of the threat posed by India. This would have to be achieved without getting Pakistan involved in an arms race that she can ill afford in her present economic condition.

Nuclear Policy

In order to be able to achieve all the objectives listed above, Pakistan's nuclear policy must be centred on the concept of responsible behaviour and must espouse the exercise of maximum restraint in the conduct of her deterrence policy. Both these aspects would go to prove that Pakistan is capable of behaving in a manner expected of a mature nuclear state. The adoption of this posture of responsible behaviour implies that Pakistan exercise maximum restraint in the conduct of its deterrence policy.

Essential Elements of Pakistan's Nuclear Policy

Though the essential elements which go to make the nuclear policy of a country have never been overtly mentioned by the Government of Pakistan officially, it stands to reason that a lot of thought, deliberation and thinking must have already gone into this aspect. Most of these elements have been referred to or alluded to by different Pakistani leaders during their speeches, statements and interviews. Also, this aspect has been addressed in quite detail by the media as well as the various think tanks, both domestic and international. In my opinion, the following could be some of the essential elements of Pakistan's nuclear policy:

- Unlike India which went ahead with the acquisition of nuclear weapons in order to further strengthen her regional power, prestige and standing, Pakistan essentially developed these weapons as a defensive counter to India. As such, Pakistan's acquisition of nuclear capability must be viewed in this context and perspective. Having no aggressive or hostile designs against anyone, it therefore stands to reason that the purposes behind Pakistan's nuclear programme are to deter the chances of aggression by any adversary and to ensure the defence of Pakistan's territorial and ideological integrity and sovereignty.

- In line with established international precepts of nuclear weapons not being employed against non-nuclear states, Pakistan's policy must also stipulate that Pakistan will neither use nor threaten to use nuclear weapons against a country that does not possess nuclear weapons capability. The incorporation of this element into Pakistan's nuclear policy would also serve to put the non-nuclear regional states at peace and promote regional stability.

- Maintenance of Credible Minimum Nuclear Deterrence is the guiding principle of Pakistan's security policy.[2] Flowing from the assertion that the raison d'être for Pakistan venturing into the nuclear domain was the imperative to balance out Indian conventional military capabilities, it stands to reason that from a defensive standpoint, Pakistan's nuclear policy must be based on the cardinal principle of deterrence.

- Pakistan will refrain from entering into any arms race. This imperative flows from Pakistan's dire economic straits. Despite the fact that Pakistan has moved back appreciably from the brink of financial ruin that it was facing a few years back, it cannot afford to venture into any arms race with India, whether conventional or nuclear. Not only would such a venture be absolutely unaffordable but it would also be entirely unacceptable to the developed countries and the International Financial Institutions that have played a significant role in bailing Pakistan out of her financial crisis.

- Pakistan will maintain an adequate conventional military force in order to raise its nuclear threshold. Notwithstanding the fact that the first purpose of a nuclear deterrent is to prevent any sort of conflict from breaking out, Pakistan is faced with an increasing conventional imbalance vis-à-vis India. The recent military acquisitions that India has ventured into from Israel, Russia, United States and France are indicative of this trend. The single most significant impact of the emerging conventional imbalance in South Asia is that this would lead to a marked lowering of Pakistan's earlier and existing nuclear weapons usage threshold. Understandably, any sharp shift in the level of nuclear threshold impacts the stability of nuclear deterrence adversely and could precipitate an arms race which Pakistan can ill afford.

- Pakistan will develop flexible and sufficient means based on a variety of delivery systems as determined by its minimum deterrence requirements. The build-up and enhancement of Pakistan's nuclear weapons capability would essentially be based on the following two imperatives:[3]

  o In order to ensure an adequate level of assuredness as regards the second strike capability, Pakistan must endeavour for a multiplicity of nuclear delivery means. The requirement here would be for Pakistan to develop and field a triad-based nuclear potential. With the land-based and air-delivered capability already in place, the emphasis must now be on the development of a sub-launched nuclear capability. This is vital from two perspectives:

  o The ease with which Pakistan would be able to ensure the dispersal of her nuclear weapons-equipped submarines would make it very difficult for the Indians to detect and effectively neutralise these. This would, therefore, lend a lot of credence to Pakistan's second strike capability.

- Being a massive territorial entity, most of India is beyond the reach of Pakistan's air-delivered and surface-launched nuclear weapons. The ability of the nuclear capable submarines to virtually deploy anywhere along the vastness of India's Ocean rim would give a tremendous boost to the reach of Pakistan's nuclear weapons. The deployment of a Pakistani nuclear capable submarine in the Bay of Bengal for instance, would threaten the Eastern reaches of India which are otherwise located well beyond the reach of the available Pakistani nuclear delivery means.

- Pakistan will not transfer nuclear weapons or weapon related material or technology to any recipient. This is an essential prerequisite for global acceptability of Pakistan's status as a responsible nuclear weapons-capable country. It would require that we refrain from establishing any overt nuclear ties with any of the countries that are suspected of actively pursuing a nuclear weapons development programme. This restraint would involve implicit adherence to all the established international non-proliferation regimes that are in force, even though Pakistan may not have formally accepted these or ratified these, such as the NPT and the CTBT.

- Pakistan will pursue a strategic restraint regime and other nuclear risk reduction measures in the region. For the first time in the history of the world, the peculiar geography of South Asia has placed two territorially contiguous nuclear weapons-capable states opposite each other. This is a situation that is far removed from the nuclear confrontation of the US and the erstwhile USSR. The proximity of these two countries reduces the warning of an impending nuclear attack by either to virtually zero. In this environment of no early warning, the institutional of safeguard CBMs emerges as an essential requirement and this need must figure prominently in Pakistan's nuclear policy. In South Asia, the following existing CBMs need to be further strengthened with the initiation of other similar measures:
- India and Pakistan have an agreement to exchange information regarding their respective nuclear installations. This information is exchanged in January every year.[4]
- The two countries also have an agreement not to attack each others' nuclear installations.[5]
- Though not yet formalised as an agreement between India and Pakistan, both the countries have also stated their resolve to implement a moratorium on further nuclear testing.
- Pakistan will continue to support international arms control and disarmament initiatives, which are universal and non-discriminatory in character. The universality and non-discriminatory aspects are interesting since both India and Pakistan are of the view that they should be treated at par with the five acknowledged nuclear weapon states and that any attempts and efforts at nuclear non-proliferation must also be made applicable to all—something that is not likely to happen for quite some time. I consider this to be just a ploy by the South Asian nuclear countries to justify their own nuclear arsenals since they are asking the accepted nuclear states for the impossible.
- Command and Control of nuclear forces will be vested in the Chief Executive (Prime Minister) and will be exercised through a National Command Authority assisted by the Strategic Plans Division as its secretariat and Strategic Commands within the three armed services.[6] Though on paper the strategic command and control infrastructure indicates a suitable mix of civilian and military participation, in effect the organisation is dominated by the military.

Conclusion

While there is a lot of criticism against the Pakistan military's dominance over the country's nuclear programme, this must be viewed against the backdrop of the role and contribution of the Pakistan armed forces in the development of the nuclear weapons. Having witnessed at first hand the mess that the politicians and the bureaucrats have made of this country, I am convinced of the fact had it not been for the continuous involvement and oversight of the Pakistan military, the country's nuclear weapons programme would still have existed merely on paper. I would, therefore, contend that Pakistan owes the success of her nuclear weapon development programme to the armed forces which not only oversaw each aspect of its development but also ensured that it was adequately funded throughout the developmental process.

Having been intimately involved in the nuclear programme from its early stages, the military has maintained its involvement and rightly so, since it trusts neither the political leadership nor the bureaucracy when it comes to something as critical for the country's security as its nuclear weapons development programme. Since the nuclear programme has been the military's baby all along, it can be expected that the Pakistan armed forces will continue to dominate it in all respects.

Notes

1. In the absence of a formal Pakistani nuclear doctrine, I have made an effort in the Chapter titled "Nuclear Weapons Development and Employment—A doctrinal roadmap for Pakistan," to address the doctrinal issue from the development as well as the employment perspective. The Nuclear Policy that I am presenting here, therefore, has a basis in the doctrinal framework suggested by me in the referred Chapter.

2. For a detailed discussion of what the terms "minimum" and "credible" mean, please refer to the Chapter "Nuclear Weapons Development and Employment Options Open to Pakistan."

3. For a detailed discussion of Pakistan's Nuclear weapons development strategy, please refer to the Chapter titled "Nuclear Weapons Development and Employment Options Open to Pakistan."

4. For the text of this agreement, please refer to the Chapter titled "Nuclear CBMs in South Asia."

5. Ibid.

6. For a more detailed discussion of the organisational structure and functions of Pakistan's National Command Authority and the Strategic Plans Division, please refer to the Chapter titled "Pakistan's Strategic Weapons Command and Control Organisation."

08 Nuclear Weapons Development and Employment Options for Pakistan

Introduction

Faced with a significantly superior adversary, Pakistan was compelled in May 1998 to respond to the Indian nuclear tests with similar tests of her own. Since then the South Asian region, with two contiguous nuclear capable neighbouring countries has been one of the world's most volatile nuclear flashpoints.

Although both India and Pakistan have been understandably cautious and reticent in talking about their nuclear employment and development doctrines, a lot can be inferred regarding their designs in this context from the various statements and speeches that their leaders and academic analysts have made and written on the subject.

While India has come out in the open with a draft nuclear doctrine that has been well publicised, Pakistan has not followed suit by announcing its nuclear posture and position. The aim of this article is to study the peculiarities of the South Asian nuclear environment and suggest not only a Nuclear Employment Doctrine but also a Nuclear Development doctrinal road-map for Pakistan. The contents of this article represent the personal views of the author and should not in any way be construed as the official viewpoint of any of the concerned agencies or departments of the Government of Pakistan.

Part I: A Nuclear Employment Doctrine for Pakistan

While this paper does not aim to present a comprehensive Nuclear Doctrine for Pakistan, it will attempt to address most, if not all, of the key determinants and elements that influence the shaping of Pakistan's nuclear weapons employment and development doctrines. As regards Pakistan's nuclear weapons employment doctrine, this will be done by focusing on the following key aspects:

- The Basis of Pakistan's Nuclear Employment Doctrine
- The Focus of Pakistan's Nuclear Employment Doctrine
- The Objectives of Pakistan's Nuclear Employment Doctrine

While discussing these three essentials, the various other considerations that influence the formulation of Pakistan's Nuclear Employment Doctrine will also be elaborated upon.

Deterrence—the Basis of Pakistan's Nuclear Employment Doctrine

Deterrence can be simply defined as the potential military capability possessed by a country that through the perceived threat and intention of its usage, serves to inhibit or restrict an adversary from adopting a particular course of military action or progressing along the ladder of escalation inherent to most military confrontations.

Pakistan's nuclear employment doctrine must embody the essence of nuclear weapons being primarily a means of deterrence. This is typical when a smaller and weaker nuclear capable country such as Pakistan is pitched against a much larger and more powerful adversary like India. It is imperative, therefore, that deterrence must form the cardinal theme of Pakistan's employment doctrine. In this context, most Pakistani leaders have already highlighted on various occasions that Pakistan's nuclear posture would be based on the possession and fielding of a "minimum credible deterrent."[1]

The words "minimum" and "credible" in this phrase both need to be elaborated since there is an element of vagueness that is normally associated with these. The subsequent text briefly addresses the vital aspect of defining "Minimality" and "Credibility" of Pakistan's Nuclear Deterrence Potential.[2]

The *Minimality* of deterrence. A nuclear deterrent is required to cater to two different situations that might warrant its use:

- The availability of a viable nuclear deterrence should deter any hostile nation from contemplating the initiation of a conventional military conflict for fear of a nuclear reprisal. This level of deterrence essentially flows from the first strike capability that a nuclear state possesses. In my opinion, the commencement of any future military conflict in the South Asian realm would see India embarking on a Low Intensity Conflict which would be also limited to a particular geographical sector, e.g., Kashmir. In doing so, India would endeavour to capitalise on her significant conventional superiority while remaining within Pakistan's conventional war threshold. This level of "minimum deterrence" could also be described as low level deterrence and is essentially contributed to by the country's first strike capability.

- In case conventional conflict has already been initiated, the availability of nuclear capability must deter our adversary from launching a nuclear first strike. Unlike the previous case, this level of deterrence pertains to the second strike capability of a country and embodies not only the possession of the requisite nuclear deterrent potential but also the ability to survive an enemy conventional pre-emptive or a first strike.

Specifically in the case of Pakistan, the various connotations of the word "minimum," among other things, imply the following:

- The "minimality of deterrence" essentially pertains to the nuclear weapons potential of a country. The deterrence potential of Pakistan's nuclear capability must be adequate to deter Indian first nuclear use because of the danger of a nuclear response. Through an approximation of the nuclear threat posed by India, Pakistan's nuclear planners can arrive at a quantification of the desired minimum nuclear potential that Pakistan needs to possess. The importance of this aspect is even more relevant in today's economy-led global environment since the determination of the minimum desired potential would also be driven by economic resource constraints. If calculated correctly, this would avoid Pakistan getting into a useless, unwarranted and unaffordable nuclear arms race with India as had occurred between the erstwhile USSR and USA during the early days of the cold war.

- The nuclear capability of Pakistan, through the implied plan and intention of its usage, must be potent enough to dissuade India from considering the prospect of an all-out conventional war.

- In the case of Pakistan, the nuclear potential must mandatorily be able to imply sufficient second strike potential. Such a capability, in turn necessitates that Pakistan's nuclear potential comprising the weapons as well as the delivery platforms must embody adequate security to survive an Indian first strike against it—whether nuclear or conventional.

The *Credibility* of deterrence. Having defined the connotations of the aspect of "minimality" in Pakistan's nuclear doctrine, we can now move on to the next important aspect, that deals with the credibility of Pakistan's nuclear deterrence potential. The credibility of nuclear deterrence, apart from its minimality, is the second key aspect of the phrase "Minimum Credible Deterrence" and implies the following:

- At the bare minimum, the credibility of a country's nuclear capability is based upon its demonstrated and proven capacity of delivering nuclear warheads. This implies possession of nuclear weapons and also the availability of effective delivery platforms for the employment of these weapons. This capability can only be demonstrated during peacetime through the conduct of test explosions and trials. Such tests and trials serve two purposes; firstly, these enhance own confidence in the efficiency of these weapons and delivery platforms and secondly, these indicate to the adversary that continuous improvements and experiments are being undertaken to further increase the lethality of one's nuclear arsenal. Pakistan has adequately proven her capability of developing nuclear weapons with the conduct of her nuclear tests and is further strengthening it by conducting periodic ballistic missile trials. The conduct of such trials indicates to the adversary one's commitment to the maintenance of a credible nuclear weapons delivery capability and as such promotes deterrence.

- The credibility of the nuclear deterrence potential of a country is also strengthened by that country's expressed policy regarding the usage philosophy of these weapons. This can be partially publicised in the form of a formal nuclear doctrine. Following the Indian example of the release of a draft nuclear doctrine document, Pakistan also needs to develop her own nuclear doctrine and publicise the relevant portions of it.

- The demonstration of national will and resolve to use nuclear weapons also contributes significantly to the credibility of a country's nuclear deterrence potential. Readers familiar with the development of nuclear weapons in France in the aftermath of the Second World War would recall that France had openly announced that any violation of French territorial frontiers by a hostile nation or army would warrant a French nuclear response. While the issuance of such a categorical nuclear threshold may not be suitable in the case of Pakistan, guarded statements implying her nuclear threshold could serve to highlight the country's resolve whilst simultaneously maintaining an element of vagueness.

- The institution of an effective nuclear command and control infrastructure and mechanism also contributes to enhancing the credibility of a country's nuclear potential. In this context, Pakistan has a distinct edge over India which must be maintained. Pakistan must ensure that her nuclear command and control structure is physically put in place as early as possible. Moreover, this command and control infrastructure must be supported with the requisite intelligence gathering apparatus and possess an extremely secure communications system. The fielding of such an effective nuclear command and control architecture should be publicised to ensure that all concerned should be familiar with its existence and structure apart from being sure about its redundancy, structural integrity and effectiveness. This requirement implies that Pakistan, which has taken a lead in establishing her nuclear command and control authority, as epitomised by the National Command Authority, must make this organisation as strong and capable as possible to respond to the operational requirements.

- The capability of one's nuclear weapons arsenal as regards its reliability, the accuracy of its delivery potential and its surety of reaching the target in the face of the enemy defences is another vital aspect that has to be considered when measuring the credibility of a country's nuclear potential. The ideal would be to have a triad-based nuclear delivery capability (air delivered, surface launched ballistic missiles and sea/submarine launched missiles). Since Pakistan only possesses air delivery and surface launch nuclear delivery capability and is still working to achieve sea-based nuclear delivery capability, her doctrine should be based on a simultaneous air and land nuclear attack so as to enhance the chances of success in the face of the strong and potent Indian air defence ground environment. In days to come, the already formidable array of Indian ground defences is likely to be boosted further with the planned acquisition and deployment of anti-ballistic missile systems such as the Arrow ABM system that she is endeavouring to purchase from Israel and the Russian S-300 PMU ABM system that she reportedly already possesses.

- Another dimension of the credibility of Pakistan's nuclear deterrence potential would lie in the range or reach of the nuclear weapons. Since India has comparatively immense strategic geographic depth by virtue of her size, Pakistan must field a nuclear deterrent that has the capacity of reaching the maximum number of Indian targets, including those that are located in depth.

- Transition from a limited conventional war to a nuclear war will be dictated by the violation of a country's nuclear threshold. The reaching of such a situation would force a resort to nuclear weapons. In view of its significance in the conduct of wars, Pakistan's defence planners must have as accurate an assessment as possible of India's nuclear threshold built into their nuclear employment doctrine. This would imply that the perceived Indian nuclear threshold must be built into all our plans so that the progress of war in all three conventional realms (air, sea and land) is regulated in a manner that India, while being kept on the back foot, is not forced beyond her threshold which would force her to resort to a nuclear strike against Pakistan. The danger of this is not difficult to contemplate when one considers what an Indian nuclear first strike could mean for Pakistan.

- Another essential aspect of a nation's nuclear potential that directly contributes to the credibility is the aspect of its survivability in the face of an enemy conventional pre-emptive attack or a nuclear first strike. In the realm of an Indian conventional pre-emptive, the main force that Pakistan would have to contend with is the vastly superior and capable Indian Air Force. The pre-emptive threat posed by the IAF to Pakistan is further exacerbated when weighed against the limited air defence capabilities that the Pakistan armed forces possess, both in the area of airborne fighter interceptors and in the realm of surface-to-air guided weapons. This imbalance has been aggravated further with the Indian acquisition of the IL-76 mounted Israeli supplied Phalcon Airborne Early Warning, Command and Control System (AEWC[2]).[3] The imperative of survivability not only requires the availability of an adequate number of nuclear weapons and delivery systems to survive the pre-emptive or first strike but also dictates that these assets should be suitably dispersed so as to reduce their vulnerability to being targeted and attacked by India. From the defensive perspective, the availability of an elaborate and integrated network of surface-to-air weapon systems also emerges as an essential. Moreover, these systems must be maintained at a very high degree of alert to guard against an Indian conventional pre-emptive offensive or an Indian nuclear first strike. The enhancement of the survivability potential of Pakistan's nuclear deterrence potential also dictates the incorporation of suitable Nuclear–Biological–Chemical protective measures in her nuclear weapons architecture. This should include not only the sites where the nuclear weapons and their associated delivery platforms are located but must also bring the entire nuclear command and control infrastructure within its ambit.

- In the peculiar nuclear environment of South Asia where both India and Pakistan are contiguous and where Pakistan, unlike India, is also straddled with the strategic handicap of having very limited geographic depth and where the proximity of the launch and target positions provides virtually no early warning, Pakistan must maintain a nuclear readiness and preparedness state that ensures the ready availability of her nuclear deterrence potential. This would imply Pakistan prepositioning her nuclear weapons and delivery platforms at a location from where the planned target inside India could be effectively engaged with a simultaneous two-pronged nuclear strike (air delivered and surface launched). The element of preparedness might dictate Pakistan dedicating the requisite number of designated strike aircraft for this express purpose so that these are easily available and are not committed elsewhere.

While defining and addressing the aspects of "minimality" and "credibility" of Pakistan's nuclear deterrence potential, one fact that must not be lost sight of is that "credibility" and "minimality" are essentially inversely proportional to each other. It stands to reason, therefore, that the higher the "credibility" the lesser would be the number of warheads required to provide the required level of "minimality."

Another important aspect that needs to be kept in mind here is the occasion that might lead Pakistan to employ her nuclear weapons, since this would also have to be built into the deterrence dimension of Pakistan's nuclear potential.

In my reckoning, there could only be two situations that might lead Pakistan's leadership to contemplate the drastic step of resorting to nuclear weapons; firstly to respond to an enemy nuclear first strike and secondly, to bring a war to an end in the face of an abject military defeat. While the first situation would be handled with Pakistan's first strike potential, the second scenario might even require the second strike forces coming into the equation. Since these situations are only likely to arise once the nuclear deterrence has failed in averting a conflict in the first place, these considerations must be dove-tailed into Pakistan's doctrine of nuclear deterrence.

India and Israel—the Focus of Pakistan's Nuclear Employment doctrine
Pakistan must be clear in determining and defining the focal points of its nuclear employment doctrine. This identification can be direct or implied. Take the example of the draft Indian Nuclear Doctrine—it does not exactly mention whom it is aimed against and never even once mentions China or Pakistan by name, but the implied inclusion of China is obvious if one browses through the statements of top Indian leaders. China was even

mentioned explicitly in the letter that Indian Prime Minister Atal Behari Vajpayee wrote to President Clinton in the aftermath of the May 1998 nuclear tests in South Asia. In my opinion, Pakistan's nuclear employment doctrine should not be as vague as the Indian draft nuclear doctrine is in defining the focus. The Pakistani nuclear employment doctrine should, therefore, include the following:

- Pakistan should openly accept and profess that her nuclear employment doctrine is India centric and India focused. This should be justified not only on the basis of our previous history but also on the fact that the conventional military balance between the two countries has reached levels of alarming asymmetry.

- Though no specific mention of Israel or any other country should may be made, the doctrine must imply its inherent flexibility in being directed and focused against other nation-states with the incorporation of suitable modifications. Israel cannot be eliminated as a focal point of our nuclear employment doctrine on the following counts:

  o The growing Indo-Israeli military nexus as evidenced by their cooperation and collaboration in the military field. Another dimension of this growing threat is the increasing US involvement with both India and Israel.

  o The earlier example of Israel having attacked Iraq's Osirak nuclear reactor in what was a blatant and unwarranted act of aggression in complete disregard to global opinion and the immense success that this hostile venture achieved indicates the possibility of Israel carrying out a similar strike with the active collusion of India and the implied or unstated agreement/encouragement of USA.

  o The recent statement of the Israeli Prime Minister regarding the possibility of Israel neutralising Iranian nuclear facilities is the latest in the series of blatant threats that the Israelis have made against the possession of weapons of mass destruction capability by any Muslim country and serves to further reinforce the assertion that Pakistan must also be figuring out fairly high on the Israeli threat list. From this it flows that Israel should remain as one of the implied focal points in Pakistan's nuclear weapons employment doctrine.

  o Israel, as the representative of the Zionist lobby, can never sit at peace with a Muslim country such as Pakistan having access to demonstrated and deliverable nuclear capability. Our nuclear potential is a thorn in Israel's side and poses a problematic situation for her. The recently emerging Indo-US-Israel nexus in the region would serve to accentuate Israel's posture of underlying hostility and antagonism against Pakistan with the situation being aggravated further by Pakistan's continued non-recognition of the Jewish state even though some of the Arab Muslim states neighbouring Israel have not only recognised the existence of the Jewish state but have also established diplomatic relations with it.

Being on a weaker military footing as compared to India, Pakistan nuclear employment doctrine should assert that since she would be fighting for her very survival as an independent nation state in any future war, it cannot afford to adopt a policy of " no first use" as India has made it appear in her draft nuclear doctrine. Pakistan, while announcing and emphasising the deterrent basis of its nuclear employment doctrine, must reserve the right of first use of nuclear weapons and this assertion could also be made a part of her nuclear employment doctrine.

By alluding to Israel as one of the possible focal target points of her nuclear employment doctrine, Pakistan would also be inducing an element of deterrence vis-à-vis the United States and any other nation that could be expected to abet Israel or India if they undertake any strike against Pakistan's nuclear potential. This is based on the assumption that Israel would never even contemplate taking out Pakistan's nuclear infrastructure without the implicit support and nod of the US. Also, the threat of a nuclear strike against Israel would not be acceptable to the US under any circumstances and as such the fear of such a strike by Pakistan might serve to deter both, Israel directly, and the USA indirectly.

Although the USA employed nuclear weapons against a non-nuclear capable country in 1945, nuclear weapons have never been employed since especially by any two countries that were both nuclear capable. Moreover, modern day geopolitics may find such a situation of nuclear weapons being employed by a nuclear capable country against a non-nuclear adversary as being entirely unacceptable. To this effect, Pakistan's nuclear employment doctrine could include the fact that Pakistan would not employ her nuclear weapons against non-nuclear adversaries or countries. This fact, by allaying the unfounded fears and apprehensions of the non-nuclear regional countries, would also serve as a confidence-building measure in the regional political situation and would promote regional stability.

Counter-Value or Counter-Force or Counter-Space—the Targeting Philosophy of Pakistan's Nuclear Employment Doctrine

The third vital aspect of Pakistan's nuclear employment doctrine that needs to be explored in detail is that pertaining to targeting. As per established nuclear doctrines, nuclear weapons targeting can essentially be subdivided into two priority areas that define the conceptual categories of targets that can be engaged without getting into the specifics—Counter-Value and Counter-Force. The first issue that one must contend with is the relevance of the concepts of Counter-Value, Counter-Force and Counter-Space (territory) targeting to South Asia and its peculiar prevailing nuclear environment.

The emergence of the two conceptual categories of targets for nuclear weapons employment must be traced back to 1945 and the mindset of the initial individuals who had to arrive at a decision regarding the employment of nuclear weapons. The Second World War had seen the launching and execution of the largest and the most massive strategic air offensive in the history of mankind. The concept of strategic aerial bombardment owed its genesis to the ideas and theories espoused by some of the early air power thinkers whose writings influenced the employment of air power in World War II, specifically Giulio Douhet of Italy and Hugh Trenchard of Great Britain. Since the events of the First World War further strengthened the idea that all future wars would be total wars involving the entire populace of the warring countries and all aspects of their national power potential, the early air power thinkers, in an effort to crystallise the role of air power, advocated strategic air attacks against the enemy population and economic/industrial targets with the prime objective of breaking the will of the enemy populace from continuing with the war. This concept was still in vogue when in 1945, the US made her decision to drop nuclear weapons on Japan. As such, the decision to engage two major population centres of Japan (Hiroshima and Nagasaki) was an obvious and predictable conclusion to arrive at. Hence the birth of the concept of Counter-Value targeting.

In the aftermath of the destruction of Hiroshima and Nagasaki and the immense toll of human life that these attacks took, the entire world was rudely awakened to the reality of the destructiveness of nuclear weapons, leading a lot of thinkers to question the nuclear targeting philosophy. The anti-counter value targeting lobby gained further strength when the Korean conflict showed that nuclear weapons were not applicable to each and every type of war. Rather than giving up nuclear weapons entirely, which was undesirable, military thinkers of the Korean era dreamt up the concept of engaging military targets with nuclear weapons—their thesis being that nuclear weapons could be employed against the enemy's military potential with little or no danger of collateral damage to innocent civilian population. This idea, however, preceded the availability of suitable technology that was required for its implementation since the nuclear weapons of that era were area rather than point weapons and the immense fallout inherent to the high-explosive power of the fusion devices of that time made the limitation and confinement of their impact difficult.

Subsequent improvements in delivery technology and accuracy and the availability of lower yield and more efficient nuclear weapons facilitated the evolution of Counter-Force targeting wherein selected and pinpoint military targets were possible to engage with an appreciably lesser chance of collateral damage. Since then, both these targeting concepts have remained in vogue throughout the cold war and even afterwards.

One of the major factors that led to this transition from counter-value to counter-force targeting was also the fact that the antagonists (USSR and USA) were not territorially contiguous and their surface wars were expected to be fought on the soils of their respective allies and not on their own territories. Though not mentioned in these words for fear of alienating the allies and their respective populace, this consideration did play a role in the evolution of the concept of counter-force targeting by the USSR and USA. The peculiar geographical environment of South Asia where both India and Pakistan have a long contiguous border, however, does not lend itself to counter-force targeting. The situation in the case of Pakistan and India is made even more serious by the fact that most of the expected areas of their surface battles (Ravi-Chenab corridor, Ravi-Beas corridor and Kashmir) are extremely densely inhabited and as such the dangers of collateral damage to innocent civilian population even from counter-force targeting, are inordinately and unacceptably high.

The above discussion would lead one to conclude that counter-force targeting per se, is not applicable to South Asia. This assertion is further strengthened by the fact that neither Pakistan nor India have weapons with very accurate delivery capability. Moreover, neither of the South Asian nuclear powers have a nuclear weapons programme so advanced that they can employ low yield nuclear weapons which have an effective destruction area that is very limited in size.

The third targetting option is that of counter-space or territory. This entails conducting a nuclear attack in a region that is sparsely populated and inhabited but still possesses some military relevance, such as a tract of desert as in Indian Rajasthan or the adjoining Pakistani Sindh. The objective here would be two-fold: to be able to conduct a nuclear attack while causing minimum damage and to contaminate the area and render it unusable for further military operations in the immediate future. In South Asia, however, the prevalent strategic thinking in both the countries revolved around the counter-force or counter-value targeting with little thought having been apparently given to counter-space or territory targeting.

The obvious assertion after reading the above discourse is to conclude that counter-force targeting is not really relevant to the South Asian scenario because of a multiplicity of factors. Pakistan and India can only employ this targeting concept while engaging military targets that are isolated from the population centres and the engagement of which poses no dangers of collateral damage to innocent civilians. Such an opportunity may not be easily available to either of the two countries. In the case of Pakistan, however, one such isolated Indian military target that comes to mind is either of the Indian Navy's two aircraft carriers. If these vessels venture outside the sanctuary of their ports during war and are in the open sea, they do offer a suitable counter-force target that Pakistan could engage with her nuclear weapons, whether air launched or surface launched. Other than this case of counter-force targeting, it is surmised that Pakistan's nuclear targeting doctrine would essentially remain confined to the counter-value realm and the same would be the case for India.

While it is vital that the targeting philosophy underlying Pakistan's nuclear weapons employment doctrine be accurately identified, the same does not essentially need to form a part of the publicised nuclear doctrine. After arriving at a finalised nuclear targeting philosophy, the subsequent steps would include the identification and selection of the preferred targets and the preparation of plans to ensure that the requisite nuclear weapons as well as the associated delivery platforms are located at sites from where the identified Indian targets can be effectively engaged.

Part II: A Nuclear Development Doctrine for Pakistan

After this discussion of the various aspects of Pakistan's nuclear weapons employment doctrine, the next step is to analyse what should be Pakistan's nuclear weapons development doctrine. Needless to say, the development doctrine must lead to the production of weapons that support the finalised nuclear weapons employment doctrine and as such both of these, the nuclear weapons development doctrine and the nuclear weapons employment doctrine, have to be necessarily complementary to each other. As was done while elaborating on Pakistan's Nuclear Weapons Employment Doctrine in Part I of this article, the objective here also is not to give a comprehensive nuclear weapons development doctrine but only to highlight its salient aspects by discussing the following areas that have an immense influence on Pakistan's nuclear weapons development doctrine:

- Type and Nature of Nuclear Deterrence Potential
- Improvements/Enhancements in Pakistan's Existing Nuclear Weapon Systems
- Development of Passive NBC Protective Measures
- Surveillance/Launch Detection Capability

Type and Nature of Nuclear Deterrence Potential
The Indian draft nuclear doctrine indicates a desire on the part of the Indian planners to aim for having a triad based nuclear force that embodies air delivered, surface launched and sea launched nuclear weapons capability. In my personal opinion, Pakistan must also adopt the triad route. This is important due to the following reasons:

- Nuclear weapons are a military instrument of last resort and as such there would be just a fleeting opportunity, if any, for their employment by Pakistan. In order to ensure that these weapons are available whenever the situation arises, possession of all three types of nuclear delivery platforms will definitely be an advantage. Moreover, the possession of nuclear delivery capability from any of the three media (air, land and sea) would serve to significantly enhance the credibility of Pakistan's deterrence potential.
- A triad based nuclear arsenal would embody a much higher degree of survivability in the face of an Indian conventional pre-emptive attack or a nuclear first strike. This again would add to the deterrence potential of Pakistan's nuclear arsenal.
- The sea-based (whether surface vessel launched or submarine launched) nuclear weapons capability would induce an element of unpredictability in Pakistan's nuclear posture that India would have difficulties in contending with. Moreover, while the Indians may be able to locate Pakistan's surface based nuclear weapons and associated

delivery platforms, the detection of a nuclear weapons delivery capable submarine would present a problem for the enemy.

- A sea-based nuclear weapons delivery capability would significantly enhance Pakistan's second strike potential. Even in the extreme case where India is able to neutralise Pakistan's entire land-based nuclear capability (aircraft as well as ballistic missiles), the second strike potential as made available by the nuclear weapons delivery capable submarines would remain an effective second strike weapon.

- The development of a sea-based nuclear weapons delivery capability for Pakistan should focus more on this capability being built into the submersible vessels rather than those that ply on the surface of the sea.

- Although the likely targeting philosophy that Pakistan will adopt is going to be counter-value targeting, the development of more accurately deliverable and low yield nuclear weapons must continue to remain a priority of Pakistan's nuclear weapons development doctrine. The availability of such weapons would significantly help in targeting smaller and more pinpoint targets with little or no danger of unwanted and undesirable collateral damage being caused.

- The availability of nuclear weapons delivery capable submarines would also necessitate the availability of a secure communication system between these vessels and the National Command Authority even when the former are at sea and are submerged. It has to be considered that like the need to dedicate aircraft for nuclear delivery and keep them aside during peacetime, the nuclear capable submarines would also have to be taken out of the Pakistan Navy's effective inventory and kept aside for the nuclear role. Since this would reduce the number of submarines that are available with the Pakistan Navy, more such platforms may need to be acquired.

The land based nuclear capable surface-to-surface missiles are currently an important component of Pakistan's nuclear potential. The immense size, transportation difficulties and huge infrastructure inherent to such systems, however, are undesirable in that these render such systems to easy detection and engagement by the enemy. Being relatively easy to detect and engage, these weapons may not survive an enemy conventional pre-emptive attack or a nuclear first strike. As such, the efficacy of these weapons as regards their second strike potential is extremely limited and questionable. In view of these serious limitations, it is proposed that Pakistan's nuclear development doctrine, apart from focusing on the development of submarine launched nuclear weapons, must also endeavour to develop aircraft launched supersonic nuclear armed cruise missiles. The SSMs already available must be maintained in the inventory till such time that the air launched cruise missiles and the submarine launched nuclear missiles are developed and subsequently these could be shifted to the second tier of nuclear forces to act as a reserve capability that could come in handy for launching a second strike or an all-out nuclear attack if the situation so warrants.

As regards nuclear weapons, Pakistan must continue to strive for the development of thermonuclear weapons and neutron weapons from the futuristic perspective. In this context, we must not lose sight of the Indian claim, although not substantiated, that one of the nuclear devices exploded during the May 1998 nuclear tests was a thermonuclear device. While the availability of a thermonuclear device would significantly enhance the lethality and yield of Pakistan's nuclear weapons, the development of neutron warheads before the Indians are able to do so would provide Pakistan with the exclusive capability of completely shifting its targeting strategy from the concept of counter-value targeting to that of counter-force targeting. The achievement of this capability would be of immense benefit when viewed in the backdrop of the huge conventional asymmetry that confronts Pakistan vis-à-vis India.

Improvements/Enhancements in Pakistan's Existing Nuclear Weapon Systems

As mentioned earlier, Pakistan's aircraft delivered or missile delivered nuclear weapons will have to contend with the entire spectrum of strong and potent Indian defences, both in the shape of effective airborne interceptor aircraft and in the form of a vast array of surface-to-air weapon systems. In order to be able to effectively contend with these threats, the development of Pakistan's nuclear delivery aircraft and nuclear equipped ballistic missiles must consider the following essentials:

- All nuclear weapons delivery capable strike aircraft must be multi-role platforms that should embody excellent self-defence capability. The availability of the requisite passive and active self-defence avionics equipment and on-board air-to-air weaponry would permit these aircraft to fight their way through the Indian air defences in their quest of reaching the desired targets. Future aircraft development programmes and induction programmes must also emphasise the incorporation of stealth technologies in these platforms. If these strike aircraft are capable of fighting their way through IAF interceptors, the requirement of this force being escorted by high technology fighters would diminish and this would reduce the burden on the PAF's already limited resources.

- Considering the high probability of the Indians acquiring an effective anti-ballistic missile system such as the Arrow, our surface launched ballistic missiles must be modified to evade detection by the incorporation of stealth technologies and characteristics. This could involve one or all of the following:

- Pakistan's SSM inventory must be the focus of an extensive size and weight reduction programme that would make these weapons that much more lighter/sleeker while enhancing their range significantly. The smaller size of these weapons, if achieved, will also make these difficult to being detected by the Indian ADGE sensors. The focus of the weight reduction and airframe redesign initiatives must be aimed at reducing the radar cross-section (RCS) of these SSMs. Another option could be to use radar absorbent paint on these missiles to make these more difficult to detect.

- The imperative of making Pakistan's SSMs leaner and meaner would also require advancements in our capability of miniaturising the nuclear warheads without really compromising on their yield. Any weight and size reductions achieved would also reduce the detectability of these weapons and offer gains in their effective range.

- The chances of the Indian ground/air defences successfully engaging a Pakistani nuclear SSM would depend largely on the time for which such a weapon remains illuminated by Indian radar systems. One of the antidotes to this lies in enhancing the cruise speed of Pakistan's SSMs. If we are able to increase the speeds of these weapons systems to the supersonic regime as is being planned by India and Russia for the Brahmos supersonic cruise missile, the time available to the Indian ground/air defences to effectively intercept and neutralise these weapons in flight would be extremely limited. All the earlier mentioned desirable developments of size and weight reduction would also facilitate the enhancement of cruising speed of these weapons.

Surveillance/Launch Detection Capability

As alluded to earlier, the contiguity of borders, the limited distance of most Pakistani targets from the border and the short time of flight of Indian ballistic missiles from launch to impact all pose very serious considerations for the Pakistani defences. While the approximate location of the Indian SSM batteries could possibly be determined through intelligence/reconnaissance and the remaining aspects calculated, the problem lies in knowing when an Indian SSM has been launched since all subsequent calculations would start from there. Since aerial and ground based surveillance means currently available to Pakistan might not be capable of detecting the launch of Indian SSMs, the only option is to rely upon a satellite based surveillance system that could detect the launch of an SSM by possibly acquiring its infrared signature at the time of launch. In order to ensure that this sort of coverage is available to us round the clock, this satellite would have to be placed in orbit so that the area of interest remains under surveillance all the time. Since Pakistan is seriously lagging behind India as regards satellite manufacture and launch technology and expertise, our efforts at acquiring this capability would have to be based upon either an off-the-shelf purchase if the same is cleared for sale to us or through leasing or purchasing this capability if the same is available on one of the existing satellites. From the long-term perspective, however, Pakistan must proceed with indigenisation as quickly as possible.

Development of Passive NBC Protective Measures

Being a new nuclear power, Pakistan is seriously deficient in the area of NBC protection systems and measures. The aspect of passive defensive measures directly complements the offensive measures and as such must form a vital component of Pakistan's nuclear weapons development doctrine. The following are the salient passive development measures that need to be incorporated within the overall nuclear weapons development doctrine:

- **Education and Awareness**. This is the most important passive measure and pertains to educating the masses regarding the possible after-effects of nuclear explosions and the steps to be taken to reduce their negative effects. Since targeting in any expected South Asian nuclear exchange is likely to be confined essentially to the counter-value realm, the need to educate the common population of all the major cities that could be likely targets emerges as an essential requirement. Commencing with these cities, this education could then be expanded to include the armed forces also. As a long-term measure, NBC Preventive Measures training and education could also be included in the syllabi of middle class students so that over a period of time each and every high school graduate is familiar with the threat that nuclear explosions pose and the means of countering these. Education and training regarding these aspects must also encompass the aspect of medical response to a nuclear explosion, specifically from the perspective of those who have been exposed to nuclear radiation.

- **Shelters**. Government agencies must develop designs of suitable structures that could be used as shelters during an attack with NBC weapons. These designs along with detailed specifications must be made available to all those desirous of obtaining these. While existing house owners could be requested to construct basements, the construction of these should be made compulsory in the case of all new buildings that are coming up. Moreover, all multi-storey complexes must be designed with adequate underground parking space so that the same could be converted into shelters whenever required.

- **NBC Proofing**. Even though the Indians are expected to focus on counter-value targeting, vital military operations centres cannot be excluded from the list of buildings that have to be made NBC proof. The same must also be done for all essential structures belonging to the NCA and other nuclear weapons related agencies. These structures must have all the essentials for those who are inside to be able to survive without any outside help for at least a few days. The top priority for NBC proofing would have to be given to own nuclear weapons infrastructure and the personnel associated with its functioning. In this context, the following would need to be accomplished in order to ensure that a potent second strike option is maintained even in the face of an Indian first strike:

  o   All nuclear SSM sites must be made NBC proof with the personnel manning these also being afforded total protection.

  o   All strike aircraft that are planned to undertake nuclear strikes and the associated manpower must be placed within NBC proof hardened shelters.

- **Protective Clothing**. While most military personnel will have their own personal NBC protective kit, efforts must be made to extend the same to those civilians who are likely to be required for the provision of medical care after an enemy NBC attack.

- **Redundancy of C2 Infrastructure.** The essential prerequisite of redundancy demands that all command and control centres must be suitably duplicated at classified but easily reachable sites. All these centres must be manned and provided with the latest war situation so that either one of these could be utilised by the national leadership to control the conduct of war.

- **Safety of National Leadership.** In order to ensure that the essential leadership of the country remains available for taking critical decisions, some predetermined elements of the national hierarchy may need to be separated from the rest and kept at a secret command and control facility right after the outbreak of hostilities. This tier of national hierarchy must have access to the latest war situation and must remain in constant communication with the other tier who would continue to remain in the capital.

The entire spectrum of NBC protective activities should be handled at the central government level by an organisation entrusted with this vital assignment. One of the options could be to re-organise and restructure the existing Civil Defence Organisation for undertaking these tasks. The same organisation could be assigned the title of NBC Defence Organisation (NBCDO) and structured with suitable representation from the civil administration, the medical fraternity, nuclear scientists and the armed forces.

Conclusion

As most readers would understand, definitising Pakistan's nuclear weapons development and employment doctrines is not a simple task because of the multitude of factors that have to be considered while drawing out these doctrines. The purpose of this chapter, as was highlighted in the preceding text, is not to offer a comprehensive doctrinal solution but rather to assess the various influencing factors and considerations that impinge on Pakistan's nuclear doctrines.

In most cases, nations embarking on a new venture into uncharted territory often resort to taking guidance from the examples of precedence that other countries have adopted. In the case of the nuclear doctrines, however, my suggestion is for Pakistan not to follow the already available nuclear doctrines since these may not be relevant for us. The stark dissimilarities between the cold war paradigm and present-day South Asia dictate that the peculiarities of our specific region must be fully taken into account while evolving our nuclear doctrines. This means developing these documents from scratch with only the threat remaining as a focal consideration.

While it may not be advisable to publicise the entire nuclear doctrine, it is proposed that relevant portions of the same may be brought out into the open so that healthy and productive discussions can be made on its various aspects in the educated environs of our think tanks. We must consider the importance of these doctrines from the following two perspectives:

- Pakistan's nuclear doctrines must serve to reassure our own countrymen of our seriousness and the capability which lends strength to our national nuclear posture. A more nuclear-aware polity and military would be able to respond to the nuclear threat posed to us by India in a far more coordinated and forceful manner. The fruits of these discussions could in time allow us to further refine our nuclear doctrine and help it evolve with the passage of time.

- The doctrinal document also serves to communicate a message to the enemy regarding our national resolve in no uncertain terms. In this context, the relevant portions of this document should be made available openly. The language to be used while drafting this document must be matter-of-fact rather than high-sounding and should be forceful enough without appearing to convey any overtly aggressive tone.

From the above discourse one could conclude that possession of nuclear capability is only the first step in becoming a recognised nuclear state. The subsequent steps of understanding the employment and development dynamics of a country's nuclear arsenal are what breed nuclear maturity and understanding. By starting to work on her nuclear development and employment doctrines, Pakistan will be well on her way to becoming an accepted and respected nuclear power of this world.

Some of the readers might wonder why the important aspect of economics has been completely ignored while writing this article. In response to this, I would submit that the economics of defence remain a paramount consideration whenever one attempts to chalk out a doctrinal road-map but I purposely deleted this aspect because I wanted to focus on what I would want Pakistan to ideally have. Needless to say, the economic constraints would cause the envisaged development plan to be undertaken piecemeal or even be phased over a number of years and there is not much that can be done about it other than to hope for and work for a dramatic turnaround in Pakistan's economy.

Notes

1. Please refer to Chapter 10 for an elaboration of the Concepts of Credibility and Minimality.
2. Please refer to Chapter 10 for a more detailed discussion of the elements of "minimality" and "credibility."
3. For a detailed analysis of the implications of the acquisition, induction and deployment of the Phalcon AEWC2 system by the IAF, please refer to the author's article titled "IAF's Acquisition of AEWC2 capability—Implications for the South Asian Air Power Scenario" published in the December 2003 issue of the *Defence Journal*.

09 Essential Elements of Pakistan's Nuclear Doctrine

The reticence of the Pakistani leadership to speak about the country's nuclear doctrine, though understandable from the perspective of Pakistan's desire to remain ambiguous, has raised more questions and uncertainties than answers.

Being on the weaker footing as regards conventional military wherewithal, Pakistan has treaded the path of nuclear ambiguity ever since she embarked upon her nuclear weapons development programme. The idea behind this has been to engender doubts and uncertainties in the minds of the Indian political and military leadership and to also cloud the perceptions of the global community regarding Pakistan's actual nuclear capabilities and its perceived employment thinking.

An aspect as vital as a country's nuclear thought process, especially in the military realm, does not get crystallised overnight. It has to traverse through an endless process of discussions and deliberations among the widest possible group of stakeholders and has to be a dynamic document that is amenable to modification and improvement. One means of achieving this in the shortest possible time is to float the policy document openly for comments and we saw this happening with the draft Indian Nuclear Doctrine immediately after it was unveiled.[1]

Despite the fact that Pakistan is quiet on the issue of her nuclear doctrine, enough details of its possible contents can be gleaned from the various statements that Pakistani leaders have been making to the public and the media so as to enable us to construct and predict its major defining characteristics. In this context, the enormous amount of scholarly writings on this subject also provide an invaluable resource which can be utilised as the springboard from where to launch into this discourse on the outline contents of Pakistan's Nuclear Doctrine. Some analysts have started describing the nuclear confrontation that currently exists in South Asia as one of "mutually assured deadlock."[2]

Rather than presenting a complete draft of Pakistan's expected Nuclear Doctrine, this paper aims at highlighting and discussing some of the essential elements which should be included in this document, as and when it is finalised and publicised by the Government of Pakistan. It must be kept in mind that most of these elements have already been alluded to at one time or the other by various individuals of the Pakistani civilian and military leadership as well as the strategic scholar community in their statements, speeches, interviews and writings.

India-Centricity

Since its creation in 1947, Pakistanis has been haunted by the inordinate fear of India being bent upon destroying their country and this apprehension affects not only the political and military leadership of the country but also its teeming millions who have been brought up in the shadow of this all-encompassing fear of India and hatred for it. So deeply entrenched is the distrust for India and anything that the Indians do that most Pakistanis tend to scoff and laugh even at genuine peace overtures that emanate from their significantly larger and powerful neighbouring country. Needless to say, these fears and apprehensions have been further strengthened due to the three wars that India and Pakistan have fought since 1947 and the numerous occasions that they have neared possible wars. For most Pakistanis, the debacle of East Pakistan and the creation of Bangladesh out of the eastern wing of the country is also attributed more to the Indians than to the Bangladeshis themselves. In the words of one analyst, "Pakistan's main concern has been with her security and territorial integrity which has been threatened and violated by India many times since 1947 when both countries became independent."[3]

Already confronted with a significant conventional military inferiority vis-à-vis India, it was but natural, therefore, for Pakistan to embark on a concerted effort at achieving nuclear weapons potential immediately after the 1971 debacle. "Pakistan's nuclear imperative originated with its defeat in the 1971 India-Pakistan war that led to the creation of Bangladesh."[4] According to Dr. Subash Kapila, "Pakistan's nuclear arsenal is India specific and designed to offset India's conventional and nuclear weapons superiority."[5] Even the Director General of Pakistan's Strategic Plans Division, Lieutenant General (Retired) Khalid Kidwai, told a team of physicists from Italy's Landau Network, an arms control institution, in late 2001 that Pakistan's nuclear weapons were "aimed solely at India."[6]

Pakistan's Quest for Security

As mentioned above, Pakistan has been plagued by insecurity right from 1947. Even today, analysts describe three main threats that are perceived by the Pakistanis to be imperilling the very existence of their state: the instability in Afghanistan to the North West, the domestic discord and turmoil and a belligerent India breathing down Pakistan's neck from the East.[7] These serious threats to the very existence of Pakistan have tended to dominate the strategic thinking not only of her leadership but also her scholars. It is not surprising, therefore to hear Lt. Gen. Kidwai saying that Pakistan would only employ its nuclear weapons "if the very existence of Pakistan as a state was at risk."[8]

Since the most serious threat to Pakistan's security is posed by India, hence it was but natural for Pakistan's nuclear weapons capability to be India-centric and focused only in that direction. Therefore, unlike the Indian nuclear doctrine which also takes unspoken and unstated cognizance of China emerging as a possible future threat which needs to be countered, Pakistan's nuclear doctrine would not envisage any threat other than India except in the case where a country other than India attacks and attempts to destroy her precious nuclear military arsenal and capability.

Here it would be relevant to have a look at the specific threats perceived by Pakistan that her nuclear doctrine could be designed to cater for:

- **Conventional Military Threat from India**. The conventional military balance which has always been in favour of India has tilted even more significantly in her favour over the past few years. The major reasons for this have been the capacity of India's booming economy to allocate more resources for defence and the willingness of not only Russia but also the West to provide her with the latest in weaponry. Lavoy and Smith assert that "India has achieved numerical and qualitative superiority in many military categories, particularly in mechanised ground forces and in attack aircraft."[9] In their opinion, "the two-to-one overall advantage in aircraft grows to almost a six-to-one advantage when one compares just the most modern and capable aircraft."[10] The increased Indian advantage in both these areas is very significant because of Pakistan's limited strategic depth which might cause it to position at least some of her strategic assets close to the border with India.[11]

  So significant is the Indian conventional advantage now becoming that it could well achieve the level of being a decisive edge over Pakistan's conventional military power and this possibility leads some to the conclusion that in South Asia, "a balance of power cannot be maintained by conventional means alone and would have to be offset by nuclear weapons."[12]

- **Nuclear Threat Emanating from India**. Although I concur with the view of most analysts that it would in all probability be Pakistan that is likely to be the first one to resort to or threaten to resort to the use of nuclear weapons, most Pakistanis do not lend much credence to the conditional clause of "no first use" contained in the Indian nuclear doctrine. They feel that this has been inserted purely for political and diplomatic reasons and India could well renege on this pledge if she thinks it opportune. Consider hypothetically, a far-fetched scenario in which Pakistani forces find themselves in a position to either cut off the Indian forces in Siachen (e.g., Kargil) or Kashmir from the rest of India. Despite the fact that India and Pakistan adopted very different routes for developing their nuclear weapons (plutonium versus enriched Uranium), most analysts agree that the number and type of weapons that both have managed to produce till date is almost comparable. It must, however, be kept in mind that in the nuclear realm, parity in numbers does not have much significance.

- **Threat to Pakistan's Nuclear Assets from India.** Since India has a significant conventional offensive potential vis-à-vis Pakistan and also possesses a markedly superior capability to conduct strikes into Pakistan which is plagued by lack of strategic depth, the Pakistan nuclear doctrine must take cognizance of the possibility, howsoever far-fetched it might be, of India contemplating a first strike against Pakistan with a view to neutralising the latter's nuclear arsenal before the same could be brought into use.

  Considering that Pakistan is not only likely to have a lesser number of smaller nuclear weapons but is also constrained by its limited nuclear weapons delivery capability, specifically in the realm of high technology attack aircraft, the spectre of an Indian first strike looms large in Pakistani military thinking and is, therefore, bound to be reflected in her nuclear doctrine.

  According to Lavoy and Smith, "If we suspect that in a crunch, India could renege on its promised no first use; and if the US, despite its pre-eminent conventional power, was unwilling to forgo this option; who would believe that Pakistan, if in trouble against a much larger adversary, would not use or threaten to use its 'force equaliser'?"[13]

- **Threat from a Country other than India to Pakistan's Nuclear Assets.** Pakistan has been living with the fear of Israel conducting an attack on Pakistan's nuclear installations similar to the one that reduced the Iraqi nuclear reactor at Osirak to dust. On numerous occasions in the past, the Pakistan Air Force went on high alert after receiving unconfirmed reports of the Israelis contemplating an air strike against the Pakistani nuclear installations around Kahuta. In some cases, fighter-interceptor aircraft even got airborne and proceeded to predetermined patrol sites in anticipation of the expected Israeli air attack.[14] Although the chances of such an eventuality occurring in the near future appear fairly remote, this is a possible threat that plays on the minds of the Pakistani leadership, especially in view of the growing India-Israel relationship and the West's continuing overall displeasure with an Islamic country such as Pakistan having gained access to nuclear weapons. Since Israel would not be able to undertake such an operation without informing and bringing the Americans on board, I feel that such an attack is highly unlikely to occur till such time that the situation in Afghanistan and Iraq has returned to normal, and also the issue of the Iranian nuclear programme has been resolved to the satisfaction of the involved parties. I am convinced, however, that this would remain an "unstated and unspoken" about part of Pakistan's undeclared nuclear doctrine.

Nuclear First Use

Unlike India which has at least made a mention of its decision of not being the first one to employ nuclear weapons in her nuclear doctrine, Pakistan has understandably refrained from making any commitment to "No First Use." Analysts have interpreted Musharraf's statements during the 2002 military stand-off that while Pakistan does not want a war with India, she would "respond with full might" if one is forced upon it, to mean that if pressed by an overwhelming conventional attack from India, which has superior conventional forces, Pakistan might use its nuclear weapons.[15]

Since Pakistan essentially considers her nuclear arsenal to be an instrument of deterrence, "a Pakistani policy of no-nuclear-pre-emption would not be credible."[16] Pakistan's ambiguity in the domain of No First Use by not ruling it out could be attributed to one or more of the following factors:

- Being significantly weak in the conventional military realm, Pakistan expects to reach her nuclear escalation threshold before India and as such wants to keep the option of Nuclear First Use open and available to it. This indicates that "Pakistan's Nuclear Doctrine would essentially revolve around the first-strike option."[17]

- By maintaining ambiguity regarding No First Use, Pakistan is actually strengthening the deterrence potential and value of her nuclear arsenal since this possibility is bound to figure very prominently in the minds of the Indian military and political leadership and could even lead to them refraining from adopting a course of action that could be construed too negatively by Pakistan.

- Pakistan's nuclear first use option, rather than being put into action immediately, could be expected to follow a scheme of graduated responses as suggested by Dr. Stephen Cohen.[18] I have taken the liberty of further expanding the stages that Dr. Cohen has mentioned in his writings and envisage the Pakistan nuclear first use to develop as follows:

  - A private warning communicated by the Government of Pakistan through unofficial channels or other countries.
  - A public warning by the Pakistani leadership in the form of a widely publicised media statement.
  - The conduct of a nuclear test explosion on Pakistani soil.
  - The conduct of a nuclear-capable ballistic missile test.
  - The counter-force employment of nuclear weapons against an Indian Navy vessel at sea which would be a legitimate military target.
  - The counter-force employment of a low-yield nuclear weapons or a tactical nuclear weapon (if Pakistan develops one) against Indian conventional forces that have intruded into Pakistani territory.
  - The use of nuclear weapons against purely military targets on Indian soil, most probably in thinly populated desert or semi-desert areas to minimise the collateral damage.

Weapon of Defensive Deterrence

There is a significant difference in the nuclear doctrinal thinking process of India and Pakistan. While both ascribe a "deterrent" value to their respective nuclear weapons arsenals, they do it for absolutely different reasons.

The Indians construe their nuclear weapons to be a weapon of response, essentially to deter the employment of nuclear weapons by any other country against India. The Indians, therefore, envisage these weapons to help deter a nuclear onslaught against them.

Pakistan, on the other hand, qualifies her use of nuclear weapons as a means of defensive deterrence with the objective of deterring the Indians from waging a conventional or limited war against Pakistan and the threat of their use is expected to dissuade India from initiating a full-scale conventional war. In this aspect, the Kargil Conflict of 1999 and the 2001-2002 Stand-Off[19] could be cited as examples where presumably, it was the Pakistani threat of employment of nuclear weapons that prevented India from escalating the conflict and gradually led to de-escalation.

Weapon for Ensuring Survival

Pakistan considers her nuclear weapons to be a means of ensuring her survival. This could also be construed to be a mechanism of denying the massive Indian conventional military a significant military victory. In this aspect of doctrinal thinking, Pakistan's nuclear doctrine could specify that Pakistan would be forced to consider the employment of nuclear weapons whenever confronted with the spectre of a major defeat in the conventional arena. Lt. Gen. Kidwai specified Pakistan's nuclear threshold in terms of the "territorial or space threshold, military threshold, economic threshold and internal stability threshold"[20] but these are very broad-based intangibles which are vague and leave a lot ambiguous.

Dr. Manpreet Sethi alludes to Pakistan's nuclear posture serving the purposes of being "a strategic equaliser of power asymmetry"[21] and a "guarantor of security in absence of support" forthcoming from her allies.

Nuclear Posture

Both India and Pakistan have openly declared their adherence to Minimum Credible deterrence as an essential foundation of their nuclear weapons philosophy. Conveniently, however, both the countries have left the quantification of the "Minimality" and "Credibility" of their respective nuclear doctrines ambiguous.

The aspect of minimality essentially refers to the number of nuclear weapons available, the number of aircraft available for delivering air-delivered nuclear weapons and the type, number and quantity of nuclear-capable ballistic surface-to-surface missiles that are available to each country. While this aspect does lend itself to be tangibly quantified, the other vital component of their nuclear posture, i.e., "credibility" remains a vague and unquantifiable entity.

It stands to reason that since her nuclear doctrine is purely Indo-centric, Pakistan's assessment of minimality and credibility would depend solely on what the Indians are able to field in the nuclear weapons domain. This linkage of Pakistan's nuclear doctrine with the evolving nuclear arsenal and thinking of India is one of the essentials that cannot be lost sight of while drafting Pakistan's nuclear doctrine.

No Arms Race

Pakistan had expected that the possession of a credible nuclear capability would permit it to reduce the expenditure on its massive conventional military machine. This, however, has not happened for the following reasons:

- The assertion in the Indian nuclear doctrine that she would continue to maintain "highly effective conventional military capabilities in order to raise the threshold of outbreak both of conventional military conflict as well as that of threat or use of nuclear weapons."[22]
- The fear and apprehension among the Pakistani leadership that a weakening of its conventional military potential vis-à-vis India would impinge directly on nuclear stability in the region by further lowering Pakistan's nuclear escalation threshold.[23]
- The emerging belief within the Indian military that "strategic space" does exist below Pakistan's nuclear escalation threshold for India to contemplate a conventional war of limited objectives. The Indian Army's Cold Start Doctrine is based precisely on this assumption and its implementation would significantly enhance Pakistan's fears of a conventional war with India.[24]

In summary, it appears, therefore, that while Pakistan is not keen on venturing into a blatant nuclear arms race with India, the latter, through her actions wants Pakistan to venture down this path despite knowing fully well that an economically unstable Pakistan would not be good for the stability of the region. Pakistan's nuclear doctrine must take cognizance of this factor.

Security of Nuclear Arsenal

Nuclear weapons are considered as the "weapons of last resort" for Pakistan. As such, their security is a paramount consideration that would figure prominently in Pakistan's Nuclear Doctrine. In ensuring the security of Pakistan's nuclear weapons, the internal or domestic as well as the external dimensions of the threats posed to it have to be taken into account. As Lavoy and Smith write, "The survival of Pakistan's strategic forces is critical to Pakistan, and a threat to them could place pressure on Pakistan to launch a nuclear attack while the strategic forces are still intact and capable of making a credible impression upon India."[25]

In the realm of internal or domestic threats to Pakistan's nuclear weapons, a lot has been said and spoken about the dangers of this arsenal being allowed to fall into the hands of Islamic extremists or other radical elements that are operating inside Pakistan. Personally speaking, I do not lend much credence to this threat since Pakistan's nuclear weapons are known to be fairly secure and under the control of the military. Additionally, with the help of the United States, Pakistan's Strategic Plans Division (SPD) which oversees the country's nuclear weapons programme on behalf of its National Command Authority (NCA) has instituted an intricate system of Permissive Action Links (PALs) and Personnel Reliability Programmes (PRP) that further obviates the chances of these weapons falling into the hands of any undesirable group of people. In a recent statement, Lt. Gen. Kidwai acknowledged the aid that the US Government had provided to Pakistan in this area, both in terms of financial assistance as well as in the domain of training for personnel.[26]

The external dimension of the threat to the security of Pakistan's nuclear arsenal emanates from India. Since most Pakistanis do not lend much credence to the Indian assertion of "No First Use" and expect India to renege on this pledge whenever it suits her, the defence of Pakistan's nuclear weapons is of great importance.[27] In this area, Pakistan's lack of geographic strategic depth also figures since even the deepest parts of the country are now within the range of the newly inducted and operationalised Sukhoi Su-30 MKI long range strike aircraft of the Indian Air Force. It stands to reason, therefore, that Pakistan's nuclear weapons, apart from being housed in suitably hardened shelters, would also be widely dispersed all over the geographic expanse of the country. Unless this is done, the danger of the Indians being able to neutralise these weapons through a First Strike will continue to haunt the minds of the Pakistani leadership, both civilian and military.

In the same vein as dispersal of nuclear weapons, Pakistan might also contemplate staggering its meagre force of F-16 combat aircraft since other than the surface-to-surface ballistic missiles, these aircraft form the prime means of nuclear weapons delivery by employing air-deliverable nuclear bombs.

Security of Communication

"Fast and secure communications is another essential factor in a nuclear environment."[28] These communications, in the nuclear realm, could be categorised into two significant albeit disparate areas: communications between the two or more adversarial countries to obviate the chances of any miscommunication that could trigger a nuclear holocaust and those within a country's nuclear command and control system. Pakistan's nuclear doctrine must highlight the importance and relevance of both.

As regards interstate communications, I believe that India and Pakistan have, in the process of their continuing Composite Dialogue, established contacts and links which could be utilised for conveying crucial messages whenever needed. Additionally, the establishment of hotlines between the Army Headquarters of the two countries also affords an effective and readily available channel of communication.

In respect of the communication channel within Pakistan's nuclear command and control system, it has to be ensured that the adopted channels of communication are secure, non-interferable, non-monitorable and possess adequate back-up redundancy. Only with the incorporation of these attributes would a communications mechanism within the country's NWCS be acceptable.

Strategic Intelligence

The geographic contiguity of India and Pakistan presents a nightmare from the perspective of early warning availability of a missile launch by either of the countries. The nuclear doctrine of Pakistan, therefore, must lay down the requirement for the establishment of a strategic intelligence gathering apparatus which is able not only to provide timely information but is also secure enough so that it cannot be interfered with by the enemy. This system would have to incorporate a variety of intelligence gathering equipment and means ranging from human (HUMINT) to signals (SIGINT) to communications intelligence (COMINT) and would require ground-based, airborne and possible space-based sensors being developed and employed in a coordinated manner.

Since raw intelligence information does not suffice by itself, an efficient mechanism for analysing the intelligence immediately and communicating it to the required individuals within the political and the military hierarchy would also require to be put in place for exploiting the advantages of strategic intelligence gathering.

Dynamic Nature

Pakistan's nuclear doctrine would need to be a "living" document which is amenable to rapid modification and adjustments based on developments taking place on the Indian side. This requirement for this document to be dynamic is also a fallout of it being entirely Indo-centric and I am positive that any change in the Chinese or the Pakistani nuclear posture would bring about a corresponding change in the Indian doctrine.

In terms of dynamism and amenability to change and improvement, Pakistan's nuclear doctrine must stay abreast of all nuclear developments that are taking place on the Indian side—whether in material terms or in thinking. This is not to say that the Pakistan nuclear doctrine would be slaved to the Indian one since it first has to fulfil the requirements stipulated earlier from the Pakistani perspective. Dr. Shireen Mazari quoted a Pakistani Government official as having said, "the direction of our nuclear weapons programme will be determined by India's actions."[29]

One example of Indian intransigence in this regard is its announced intent to develop a triad-based nuclear deterrent that she really does not need vis-à-vis her confrontation with Pakistan but which might force Pakistan to also expand her nuclear arsenal. Similarly, the rapidly widening gulf in the air attack potential of the two countries in India's favour could also lead Pakistan down the road of additional nuclear weapons development.

Ambiguity

"Ambiguity deters" is the canon of all nuclear creed[30] and both India and Pakistan have resorted to it for their own ends. The views of the delegates at the Pugwash Workshop held at Lahore in early 2003 were split amongst the nuclear optimists and nuclear pessimists on the aspect of nuclear ambiguity. While the former supported opacity on the grounds that declared thresholds undermine operational flexibility and increase nuclear risks during crises, the latter argued otherwise. While compiling the report of this Workshop, Samina Ahmed summarised this controversy in these words, "By keeping deterrence vague and by avoiding explication of red lines, Pakistan can also avoid a nuclear arms race with India and keep its weapons un-deployed. This nuclear restraint, reflected in Pakistan's policy of minimum nuclear deterrence, has helped to buttress nuclear crisis stability in South Asia."[31]

The report cited above goes on to mention that "Pakistan's emphasis on opacity and its rejection of a no-first use doctrine reflects its concerns about conventional inferiority vis-à-vis India."[32]

Specifically, among other things, Pakistan needs to continue maintaining an ambiguous stance regarding the number and type of nuclear weapons that it possesses, its nuclear escalation thresholds, nuclear development plans, nuclear targeting philosophy and strategic nuclear intelligence gathering capability since the uncertainty that lack of knowledge regarding these that is created in the minds of the Indian civilian and military leadership actually strengthens Pakistan's deterrence potential and could well prevent the initiation of conventional hostilities by India in the future.

Adherence to the International Norms of Non-Proliferation

The immense international hue and cry over the disclosure of the alleged involvement of Pakistan's A. Q. Khan network in unauthorised and illegal nuclear proliferation was warranted and required the Pakistan Government taking appropriate corrective action to obviate the chances of any recurrence. As an immediate step, not only was Dr. Abdul Qadeer Khan upbraided and questioned by the Government but also a law was promulgated to prevent any recurrences.

Since this episode is fairly fresh in the minds of the international community, it is imperative that a mention of this be included in Pakistan's nuclear doctrine in order to convince the World that Pakistan would ensure compliance with all the accepted international norms of nuclear non-proliferation and would do its utmost to ensure that the unauthorised disclosure and provision of nuclear technology and expertise to other countries is prevented. This requirement could also form a part of the security imperatives of Pakistan's nuclear weapons programme.

In addition to stipulating adherence to the accepted international norms of non-proliferation, Pakistan's nuclear doctrine must also include a commitment from the leadership of the country expressing its intention and desire to support the success of other international agreements and conventions related to controlling the spread of weapons of mass destruction.

Command and Control of Nuclear Weapons

A nuclear doctrine is essentially just a document and it needs the putting in place of an effective and efficient Nuclear Command and Control System (NCCS) to oversee not only the country's nuclear programme but also the implementation of its nuclear doctrine. Both Pakistan and India have put in place what they respectively consider to be suitable nuclear command and control systems and these appear to be functioning as per the requirements.

One major anomaly that currently exists in the Pakistan NWCS is that it is dominated by the country's military which holds the rein at each and every tier of the system. This has happened despite the initial law stating that the command of the NWCS would rest in the Chief Executive of the country who would normally be the elected Prime Minister of Pakistan. Subsequent arbitrary changes to the regulations have altered the shape and content of the NWCS and handed over its reins to the Pakistan Army. In Pakistan, "civilian leaders have thus far, despite official claims, been largely excluded from nuclear decision-making by a military establishment that controls the country's nuclear assets."[33] It is imperative that the control of this devastating weapon must rest firmly in the hands of the highest political authority in the country—in the case of Pakistan this would be the elected Prime Minister of the country.[34]

Pakistan's nuclear doctrine must address this vital issue in earnest and ensure that suitable legislation is enacted to preclude any arbitrary changes being brought about in the NWCS by any individual or institution of state. This is essential if Pakistan wants to live up to its desired image of being a responsible nuclear weapons capable state.

In order to bestow an element of uninterruptible continuity on the working of the NWCS, the Pakistan nuclear doctrine should also include details on the delegation of responsibility within the critical elements of the nuclear decision-making chain of the country. This must cater for the non-availability of one of the key links or his/her incapacitation.

In her report on the Pugwash Workshop held at Lahore in 2003, Samina Ahmed cites one of the participants as having asserted that "it is intellectual arrogance to assume that military and intelligence services fully comprehend the dynamics of crisis escalation." She goes on to elaborate that nuclear adventurism would be forestalled if the political leadership and the public were able to comprehend the implications of nuclear war but unfortunately the situation in India and Pakistan is such that while the masses continue to remain ill-informed, the leadership is often ill-advised by the bureaucracies that control the nuclear weapons establishment.[35] These are precisely the issues that Pakistan's NWCS and its nuclear doctrine must cater for.

Commitment to further India-Pakistan Nuclear CBMs

India and Pakistan have already made a promising start in the area of nuclear CBMs by agreeing to exchange a list of each other's nuclear installations every year, by providing advance notification of any missile test to the other and by agreeing not to attack each other's nuclear installations. This encouraging process of bilateral nuclear CBMs must be continued and the Pakistan nuclear doctrine should incorporate a provision for this.

Nuclear Targeting Philosophy

Though the aspect of targeting would be too classified and secret to be included in the public version of the nuclear doctrine, adequate thought must be given to the options of counter-force, counter-value and counter-space targeting options while preparing Pakistan's nuclear doctrine.

Developmental Strategy

Nuclear weapons development would be an ongoing process with the incorporation of newer technologies as and when these become available. Since a nuclear doctrine cannot elaborate on the classified and secret aspects of her nuclear weapons development plans, a reference to the fact that Pakistan would actively pursue the process of development and improvement of her nuclear weapons needs to be incorporated in the nuclear doctrine. It goes without saying that Pakistan's nuclear weapons development strategy would be shaped and influenced to a great extent by what India does since some believe that "by mimicking Indian policy, Pakistan can be relatively certain of enforcing a stable nuclear deterrent relationship."[36]

Will to Use Nuclear Weapons

Nuclear weapons are essentially designed to serve a psychological purpose and nuclear deterrence works best by influencing the perceptions of the adversary. Not being actual weapons of war in the true sense, these are supposed to achieve the desired end without being fired but cannot do so unless the one possessing these is prepared for and has the will for their ultimate use.

The Pakistan nuclear doctrine must assert the national resolve and will of the Pakistani Government and its people to resort to the use of nuclear weapons if the situation so warrants. This would serve two purposes: it would strengthen the credibility of Pakistan's nuclear deterrence and also assure the people of Pakistan regarding the will of the Government to go to any extreme to assure the survival of their homeland in the face of any aggression. In the words of Lt. Gen. (retired) Durrani, "We wish to reassure our people that we have the will to pull the nuclear trigger, and we want them to be prepared if we did."[37]

Summary

In summarising the contents of this paper, I would confine myself to listing the eighteen elements that, in my reckoning and belief, merit consideration for inclusion in the Pakistan Nuclear Doctrine:

- India-Centricity
- Quest for Security
- Nuclear First Use
- Weapon of Defensive Deterrence
- Weapon for Ensuring Survival

- Nuclear Posture
- No Arms Race
- Security of Nuclear Arsenal
- Security of Communications
- Strategic Intelligence
- Dynamic Nature
- Ambiguity
- Adherence to International Norms of Non-proliferation
- Command and Control of Nuclear Weapons
- Commitment to Indo-Pak Nuclear CBMs
- Nuclear Targeting Philosophy
- Developmental Strategy
- Will to Use Nuclear Weapons

Conclusion

"A doctrine could be defined as a set of principles formulated and applied for a specific purpose, working towards a desired goal or aim. A nuclear doctrine would consequently consist of a set of principles, rules and instructions for the employment or non-employment of nuclear weapons and other systems associated with those weapons."[38]

Nuclear weapons are here to stay in South Asia since there is no going back for either India or Pakistan. Encumbered with this additional burden, therefore, it is imperative for the political and military leadership of both the countries to learn to live with nuclear weapons and one of the first steps in this direction entails being fully conversant with the nuclear doctrines of each other.

Two Separate Nuclear Doctrine Publications. Since ambiguity and secrecy of operational plans does not permit the inclusion of certain of classified and secret aspects in the publicised version of the nuclear doctrine, it would be worthwhile for Pakistan to consider preparing two separate nuclear doctrine documents—a generic one that could be released to the domestic public/international media and another that would remain classified and be distributed strictly on a need-to-know basis within Pakistan's NWCS, its political leadership and its military hierarchy.

Readers would appreciate that most of the contents of this paper are based on statements and comments of Pakistani Government officials and scholars. This indicates that notwithstanding the non-publication of an official Nuclear Doctrine, the Pakistani leadership and intellectual community have actually spoken about most of its contents at one time or the other. Therefore, rather than saying that Pakistan does not have an announced nuclear doctrine, it would be better to describe the situation as being akin to that of the unwritten British Constitution—it might never have been actually put down on paper or officially published but there is no denying the fact that it does exist. One just needs to know where to look!

Modified Pakistani doctrine restating the old

In a recognition of the importance and relevance of Pakistan's nuclear weapons, one of the first priorities of the newly elected Prime Minister Mian Muhammaf Nawaz Sharif was to convene a meeting of the country's National Command Authority (NCA). Accordingly, the new Government organized the first meeting on the National Command Authority on 05 September - just a day before the Pakistani nation celebrated the Defence of Pakistan Day. Other than the relevance of the subject, the following also contributed to this meeting being organized:

- The disclosure of Edward Snowden that despite its best efforts, the US Intelligence agencies had not been able to fully unravel the secrets regarding Pakistan's nuclear weapons.
- The fact that according to Snowden, a fair amount of the US$ 52.6 billion black budget was being spent on collecting information on Pakistan's nuclear arsenal.
- Prime Minister Nawaz Sharif wanted to assert and visibly demonstrate that he was indeed controlling the country's nuclear arsenal.

Having chaired this meeting, PM Nawaz Sharif left for the US to attend the meeting of the UN General Assembly and immediately after his return from the US, he paid an unprecedented visit to Pakistan's Nuclear Command and Control Headquarters on 04 October 2013. During this visit, the Prime Minister saw a secret weapons storage facility and a "technical site" where he received the most comprehensive briefing ever given to a Prime Minister by the Pakistan Army's Strategic Force Command. It was reported that the Prime Minister also visited a Uranium Enrichment facility located at Kahuta, in the outskirts of the capital city of Islamabad where fissile material and metal cores for Pakistan's nuclear devices are manufactured.

Statement issued after the September 5 NCA Meeting

A statement of the NCA was held under the chairmanship of the PM on

September 5. The meeting was attended by all the members of the NCA, Federal Ministers of Finance and Interior, the Adviser to the PM on National Security and Foreign Affairs, Special Assistant to the PM on Foreign Affairs, the Chairman Joint Chiefs of Staff Committee and the three Service Chiefs.

The NCA reaffirmed the centrality of Pakistan's nuclear programme for the defence of the country. The NCA reposed full confidence in Pakistan's robust Command and Control structure and all the security controls related to the strategic assets of the country. The NCA paid rich tributes to the various scientists as well as the security and policy level officials and diplomats who are associated with Pakistan's strategic programme.

The NCA reviewed developments at the regional level and reiterated that as a responsible nuclear weapon state, Pakistan would continue to adhere to the policy of Credible Minimum Deterrence, without entering into an arms race with any other country. Pakistan, however, would not remain oblivious to the evolving security dynamics in South Asia and would maintain full spectrum deterrence capability to deter all forms of aggression.

The NCA also reviewed the developments at the international level and took note of the discriminatory trends and policies that could have serious implications for Pakistan's national security and the global non-proliferation regime. The NCA reiterated that while maintaining its principled position on various arms control and non-proliferation issues, Pakistan would continue to oppose any arrangement that is detrimental to its security and strategic interests. As for the Fissile Material Cut-off Treaty FM(C)T, Pakistan's position will be determined by its national interests and the objectives of strategic stability in South Asia.

The meeting underscored Pakistan's commitment to play its due part as a mainstream partner in the global non-proliferation regime, and renewed Pakistan's keen interest in joining the multilateral export control regimes on a non-discriminatory basis. Pakistan has the requisite credentials for full access to civilian nuclear technology for peaceful purposes to meet its growing need energy needs for continued economic growth. The meeting noted the importance of Pakistan's positive outreach and enhanced engagement with all the multilateral export control regimes including membership of the Nuclear Suppliers Group (NSG).

The NCA emphasised that Pakistan will continue to participate constructively in the Nuclear Security Summit (NSS) process. As a responsible nuclear weapon state with advanced technology and four-decade long experience in safe and secure operation of nuclear power plants, Pakistan is ready to share its expertise with other interested states by providing fuel cycle services under IAEA safeguards and by providing placements at its Centres of Excellence on Nuclear Security.

Analysis

On the surface, the phrase that Pakistan "would maintain full spectrum deterrence capability to deter all forms of aggression" does appear to have an escalatory connotation but as has been the case with most of Pakistan's declaratory pronouncements regarding nuclear doctrine, the use of these meaningful phrases could well be construed to conceal more than it reveals. For instance, "full spectrum" could mean the entire spectrum of military operations from the tactical to the strategic and could also be indicative of Pakistan's desire to establish a triad-based nuclear deterrent capability. Similarly, the phrase "all forms of aggression" could, by some stretch of imagination be indicative of being applicable to all categories of conflict ranging from the sub-tactical to the strategic.

In my personal opinion, however, too much meaning should not be understood from these phrases which are primarily meant to strengthen Pakistan's deterrence by restating it more forcefully. This statement could also be considered to be a quantification of Pakistan's low nuclear threshold by insinuating that this threshold is quite low since its nuclear deterrent is designed to cater to "all forms of aggression". The same very phrase could also be considered to be an assertion of Pakistan's continuing adherence to the policy of nuclear first use since it talks of the nuclear weapons being used to deter all forms of aggression-not merely the nuclear one.

Also not to be lost sight of is the fact that this statement issued by the Pakistan NCA also laid inordinate emphasis on Pakistan's role as a legitimate exporter of civilian nuclear technology. The Pakistan Government has probably been forced to highlight this due to India having been accorded a membership of the Nuclear Suppliers Group (NSG) in the aftermath of the US-India Nuclear Co-operation Agreement while Pakistan has been denied this privilege. Moreover, in its current economic predicament, Pakistan could benefit financially to a significant extent if she is permitted to export peaceful nuclear technology to other friendly countries.

Pakistan has been expressing its continuing disappointment and concern over the discriminatory character of the global nuclear proliferation mechanism and this statement of the Pakistan NCA also mentions the same, specifically in the manner in which India has been accorded preference over

Pakistan and has been permitted to benefit from waivers and exceptions while Pakistan continues to be subjected to sanctions and restrictions in one form or the other.

Notes

1. The draft Indian Nuclear Doctrine was prepared by the 27-member National Security Advisory Board (NSAB) and was released by Mr. Brajesh Mishra, India's National Security Adviser on August 17, 1999 in New Delhi. According to the Government of India, this draft proposal was released to encourage public debate and would be considered by the government in due course for a final decision. The text of this document is available from numerous websites but the author downloaded it from http://www.pugwash.org/reports/nw/nw7a.htm.

2. Samina Ahmed, Workshop Report on the Pugwash Workshop on "Avoiding an India-Pakistan Confrontation" held at Lahore on March 11-12, 2003. Available on the internet at http://www.pugwash.org/reports/rc/sa/march2003/pakistan2003-workshop-report.htm.

3. Lt. Gen. (Retd) Sardar F. S. Lodi, "Pakistan's Nuclear Doctrine", *Defence Journal*, Karachi, April 1999. Available on the internet at http://www.defencejournal.com/apr99/pak-nuclear-doctrine.htm.

4. Brigadier (Retired) Feroz Hasan Khan, Report of Round Table organised by CAPP (RAND) on "Pakistan's Nuclear Future: How to Maintain Stability in an unstable Region." Available on the internet at http://www.rand.org/international_programs/capp/events/02/ferozkhan.html.

5. Dr. Subhash Kapila, "India and Pakistan Nuclear Doctrine: A Comparative Analysis." Available on the internet at http://www.ipcs.org/India_Pak_articles2.jsp?action=showView&kValue=573&status=article&mod=a.

6. Paolo Cotta-Ramusino and Maurizio Martellini, "Nuclear safety, nuclear stability and nuclear strategy in Pakistan." *A concise report of a visit by Landau Network—Centro Volta.* Available on the internet at http://www.mi.infn.it/~landnet/Doc/pakistan.pdf. Also quoted in a newspaper article titled, "Pakistanis see new aggression in Indian nuclear doctrine" that is available on the internet at http://www.dailytimes.com.pk/default.asp?page=story_24-1-2003_pg7_39.

7. Brigadier (Retired) Feroz Hasan Khan, op. cit.

8. Paolo Cotta-Ramusino and Maurizio Martellini, op. cit.

9. Peter R. Lavoy and Major Stephen A. Smith, "The Risk of Inadvertent Nuclear Use Between India and Pakistan." Available on the internet at http://www.ccc.nps.navy.mil/rsepResources/si/feb03/southAsia2.asp.

10. Ibid.

11. Ibid.

12. Lt. Gen. (Retd) Sardar F. S. Lodi, op. cit.

13. Peter R. Lavoy and Major Stephen A. Smith, op. cit.

14. The possibility, howsoever remote it might be, of Israel attempting to attack and destroy Pakistan's nuclear infrastructure have figured prominently in Pakistani

military thinking since as far back as the mid-1980s. In one instance, there were unconfirmed and unsubstantiated reports of Israeli aircraft even having been deployed to IAF bases in Indian Occupied Kashmir (Srinagar, Awantipura, etc.) for conducting such a strike. So seriously was this threat taken by the Pakistan Air Force that it drew up contingency plans to counter this particular eventuality and practised it on a regular basis.

15. "Pakistan's Nuclear Doctrine." Available on the internet at http://www.fas.org/nuke/guide/pakistan/nuke/index.html.

16. Peter R. Lavoy and Major Stephen A. Smith, op. cit.

17. Lt. Gen. (Retd) Sardar F. S. Lodi, op. cit.

18. Dr. Stephen Cohen's graduated response scheme has been quoted in Lt. Gen. (Retd) Sardar F. S. Lodi, op. cit. and is also referred to in the write-up available on the internet at http://en.wikipedia.org/wiki/Nuclear_Doctrine_of_Pakistan. Rather than going exactly by what has been quoted in these texts, the author has attempted to expand slightly by including certain additional steps in the scheme.

19. The author had the privilege of being very closely involved in both these events. During the Kargil conflict, he was the Base Commander of the Pakistan Air Force Base at Skardu which was the only PAF Base in the vicinity of the Kargil theatre of operations while during the period of escalated tensions in 2001-2002, he was serving as the Assistant Chief of Air Staff (Operations) of the Pakistan Air Force. In this assignment, he oversaw the entire process of deployment and response plans of the Pakistan Air Force and even presented the same to President Pervez Musharraf during his visit to the Command Operations Centre in December 2001.

20. Paolo Cotta-Ramusino and Maurizio Martellini, op. cit.

21. Dr. Manpreet Sethi, Paper read at a seminar on "Pakistan's Nuclear Doctrine and Strategy" at the Institute for Peace and Conflict Studies (IPCS) on August 16, 2007. A report of the proceedings of this seminar can be accessed on the internet at http://www.ipcs.org/Nuclear_seminars2.jsp?action=showView&kValue=2377.

22. Please refer to paragraph 2.7 of the draft Indian Nuclear Doctrine, available on the internet at http://www.indianembassy.org/policy/CTBT/nuclear_doctrine_aug_17_1999.html.

23. Lt. Gen. (Retd) Asad Durrani, "Doctrinal Doublespeak." Paper read at the Pugwash Meeting No. 280 (Pugwash Workshop on "Avoiding an India-Pakistan Confrontation") held at Lahore on March 11-12, 2003. Available on the internet at http://www.pugwash.org/reports/rc/sa/march2003/pakistan2003-durrani.htm.

24. For a detailed analysis of the Indian Army's Cold Start Doctrine, please refer to Air Commodore Tariq Mahmud Ashraf, "Doctrinal Reawakening on the Indian Armed Forces," US Army Military Review, November/December 2004. The complete text of this article is available on the internet and can be downloaded from usacac.army.mil/cac/milreview/download/English/NovDec04/ashraf.pdf.

25. Peter R. Lavoy and Major Stephen A. Smith, op. cit.

26. John M. Glionna, "Pakistan says its nuclear weapons are secure" published in the Los Angeles Times, January 27, 2007. This article can be accessed and downloaded from the internet at http://www.latimes.com/news/nationworld/world/la-fg-

nukes27jan27,1,5490429.story.
While acknowledging the "less than US$ 10 million US assistance to Pakistan for bolstering its nuclear security," Kidwai stated that Pakistan now had a foolproof nuclear security system in place with over 10,000 troops deployed on safeguarding her nuclear assets. As such, he asserted that there was no chance whatsoever of these weapons falling into unauthorised hands.

27. Lt. Gen. (Retd) Asad Durrani, op. cit. The General thinks that "if India were ever to get desperate, the policy (of no first use) alone would not hold it back from firing the first nuclear salvos."

28. Lt. Gen. (Retd) Sardar F. S. Lodi, op. cit.

29. Dr. Shireen Mazari's statement at a seminar jointly organised by the Institute of South Asian Studies and the Institute of Defence and Strategic Studies in Singapore on June 2, 2005. Available on the internet at http://www.rsi.sg/english/comment/view/20050602172517/1/.html.

30. Lt. Gen. (Retd) Asad Durrani, op. cit.

31. Samina Ahmed, op. cit.

32. Ibid.

33. Ibid.

34. Lt. Gen. (Retd) Sardar F. S. Lodi, op. cit.

35. Samina Ahmed, op. cit.

36. "The Nuclear Doctrines of India and Pakistan." Available on the internet at http://www.nti.org/f_WMD411/f2i3.html.

37. Lt. Gen. (Retd) Asad Durrani, op. cit.

38. Lt. Gen. (Retd) Sardar F. S. Lodi, op. cit.

10

"Minimality" and "Credibility" in the South Asian Nuclear Milieu[1]

"The strategic benefit of nuclear weapons derives not from how many a state has, but what the state is able to do with them, and how the state's standing in the international community improves when it has a nuclear capability."[2] Pakistan and India appear to have not only recognised the truth of this statement but also the validity and relevance of one of the key lessons of the Cold War that there is little point in having large numbers of nuclear weapons.

Although both India and Pakistan went overtly nuclear in May 1998, it is an accepted fact that they had both achieved the capability of producing nuclear weapons much earlier. Cotta-Ramusino and Martellini quote General (Retired) Mirza Aslam Beg as saying that Pakistan possessed 6 nuclear devices in 1989 and this number had risen to 15 by 1991[3] while India, in Basrur's reckoning, probably achieved nuclear weapons capability in or about 1990.[4]

In the nuclearised South Asian milieu, both Pakistan and India have declared their respective commitments to the tenet of maintaining a "minimum credible nuclear deterrent."[5] Since both the countries have tended to take advantage of the cloak of ambiguity and have not elaborated on what they construe the terms "Minimum" and "Credible" to mean, an analysis of both these terms and how these could be interpreted by India and Pakistan warrants a study.

This Chapter would aim to define the terms "Minimum" and "Credible" as these pertain to nuclear matters and attempt to elaborate each with the objective of attempting to understand not only how these terms are being interpreted in South Asia but also to highlight their implications on the cherished goal of nuclear stability in South Asia. In simplistic terms, "minimality" and "credibility" could be described respectively as the quantitative and qualitative dimensions of a country's nuclear potential. Considering that minimality and credibility are two distinct albeit interlinked areas, they could also be seen as a staged or phased process.

Minimality and Credibility as Phased Processes
One can consider the achievement of a "minimum credible" nuclear deterrence to a two-staged process: in the first stage, the aspect of minimality has to be addressed while in the second stage, having achieved the minimality, the focus has to be shifted towards the achievement of greater "credibility." Therefore, in my understanding, both India and Pakistan initially endeavoured during Stage 1 to develop the required number of

weapons with the credibility of being able to deliver these being accorded a lower priority. Having developed what they considered to be meeting the requirements of their respective minimum nuclear deterrent, they both embarked on Stage 2 wherein the emphasis now shifted to the enhancement of the "credibility" aspect of their nuclear arsenals. I will now discuss each of these terms separately before attempting to present a consolidated summary of the salient conclusions emerging from this analysis.

"Minimality"

Minimality is a more quantifiable aspect since it pertains, directly or indirectly, to the number of deliverable nuclear warheads that each country possesses in its nuclear arsenal. Since this is a classified piece of information that neither India nor Pakistan would want to be disclosed, the specific quantities of weapons that constitute a minimum deterrent potential in their respective reckoning have never been alluded to by either.

Unlike conventional military potential that lends itself to a fairly accurate comparison based on the numbers of personnel, aircraft, ships and tanks, etc., parity in the nuclear military realm is not as simple. "The magnitude of an arsenal matters but the nuclear game is more than a matter of numbers."[6]

From the Pakistani perspective which considers India as the sole nuclear-armed threat to its security, minimum nuclear deterrent potential could be defined as that which after surviving an Indian first strike, is still able to react and inflict an unacceptable degree of damage on India. As such, "Pakistan intends to build a capacity that would create at least a 'reasonable doubt' that it could do so."[7] Pakistan's minimum nuclear arsenal, therefore, should not be too small a nuclear force which can be wiped out by a single Indian strike.[8] Minimality, therefore, is influenced significantly by the survivability of the nuclear arsenal and it stands to reason that the lower the number of nuclear weapons, the greater these would have to be dispersed while being deployed. This would create additional problems of command, control and communications as regards these weapons.

India on the other hand, is faced with two nuclear threats—one from Pakistan that she openly accepts and another from China which is often alluded to but never officially. "India's nuclear weapons are used to deter not only Pakistan but China as well. Hence, there is a need for a higher overall capability."[9] India, therefore, considers herself to be faced with a two-front nuclear threat scenario and accordingly, her assessment of what constitutes the minimum nuclear deterrent potential would be significantly more than nuclear threat remains and accordingly, her assessment of what constitutes the minimum nuclear deterent potential woudl be significantly more than that of Pakistan. India's minimum nuclear deterrent potential, therefore, "must have the ability to deter both of them."[10]

The above discussion has been made considering that India and Pakistan would only contemplate the employment of their respective nuclear weapons in the defensive mode, unlike the plans of NATO and Warsaw Pact countries to attempt to neutralise each other's nuclear potential through a first strike option. The possibility of either India or Pakistan adopting such an option appears remote because of the following considerations:

- Both India and Pakistan have clearly stated in unequivocal terms that their nuclear weapons are considered as instruments of deterrence or retaliation and not offence.
- Contemplating a first strike with a fair degree of success involves extremely accurate and current information on the entire array of nuclear weapons that the adversary possesses. The availability of this information in an accurate manner is currently well beyond the intelligence gathering potential of India and Pakistan.
- Since the chances of total success of a first strike appear very remote, the risk of the adversary being left with a number of nuclear weapons even after the attack, howsoever small the quantity might be, presents a horrifying danger of devastating nuclear retaliation.
- The experience of the Cold War highlights that NATO and Warsaw Pact countries were never sure of being able to neutralise the other's nuclear arsenal in its entirety and ended up getting embroiled in a mad and senseless nuclear weapons race which ultimately led them to a state where their stand-off started being referred to as one of Mutually Assured Destruction more appropriately referred to by its acronym of MAD.
- The possibility of an India-China nuclear confrontation which currently appears remote could lead to India developing greater nuclear weapons capability. Such a move would be extremely destabilising for South Asia since it could well lead to Pakistan increasing the number of weapons that it considers as being adequate for maintaining its stated nuclear posture of minimum credible deterrence vis-à-vis India. It would be relevant to point out here that most Pakistanis consider India's veiled references to the Chinese threat as merely being a ploy that would justify her amassing a significantly larger nuclear arsenal including sea-based and launched weapons which she definitely does not need to counter Pakistan.

Since Pakistan's nuclear weapons programme is entirely India-specific, the determination of the number of nuclear weapons that afford it the desired minimum level of deterrence vis-à-vis India would continue to be dictated by events across the border. While the minimality of Pakistan's minimum credible nuclear deterrence remains an undefined quantity, it is a dynamic concept based on India's capabilities of pre-emption and interception. It stands to reason, therefore, that as the threat perceptions in terms of pre-emption and interception from India changes, Pakistan will seek to accordingly adjust its minimum deterrence capability.[11]

Quantifying the Minimality in South Asian Deterrence. Writing in the Armed Forces Journal of September 1998, Amit Gupta estimated that India would require between 100 to 150 nuclear weapons in order to be able to field a viable deterrent against both China and Pakistan. For Pakistan, most analysts agree that the minimum deterrent could be quantified in tangible terms to range between 30 and 50 nuclear weapons.[12] General (Retired) Mirza Aslam Baig, the person who succeeded late General Zia-ul-Haq as the Chief of the Army Staff of the Pakistan Army, estimated that Pakistan would need a minimum of 75-90 nuclear weapons to redress the conventional imbalance with India.[13] Samar Mubarak Mund, who headed the Pakistani nuclear test team in 1998 and recently retired as the Chairman of NESCOM, stated in an interview with Dawn that 60 to 70 nuclear warheads would be good enough for Pakistan to have a credible nuclear deterrence against India.[14] According to P. R. Chari, the figures debated among Indian strategists quantify the minimality of the Indian deterrence posture to mean a number anywhere in-between 70 and 150 nuclear weapons.[15]

In fact even prior to the May 1998 nuclear tests, some Indian strategic analysts including former Indian Army Chief of Staff, General K. Sundarji, and Subrahmanyam had endorsed the view that numbers of 100 or even less would be adequate for India's deterrence requirements.[16]

What is disturbing in the determination of a balance nuclear deterrence potential is the fact that while India is harping on its pledge of maintaining a minimum nuclear deterrent, on the other hand, her new maritime doctrine unveiled in May 2004 calls for the deployment of 24 ballistic missile submarines by 2030.[17]

Lavoy and Smith have calculated the numbers of nuclear warheads presumably held by India and Pakistan in their respective arsenals as depicted in the subsequent Table.[18]

	India			Pakistan		
	Low	Med	High	Low	Med	High
Weapon-grade Plutonium	280	400	600	5	15	45
Weapon-grade Uranium	U/K	U/K	U/K	815	1,020	1,230
Weapon Capability	**40**	**70**	**120**	**35**	**60**	**95**

In a more recent paper, Dr. Lavoy puts the low end of the estimate for Pakistan's nuclear weapons at 70, the medium at 90 and the higher one at 115 nuclear weapons.[19]

If the figures of 100-150 nuclear weapons being the minimum required by India and 70 for Pakistan are taken as a datum, most estimates indicate that while Pakistan has definitely reached the desired minimum number of nuclear weapons, India has also reached it or is about to reach.

It appears, therefore, that the Phase I of achieving a "credible minimum" nuclear posture, i.e., ensuring the availability of the minimum number of nuclear weapons has been completed by both the countries since they now possess at least that number of nuclear warheads which meets the requirements of the minimality aspect of their doctrines of "minimum credible" nuclear deterrence. Having met the requirements of the first stage, the emphasis in both India and Pakistan has now shifted understandably towards enhancing the "credibility" of their respective nuclear arsenals, i.e., they have entered the second stage of achieving the desired "minimum credible" nuclear deterrent potential.

Although there have been no statements from India and Pakistan regarding the number of nuclear weapons that each country considers to be constituting the minimal element of its deterrence capability, a purview of the available literature on the subject indicates that this quantity would be around 150 weapons for India and around 90 weapons for Pakistan.

Credibility

Whereas the minimality of deterrence is a quantifiable entity that lends itself to quantitative comparative analysis, credibility pertains more to the qualitative aspect of nuclear weapons potential. In order for an arsenal to be accepted as credible enough for an adversary to be deterred, several factors have to be taken into account. These include the following:

- Assurance of adequate nuclear potential being able to survive a first strike by the adversary.
- Nuclear weapons delivery capability potential, i.e., air-delivered weapons, nuclear-armed surface-to-surface missiles and sea-launched nuclear weapons.

- The ability of the nuclear weapons delivery systems to reach strategic targets located in depth. This aspect pertains to the reach of the nuclear-armed missiles and the operational radii of action of nuclear weapons carrying strike aircraft.
- The degree of accuracy with which the nuclear weapons can be delivered on the desired target or are able to navigate to the desired target.
- The degree of assurance with which the nuclear-armed strike aircraft and the nuclear missiles can negate or evade the en route air defence environment and still make it to the desired target.
- The level and correctness of strategic information that is available to the adversary leadership.
- The national will and resolve of the adversary must be strong enough to take the decision of going nuclear since a nuclear attack is bound to invite retaliation in kind with devastating consequences.

Another facet of "credibility" that has not been talked about much is "Readiness" or the status of alert or preparedness of a country's nuclear arsenal. If a country expects the enemy to launch a first strike against its nuclear weapons, it has to be prepared to respond immediately. This might require the nuclear weapons being maintained at a high status of alert and preparedness which is destabilising in itself. Considering the geographic contiguity of India and Pakistan, the amount of early warning available to either side is virtually negligible. It can be stated, therefore, that a certain level of nuclear preparedness is necessary for communicating the "credibility" of one's nuclear arsenal to the adversary. One of the means available for influencing the perception of the adversary in this regard could be through the holding of regular exercises involving the nuclear elements of one's military.

Credibility, apart from being a function of the quantity of nuclear weapons available, their reach, their accuracy, their potential of evading defences and the will of the country's leadership to resort to the use of nuclear weapons, is also influenced by the survivability of these weapons in the same fashion as minimality is affected by it.

This situation is especially hazardous from the Pakistani perspective. Being constrained and limited in terms of being able to detect the launch of an Indian first strike due to the lack of her strategic depth, she could well construe any missile launch from the Indian side to be a nuclear weapon and respond accordingly. The danger here is whether this concern could lead Pakistan to adopt a launch-on-warning or launch-under-attack posture whenever any Indian missile attack is detected. The danger of this eventuality being interpreted as a pre-emptive strike could well precipitate a Pakistani nuclear response.[20] Needless to say, such a heightened state of alert and readiness of Pakistan's nuclear weapons does not augur well for South Asian strategic stability and, therefore, must be avoided.

One example of Indian actions that could cause Pakistan to raise the readiness and preparedness level of her nuclear forces is the Indian Army's adoption of the new Cold Start Doctrine. The fact that this new doctrine is based on swift and rapid ingresses into Pakistani territory, while exploiting the "strategic space" that the Indian Army perceives to be existing between a limited war and a Pakistan's nuclear escalation threshold, has implications for Pakistan which could influence her to increase the readiness level of her nuclear forces. The previous Indian Army doctrine entailed the strike elements forming up at their locations in depth and then moving forward to the border. This provided the Pakistan Army with adequate warning and reaction time which would not be available now after the implementation of the Cold Start Doctrine.

Considering that India has presumably been thwarted from launching meaningful conventional offensives against Pakistan at least a couple of times due to the latter's access to nuclear weapons and the fact that the two countries have a history of trying to pay each other back in the same coin, e.g., Pakistan's action in Kargil as a response to earlier Indian moves in Siachen, the Cold Start doctrine could well be designed by the Indians to exploit the perceived strategic space below Pakistan's nuclear threshold through superior conventional forces backed up by a credible nuclear weapons arsenal.

Relationship between Minimality and Credibility

Notwithstanding the possibility that minimality and credibility of nuclear deterrence in the South Asian scenario have been considered in isolation to each other, there is a definite linkage and relationship that exists between the two. In fact the term "minimum credible deterrence" implies achieving the maximum credibility of one's nuclear arsenal with the least possible quantity of nuclear weapons. In this aspect, the South Asian nuclear doctrines are very similar to the British nuclear doctrine which "can be characterised as trying to do the most with the least."[21]

At the first glance, the two aspects appear to be directly proportional to each other, i.e., the more the number of nuclear weapons, the greater a country's deterrence potential. While this would be true during Stage 1 of the deterrence build-up, a more detailed analysis leads one to conclude that after both the countries have reached a certain quantitative level as regards nuclear weapons, the credibility aspect becomes more significant and at this stage, credibility and minimality appear to be inversely proportional to each other, i.e., as the credibility of nuclear deterrence continues to increase, a country could afford to reduce the number of weapons that it considers as constituting a minimum level of nuclear deterrence and vice versa. What is more significant here to understand is that any change in the adversary's military posture, whether conventional or nuclear, that impinges on credibility, would also have an impact on the minimality since the two are interlinked and connected. The same would also hold valid if any move of one of the countries impinges adversely on the minimality of deterrence of the other.

As regards South Asia, India and Pakistan have passed the first stage where the numbers of nuclear weapons played a more significant role and have now entered a phase where greater credibility through any of the means elaborated above could lead to a reduction in the number of nuclear weapons that each needs to possess. This indicates that like most other facets of nuclear doctrine, "credibility" and "minimality" are also dynamic concepts which would keep getting changed and adjusted as the situation on the ground keeps changing.

The recent surge of conventional military acquisitions such as the high-technology and very long range Sukhoi Su-30 strike aircraft capable of reaching the farthest depth of Pakistan and the increasing emphasis of the Indians on fielding ballistic missile defences are two cases in point.

While the induction of the Su-30 and similar offensive weapon platforms increases the threat of first strike posed to the Pakistani nuclear arsenal and impinges directly on both, the minimality and the credibility dimensions of Pakistan's nuclear posture, the expected induction of defensive weapons such as the Russian S-300, the US Patriot, the Israeli Green Pine radar system and the Airborne Early Warning and Control aircraft (AWAC) directly reduces the credibility of the Pakistani nuclear weapons by significantly increasing the chances of these weapons being intercepted and neutralised before they can reach the desired targets. In both these examples, Pakistan would be forced to seriously consider the number of nuclear weapons in its arsenal while simultaneously attempting to improve their credibility.

The above discussion indicates that minimality and credibility, therefore, are both dynamic concepts. Thus both India and Pakistan need to stay abreast of developments taking place in each other's nuclear capability so that they can suitably modify their own nuclear military potential to ensure its continued relevance in the strategic military equation. In the South Asian Nuclear milieu, therefore, it can be stated that while Pakistan's nuclear posture would continue to be shaped by that of India's, the latter would adjust its nuclear posture in line with the developments that take place in the nuclear weapons arena in China and Pakistan.

Conclusion

Since both India and Pakistan have declared that their respective nuclear postures would be based on fielding a "minimum credible" nuclear deterrent potential, it is important to study the two key determinants of their nuclear doctrines, i.e., "Credibility" and "Minimality."

This chapter has been an attempt to elaborate on these two key determinants by elaborating on these, attempting to quantify these where possible, analysing their linkage and interconnectedness and studying some of the factors that could bring about a change in these two determinants. It has also endeavoured to put forward the idea of these two determinants being a part of a phased process of building a country's nuclear deterrence capability wherein both Pakistan and India, having met the requirements of Stage 1 (ensuring the minimality), are now proceeding ahead with Stage 2 (ensuring the credibility).

In order to ensure and also enhance the nuclear stability of South Asia, it is important for Pakistan and India to establish channels of intergovernmental communication that provide prior information regarding any action by either of them that could possibly influence the other's notions of minimality and credibility.

Notes

1. Please refer to Chapter 8 for a brief introduction to the Concepts of Credibility and Minimality.
2. Dr. Patrick M. Cronin and Dr. Audrey Kurth Cronin, "Strategic Stability in the 21st Century." A Special Joint Report of the International Institute for Strategic Studies and the Oxford University Changing Character of War Programme, February 2007, page 18.
3. Paolo Cotta-Ramusino and Maurizio Martellini, "Nuclear safety, nuclear stability and nuclear strategy in Pakistan." A concise report of a visit by Landau Network-

Centro Volta. Available on the internet at http://www.mi.infn.it/~landnet/Doc/pakistan.pdf.

4.   Rajesh Basrur, "Minimum Deterrence and India Pakistan Nuclear Dialogue: Case Study on India." LNCV South Asia Security Project Case Study 2/2006, Landau Network-Centro Volta, Italy, March 2006, p. 9.

5.   India has clearly enunciated its adherence to "Minimum Credible" nuclear deterrence in her nuclear while Pakistani leaders have, in the absence of any published doctrine, indicated their adoption of the same basic theme, in numerous statements and proclamations.

6.   Lt. Gen. (Retd) Asad Durrani, "Doctrinal Doublespeak." Paper read at the Pugwash Meeting No. 280 (Pugwash Workshop on "Avoiding an India-Pakistan Confrontation") held at Lahore on March 11-12, 2003. Available on the internet at http://www.pugwash.org/reports/rc/sa/march2003/pakistan2003-durrani.htm.

7.   Ibid.

8.   Dr. Manpreet Sethi, Paper read at a seminar on "Pakistan's Nuclear Doctrine and Strategy" at the Institute for Peace and Conflict Studies (IPCS) on August 16, 2007. A report of the proceedings of this seminar can be accessed on the internet at http://www.ipcs.org/Nuclear_seminars2.jsp?action=showView&kValue=2377.

9.   Ibid.

10. Lt. Gen. Asad Durrani, op. cit.

11. Dr. Manpreet Sethi, op. cit.

12. As quoted in Lt. Gen. (Retd) Sardar F. S. Lodi, "Pakistan's Nuclear Doctrine." *Defence Journal*, Karachi, April 1999. Available on the internet at http://www.defencejournal.com/apr99/pak-nuclear-doctrine.htm.

13. As quoted in Smruti S. Pattanaik, "Pakistan's Nuclear Strategy," *Strategic Analysis*, vol. 27, no. 1, Jan-Mar 2003, Institute for Defence Studies and Analyses. Available on the internet at http://www.idsa.in/publications/strategic-analysis/2003/jan/Smruti.pdf. This estimate of General (Retd) Baig of what constitutes a minimum number of nuclear weapons for Pakistan has also been quoted in Paolo Cotta-Ramusino and Maurizio Martellini, "Nuclear safety, nuclear stability and nuclear strategy in Pakistan." A concise report of a visit by Landau Network-Centro Volta. Available on the internet at http://www.mi.infn.it/~landnet/Doc/pakistan.pdf.

14. Bhumitra Chakma, "Pakistan's Nuclear Doctrine and Command and Control System: Dilemmas of Small Nuclear Forces in the Second Atomic Age," *Security Challenges*, vol. 2, no. 2 (July 2006), p. 122.

15. P. R. Chari, "India's Nuclear Doctrine: Confused Ambitions," *The Non-Proliferation Review*, Fall/Winter 2000, p. 133. Available on the internet at http://www.cns.miis.edu/pubs/npr/vol07/73/73chari.pdf.

16. Rodney Jones, "Minimum Nuclear Deterrence Postures in South Asia: An Overview." Paper prepared for the US Defence Threat Reduction Agency (DTRA), October 1, 2001, p. 12.

17. Monterey Institute's Centre for Non-Proliferation Studies, "The Nuclear Doctrines of India and Pakistan," updated November 2006. Available on the internet at http://www.nti.org/f_WMD411/f2i3.html.

18. Although there are numerous estimations of the number of nuclear weapons that India and Pakistan could possess, most of these estimates indicate similar figures. The data for this Table has been extracted from Peter R. Lavoy and Major Stephen A. Smith, "The Risk of Inadvertent Nuclear Use Between India and Pakistan." Available on the internet at http://www.ccc.nps.navy.mil/rsepResources/si/feb03/southAsia2.asp.

19. Peter R. Lavoy, "Pakistan's Nuclear Posture: Security and Survivability." Available on the internet at http://www.npec-web.org/Frameset.asp?PageType=Single&PDFFile=20070121-Lavoy-PakistanNuclearPosture&PDFFolder=Essays.

20. Peter R. Lavoy and Major Stephen A. Smith, "The Risk of Inadvertent Nuclear Use Between India and Pakistan." Available on the internet at http://www.ccc.nps.navy.mil/rsepResources/si/feb03/southAsia2.asp.

21. Patrick and Audrey Cronin, op. cit. p. 18.

11

The Impact of Nuclearisation on Pakistan's Military System[1]

Introduction

The military system of a country is the sum total expression of its military capability. While Pakistan's existing and prevalent military system was designed to cater for the conventional weapons scenario, it is now being suitably modified to cater for the inclusion of nuclear weapons in the military confrontation equation. One cannot lose sight of the fact that the "military system to be adopted is linked with the power potential of a country."[2] Considering its vital significance, the military system to be adopted by a country must fulfil certain essential requirements and imperatives. These imperatives span from the military area to command requirements, national imperatives, coordination prerequisites and financial considerations.

Basic Requirements of a Military System

Military Imperatives. A military system must exhibit adequate military power to deter the aggressive designs of any hostile country with a view to avoiding war. In case war becomes unavoidable or is thrust upon us, the military system should be able to face up to the threat and bring the war to an end on a favourable note. This means that the military system has to be threat specific as regards its quantum and its capabilities.

   National Imperatives. The military system must act as a uniting force for the various communities residing in the country by ensuring national participation. A military system must be responsive enough to react during periods of national emergencies and flexible enough to be mobilised for nation building projects during peacetime.

   Coordination Requirements. The military system must be able to assimilate the entire strength of the nation in times of need, i.e., economic potential, diplomatic prowess, military force, technological and industrial capability, etc., and apply the same in a concerted manner. It is required for a military system to embody a suitable mix of civilian and military control.

   Command Imperatives. A military system must embody a Unity of Command in its hierarchical structure. It should be able to react as a whole rather than in penny packets where the individual services do not operate in unison.

   Economic Imperative. Be affordable for the national exchequer to be able to sustain. Due to its weak economy, it is extremely difficult for Pakistan to afford a huge defence budget. Whatever allocation that has to be made for the defence by the Pakistan Government has to be made at the cost of reducing the expenditure for other essential sectors of the national economy such as education, and health.

Does Pakistan's Existing Military System Meet the Requirements?

Analysis vis-à-vis Military Requirements. The military requirements relate to the military capability of the military system which would enable it to deter war and also negate the enemy in case a war is thrust upon us. In this realm we can safely conclude that while our conventional potential is adequate to meet the Indian threat, our nuclear potential is under development. While the nuclear weapons would play the main role in deterring war, our conventional capability would be able to withstand any enemy offensive short of the use of nuclear weapons. It is interesting to note that whereas the deterrence is now being ensured by the nuclear component of our military system, the role of the conventional component would now be to avert the reaching of our nuclear threshold in case of war. Since the nuclear control mechanism is already being put into place and the conventional forces are capable of meeting the threat posed by India under the present circumstances, our military system does not need any major changes because of these two requirements except for an analysis of the requirement for maintaining such a large standing conventional armed force in the presence of the nuclear capability.

Analysis vis-à-vis National Requirements

The national imperatives relate to the very character of the military system being of a participatory nature and the imperative need for this system to be able to support the government during times of national crises and emergencies as well as for other nation building projects. In all these areas, the existing military system meets the requirements adequately and needs no major overhauling or modifications.

Analysis vis-à-vis Coordination Imperatives

As for the coordination requirements, Pakistan's military system, being a vestige of the colonial era, is designed to operate and function with a very high level of independence and even disregard at times the other facets and elements of national power. Over the last half a century, it has also become fairly obvious that owing to its strong institutional character, our military system has a propensity for acting independently of the political machinery of the country. Both these factors go against the requirements of the day. Encouragingly, the creation of a joint civilian-military National Security Council (NSC) at the very highest level is a very good step in this direction. This institution will help not only in coordinating all the elements of our national power but also in involving the civilian hierarchy in military decision making, specifically when it comes to the decision to use nuclear weapons. The creation and institutionalisation of the NSC would go a long way in meeting both these requirements.

Analysis vis-à-vis Command Requirements

In the realm of Command Imperatives, Pakistan's existing military system is seriously lacking. The high degree of freedom that is available to the Service Chiefs precludes an integrated approach to situations demanding a military response. The main reason for this is the inordinate power and influence of the Army and the inherent weaknesses of the MOD/Joint Staff Headquarters.

Analysis vis-à-vis Financial Imperative

The last and perhaps the most bothersome requirement confronting our existing military system is its financial affordability. Needless to say, the drain that our military system imposes on the national exchequer is an area of great concern specially when viewed in the context of the dire economic straits that we find ourselves in today. The problem is bound to get accentuated further due to the imperatives of weaponisation of our demonstrated nuclear capability. The bottom line is that unless we prune the existing military system in a serious manner, we are going to further worsen the country's economic plight by incurring an appreciable expenditure on the creation of a credible nuclear deterrent even if it is kept at the minimum possible level.

Factors Warranting a Review of the Existing Military System

From the above discussion, it is evident that the prime influencing factor which dictates a review of Pakistan's Military System is the overt nuclearisation of South Asia. This necessitates an examination of not only how nuclearisation has altered the regional military scenario and the nature of future Indo-Pak wars but also the modifications and improvements that need to be implemented in Pakistan's military system in order to make it compatible with the dictates of nuclearisation. These aspects are elaborated upon in this Chapter.

Nuclearisation, the Altered Regional Military Scenario and the Nature of Future India-Pakistan Wars

The military system of a country is defined primarily by its security concerns. Pakistan's security concerns are driven by the imperatives of the maintenance of its territorial sovereignty and its identity as an independent Muslim state.

Pakistan's security concerns stem from the nature and magnitude of the military threat that it is confronted with. "In addition to the direct military build-up, another facet is that of an indirect multidimensional threat. This encompasses the economic, political, ideological and social aspects, with the economic threat occupying the centre stage."[3]

The principal military threat facing Pakistan, at least in the immediate future, is India. Its military system has to consider the threat that India poses to Pakistan's sovereign existence. While the existing military system was designed with India primarily in mind and has borne the pressure of three major conflicts well, the imminent weaponisation of nuclear capability by both India and Pakistan has altered the situation significantly. Pakistan's military system must now be able to cater for a nuclear India which, because of its earnest desire for global recognition, is now going to be even more averse to the presence of any significant opposition, at least in its immediate neighbourhood.

Impact of Nuclearisation

While carrying out a detailed review of Pakistan's present military system with the purpose of suggesting suitable modifications to it, the following relevant aspects of the recent developments will have to be considered:

- **The Quantum and Magnitude of Indian Conventional Military Threat**. This is a known equation that has been a constant factor in influencing the creation of Pakistan's existing non-nuclear military system. Pakistan's military planners have realised that India's booming economy has made it virtually impossible for Pakistan to match it in the conventional domain and as such, the development of nuclear weapons has become essential from the point of view of balancing Indian conventional military superiority.

- **India's Nuclear Weapons Inventory**. A mere counting of the nuclear warheads available with the antagonist is an entirely academic discussion. "The central strategic significance of nuclear weapons is that they do away with the traditional quest for military parity with an adversary."[4] The factors determining the nuclear threat, therefore, are not the number of nuclear weapons held but a consideration of several key factors which are discussed in the subsequent paragraphs.

Factors Determining the Nature of the Nuclear Threat Faced by Pakistan
Enemy's Will and Design to Employ Nuclear Weapons. Whether the enemy is likely to exercise the "first strike option" or is his nuclear threshold so high that

he could avert the achievement of the same with his considerable conventional military might. In the second case, it would be vital to assess the capability of the enemy's nuclear forces to be able to withstand a nuclear first strike and be able to launch a credible second strike. In the regional scenario, India's conventional superiority over Pakistan and its geographic strategic depth indicate that Pakistan is more likely to reach its nuclear threshold earlier than India. This would entail a detailed study of whether the Indian nuclear arsenal could still maintain a credible level of effectiveness after a Pakistani nuclear "first strike." Another significant manifestation of the evaluation of the Indian nuclear threat would be their targeting strategy—would the Indians opt for counter-force or counter-value targeting. This aspect would not only influence Pakistan's own nuclear targeting policy but would also govern the defensive measures that the country would have to undertake to minimise the effect of an Indian nuclear launch. As regards deterrence, it has to be kept in mind that "it is basically a fragile concept based on the somewhat naive or innocent belief that the possession of nuclear hardware by potential antagonists and the knowledge thereof would prevent a nuclear war."[5]

Type and Nature of Future Indo-Pak Wars. A lot of analysts are of the opinion that in the wake of weaponisation of their respective nuclear capabilities, both India and Pakistan are headed for a "cold war" similar to the confrontation between the USA and the erstwhile USSR. This analogy, in my opinion, does not fully apply to the regional scenario where geographical contiguity reduces the early warning time to virtually nothing. This would entail a very high level of conventional force readiness and does not preclude the possibility of skirmishes on the border. Moreover, "nuclear development would not reduce either side's dependence on conventional forces, because war in South Asia would most likely begin with a conventional confrontation."[6] It also has to be kept in mind that, "the escalation of a conventional war is the most likely route for a nuclear war to break out."[7] This indicates that a cold war in South Asia would be one in which the temperatures are going to be running very high and as such rather than using the term "cold war" to define it, one could possibly classify it as a sort of "simmering" or "dormant war." In my assessment, the future Indo-Pak war could possibly take the following shape:

Dormant Phase (Economic Confrontation)

This phase, similar to the "cold war" that ensued between the USA and the erstwhile USSR, would be the one that would prevail all the time. During this phase, the priorities of the two countries would be to:

Ensure the level of military balance and not allow either of the two countries to gain a significant edge. At present, "the crux of Pakistan's security dilemma is the progressive weakening of its conventional defence capability."[8] While Pakistan would be vying more for maintenance of the status quo as regards military balance, India's quest would be to forge ahead in a significant manner. Needless to say, Pakistan would feel obliged to keep pace with India's development of its military arsenal to the extent that is necessary to be able to field a credible deterrence and "has to objectively assess to what extent it can limit its nuclear capability without jeopardising its security imperatives."[9]

The emphasis during this phase would be on economic confrontation. India, being significantly stronger in the economic arena, would mount a concerted campaign to strangulate Pakistan's beleaguered economy. The simplest means of doing this would be to embroil Pakistan in an endless arms race and not allow it to concentrate on its nation building ventures. "The pace of nuclearisation will be set by India because Pakistan has neither the intention nor the resource base to enter a nuclear arms race with India."[10]

Both the countries during this phase would be forced to maintain and demonstrate the existence of a viable second-strike capability in the face of a first strike being launched by the enemy.

The requirements of this phase would need for the strategic response forces of both the countries being kept at a high state of readiness while the conventional military apparatus would continue operating on a peacetime footing.

The duration of this phase would be very long. It could stretch, as was the case with the erstwhile USSR, till economic collapse of one of the antagonists (in this case Pakistan) occurs.

Preparatory Phase (Diplomatic Confrontation)

As and when a military conflict appears imminent, the antagonists are going to shift from the dormant to the preparatory phase. This shift could be brought about by an impending economic collapse of Pakistan, which would force the hand of the Pakistani leadership or a realisation on the part of India that Pakistan no more has a credible second launch capability. The significant aspects of this phase would be:

- Both the countries would raise the readiness of their military forces and move these to the war locations.

- The strategic forces would be placed on the highest level of alert and preparedness.

Main emphasis during this phase would be in the diplomatic arena. While Pakistan could undertake a diplomatic offensive to highlight to the world the imminence of a devastating war and urge it to intervene, India could possibly be marshalling allies to acquiesce to its decision to go to war against Pakistan.

Another purpose of the diplomatic confrontation would be to gain time not only for the world opinion to play its role in preventing the war, but also for both Pakistan and India to be able to bring their military might to a war-preparedness level.

Depending upon the prevalent situation and circumstances, the duration of this phase could span from a few weeks to a few months at the most.

Conflict Phase (Military Confrontation)

In the event of the diplomatic confrontation failing to dissuade both the countries from embarking on a potentially devastating military confrontation, the third phase of the envisaged future war involving the actual employment of military potential would commence. The salient aspects of a future India-Pakistan war could be expected to include the following:

A limited intensity conventional war instigated by India with all the care that the situation does not deteriorate to a stage where Pakistan's nuclear threshold is reached.

Fighting a prolonged limited conflict such as mentioned above would not be in India's interest but may be waged to impose unbearable financial burdens on Pakistan's beleaguered economy.

Since the conflict would be designed by the Indians to stay within the conventional domain and not allow Pakistan to resort to the nuclear option, the conflict would be "destruction oriented and not space oriented."[11] The Indians, therefore, would endeavour to inflict maximum destruction and attrition without attempting to gain a significant advantage in terms of occupation of space.

Possible War Scenarios

Notwithstanding the above aspects, any future India-Pakistan war could take a variety of shapes—some of the possible scenarios that could emerge are:

- Pakistan, in the face of overwhelming Indian conventional and nuclear preponderance, opts to pre-empt the outbreak of hostilities. This could, at the worst, take the form of a nuclear first strike but considering the force with which India could retaliate, such a move is extremely unlikely. Moreover, it has to be considered that Pakistan, with the limited means available at its disposal, cannot possibly hope to neutralise India's relatively bigger and much more dispersed nuclear capability with a first strike.

- India, if it is assured of being able to effectively neutralise Pakistan's entire nuclear arsenal and denude it totally of any second strike option, could also resort to a nuclear "first strike." This, however, is also a far-fetched option since even in the most ideal circumstances, India could not possibly be assured of taking out Pakistan's entire nuclear weapons potential. The development of a triad-based nuclear deterrence on the Pakistani side makes this option even more difficult to consider.

- India launches a conventional offensive in a crucial sector with the objective of gaining a significant foothold in Pakistani territory. Possible areas could be in northern Punjab or Southern Punjab/Northern Sindh. The Indian premise would be to gradually bring Pakistan close to its nuclear threshold without overstepping it. This would present Pakistani leadership with a dilemma—should they resort to the nuclear option or should they remain with the conventional one only. India, being well aware that the rest of the world would be closely monitoring the ground situation, could safely expect that its action, under the garb of punitive measures, would be condoned, while the opposition to Pakistan's unleashing of its nuclear capability would be tremendous and swift. This is possible since the world will view a conventional war more detachedly than the spectre of a nuclear conflict with its aspects of nuclear fallout, etc. The active intervention of the global powers could bring the conflict to an end with India in control of the captured Pakistani territory, and Pakistan not having been afforded the opportunity of a nuclear response. This highlights the requirement for Pakistan's nuclear doctrine to be dynamic as regards the determination of its nuclear threshold. During actual military confrontation, Pakistan may be required to continuously modify and publicise its nuclear threshold in order to dissuade the Indians and prevent such a scenario as illustrated above from taking place.

- Pakistan, with its back to the wall, opts to initiate hostilities through pre-emption in a key land sector such as Indian Held Kashmir while maintaining an effectively defensive posture elsewhere. While reminiscent of the recent Kargil debacle, this operation would be on a much wider scale on the lines of the ill-fated Operation Gibraltar of 1965. The initiation of hostilities would be undertaken by marshalling the Kashmiri Mujahideen active within IHK and providing all-out logistic support to them including beefing up their ranks by facilitating the infiltration of volunteers from Afghanistan and other countries. Pakistan's intentions in this case would be firstly to highlight the imminence of a military conflict and force the world powers to intervene and bring the increasing tensions under control. Secondly, such an operation would not violate India's expected nuclear threshold and prevent a nuclear outbreak. Needless to say, Pakistan's primary effort in this eventuality would be on localising and limiting the conflict to prevent an all-out war. This possibility has to be carefully considered in the backdrop of the 1965 situation where Pakistan failed to prevent the escalation of the hostilities into a full-fledged war between the two countries. Moreover, India's determined resolve during the recent Kargil crisis should also be an indicator that should prevent the consideration of such an option by Pakistan. It also has to be considered that India's desperation against the Mujahideen can result in irresponsible action across the LOC at places where Pakistani salients offer advantage to India, such as Bagh, Poonch, Kotli and Bajawant Salients.[12]

- Another option available with India is to exercise coercion by embarking on measures designed to achieve economic strangulation through the marshalling of global opinion against Pakistan at one end and the possibility of a naval blockade or quarantine at the other end of the spectrum. Such an eventuality would be designed to force Pakistan into a military response and would allow India to brand it as an aggressor and justify its response to the global community at large. Needless to say, Pakistan, while specifying its nuclear thresholds, must also not lose sight of the aspect of economic dominance and strangulation carried out by India. In this scenario of the Indian Navy attempting to impose a blockade, the operationalisation of the joint Sino-Pakistan naval port complex at Gawadar has altered the situation significantly in Pakistan's favour.

Nuclear Imperatives
Status and Potential of Pakistan's Nuclear Deterrence Capability. The concept of deterrence has become the central feature of strategy in the nuclear

age.[13] Pakistan's nuclear capability, should ideally be triad-based. In the immediate future, while actively endeavouring to create the third dimension of a naval based deterrence, Pakistan must maintain a two-dimensional nuclear deterrence in the form of a land-based missile capability and an air-delivered nuclear bomb capability. Nuclear "force structure options exist in Pakistan's tactical aircraft and missile acquisitions. Aircraft can be recalled, are flexibile and have precision of attack potential, but the air power asymmetry that prevails in South Asia will make Pakistan's aircraft more vulnerable to surprise attack on their bases as well as air defence attrition after launch, than India's dispersed and larger air force."[14] On the other hand, "ballistic missiles are more assured of penetration but may be less accurate and, once launched, cannot be recalled."[15] Adequate safeguards, therefore, need to be built-in into both these capabilities, in order to ensure their safety against an Indian first strike materialising. Based on the above, it can be conjectured that Pakistan "would allocate its limited nuclear arsenal about equally between aircraft and mobile ballistic missiles."[16]

Determination of Nuclear Threshold. "Credible deterrence depends on some prospect of use."[17] The credibility of a nuclear deterrent is based on the will to use it. This makes the determination of a plausible and credible nuclear threshold a cornerstone of any country's nuclear doctrine. It has to be based on national security imperatives and should be clearly and unambiguously spelt out in order to dispel any doubts or misapprehensions regarding the nation's will to resort to the use of nuclear weapons when its national aims and objectives are threatened. Needless to say, the exact contents of this threshold would have to be kept secret and vague so as to keep the enemy guessing. Despite being subject to regular periodic reviews, the determinants of Pakistan's nuclear threshold are expected to remain relatively constant during peacetime. During wartime, however, Pakistan's leadership may have to debate modifications in this paradigm in consonance and accordance with the changing shape of the war situation. A nuclear deterrence should not only be able to avert a war in the first place, it should be able to avert an abject defeat in the event of a war materialising and not going well. Pakistan's nuclear threshold must keep these considerations in mind. If the war is not going well, Pakistan could well threaten to employ her nuclear weapons in an effort to avert an abject defeat.

Formulation of Nuclear Doctrine.[18] The weaponisation of the nuclear capability by Pakistan has drawn the political hierarchy of the country into the military arena in an active and unavoidable manner. The promulgation and formulation of a nuclear doctrine falls within the purview of the political government with the active involvement of the senior military leadership of the country. Considering the existing defence hierarchy, the formulation of the nuclear doctrine is the responsibility of the Defence Committee of the Cabinet or the National Security Council. A nuclear doctrine must address the following main aspects:

The Nature and Quantum of Nuclear Capability required. The nuclear doctrine must spell out the type of capability, i.e., triad-based, dual dimension or single dimension and also specify the number of warheads that need to be developed for each delivery option.

A decision should also be forthcoming from the nuclear doctrine whether Pakistan needs to restrict itself purely to the development of strategic nuclear weapons capability or does the situation also warrant the development of tactical nuclear weapons. In this context, the development of miniaturised low-yield artillery delivered nuclear warheads also needs to be taken into serious consideration. This question is of vital significance when viewed in the Indo-Pak context. All the previous wars in this region have indicated that both the countries generally refrain from engaging civilian populace and civilian targets during wars. If this trend is going to continue then the development of low-yield nuclear weapons which can be employed in the tactical scenario with little or no collateral damage needs to be seriously considered. Needless to say, a decision to develop nuclear weapons which can be effectively employed in the tactical scenario, must be consciously taken and arrived at since it is bound to drastically alter the requirements of Pakistan's military system.

The nuclear doctrine also needs to spell out the size of Pakistan's nuclear weapons inventory. For a determination of the number and types of warheads needed to pose a credible nuclear deterrent capability in the face of the Indian threat, the following aspects need to be considered:

- The number of weapons held by India should not be the consideration. Pakistan does not need to balance out the number of weapons fielded by India as long as it possesses adequate nuclear weapons to ensure survival in the face of an Indian "first strike" against its nuclear weapon sites and still retain enough potential to target selected Indian cities.
- India must be convinced that it cannot destroy Pakistan's entire nuclear arsenal through a nuclear "first strike."

The decision whether to go for a triad-based deterrence or just restrict the capability to either one or two delivery mediums out of sea, land and air, is an academic question. Needless to say, Pakistan must prefer a triad-based nuclear deterrence but for the time being, in consideration of the phenomenal costs involved, it should be satisfied with just the land and air based deterrent. What follows is the need for these land and air-delivered weapons to be adequately secure to survive the enemy's "first strike."

Economic Aspects of the Weaponisation of Nuclear Capability. The imperative need to avoid getting involved in a nuclear arms race with India must not be lost sight of. Pakistan's fragile economy can ill-afford such a luxury. In all fairness to and in due consideration of its economic plight, Pakistan must endeavour to enhance its nuclear capability and build up its nuclear deterrence while staying within the existing defence budget. Estimates prepared by the Strategic Plans Division indicate that the funds required for the development of the desired level of nuclear deterrence are less than initially expected and no problems are anticipated in meeting these for at least the next eight years.[19]

- **Determination of the "Nuclear Threshold."** The nuclear threshold of a country defines the event that would see it stopping to rely purely on its conventional capability and bringing its nuclear wherewithal into action. This has a singular influence on the formulation of the nuclear strategy of a country and as such, needs to be stipulated in unequivocal terms. It should be remembered that, "Pakistan's nuclear option is connected with its national security requirements and any sacrifice of this option would mean jeopardising its geographical integrity."[20] It also stands to reason that the nuclear threshold level has to be credible and vague enough to be visible yet not identifiablenot only by the enemy but also by the world at large. The nuclear threshold, ideally speaking, should be based on occurrences which endanger the very existence of a country, i.e., events which are expected to lead to the destruction of a country's existence through violation of its independence. This element of a country's independence, has to be studied in all its manifestations—ranging from territorial integrity to economic freedom to the very raison d'être of a country's existence.

- **Creation and Establishment of a Nuclear Command Structure.** The nuclear doctrine must also spell out the responsibility and the mechanism for the command and control of a country's nuclear arsenal. The ultimate responsibility for the decision to resort to the employment of nuclear weapons, must rest in the Chief Executive of the country while the implementation of this decision should be the responsibility of the military apparatus. The entire nuclear C⁴I organisation has to be made completely interference proof with adequate levels of redundancy being built into it at all levels. All the above has to be achieved while not losing sight of the fact that, "the cost of establishing an effective nuclear command and control structure has been estimated to be up to half or more of a nuclear weapons programme."[21]

Impact of Pakistan's Nuclear Doctrine on Its Military System. As mentioned earlier, the post-nuclear weaponisation military system of a country would have to be evolved in the light of its nuclear doctrine. The military system of Pakistan, therefore, has to be suitably modified, both structurally and organisationally, in keeping with the dictates of the country's nuclear doctrine.

In summary, the essence of the foregoing is an analysis of the implications of the Indian nuclear military threat for Pakistan. These implications, which are of prime importance for the formulation of Pakistan's new military system, are:

- In view of the nuclearisation of South Asia and the emergence of destruction oriented rather than space oriented conflicts,[22] the focus of "military doctrine will shift from defence of territory to defence of national interests."[23]
- In its desire for regional hegemony, "India is now seeking to move beyond South Asia to a Southern Asian framework."[24] This is bound to make the regional climate even more unfriendly and hostile.
- India's "offensive orientation will hasten the shift towards modernisation."[25]
- India's "nuclear doctrine increases the possibility of a nuclear conflict."[26]
- India's "emerging nuclear doctrine makes no mention of a conventional force reduction."[27] In fact, it "makes it clear that India's nuclear escalation will be accompanied by the further build-up of India's conventional warfare capabilities."[28]

Implications of Nuclearisation for Pakistan's Existing Military System
While Pakistan's existing and prevalent military system has been designed to cater for the conventional weapons scenario, it will now have to be suitably modified to cater for the inclusion of nuclear weapons in the military confrontation equation. One cannot lose sight of the fact that the "military system to be adopted is linked with the power potential."[29]

In this context, the military system needs to be reviewed in light of the following:

Restructuring of Conventional Military Capability. Considering the economic situation, any significant increase in the defence expenditure appears to be a mirage and borders on wishful thinking. Since the weaponisation of Pakistan's nuclear prowess is going to be an expensive proposition in monetary terms, there would be a requirement to cut down the expenditure on the maintenance of our existing conventional forces. This would be required in order to bring about significant savings which could then be diverted towards the development of nuclear weapons capability. This assertion begs the question—can we really afford to lower our conventional guard?

A decision on the level of conventional forces required by Pakistan to face up to the Indian conventional might could very well end up becoming a double-edged sword. The greater our conventional capability, the lesser the chances of our reaching the nuclear threshold and vice versa. Conversely, the maintenance of a large conventional force would not be economically possible when we add the additional expenditure of nuclear weapons development to the defence budget. This Catch-22 situation could best be catered by a balancing act which permits us to retain the current level of conventional effectiveness or capability through reducing the conventional forces in numbers but enhancing their fighting capability by the provision of greater firepower and increased mobility. Needless to say, this would entail an extra financial burden on the defence exchequer initially but the same will be balanced out by the savings in the long run. In this context the effects of the advent of nuclear weapons on conventional force structure should first be analysed with regard to the three services.

Effects of Advent of Nuclear Weapons on Conventional Force Structures. The initial euphoria on development of nuclear weapons provided reasons to consider conventional forces redundant. But owing to their menacing character, the realisation developed that nuclear weapons were not just another type of weapon. "If one examines the debate about the relevance of conventional weapons in the post-nuclear tests environment, two important questions are taken into account. First, can nuclear weapons ensure maximum security to our territorial integrity in case of war and second, will it be possible for us to modernise our nuclear arsenal in such a manner that there is a little need for a huge conventional set-up?"[30] Some analysts believe that while nuclear capability makes, "a regression from military stance affordable but it does not permit any sizeable reduction in forces."[31]

Deterrence is likely to play an increasingly important role in future arms conflicts. It is not likely that even with possession of a large amount of nuclear weapons, in the present state of parity, anyone is going to resort to their use unless conventional defence has virtually broken down. Even in this situation, there is a possibility that nuclear weapons will not be used. However, this puts a great burden on the conventional forces. These forces now would be required to prevent the reaching of a stage where the use of nuclear weapons becomes unavoidable. Hence, these must continue to be employed as long as they possibly can. The best way to address this requirement would be to address the issue of induction of nuclear weapons with regard to their impact on the three tiers of the military system:

- At the government or national level, i.e., the Defence Committee of the Cabinet (DCC) or the National Security Council (NSC).
- At the tri-services or the Joint Staff Headquarters Level.
- At the level of the three individual services.

Impact on the Military System at the National Level. At the national level, the necessary mechanism to deal with the nuclear weapons issue already exists in the form of the erstwhile Defence Committee of the Cabinet (DCC) which has now been replaced by the National Security Council (NSC) with its ancillary think tank component. The need is to formalise the existing structure and allocate it the required responsibilities. The decision of opting for the employment of nuclear weapons would vest directly in the Chief Executive (Prime Minister). In terms of nuclear command authority, the channel would flow directly from the Chief Executive to the Chairman of the Joint Chiefs of Staff Committee. This would now be performed by the National Command Authority (NCA) which has a balanced civilian and military representation.

Impact on the Military System at the JSHQ Level. Nuclear weapons, at least for the time being and even in the foreseeable future, are expected to remain confined to being employed in a strategic role only within the South Asian regional scenario. Even if Pakistan and India do develop tactical nuclear weapons in the future, the control of these tactical weapons will continue to be exercised at the strategic level. Since effective military leadership essentially revolves around the principle of Unity of Command, the control of the country's nuclear arsenal must also rest with one organisation. In the case of Pakistan, Joint Staff Headquarters would be the ideal such institution which could be tasked to perform this function. The following are some of the reasons for and advantages of involving the JSHQ in this role:

- JSHQ happens to be a tri-service organisation, albeit with unequal distribution of manpower from the three component services.

- The JSHQ has not been accorded its rightful place of importance in the military affairs and needs to be strengthened and made more responsible. Currently, it is only coordinating on various matters between the three Services and that too not in a very effective or forceful manner. The need is for this headquarters to be immediately assigned the responsibilities of the integrated development programme for the three Services and also of the integrated training requirements of the three Services. This role could, subsequently, be further enhanced. This measure would contribute significantly to the development of joint and tri-service understanding. In line with its increased role in strategic military matters the word "Staff" in JSHQ could well be replaced by the word "Services" in order to project its correct image and span of control.

- The JSHQ, with the Chairman JCSC at the helm of its affairs, is ideally suited to be the sole military point of contact with the civilian government hierarchy as regards nuclear policy and employment matters.

Nuclear Command and Control Structure. The involvement of the Chief Executive of the country in the heretofore exclusively military decision loop during war, is a sign of maturity of our politico-military system and must not be lost sight of. At the military level, what was needed was the establishment of a Strategic Nuclear Command under the aegis of the Chairman Joint Chiefs of Staff Committee. He would be the sole link of the military apparatus with the country's Chief Executive as regards nuclear weapons employment is concerned. This has already been actioned with the creation of the Strategic Plans Division at the JSHQ which would function as the Secretariat of the National Command Authority (NCA). Additionally, the three Services are in the process of setting up their independent Strategic Forces Commands (SFCs).[32]

Impact of Nuclearisation on the Military System at the Services Level
Sophistication of Conventional Weapons versus Manpower Reduction. Today's sophistication and lethality of conventional weapons can be called the spin-off from nuclear weapon production. The spin-off from nuclear

research and development enhances the accuracy and effectiveness of conventional weapons. Now smart and intelligent munitions can be employed with surgical accuracy to attack military targets without fear of much collateral damage. The "one weapon one target concept" has given great strength to conventional forces. The increased lethality and range of conventional weapons along with the increased level of computerisation has contributed to the creation of smaller conventional units which have the same or even greater firepower than their much larger predecessors of yesteryear.

The most significant aspect of the technological breakthroughs and the increasing sophistication has been to make war more impersonal. This has led to it being less reliant on the human component and more dependent on weapons. An obvious corollary that emerges from this statement is that if the role of human beings in wars has been reduced then the first impact of technology should be to bring about a significant reduction in the quantum of manpower that is available with the forces. Though not entirely true, this assertion has gained further advocates in the wake of the increased burden that the defence apparatus is imposing on the national exchequer in the developing countries of the world. While tackling this ticklish issue, one must consider the following aspects:

While the high levels of technology have made smaller fighting formations a distinct possibility in the developed countries, the level of sophistication in the armed forces of most of the developing countries is still too low and insignificant to warrant any sharp across the board cuts in manpower strength.

Even in the developed countries, while one can see a distinct reduction in the area of land-based conventional forces, one also simultaneously witnesses almost a proportional and corresponding increase in the manpower strength of either both the air and naval forces or at least one of the two Services. A case in point is the United Kingdom, which in the aftermath of having gone nuclear, today fields an air force which is bigger in size than the British Army. This is a significant change from the time of the Second World War when the British Army was bigger than the RAF several times over. A similar trend is also noticeable in France while in the case of USA, the situation is slightly different. USA, because of its global involvement in several military conflicts and the need to position significant forces overseas, has continued to maintain a large army. Significantly, however, the USA has brought about a major increase in the manpower strength of both its air force and its navy.

This indicates that one of the results of nuclearisation has been the increase in importance of the air force and the navy which has brought these two Services almost at par with the Army as regards manpower strength. Before embarking on such a move, however, we have to be cognizant of the fact that our threat environment is starkly different from these countries and will influence our force restructuring plans.

Pakistan's army, which is by far the biggest Service in terms of manpower, is India-specific. It is noticeably smaller in size than the Indian Army and any further reduction would tilt the balance critically in favour of the Indian Army. A similar situation exists with both the PAF and the PN which are already much smaller than their adversaries in India. In fact, going by the changes in the military systems of the nuclear states, one can discern that while the army has been reduced or at the best maintained at the current levels, the other two Services have increased their personnel strength. Notwithstanding the above, there exists a definite requirement to prune the defence establishment. A significant reduction could be made in the ranks of the armed forces by getting rid of non-essential manpower. It has to be kept in mind that having someone in uniform costs the government at least twice if not more as compared with a rank outsider who is employed on a contract or civilian basis. Some of the options which could be exercised in this context, are:

Troops employed as orderlies and batmen. This alone would reduce the strength of the Army by around 60,000. In lieu of this arrangement, the Army officers and JCOs who are entitled to the services of an orderly could be paid the equivalent of their salary as a part of their own pay package. Though this measure would not bring about any significant savings straight away as regards salary, the ultimate savings on account of pensionary and other benefits for 60,000 troops would be staggering. The same applies to a certain extent to the PAF where the officers are authorised to employ a servant who is then enrolled in the ranks of the PAF and gains a pensionable job. It would be far simpler to just pay the officer the salary of the servant and not get encumbered with another budding pensioner. A similar system could then be applied to the Pakistan Navy.

Individuals from those areas of expertise could be made redundant where people with equivalent qualifications are available in the civilian sector. One possibility could be the Military Engineering Services (MES) which already has a sizeable civilian establishment. Other categories of individuals which could be hired from outside could include drivers for those vehicles which are not expected to operate outside peacetime stations, doctors and medical staff at the fixed location, hospitals, etc. This is especially relevant in the case of female doctors and nursing staff whose charter of duties anyway is limited to peacetime stations. Once again the savings in pensions, retirement benefits and expenditure incurred on in-service training both in-country and abroad would amount to a phenomenal figure.

Another option which needs to be actively considered by all the three Services is the possibility of contracting out certain areas of activity to the civilian sector. For example, asking any one of the main banks to handle the salaries of the personnel would virtually obviate the requirement for having hordes of accounts personnel eating out of the meagre defence budget. Several other similar areas of activity could be defined but this needs a much more detailed study and is beyond the purview of this paper.

The impact of the adoption of the above-mentioned manpower reduction measures on the combat potential of the armed forces would be negligible while the savings that would accrue over the long term would be substantial. These savings could then be channelised into other areas as required.

Other Aspects Applicable to All Three Services. The increased effectiveness of conventional forces and the relatively longer ranges of their smaller size weapons have brought about conceptual changes in the art of waging conventional wars. For a conventional force to meet the challenges of a nuclear environment is by no means an easy task. It needs to re-evaluate its war-fighting concepts, modify its organisational structure and enhance its ability to operate under the threat of a nuclear strike. While the generic aspects of Survivability, C^3I and Control/Denial of the Electromagnetic Spectrum and Air Defence have been dealt with here, the specific aspect of organisational and structural changes pertinent to each of the three Services has been discussed subsequently in the sections pertaining to each individual Service.

Centralised Control of Air Defence. The induction of ballistic surface-to-surface missiles in the Indian inventory adds a new dimension to the threat faced by Pakistan's air defence. The Indian SSM capability highlights the need for an effective anti-missile system which needs to be coordinated with the early warning radars. This new threat makes it imperative that the air defence of the entire country is centralised under one agency—the PAF. "Air Defence Commands on geographical basis, suitably augmented, should be responsible to trace, identify and destroy incoming enemy missiles and to launch our nuclear weapons."[33] This would enable the most effective conduct of air defence operations at all levels.

Survival. To increase the survivability factor and generate adequate confidence level in the conventional forces, it would be essential to do the following:

NBC Equipment. Provision of Nuclear-Biological-Chemical (NBC) defensive equipment for personnel and combat vehicles. This, because of the prohibitive costs, may have to be done piecemeal and also extended to all strategic weapons sites.

Protective Measures. Hardening of communication systems to reduce collateral failures and maintenance of command and control centres and posts. This hardening should not only include an increased resistance to enemy electromagnetic interference but should also afford the required levels of redundancy in communications. The degree of redundancy that would be built-in into the system would be proportional to the criticality of that particular channel or circuit to the conduct of overall military operations.

Infrastructure. Creation of hardened NBC proof command posts in preselected areas. This would be applicable to all the three Services. Whereas the army would include its operational and field headquarters in this domain, the PAF may have to safeguard some of its strategic assets including aircraft while the PN would need for the Maritime Headquarters and key shore establishments to be similarly protected. The hardening of the key structures should be carried out in addition to the routine camouflage and concealment measures which are undertaken to conceal these.

Monitoring and Detection Equipment. Suitable equipment to monitor radioactive fallout. This would be a generic requirement for all three services as also for the civil defence set-ups all over the country.

C³I Network. Command and control of these smaller but spread-out units will have to be tightened up considerably if they are to be employed to maximum advantage. To make the command and control meaningful, a comprehensive C³I network is essential. In the United States, the command and control problems associated with the employment of strategic nuclear forces were tackled through the development of the Airborne Command Post, Joint Surveillance Target Acquisition Radar System (JSTARS) and Joint Tactical Information and Distribution System (JTIDS). These types of C³I systems have become a reality. Now even a conventional force commander can exercise control over each and every tank employed in the tactical battlefield or fighter aircraft deployed, apart from having a complete theatre picture in real time. This has projected the art of warfare in the fourth dimension, i.e., the struggle for supremacy in the electromagnetic spectrum.

Electromagnetic Spectrum. Deception units, equipped to generate audio-visual and electronic emissions to deceive the enemy on actual battle plans and movements, would increase the degree of difficulty in the decision-making process for the adversary. The efficient use of EMS or successful denial of its use to the enemy has become a battle-deciding factor. This activity over the EMS should span all the three key aspects including Electronic Counter Measures (ECM), Electronic Counter-counter Measures (ECCM) and Electronic Support Measures (ESM). Both ground and air-based assets would be employed for this task which also needs to be centrally directed and controlled by a single agency preferably functioning within the ambit of the JSHQ.

Impact on the Army or Land Forces Component
In the aftermath of the Cuban missile crisis, there was a realisation within the American leadership that their massive nuclear arsenal has to be supplemented by an adequate conventional capability. This was borne out by the growing feeling that a nuclear arsenal does not obviate the retention of a viable conventional military capability. President Kennedy, in a message to the US Congress on May 25, 1961, highlighted the following key points as regards the restructuring of conventional forces:

"... I have directed a *further reinforcement of our own capacity to deter or resist non-nuclear aggression.* In the conventional field, with one exception, I find *no need for large new levies of men.* What is needed is rather a change of position to give us still further increases in flexibility.

"Therefore, I am directing the Secretary of Defence to *undertake a reorganisation and modernisation of the Army's divisional structure,* to *increase its non-nuclear firepower, to improve its tactical mobility* in any environment, to *insure its flexibility to meet any direct or indirect threat ...*

"And secondly, I am asking the Congress for an additional ... [funds] to begin the procurement task to *re-equip this new army structure with the most modern material.* New helicopters, new armoured personnel carriers, and new howitzers, for example, must be obtained now.

"Third, I am directing the Secretary of Defence to expand rapidly, ... the *orientation of existing forces for the conduct of non-nuclear war, para-military operations and sub-limited or unconventional wars.*"[34]

Most of the assertions contained in President Kennedy's letter to the Congress are applicable to Pakistan's current situation vis-à-vis the restructuring of its conventional military forces. What this means is that conventional forces now need to be assessed in terms of effectiveness and combat potential and not just in numbers.

The essence of organisational changes in the military system as regards the Army, could encompass the following:

Reduction in Size of Fighting Formations. Reducing the size of existing units without degrading the existing kill potential/operational efficiency. This would entail greater mechanisation and increased firepower. One of the options in this regard could be the integration of all arms concepts at the unit level. This would help in the creation of a composite fighting formation that would be able to exhibit tremendous autonomy and flexibility in operations. In the realm of the land forces, this could possibly translate to a formation having its own integral components of infantry, armour and artillery as well as the supporting arms and services. Though a bit far-fetched under the prevailing economic crunch, these highly mobile army formations should preferably be provided with integral attack and cargo helicopter assets also to further augment their firepower and mobility.

Rehashing the entire training infrastructure would be required to meet new doctrinal compulsions. This would include special psychological training programmes, including confidence building for troops to operate in the new scenario. Personnel would now need to be made aware of the nuclear threat and the impact that the presence of this capability with the enemy could have on the conduct of their operations which up until now were confined only to the conventional ambit.

Introduction of specialist units to cater for damage limitation and casualty evacuation of troops operating in areas where nuclear strikes may be initiated. Special medical facilities will also be required to evacuate, receive and treat personnel exposed to a nuclear strike.

The requirement of surveillance units equipped and organised to provide early warning of incoming aircraft and missiles will also have to be met. The existing air defence radar infrastructure of the PAF would now need to be supplemented with the necessary equipment capable of not only detecting incoming missiles but also engaging these before they reach their designated targets. This highlights the need for the induction of an effective anti-missile system such as the Patriot or an equivalent indigenous equipment. Due to the contiguous borders between India and Pakistan, this early warning and anti-missile system would have to be designed for extremely quick reactions in the face of extremely limited warning time.

Special forces will have to be created and trained undertaking special operations well inside enemy territory to neutralise missile launch sites. This is especially pertinent in the Indo-Pak scenario where the Indian Prithvi missile launch sites will be located within 100-150 kilometres of the border and would be vulnerable to such raids.

Provision of the requisite manpower from within the existing resources as required to establish the Nuclear Command Structure.

Under nuclear environment, the smaller units and larger area equation place a much greater emphasis on mobility. Since mobility on the battlefield is essential for rapid concentration and dispersal, the conventional forces need to be afforded greater mobility through mechanisation and provision of aerial mobility assets such as helicopters.

Impact on the Pakistan Navy
The Pakistan Navy is perhaps the least effected of the three services after the weaponisation of nuclear capability has taken place in South Asia. This assertion is borne out by the following facts:

The Indian strategic nuclear capability cannot be or would not be targeting the Pakistan Navy combat potential except for some of its shore establishments and that too in the case of an all-out nuclear exchange.

The Pakistan Navy's role as far as Pakistan's strategic nuclear deterrence is concerned is also negligible till the time that a viable submarine launched nuclear ballistic missile capability is achieved. Considering the high cost and the time required for this to materialise, the Pakistan Navy is not expected to be playing any meaningful role in the near future in projecting Pakistan's nuclear deterrence.

In view of the above considerations, the Pakistan Navy's role and threat would both remain limited to conventional wherewithal and roles with its system not having to undergo any significant change in the near future.

In terms of the future, however, the requirement of having a submarine-based nuclear capability must be pursued in earnest since "such weapons give flexibility in the ability to respond to a first strike."[35] This should, however, only be done when other similar requirements have been met and funds are available for undertaking this venture. One option that could be pursued in this context is to develop missiles which could be launched from the submarines that currently are carrying the Harpoon missiles with the same tubes being used for the nuclear missiles. Since the size constraints of both the missile and the warhead would need a lot of technological development, it stands to reason that a lot of time and effort would be required in developing such a weapon from scratch. Moreover, this weapon must have a lethal range significantly more than the Harpoon in order to be able to pose a viable threat to India. After such a weapon system has been developed, the Pakistan Navy would need to keep at least two nuclear missile equipped submarines on patrol round the clock. This could be expected to increase the requirement for the number of such vessels in the Pakistan Navy's inventory. This last requirement is also going to be prohibitively expensive in monetary terms and as such, cannot be expected to be fulfilled in the immediate future.

Impact on the Air Force

The PAF, of all the three services would be the one which would be most affected by the development and induction of a strategic nuclear capability by India. "While each of the three Services would have a vital role to play, PAF will stand out as the main deliverer of goods by aircraft and missiles."[36] The situation will only change once the enemy has also embarked successfully on the development and subsequent induction of a tactical nuclear capability since such a development would bring the other armed services also into sharper focus.

An equally vital aspect not to be lost sight of is the dire straits that the PAF finds itself in today vis-à-vis the much more powerful and high-tech Indian Air Force. The vital role that the PAF will have to play in any future conflict is recognised by one and all and urgent measures are needed to beef up this vital component of the nation's military potential.

The PAF's role in a future conflict has to be viewed in the context of the realities of its nature. Considering that the future conflict would commence with conventional resources and would be destruction and not space oriented, the PAF's envisaged role could be:

- The PAF would be required to act as the spearhead of Pakistan's military operations.
- It would provide Pakistan with the capability of inflicting maximum damage on the enemy even during a conflict of relatively short duration.
- Possession of the nuclear aerial bombing capability would enable the PAF to exhibit an unrivalled multiplicity in terms of delivery of strategic weapons. This is an inherent manifestation of air power's primary characteristic of flexibility which permits it to engage a wide variety of targets and even change targets at a short notice.

The above aspects all serve to indicate the significant enhancement in the PAF's role which any future India-Pakistan conflict is expected to see. The PAF's greater involvement during the period when both Pakistan and India, especially the latter, are restricted only to strategic nuclear weapons, is borne out by the following:

- The PAF, by virtue of being solely responsible for the air defence of the country's airspace, would be required to maintain a round the clock vigil for signs of an impending enemy nuclear first strike. This would entail the following:

- The establishment of an effective ground-based early warning system that could provide early warning of the approach of enemy missiles and aircraft. Since the PAF also has a viable air defence early warning system in place, it would, apart from upgrading it, also need to modify its sensors or induct new ones that are capable of not only detecting but also tracking enemy ballistic missiles in flight.

- Being responsible for air defence of the homeland, the PAF would also be required to set-up a coordinated ground-based anti-missile defence against incoming enemy ballistic missiles. This would need such weapon systems either being procured from abroad or developed indigenously without any further loss of time.

- Like the other services, the PAF would also be required to allocate the necessary manpower needed for the establishment of the Strategic Nuclear Command and its subordinate units.

- At least for the foreseeable future, or till such time that Pakistan is able to field a credible sea-based nuclear capability, its nuclear deterrence would be two-dimensional, i.e., it would be based on land-based strategic nuclear missiles and air-delivered nuclear bombs. Understandably, the PAF would be responsible for handling the air-delivered nuclear weapons. This additional responsibility would also bring along the following requirements, which would have to be addressed:

  o The PAF would have to dedicate a number of long-range aircraft (F-16s) and undertake to modify these for the carriage and employment of nuclear bombs.

  o During any future war against India, the PAF would have to ensure that this strategic strike capability remains viable and on-call till the last day of the conflict. During war, as directed by the government or the higher military authorities, this force may have to be made available at a short notice.

- o   Even during peacetime, the aircrew and the aircraft may have to be maintained on standby status at a high state of readiness as dictated by the situation or specified by the government.
- o   Considering the vital nature of the mission that these aircraft would be undertaking, it is imperative that a set of aircrew be designated and trained to the highest possible standards as regards the peculiarities of nuclear weapons delivery.
- o   The strategic strike force must contain a sizeable integrated fighter escort element also comprising F-16 aircraft.
- o   After identification by the government of the expected targets that this strategic strike force could be required to engage, all the requisite target details and delivery profile geometries would be worked out and rehearsed during peacetime.
- o   Catering for the chances of an enemy nuclear strike against PAF command and control infrastructure, the PAF would have to ensure that all vital nerve centres and critical areas are made nuclear proof.

Economic Impact of Proposed Military System

The aspect of economics will play a crucial part in the determination of the priority which is accorded to the various components of the proposed military system. "In order to manage our nuclear forces without they becoming a burden on our limited resources, we need to ensure that they are kept to an absolute minimum commensurate with the need of maintaining a credible deterrence against our potential enemy."[37] The proposed military system does not promise any significant savings except for the aspect of reduction of non-essential military manpower and savings that may be accrued due to the involvement of civilian contracted manpower wherever possible.

Though these savings would be substantial, they would be a mere pittance when considered in the backdrop of the total projected expenditure. It is obvious, therefore, that the national exchequer would have to dole out even more funds for the defence budget—something that appears virtually impossible for Pakistan's debt-ridden economy.

In order to resolve this problem in the long term, thought has to be given to the possibility of reducing the strength of the active armed forces with greater reliance on ready reserve forces as is being done in several developed countries of the world such as Israel and Singapore. Such a major change, however, will take a substantial time period to implement and must be considered in all its manifestations before any final decision is taken.

The creation of a readily available reserve component of the armed forces would also usher in the need for an effective mobilisation system which should be able to operate on the national level and take the minimum possible time to execute.

The other aspect which could be considered is to stagger the development of the new military system over a period of a few years so as to distribute the resources required over a longer time span and make the entire scheme somewhat affordable even for our beleaguered economy.

In the final analysis, however, the solution lies in bringing about a radical turnaround in Pakistan's economy so that the increased burden of the defence expenditure becomes affordable for the country. While not losing sight of the military and security imperatives, Pakistan must devote its fullest attention on improvement of the economy.

Measures to Adapt Pakistan's Military System to the Imperatives of Nuclearisation

Long-Term Measures

- Lay the fullest possible emphasis on the improvement of the national economy.
- Reduce the active component of the armed forces and replace the same with a ready reserve. A detailed study would need to be undertaken to chalk out the strategy and mechanics of this measure. The ready reserve could either take the shape of a territorial component or, preferably, the form of a comprehensive national service scheme.
- Institute a rapid mobilisation mechanism on a countrywide basis which would facilitate the rapid marshalling of the rapid reserve.
- Develop a submarine launched ballistic nuclear weapon to complete the triad of nuclear deterrence.

Short-Term Measures

- Formulate a Strategic Nuclear Doctrine—define in detail the composition of the short-term and the long-term nuclear deterrence force as well as unequivocally determine the nuclear threshold parameters. The latter would obviously be kept vague to increase the uncertainty of the enemy.
- Formalise the NSC, the NCA and the strategic nuclear organisation.
- Allocate necessary resources and intensify efforts for the acquisition of a sizeable fleet of high-technology aircraft (at least 2 Squadrons) equipped

not only with beyond visual range (BVR) air-to-air missiles but also with anti-radiation missiles (ARMs).

- Undertake a restructuring of the armed forces with a view to making all non-essential manpower redundant and taking in replacements from the civil sector, wherever possible, as contract employees.
- Centralise the control of air defence under the PAF.
- Reduce the strength of the army's combat formations without affecting their combat power and potential. Provide these composite formations with the latest in equipment and greatly enhanced mobility.
- Induct the necessary ground-based radars and anti-missile systems to put up a viable defence against the threat of Indian ballistic missiles.
- Make arrangements for the provision of necessary NBC protective clothing and personal use items to the combat troops.
- Concentrate on enhancing the security and readiness of a two-dimensional nuclear deterrence—land-based ballistic missiles and air-delivered nuclear bombs.
- Establish a secure and adequately redundant communications infrastructure for Strategic Nuclear Command.
- Undertake an extensive military-wide training programme for educating personnel about the nature of the nuclear threat.
- Establish the requisite medical support organisation to cater for casualties after an enemy nuclear attack.

Conclusion

As mentioned in the discussion on the economic fallout and implications of incorporating the proposed changes in the existing military system, economic imperatives would and should govern the pace and time span during which these can be fully implemented. Economics will serve to accord the priority with military considerations playing second fiddle to the economic dictates except where a certain step is absolutely necessary for preserving national security and cannot be done without.

While the above long list of changes that need to be brought about in the national military system may appear to be a wish-list and a bit too far-fetched, it has to be considered that these are nothing but the absolutely unavoidable measures which Pakistan cannot do without. It is vital therefore, that these be viewed in the correct perspective without any bias or prejudice towards any particular Service in general and the armed forces of the country in specific. Notwithstanding the fact that this restructuring of conventional force would be capital-intensive in the beginning, one must not lose sight of the savings that would accrue over the long term since these would assuage the financial pain.

While the rest of the world continues to move towards economic emancipation for welfare of the populace, the South Asian region still continues to be haunted by the spectre of a nuclear and missile race due to India's relentless quest for economic and military dominance. With the passage of time and due to the changed international environment, the means may have changed yet the desirable ends for India remain the same. Her hegemonic dream has put tremendous strain on the meagre resources of India's smaller neighbours. "While Pakistan strives for a peaceful resolution of all its disputes with India, it cannot afford to ignore the looming threat from conventional and non-conventional forces of India which have grown beyond her legitimate security requirements."[38]

For Pakistan, as for any other country in the world, there is nothing more precious than its independence and sovereignty. This indicates the paramount importance of maintaining national security through the ready availability of a potent military system which can be brought to bear against any aggressor to thwart his nefarious designs.

The threat faced from the Indian side was always a sizeable one and it has gotten accentuated even further after the Indian development of nuclear weapons. While Pakistan has been fortunate enough to respond with ample proof of its own nuclear capability, the respite that our nuclear potential has afforded us is not perennial in terms of time.

The initial thinking that possession of nuclear capability obviates the maintenance of large standing conventional military forces is a fallacy which is more than amply borne out by events that have taken place in the nations which preceded Pakistan's and India's almost simultaneous entry into the exclusive nuclear club. Paradoxically, while some analysts ascribe great war-avoidance qualities to nuclear weapons, others are "worried that too great a commitment to conventional defence would signal a reluctance to cross the nuclear threshold, thereby weakening deterrence."[39]

The need for Pakistan now is to take all necessary steps to restructure and re-equip its military system and bring it in accordance with the dictates of the radically altered strategic situation in the South Asian region. This would entail the accordance of priority to the economic development of the country so that over a period of time, the exorbitant expenditures likely to be incurred on the upgradation of the military system become affordable for the national exchequer. It is equally vital that till such time that the economy improves and the proposed military system is effectively put in place, Pakistan must not only maintain the current level of conventional military prowess but also develop a credible level of nuclear deterrence which would be required to forestall any Indian nefarious designs in the foreseeable future. "Pakistan must avoid getting into an arms race with India."[40]

Notes

1. The contents of this chapter have been extracted from an essay titled "Controlling Nuclear Proliferation in South Asia" that the author wrote while undergoing the Advanced Staff Course at the Royal Air Force Staff College, Bracknell, UK in 1992. This essay went on to be declared the best research essay written by a non-British officer on the course and the author was awarded the coveted "Andover Prize" for it. Since this essay predates South Asia's overt nuclearisation by almost six years, it must be read from that perspective. Readers might find statements such as "The eventuality which scares the West most, is the possible though highly unlikely prospect of Pakistan exporting its nuclear expertise to other Islamic countries" might sound very perceptive and almost visionary when viewed against the backdrop of the recent incidents of nuclear proliferation.

2. Lt. Gen. Khalid Maqbool, Lecture on "Military System" delivered at NDC.

3. Muhammad Saleem, DG(A), ISI. Lecture on "External Threat to the Security of Pakistan" at NDC.

4. Afzal Mahmood, "Pakistan's Quest for Security," *Dawn*, December 14, 1998.

5. Brig. (Retd) A. R. Siddiqui, "The Post-Nuclear Test Scenario–I," *Nation*, June 16, 1999.

6. Amit Gupta, "South Asian Nuclear Choices: What Types of Force Structures May Emerge?" *Armed Forces Journal International*, September 1998.

7. Afzal Mahmood, "What Nuclear Sanity Demands," *Dawn*, May 31, 1999.

8. Tanvir Ahmad Khan, "Averting an Arms Race," *The News*, October 21, 1998.

9. Gen. (Retd) Mirza Aslam Beg, "Pakistan's Nuclear Propriety," *Pakistan Observer*, April 9, 1999.

10. Dr. Maqbool Ahmad Bhatty, "Nuclear South Asia: Impact on Conventional and Nuclear Arms Race," *Margalla Papers*, December 1998.

11. Air Marshal Zahid (late) Anis, Lecture on "Air Strategy" delivered at NDC.

12. Gen. (Retd) Mirza Aslam Beg, "Deterrence, Defence and Development–II," *Pakistan Observer*, June 30, 1999.

13. Col. Naeem Ahmed Salik, "Advent of Nuclear Weapons and the evolution of Nuclear Strategy," *Margalla Papers*, December 1998.

14. Rodney W. Jones, "Pakistan's Nuclear Posture," *Dawn*, September 14, 1999.

15. Ibid.

16. Ibid.

17. Nasim Zehra, "Pakistan's Security Options," *The News*, February 12, 1999.

18. See Annex "A" for the contents of India's "draft" nuclear doctrine.

19. Maj. Gen. Khalid Kidwai, Lecture at the NDC on "Management of Nuclear Capability."

20. Dr. Samiullah Koreshi, "Nuclear Blinds and Hypocrats–I," *Pakistan Observer*, June 14, 1999.

21. Col. Gurmeet Kanwal, "Command and Control of Nuclear Weapons," *Indian Defence Review*, October 1998.

22. Air Marshal Zahid (late) Anis, Lecture on "Air Strategy" delivered at NDC.

23. Lt. Gen. Khalid Maqbool, Lecture on "Military System" delivered at NDC.

24. Ibid.

25. Ibid.

26. Ibid.

27. Ibid.

28. Shamshad Ahmed, as quoted in Umer Farooq, "Pakistan to Operationalise Nukes if India did so," *The Nation*, August 1999.

29. Lt. Gen. Khalid Maqbool, Lecture on "Military System" delivered at NDC on November 4, 1999.

30. Moonis Ahmar, "Nuclear South Asia: Impact on Nuclear and Conventional Arms Race," *Margalla Papers*, December 1998.

31. Lt. Gen. Khalid Maqbool, Lecture on "Military System" delivered at NDC on November 4, 1999.

32. Maj. Gen. Khalid Kidwai, Lecture at NDC on "Management of Nuclear Capability" on January 14, 2000.

33. Lt. Gen. (Retd) F. S. Lodhi, "Pakistan's Nuclear Structure," *Margalla Papers*, December 1998.

34. John F. Kennedy, as quoted in Seymour J. Deitchman, *Limited War and American Defence Policy* (Cambridge, Massachusetts, USA: The MIT Press, 1964).

35. Air Marshal (Retd) B. D. Jayal, "Higher Defence Organization in India: The Strategic Dimension," *Indian Defence Review*, April-June 1998.

36. Brig. (Retd) A. R. Siddiqi, "Post Nuclear Environment—Strategy and Doctrine for Pakistan," *Margalla Papers*, December 1998.

37. Kamal Matinuddin, "Managing Nuclear Forces," *The News*, May 26, 1999.

38. Lecture by Mr. Muhammad Saleem, DG(A), Inter-Services Intelligence, on "External Threat to the Security of Pakistan" at NDC on November 3, 1999.

39. Philip A. G. Sabin, "Shadow or Substance? Perceptions and Symbolism in Nuclear Force Planning," Adelphi Papers, No. 222, International Institute for Strategic Studies, London, 1987.

40. Kamal Matinuddin, "Managing Nuclear Forces," *The News*, May 26, 1999.

12 Assessing Pakistan's Nuclear First Use Option

Introduction

The draft Indian nuclear doctrine lays a lot of emphasis on India's adherence to the precept of "No First Use" in the context of being forced to employ nuclear weapons and there have been repeated calls from the Indian leadership for Pakistan also to renounce the "First Use" option. This, however, is a contentious issue and must be weighed and assessed in the context of why has India renounced the first use of nuclear weapons and also whether Pakistan can and should follow suit by doing the same.

The draft Indian Nuclear Doctrine states:

- India will not be the first to initiate a nuclear strike, but will respond with punitive retaliation should deterrence fail.[1]
- Since no-first use of nuclear weapons is India's basic commitment, every effort shall be made to persuade other States possessing nuclear weapons to join an international treaty banning first use.[2]

India's renunciation of Nuclear First Use (NFU) is essentially predicated on the following aspects:

- India is convinced that in the near future, the only adversary against which she might be required to employ nuclear weapons is Pakistan since it will take India several years before she can even contemplate any confrontation with China.
- Having a phenomenal advantage in conventional military wherewithal vis-à-vis Pakistan, Indian defence planners can confidently, and I believe rightly, predict that Pakistan with her limited and inferior conventional military potential, would never be able to force India into overstepping her nuclear threshold as long as the military conflict between the two countries remains confined to the conventional spectrum.

While certain recent statements of the Indian leadership have tended to mask this earlier overt assertion of NFU in a cloud of vagueness and doubt, I perceive that relying on her immense conventional military advantage, India would continue to conform to her earlier declared stance of NFU.

The NFU Option and Pakistan

Precisely because of the same reasons that have earlier been cited as being India's motivation for adopting NFU, Pakistan cannot afford to renounce this policy. Highly effective conventional military capabilities shall be maintained to raise the threshold of outbreak both of conventional military conflict as well as that of threat or use of nuclear weapons.[3]

- Unlike India which keeps making a reference to China also as one of the reasons for her having gone nuclear, Pakistan's nuclear programme in entirely India-centric and India-focused. While India is not expected to embark on any military adventures against China in the foreseeable future, the same cannot be said of India's designs against Pakistan.

- Pakistan has some serious handicaps when compared with India that significantly enhance the possibility of her being forced to overstep her nuclear threshold and this possibility suggests that Pakistan cannot afford to renounce NFU.

- From the Pakistani perspective, the use of nuclear weapons is essentially a defensive rather than an offensive option. As such, for Pakistan, the NFU option is a basic element of her deterrence strategy. By not renouncing NFU, Pakistan could attempt to reduce the scale of the Indian military offensive or conventional military gains.

- Pakistan suffers from some very serious strategic imbalances relative to India which could lead to Pakistan reaching her nuclear threshold in a time frame much earlier than India; firstly, her limited territorial and geographic depth and secondly, her tremendous conventional inferiority. Both these stark realities lead one to the conclusion that Pakistan is far more liable to reach her nuclear threshold before India does during any future conflict. While comparing the conventional military potential of the two antagonists, one must not lose sight of the fact that while Pakistan's Army can mount an effective defence against the Indian Army, India enjoys an almost absolute superiority when it comes to the Air Force and the Navy.

- Since her nuclear weapons are essentially instruments of deterrence and are aimed at avoiding a war with India, by not renouncing the first use option, Pakistan is actually strengthening her deterrence.

Adoption of the NFU policy translates essentially to the incorporation of an element of nuclear restraint in one's military thinking and planning. This can only be done if a country does not suffer from such serious handicaps as have been highlighted above regarding Pakistan. In a confrontation between two unequal countries, this policy can only be adopted by the militarily stronger one since it could endeavour and expect to successfully repel the conventional military endeavours of the weaker antagonist without having to resort to nuclear weapons. From this it flows that while India can profess the adoption of a NFU policy vis-à-vis Pakistan, I seriously doubt whether she could even contemplate a similar stance when faced with a stronger adversary such as China.

Offensive and Defensive connotations of Nuclear "First Use"

There is a stark contrast between how countries can interpret the Nuclear First Use Option depending on their relative conventional military strength when compared with the expected adversary. While a conventionally stronger country is likely to ascribe an offensive overtone to its nuclear first use policy, one that is conventionally weaker in military terms would basically consider the adoption of this option as a primarily defensive action—more of an extension of its deterrence posture.

Being fairly confident of her conventional military might against Pakistan, Indian defence planners are expected to conform to the above. For India, with its immense conventional might, the nuclear weapons are not weapons of defence since the conventional military wherewithal should be able to look after that. Conversely, for nations suffering from a conventional imbalance such as Pakistan, nuclear weapons are more of a weapon of defence rather than offence. This would support the argument that only nations that are weaker when compared with their adversaries can be expected to develop nuclear weapons as weapons of deterrence. This is particularly true of Pakistan but does not apply to India. Being weaker conventionally, Pakistan was forced down the nuclear path since she required nuclear weapons to deter a much stronger India whereas for the latter which enjoys conventional superiority, the motivation to go nuclear had no defensive connotations.

The recent spate of large-scale Indian military acquisitions from Russia, United States, France and Israel has served to further widen the conventional gap between India and Pakistan. The most marked impact of this on the stability of the South Asian region has been a resulting lowering of Pakistan's nuclear threshold, making it more likely for Pakistan to be forced into a situation where she has to resort to employing nuclear weapons in an earlier time frame during a military conflict with India.

A direct fallout of Pakistan's increased likelihood of going nuclear first has been India's demonstrated desire and concerted efforts for the acquisition of a modern anti-ballistic missile system such as the US-Israeli Arrow-2 ABM system. Significantly, Pakistan has as yet not taken any steps in this regard.

From the above it can be surmised that in any South Asian military conflict in the foreseeable future, Pakistan can be expected to be forced into a situation of employing nuclear weapons much before India could be expected to reach such a situation. It is vital, therefore, to view the implications of Pakistan's first use of nuclear weapons in light of the expected Indian response.

Indian Response to a Pakistan Nuclear First Use

The draft Indian Nuclear Doctrine is emphatic in stating that India would meet any nuclear strike against it with massive punitive retaliation against the aggressor. This posture is designed primarily to deter Pakistan from going nuclear. While it is absolutely understandable that the circumstances that could lead to Pakistan going nuclear would have to be dire in the extreme, it is also obvious that the Pakistani leadership that is driven to the stage of contemplating the usage of nuclear weapons would be well aware of the Indian response and the ensuing terrible consequences.

A Pakistani Nuclear First Use

In the face of an almost certain defeat staring them in the face and the spectre of a massive retaliatory nuclear strike by India, Pakistan's leadership would be in a bind when faced with no option but to use the nuclear weapons. In all possibility, the Pakistani nuclear first strike would be aimed against a counter-value target—probably one of the major Indian cities such as Mumbai.

Since it is almost certain that India would respond to any Pakistani nuclear overtures in kind, its first strike will probably be the last military action that Pakistan would undertake. The obvious question here is—since this is the only option that Pakistan will be left with, why should it limit its option of a nuclear first strike to just one city or a limited number of targets. Instead, why should Pakistan not launch her nuclear first strike on a massive scale so as to cause immense devastation over as much of India as lies within the reach of its nuclear-capable fighter bombers and surface-to-surface strategic missile systems.

The obvious corollary to this argument is the fact that just as India has renounced first use but asserted the right to mount a massive punitive retaliation, should Pakistan's nuclear doctrine not highlight the defensive nature of its nuclear arsenal and also indicate in unequivocal terms that being likely to resort to the first usage of nuclear weapons, Pakistan contemplates a nuclear first strike on a massive and not on a selective dimension. If nothing else, this would enhance the deterrence potential of Pakistan's nuclear capability by deterring India from overstepping Pakistan's territorial, military or economic threshold of nuclear weapons employment.

Conclusion

The following salient conclusions emerge from the foregoing analysis:

- Unlike India, Pakistan cannot afford to renounce the no first use policy as regards its nuclear capability. Its nuclear doctrine, therefore, must clearly mention this fact as one of the basic tenets.
- Since Pakistan is likely to be the first to resort to nuclear weapons in any future India-Pakistan military conflict, she must clearly highlight in her nuclear doctrine that her nuclear first use would be on as massive a scale as is possible within her capability constraints.

Though the above assertions might appear excessively belligerent and irrational, one has to understand that Pakistan would be fighting the battle for its survival during any future Indo-Pakistan war. Being cognizant of the fact that her first nuclear strike would in all probability be also her last one, Pakistan should consider going full bore rather than remaining piecemeal in her nuclear employment options. This is because of the following:

- Since going nuclear would be an option of last resort, only an imminent scenario of abject defeat could force Pakistan to that stage. In this sort of a critical situation, Pakistan's leadership would have exhausted all other options of averting defeat and would have their backs to the wall. Also, Pakistan's nuclear threshold would have been overstepped by India.
- In the face of an expected massive retaliation by India, Pakistan is likely to only get one opportunity of employing her nuclear wherewithal. Since a nuclear response from India would anyway mean total destruction, why should Pakistan not consider making her nuclear first strike also massive in size, content and number of targets. An indication of this operational concept in Pakistan's nuclear doctrine would serve to further enhance the degree of deterrence dividend for Pakistan against India.

Notes

1. Reference paragraph 10 of the draft Indian Nuclear Doctrine document that is available on various websites on the internet and is also included in Chapter 13 of this book.
2. Ibid., paragraph 29.
3. Ibid., paragraph 13.

Section IV

Indian Doctrinal Thinking

13 Transformation in Doctrinal Rethinking of the Indian Armed Forces

Introduction

Indian and Pakistani military doctrines have had distinctive defensive undertones ever since the two countries gained independence from the British in 1947. Notwithstanding the three wars and several "near" wars that these two countries have engaged in over the period of their existence as independent nations, no significant shift in their respective military and war-fighting doctrines has come about.

Lately, however, some events that have taken place in the region and also elsewhere that have highlighted to both the countries that their existing doctrines need to be modified in order to cater for the altered situation and the emerging scenario.

Events precipitating doctrinal rethinking

Regional events. Some of the regional events that have triggered this review of military doctrines are:

- The nuclearisation of the subcontinent and its impact on the nature of war in the region and the roles of the three military services, Army, Navy and Air Force.
- Lessons of the 1999 Kargil crisis and the possibility of waging limited conventional warfare under a nuclear umbrella.
- The 2001/2002 period of massive military mobilisation and forward military posturing identified and referred to by the Indians as "Operation Parakaram."

Global events. At the global level, the following events that have occurred have also impacted doctrinal thinking in the South Asian militaries:

- The post 9/11 events and America's War on Terror, manifested in her invasion, initially of Afghanistan and later of Iraq.
- The doctrine of pre-emption espoused by President Bush in his National Security Strategy.

So pronounced has been the impact of these events that not only the Pakistan Air Force but also all three Indian Services have either come out with new doctrinal documents and manuals or modified editions of existing ones during the few years. It would be interesting to assess as to what were the factors that led to this spurt of doctrinal pronouncements and why at this particular stage of history when both India and Pakistan have expressed intentions to enter into a Composite Dialogue process. Referring specifically to the timing of announcement of Indian Army's new "Cold Start" doctrine, Hali asks, "The timing of this 'disclosure' of India's new war doctrine is of interest. Why have India's top military commanders returned to their drawing board to work on this new war doctrine: the 'Cold Start' strategy while a highly hyped peace process is underway?"[1]

Analysis of Factors Precipitating Doctrinal Rethinking in Indian Military

Doctrinal Impact of Nuclearisation of South Asia

The first and the foremost factor has been the emergence of the nuclear genie out of the closet in South Asia in 1998. The availability of nuclear capability has not only altered the very nature of war in the region but has also significantly altered the role of the three military services in their respective realms of warfare.

In both India as well as Pakistan, the first of the military services to be "nuclearised" was the Air Force since attack aircraft capable of being configured with nuclear weapons emerged as the first nuclear delivery platforms for both the countries. This ushered the IAF and the PAF into the limelight of the strategic military equation whilst simultaneously reducing the strategic significance of the Indian and Pakistani armies and navies.

Realisation of the fact that the Air Force was likely to lay claim to a lion's share of the strategic military expansion necessitated by the nuclearisation, the Army and the Navy started campaigning for their own respective strategic roles; the Army by laying claim to the surface-to-surface ballistic missile force and the Navy by harping on the theme of the sea-based dimension of the nuclear deterrence triad.

In both India and Pakistan, the armies were able to subsequently garner a strategic role for themselves by gaining control of the nuclear tipped SSMs but the navies are still endeavouring to develop a nuclear capability to justify their strategic role in the nuclear environment.

Another significant impact of nuclearisation was the shift in the objective of war in the region from territorial occupation to destruction based operations. This occurred because annexation of sizeable territory by the adversary was considered much more likely to end up violating the other side's nuclear threshold than a controlled campaign of destruction of the latter's military and economic potential. This transformation in the purpose for which military operations were conducted during war also served to reduce the significance of the large armies possessed by India and Pakistan while enhancing the importance of the air forces since the latter were more suitably equipped and configured to undertake selective and effective destruction campaigns against the adversary. Elaborating on the above theme, Dr. Subhash Kapila says that India's strategic military objectives need to:

"Shift from capturing bits of Pakistan territory in small scale multiple offensives to be used as bargaining chips after the ceasefire and focus on the destruction of the Pakistani Army and its military machine without much collateral damage to Pakistani civilians."[2]

It can be summarised, therefore, that nuclearisation of South Asia has precipitated a serious review of the military doctrines prevalent in the region by not only altering the very nature and manner in which future military conflicts will be fought but also by disturbing the balance of relevance of the three established services of the military—the army, the navy and the air force. Military doctrines thus had to be reviewed not only to cater to the changed dynamics of future wars but also to restore a semblance of balance in the respective importance of the three military services.

Doctrinal Lessons of the 1999 Kargil Conflict[3]
Occurring barely a year after the overt nuclearisation of the South Asian subcontinent, the Kargil conflict of 1999 signified perhaps the moment when India and Pakistan came the closest to an all-out conventional war that could well have developed into a nuclear exchange. The lessons learnt from this war, though different for India and Pakistan, did highlight the imperative for doctrinal adjustments and modifications that the militaries of both the countries were required to adopt and incorporate in their doctrines.

In my personal opinion, the foremost doctrinal lessons for India and Pakistan to learn from the Kargil conflict include the following:[4]
- No military operation of significance can or should ever be undertaken without adequate pre-commencement coordination with all agencies that are likely to be involved in the operations. This is particularly applicable to Pakistan where it appears that the lack of coordination between the political leadership and the military elite caused a certain degree of discord especially after President Clinton was able to coerce or cajole Prime Minister Nawaz Sharif in declaring a unilateral withdrawal without really taking the military into confidence and against its desire.[5]

- During any military operation, the maximum and not the minimum possible reaction of the enemy should be expected and a suitable response to it must be built into the plan itself to enable some degree of operational flexibility.
- In an environment where both adversaries have access to nuclear weapons, the active involvement of the Air Force, especially in the offensive role, is a step of immense escalatory dimension which could well end up escalating the conflict to a higher level, and as such, should be avoided. Neither India nor Pakistan opted to employ their air forces in a significant manner throughout this conflict, primarily due to apprehensions over enhanced chances of the conflict escalating into an all-out conventional war.
- Though the element of surprise can lead to extremely favourable initial results, especially in an environment as asymmetric as Kargil, the advantages accrued due to surprise lose significance immediately after the outbreak of hostilities and, in fact, could well precipitate an overreaction on the part of an adversary who has ended up being surprised.
- In regions as remote and inaccessible as Kargil, logistic sustenance through an efficient stocking and resupply system assumes critical proportions due to the inherent difficulties of transportation.
- Some analysts of Kargil have expressed the belief that the conflict highlighted that even in a confrontation between two nuclear capable militaries such as the Indian and Pakistani defence forces, there is some space that is available for both to indulge in a limited conflict while remaining short of an all-out conventional war that could in turn precipitate a possible, albeit extremely undesirable, nuclear exchange. It would be imperative, however, to keep such a limited conflict within each other's nuclear thresholds. Essentially, even after getting embroiled in a limited conflict, both the antagonists would be required to exercise a very high level of restraint on the actions of their respective militaries so as to preclude an escalation. The exercise of such a restraint by both India and Pakistan was fairly obvious throughout the duration of the Kargil conflict.[6]
- While contemplating a limited conflict under a nuclear umbrella, it must be kept in mind that even a tactical scale offensive that promises strategic dividends could cause the adversary to overreact with significantly greater chances of the situation developing into an all-out war/nuclear exchange.

- The lack of real-time and year-round surveillance capability to monitor the enemy's activities in the vicinity of the border could lead to one getting surprised. This is especially true in South Asia where Pakistan and India share a long contiguous border stretching from the icy wastelands of the northern mountain ranges to the blue waters of the Arabian Sea and the Indian Ocean.

- The possibility of the enemy managing to achieve surprise necessitates the maintenance of a high state of military alert and readiness as regards the back-up forces and would also require the ready availability of adequate airlift potential to rapidly bring these forces to bear on the enemy in the required theatre of operations. This requirement could well dictate the forward positioning of the important combat elements of the armies even during peacetime. While selecting these locations, thought must be given to their proximity to the expected theatres of military operations and their communication links with the area of interest.

- Due to the inaccessibility and remoteness of the icy wastelands of Siachen and the area adjoining the snow-covered mountains in the Himalayan, Karakoram and Hindukush mountain ranges, the tenuous lines of communications extending into these parts become targets that assume strategic significance. Even the destruction or denial of one minor bridge could well end up isolating the forward forces from any resupply or reinforcement efforts from the rear.

- Combat in the high altitude environment has radically different requirements when compared to similar operations in the plains and at lower elevations. The Kargil conflict brought to the fore several deficiencies not only in the equipment inventories but also in the operational philosophies of the Indian and Pakistani armies and air forces that need to be tailored into the future development doctrines of these services in order for them to undertake effective military operations in the hostile environment that prevails in the region.[7]

- International involvement, especially by a country like the US that is the sole superpower in the world today, can be instrumental in not allowing a potential conflict from escalating into an all-out war or a nuclear exchange. The clout that the US enjoys under the prevailing global environment places an enormous responsibility on her shoulders as regards the avoidance of a conflict of nuclear proportions in South Asia. For India and Pakistan, the sceptre of an inevitable US intervention to avert a nuclear exchange also has doctrinal connotations that need to be catered for in the doctrines of their respective militaries.[8]

Doctrinal Lessons of the 2001-2002 Brinkmanship Episode

Coming soon after the Kargil conflict, the massive mobilisation of their respective militaries accompanied with a stance of exaggerated forward posturing during the later part of 2001 and the early part of 2002 once again brought South Asia to the verge of war. Harping on the theme of Pakistan's involvement in "cross-border terrorism," the right-wing BJP dominated Indian Government decided to deploy its military against Pakistan in an obvious attempt to coerce and browbeat Pakistan into refraining from providing any support to the Kashmiri freedom fighters operating inside Indian Held Kashmir (IHK).

In response to the Indian military's mobilisation and forward deployment all along the international border, Pakistan marshalled her military also by bringing it to the highest state of readiness and deploying it as per the war plans. This face-to-face confrontation of over a million strong military personnel once again brought India and Pakistan to the brink of war. It was only after 10 tense months of this stand-off that the forces were gradually withdrawn by both the countries to the peacetime footing.

Following are some of the salient lessons that emerged from this period of brinkmanship which have also caused the military doctrines of both the countries to be seriously reviewed and formulated afresh:

- As was the case during the Kargil conflict, both the countries, realising that they faced the dangers of a devastating nuclear exchange, exercised a high degree of restraint. This aspect of restraint was taken so seriously that the Indians removed one Army and two Air Force commanders who had overstepped the specified degree of restraint imposed on them and on the troops under their command.[9]

- Pakistan's geography came to its rescue. Being a country lacking in geographical depth, its forces were located fairly close to their planned wartime deployment sites and as such, were deployed in a very short period of time. On the other hand, the Indian Army took almost 30 days to mobilise and deploy to the wartime locations.[10]

- Most Indian analysts contend that it was the delay inherent in Indian mobilisation and deployment that provided Pakistan the manoeuvring space for seeking international (read US) involvement as a mediator. Also, Pakistan's ability to mobilise and deploy her forces much more quickly placed the Indian military leaders on the back foot. From this realisation flows the requirement for the Indian military to adopt a posture that reduces its mobilisation and employment time to a level whereby the space that is currently available to Pakistan for seeking extra-regional intervention does not remain. This implies that the Indian military must be able to achieve "near decisive results" so early in the conflict that any foreign intervention of mediation is precluded.

- From the Indian perspective, the most important lesson that emerged from this stand-off related to the need for the political and the military instruments to work together in a synchronised manner. As events unfolded, it was evident that the decision to adopt a pronounced forward and aggressive military posture aimed at coercing Pakistan was basically a political decision and the Indian military, having been excluded from the decision loop, was not in a position to immediately adopt the posture desired by their political masters. In the words of General (retired) S. Padmanabhan, the then Chief of the Indian Army, it was not possible for him to go on the offensive against Pakistan immediately after the political decision for the mobilisation and exaggerated forward posture had been taken because:

"War is a serious business, and you don't go just like that. When December 13 happened, my strike formations were at peace locations. At that point, I did not have the capability to mobilise large forces to go across."[11]

- The US military invasion of Afghanistan and the presence of large US and Coalition military forces in proximity to South Asia and also on Pakistani territory also posed a problem of immense magnitude for India. Notwithstanding the reports of the elusive US naval fleet that was supposedly approaching the Bay of Bengal during the dying days of the 1971 Indo-Pak War, South Asian countries have never had to contend with the actual presence of Extra-Regional Forces (ERF) on their soil or doorsteps. The presence of US troops in Pakistan and the Arabian Sea severely constrained the degree of freedom available to both India and Pakistan to go to war and, in my opinion, not only discouraged them from going to war but also encouraged the US to play a more active than it has ever played earlier in attempting to resolve imminent military confrontations in South Asia.[12]

- The impact of geopolitics on regional conflicts also emerged as a significant lesson although not for the first time. Pakistan's decision to side with the US in its "War on Terror" against the Taliban in Afghanistan by permitting US forces the unrestricted use of its airspace and also providing them with prepared launching pads for the conduct of military operations made Pakistan emerge as a crucial "frontline" state for the US. During this time period, the US needed Pakistan much more than it needed India, and as such viewed the possibility of an Indo-Pak military conflict with immense disapproval. Try as she did by harping on the theme of Pakistan's involvement in "cross-border terrorism" in IHK, India could not dent Pakistan's new found relevance to the US and the West in any significant manner. In the modern-day globalised environment, it has become virtually impossible to either stay aloof from what is happening in the world or to completely isolate one's regions from the surroundings.

- In line with her hegemonic designs towards Pakistan in particular and the entire region in general, the Indian government hailed the announcement of President Bush's national security strategy that incorporated the element of "pre-emption." Some of the hardliners in the Indian establishment even espoused the idea that just like the US had announced this policy of pre-emption and was employing it in Afghanistan, India could also adopt it to ensure that Pakistan refrains from supporting the freedom fighters in IHK. A brazen attempt was even made by the Indians to group Pakistan as one of the target countries in the US "War on Terror."

- Geostrategic location of a country influences its relevance for the major powers. Although India also offered the US the use of her airfields and logistic facilities, Pakistan was a much more suitable option for the US by virtue of her location and proximity to the theatre of operations.

Summary

The objective of this Chapter has been to examine how some of the significant events of the recent past have influenced and brought about a major process of rethinking as regards the doctrines adopted and practised by the militaries of South Asia.

South Asia, notwithstanding the numerous wars and "near wars" that it has experienced, has essentially remained a "status quo" region as regards the evolution of military doctrines. Recent events, however, have been of such significance and magnitude that these have caused the South Asian militaries to wake up from their "doctrinal slumber" and re-examine how they plan to prepare for fighting any future war that might occur in this highly volatile region of the world.

This doctrinal "reawakening" amongst the South Asian military establishment is evidenced by the following recent events:

- In Pakistan, the only doctrinal document to be issued prior to 1998 and made openly available was the one issued by the Pakistan Air Force in 1987. In January 2004, the PAF came out with a new and revised version of its Basic Air Power Doctrine.

- The Indian Army announced its new doctrine, euphemistically titled "Cold Start" in early 2004. The contents of this document remain classified to this day with only the statements of some of the senior Indian Army leaders providing some indicators of its contents.

- The Indian Navy has also come out with its "Maritime Doctrine" recently and while some portion of it remains classified, the remaining has been made available to the public.

- On the nuclear side, while India did reveal the initial draft of its nuclear doctrine, Pakistan still has to follow suit. It can be safely expected that in line with its existing policy, Pakistan would continue maintaining ambiguity regarding her nuclear policy and plans.

One important aspect of the doctrinal openness process in South Asia is the desire of the military services to enhance awareness about their roles, functions and importance for the common public since they feel that increased public awareness regarding their roles would translate into greater public participation in security affairs and would also influence decisions of their government regarding funding for national security. Through measures such as these, the Armed Forces are attempting to convince the Government to allocate them the funds required for their ambitious development plans.

Notes

1. Gp Capt (Retd) S. M. Hali, "India's war doctrine: 'Cold Start'—implications for its neighbours? The implications of India's new war doctrine for Pakistan and China." Article can be accessed at http://www.pakdef.info/forum/showthread.php?t=5314.

2. Dr. Subhash Kapila, "India's new 'Cold Start' doctrine strategically reviewed." South Asian Analysis Group (SAAG) Paper No. 991 dated May 4, 2004. Can be accessed on the internet at http://www.saag.org/papers10/paper991.html. It is suggested that this paper be read in conjunction with a sequel by the same author which has been printed as SAAG Paper No. 1013 and is accessible on the internet at http://www.saag.org/papers11/paper1013.html.

3. For an analysis of the 1999 Kargil conflict, the author, among several other openly available sources, has relied on the following documents, all of which are available on the internet:

    •   Rand Organisation Report No. MR 1450 titled "Limited Conflict Under the Nuclear Umbrella: Indian and Pakistani Lessons from the Kargil Crisis," authored by Ashley J. Tellis, C. Christine Fair and Jamison Jo Medby. This document is accessible on the Rand Organisation website at www.rand.org.

    •   Master's thesis titled "High altitude warfare: The Kargil conflict and the future," written by Marcus P. Acosta in June 2003 at the Naval Postgraduate School, Monterey.

    •   Brigadier (Retired) Shaukat Qadir, "Analysis of the Kargil Crisis 1999" printed in the RUSI Journal for April 2002.

    •   Article titled "War in the High Mountains: The Kargil Operations, 1999" available on the Bharat Rakshak website at www.bharatrakshak.com.

    •   Editorial in *Daily Dawn*, Karachi, Pakistan dated May 27, 1999, titled "Kargil Conflict: A Pakistani Perspective."

    •   Lisa Hwang, "Unraveling Pakistan's Actions in Kargil" published in CSIS Prospectus, Volume 1, Number 1, Fall 1999.

    •   Article titled "1999 Kargil Conflict" available at www.globalsecurity.org website.

4. The enormous international interest that the Kargil conflict of 1999 aroused is evident from the fact that the Centre for Contemporary Conflicts of the US Naval Postgraduate School, Monterey undertook a detailed analysis of this conflict by running a research project titled "Kargil Project." The highlights of this project included two major conferences; the first one being held in Monterey from May 29, to June 1, 2002 and the second one being held in New Delhi on September 26-27, 2002. Reports of the proceedings of both these reports are available at http://www.ccc.nps.navy.mil/events/recent/sept02Kargil_rpt.asp for the September 2002 conference and at http://www.ccc.nps.navy.mil/events/recent/may02Kargil_rpt.asp for the May 2002 conference. These two conferences, through the medium of an international selection of conferees, were aimed at highlighting not only the factors and causes that led to the Kargil conflict but also attempted to analyse the possible lessons that both Pakistan and India could learn from it.

5. According to an article titled "Kargil Conflict 1999" that is available at www.globalsecurity.org, "Apart from keeping the plan top secret, the Pakistan Army also undertook certain steps to maintain an element of surprise and maximise deception." Some analysts argue that this element of secrecy was overplayed with some key individuals/organisations who needed to be kept in the loop also being totally excluded from it.

6. For a detailed overview of the possibility of waging a limited war in South Asia under the nuclear umbrella, please refer to the report of a conference on "Asymmetric Conflict in South Asia: The Cause and Consequences of the 1999 Limited War in Kargil" that was held under the auspices of the Centre for Contemporary Conflicts of the US Naval Postgraduate School, Monterey from May 29 to June 1, 2002. The text of this report can be accessed at http://www.ccc.nps.navy.mil/events/recent/

may02Kargil_rpt.asp.

7. Master's thesis titled "High altitude warfare: The Kargil conflict and the future" written by Marcus P. Acosta in June 2003 at the Naval Postgraduate School, Monterey.

8. For a first-hand account of the deliberations that took place between President Bill Clinton and Prime Minister Nawaz Sharif on the Kargil issue on July 4, 2000, please refer to a Policy Paper issued by the Centre for Advanced Study of India (CASI) at the University of Pennsylvania. This paper titled "American Diplomacy and the 1999 Kargil Summit at Blair House" has been authored by Bruce Reidel who was Special Assistant to the President and Senior Director for Near East and South Asia Affairs in the National Security Council at the White House from 1997 to 2001 and issued in May 2002. In that role, Mr. Riedel was President Clinton's senior adviser on South Asian issues and travelled with the President to India, Pakistan and Bangladesh in March 2000. His prior office was Deputy Assistant Secretary of Defence for Near East and South Asia Issues in the Pentagon. The complete text of Bruce Reidel's Policy Paper can be accessed and downloaded in pdf format from www.sas.upenn. edu/casi/reports/ReidelPaper051302.pdf.

9. Rajesh M. Basrur in a paper titled "India: Doctrine, Posture and Stability" written for the International Conference on "Strategic Stability in South Asia" held at the Naval Postgraduate School, Monterey from June 29 to July 2, 2004, highlights two incidents where senior Indian military commanders were removed from their command assignments for taking steps that could have been construed as being escalatory by the Pakistan military. He writes, "In January 2002, Lieutenant-General Kapil Vij, commander of India's 2 Corps, a strike corps, was abruptly shifted from his post for positioning his forces too close to the border. In March, Air Marshal V. K. Bhatia was transferred out of the LoC/border region after his aircraft strayed into Pakistani air space, and was hit by Pakistani fire. "Lt-Gen Vij Moved Forces 'Too Close' to Border," *Times of India*, January 21, 2002; Sandeep Dikshit, "Air Marshal Bhatia Shifted," *Hindu*, April 25, 2002.

10. In a recent interview General (retired) S. Padmanabhan, the Indian Army Chief during the 2001-2002 stand-off, said, "significant military gains could have been achieved in January 2002, had politicians made the decision to go to war." These objectives, he says, could have included "degradation of the other force, and perhaps the capture of disputed territory in Jammu and Kashmir. They were more achievable in January, less achievable in February, and even less achievable in March. By then, the balance of forces had gradually changed." This statement clearly indicates that had the Pakistan Army not been able to mobilise quickly and had the Indian Army not taken so long to deploy to the front, the latter could well have struck Pakistan a decisive blow. Please refer to Praveen Swami, "Gen. Padmanabhan mulls over lessons of Operation Parakram" athttp://www.hinduonnet.com/thehindu/thscrip/print.pl?file=2004020604461200. htm&date=2004/02/06/&prd=th&.

11. Ibid.

12. Pakistan's decision to completely support the US War on Terror operations against the Taliban in Afghanistan was one of monumental significance. Pakistan not only permitted US military aircraft including transport aircraft and AWACS platforms to

14

Indian Army's
"Cold Start" Doctrine

Introduction

In light of the lessons learnt from the 1999 Kargil crisis and the 2001-2002 period of brinkmanship between India and Pakistan,[1] the Indian Army felt a dire need to alter its doctrine and while work on this began even during the two conflicts mentioned above, the new doctrine was officially announced on April 28, 2004 during an Army Commander's Conference.

Since the doctrine still has to be fine-tuned and discussed at the various tiers of the Indian Army, its complete text was not disclosed to the public because of security considerations.

The aim of this article, which constitutes the second part in a series of three articles on the doctrinal reawakening that is currently being witnessed amongst the Indian military, is to evaluate the Indian Army's recently announced "Cold Start" doctrine.[2] A study, an analysis of the factors that have precipitated the recent doctrinal reawakening in the Indian armed forces, was covered in Chapter 13 while Chapters 14 to 17 will deal with the Indian Army's Cold Start Doctrine, the Indian Navy's Maritime Doctrine, the IAF's Aerospace Doctrine and the Indian Draft Nuclear Doctrine.[3]

Factors Leading to the Enunciation of the Indian Army's "Cold Start" Doctrine

The Indian Army's first doctrine has been a long way in coming. While it has been in preparation for a long time,[4] the immediate impetus for its drafting was provided primarily by the nuclearisation of South Asia, the events of the 1999 Kargil crisis and Operation Parakaram. These influences have been adequately highlighted in Part 1 of this series and as such will not be repeated here other than being alluded to in the passing while elaborating on the salient aspects of the new doctrine.

Delays in Mobilisation and Deployment. During Kargil, the Indian Army got surprised and was caught unprepared. Although it did ultimately manage to mobilise and deploy in adequate numbers, the time lost during this process was an issue of great concern since according to some analysts, it permitted space for the US to intervene by bringing about a Pakistani withdrawal. Subsequently, during Operation Parakaram again, the time taken by the Indian Army to mobilise and deploy permitted the Pakistani military to adopt a forward deployed posture and precluded any attempt to achieve a military edge.

Based on these essential lessons, the Indian Army commanders realised that in order to be able to mobilise and deploy early enough, the Indian Army's three Strike Corps needed to be stationed much closer to the international border with Pakistan than their current locations.[5] Reports suggested that the mobilisation and movement of these designated offensive elements of the Indian Army to locations from where these could launch an offensive against Pakistan consumed as much as an entire month—time enough for the Pakistani forces to move to their wartime locations.

Moreover, the creation of these Strike Corps in accordance with the Sundarji doctrine had denuded the rest of the Indian Army of any meaningful offensive punch. This was especially true for the "holding" or the defensive corps that are normally stationed much closer to the border. Had these defensive elements been suitably configured for undertaking limited scale offensive operations, a lot of time would be saved in going on the offensive. These small-scale offensives could then be supplemented by the Strike Corps which could be inducted as and when these became available.

In his series of two analytical articles that focus on analysing the "Cold Start" doctrine, Dr. Subhash Kapila opines that "since the most significant aim of the new war doctrine is to strike offensively without giving away battle indicators of mobilisation, it is imperative that all strike formations headquarters, Armoured Divisions and Armoured Brigades are relocated from their existing locations in Central India and in-depth in Punjab to forward locations."[6] He further suggests that these offensive formations of the Indian Army should preferably be moved from their current in-depth locations to positions forward of a line joining Barmer–Jaisalmer–Bikaner–Suratgarh.

In the aftermath of the 1999 Kargil crisis, Indian Army leaders were convinced that this conflict had proven that it was still possible to wage a limited war even after nuclearisation of South Asia provided that the adversary's nuclear threshold was not violated. The possibility of this concept was quite enticing for the armies, both in Pakistan and in India, since they were apprehensive that the thesis of a conventional limited war having become impossible after the nuclearisation of the subcontinent was gnawing at their relevance and importance in affairs of national defence. Both the land forces possibly thought that in order to ensure the place of importance that they had hitherto enjoyed in their respective countries, they needed to justify that the possibility of a limited conventional war could not be ruled out. Failure to do so would have further strengthened the position of the lobby that was asserting that like it happened during the Cold War, the availability of nuclear weapons on both sides had virtually reduced the chances of them getting involved in a limited conventional war.

Other Doctrinal Lessons from Kargil 1999 and the 2001-2002 Confrontation. As has been highlighted above, having assimilated the lessons of the 1999 Kargil conflict and the 2001-2002 confrontation, the

Indian Army's leadership thought it necessary to modify the Indian Army Doctrine based on the following precepts:

- Since the designated defensive elements that are normally located close to the border and can be brought into offensive action at a very short notice but could not do so because of their possessing very limited offensive wherewithal and capability, there was a dire need to position some offensive elements of the Indian Army near the border. In fact, the offensive elements of the Indian Army, as manifested by the three Strike Corps, despite being the prime assets, have not been brought into operation during any of the three wars that India and Pakistan have fought primarily because their location in-depth precluded their timely committal into combat. The adoption of this course of action would allow for and cater to the following requirements:
  - It would minimise the time required for bringing the Indian Army's offensive elements to bear on Pakistan.
  - By reducing the deployment and mobilisation time, it would deny the time space available to Pakistan to move her own forces forward and also not allow it to seek international intervention in order to force India to back-off. "The idea is that the international community should not get the opportunity to intervene. Hence, the need for swift action starting from a 'cold start' instead of slow mobilisation."[7]
  - Having offensive elements located close to their launching pads for attacks against Pakistan would reduce the reaction time/early warning that is normally available to Pakistan.
  - Having offensive elements in a position from where these could immediately launch an offensive would permit the Indian Army to achieve surprise since in the earlier situations, the massive mobilisation and deployment activity was liable to not only give its plan away but also forewarn the Pakistan Army.
  - Since the three Strike Corps of the Indian Army were the prime focus of Pakistan's intelligence gathering apparatus, it was extremely difficult for the Indian Army to alter their disposition in any significant manner without the Pakistan Army coming to know of it.
  - Although some offensive elements were also normally made available to the designated defensive Corps of the Indian Army, these were inadequate by themselves to launch any meaningful offensive.
  - The attachment of limited offensive elements with the designated defensive/holding Corps was resulting in a dissipation of precious offensive capability of the Indian Army and was preventing a judicious utilisation of the available offensive assets.

o   With its offensive elements being able to be brought into action at a very short notice and with the element of surprise being partially in its favour, the Indian Army could possibly achieve a decisive degree of degradation of Pakistan's military potential without crossing the latter's nuclear threshold and by also not affording the international community adequate time or opportunity to intercede. Essentially, this boils down to the Indian Army being able to conduct a limited war while adequately catering for the threat of a Pakistani nuclear response.

Essential Features of the "Cold Start" Doctrine

In view of the reasons and motivations highlighted above, it becomes apparent that there existed a need for the Indian Army to modify its doctrine in a manner that not only removed all the above-mentioned weaknesses but also incorporated all the lessons that had been learnt during Kargil in 1999 and during the ensuing confrontation two years later.

In order to address all these issues, the Indian Army's "Cold Start" doctrine embodies the following salient features:

- As reported in the Indian media, the "Cold Start" doctrine visualises the creation and subsequent employment of eight "Integrated Battle Groups (IBGs)." According to Dr. Kapila, these eight IBGs could mean eight integrated armoured division/mechanised infantry division sized forces with varying composition of armour, artillery, infantry and combat air support—all integrated.[8]
- The eight envisaged IBGs, other than possessing the integral army units (infantry, armour, artillery, etc.), would also be provided with dedicated army aviation support in the form of utility as well as attack helicopters and would also be assured the provision of comprehensive air support by pre-designated squadrons of the IAF.
- The creation of the IBGs would facilitate a judicious utilisation of the Indian Army's offensive assets, since those of such assets that are deployed along with the defensive formations could also be pulled out and incorporated in the IBGs. The Indian Army's combat potential would be fully harnessed. The distinction between "strike corps" and "defensive corps" in ground holding role would be gradually diminished.[9]
- Unlike the Strike Corps that are located in-depth, the IBGs would be situated well in front and fairly close to the border. From these locations, the IBGs could be brought into action without Pakistan getting any early warning or preparatory time.
- The exaggerated forward offensive posture of the Indian Army as envisioned by the "Cold Start" doctrine makes it important for the political leadership

to decide right at the outset and once and for all regarding the military action that is to be taken against Pakistan. This is because the immediacy of the action would not leave any time for the Indian political leadership to rethink or modify their decision in any manner.

Implications of "Cold Start" Doctrine for Pakistan

A change as radical as the "Cold Start" doctrine of the Indian Army necessitates a response from Pakistan since the focus of this doctrinal transformation remains the Pakistani military in general and the Pakistan Army in particular. Some obvious and not so obvious implications that come to mind are listed and discussed below:

- Through the suitable strategic positioning of these eight IBGs, the Indian Army would retain the option of launching a sizeable offensive in eight different sectors. This would resultantly thin out and dissipate the defensive potential of the Pakistan Army and the Pakistan Air Force.
- The launching of eight simultaneous offensives by the Indian Army would necessitate the creation and maintenance of sizeable strategic reserve elements that could easily be moved into the sector where needed. These strategic assets, being crucial to the success of the Indian Army's offensives, would also figure prominently among the list of targets for the PAF as well as Pakistan's SSM inventory.
- Spreading the Indian Army's offensive potential across as many as eight possible sectors would enable the Indians to capitalise on the tremendous numerical superiority of the IAF. While the numerically inferior PAF would be hard-pressed to meet the support requirements of the Pakistan Army in all the sectors, the IAF could do the same with a much greater degree of freedom because of its significantly larger fleet. Considering the crucial role that air power plays in determining the outcome of modern-day land battles, the availability of adequate air support would definitely prove to be a major advantage for the Indian Army. Indian analyst Firdaus Ahmed writes, "The idea is to paralyse Pakistani leadership with this decision dilemma while making quick territorial gains to be bartered post conflict on the negotiation table in return for Pakistan's promise of good behaviour with regard to Kashmir."[10]
- Since the Pakistan Army is also confronted with an adversary that is more than twice its size, it needs to first identify the eight possible sectors in which the Indian Army could mount simultaneous offensives. This is vital from the perspective of disposition of own forces since the distribution of Pakistan Army's assets over eight sectors would also eat into its own offensive potential, because the defensive elements

would also be requiring some integral offensive potential which would probably have to come from the existing assets of Pakistan Army's designated Strike elements. As a consequence, the Pakistan Army's offensive potential might get marginalised to some extent.

- The availability of integral army aviation and air force combat support assets would permit the Indian military to function as a much more responsive and integrated tri-Service military machine by addressing the common problems of inter-Service coordination and communication. The ready availability of helicopter and fixed-wing assets to the Indian Army's offensive elements would pose an additional burden for the already stretched-out PAF, while simultaneously enhancing the need for the main elements of the Pakistan Army to be provided with adequate air defence weapons.

- Since the forward location of the Indian Army's offensive IBGs reduces the early warning that is currently available to the Pakistan Army, there would be a dire requirement for round-the-clock and all-weather surveillance and reconnaissance capability of all eight IBGs at all times. This is necessary to preclude the possibility of the Pakistan military being taken by surprise. Needless to say, aerial reconnaissance by PAF reconnaissance assets as well as UAVs would be needed for this purpose. Moreover, these assets would also have to be supplemented by human intelligence assets that could be expected to play a vital role in maintaining a constant watch on the movement and disposition of the Indian Army's IBGs.

- Due to the limited reaction time available to the Pakistan military, designated elements of the Pakistan Army and the PAF would either have to be maintained at a higher state of readiness/preparation, or these would have to be stationed at locations much closer to the border with India so that these can react almost immediately on the first sign of an impending Indian Army offensive.

- As happened with the peacetime location of the Indian Army's three Strike Corps, knowledge about the locations of the eight Indian Army IBGs could provide an indication of the expected sectors of operation in which the Indian Army could be contemplating offensive action during any future military conflict.

Analysis of the Indian Army's "Cold Start" Doctrine

Although the preceding portion of this chapter has also been an attempt to analyse the "Cold Start" doctrine, it is felt that some of the contentious issues that could not be covered in the portions discussed above needed to be summarised in a consolidated manner separately.

- Implementation of the "Cold Start" doctrine requires a very high degree of coordination between the political and the military leadership of India. This is because the speed with which the military action is likely to unfold would not afford the political leadership time to waver or detract once the decision has been taken.

- The element of the Indian Army attempting to regain the supremacy within the Indian military structure that it enjoyed prior to the nuclear tests of 1998 must not also be lost sight of. By creating the eight IBGs which also involve elements from the IAF and the IN, the Indian Army could well be trying to indicate the subservience of the other two arms. Although not openly spelled out during the announcement of the new doctrine, it can be expected with a very high degree of certainty that all eight IBGs would be commanded by Indian Army Generals with the attached IAF and IN units being placed under them. It remains to be seen whether this sort of an arrangement would be acceptable to the other two Services, especially under the prevailing circumstances where all three Services are competing against each other for gaining a bigger share of the Indian nuclear military capability. It is significant to note that in order to dispel any such doubts about the intentions of the Indian Army, the Chiefs of Staff of the IAF and the Indian Navy also attended this session of the Army Commanders Conference and remained present while the "Cold Start" doctrine was being announced. One Indian journalist has captured it by writing, "In a sense, the new doctrine could be a new push for integrated command by one of the forces."[11]

- While it is possible for the Indian Army to achieve some territorial gains or cause destruction on the Pakistani military through massive surprise attacks, the ever-present factor of Pakistan's nuclear threshold has to figure very high in the Indian Army's offensive calculus. The imperative of not violating Pakistan's perceived nuclear threshold, therefore, emerges as one of the major constraints in any decisive application of the "Cold Start" doctrine.

- Considering the threat of the India Army being able to spring a major surprise on the Pakistan Army, the latter must not completely rule out the option of pre-emption by attempting to take-out the Indian Army's IBGs before these can be brought to bear on the Pakistani defences.

- Another significant aspect of the "Cold Start" doctrine is the visible move away from the erstwhile defensive mindset that the Indian Army leadership has maintained ever since independence. This shift to an offensive frame of mind needs significant adjustments being made in the entire leadership and training philosophy of the Indian Army, which is easier said than done. The problem with going on the offensive right at the outset is that the adoption of this course of action is inherently risky and as Brigadier (retired) Shaukat Qadir writes, "Neither Indian nor many Pakistani commanders ·are comfortable taking risks. There is far too much at stake! It is for this reason most of all that I consider it unlikely that such a concept (Cold Start) might actually be tried. If it ever is, I would like to witness it."[12]

- The Cold Start doctrine permits the efficient utilisation of the technological and numerical advantage that the Indian military enjoys over the Pakistani military and as such, aims to exploits these advantages to the fullest. The doctrine specifically talks of the immense firepower that the IAF combat assets, the Indian Army's long-range artillery assets and its SRBMs can bring to bear against Pakistan.

- The adoption of an offensive doctrine by the Indian Army could also be an effort on its part to reiterate and re-establish the fact that it also has a strategic military potential, like the IAF and the IN (subject to the development and induction of submarine-launched nuclear-tipped missiles). Significantly, just two months after announcing the "Cold Start" Doctrine, the Indian Army announced the establishment of a nuclear capable missile unit that is expected to be armed with Agni-1 and/or Agni-3 surface-to-surface missiles (SSMs).[13]

Summary

This Chapter has attempted to conduct a brief analysis of the Indian Army's "Cold Start" doctrine that was announced on April 28, 2004 and is expected to be implemented as soon as its contents have been finalised in the light of the feedback received by the Indian Army Headquarters from its various subordinate Commands and the operational elements in the field. It could be expected that these inputs could contribute to the initial proposal being fine-tuned and adjusted in accordance with the realities on the ground.

Once this doctrine has been finalised and implemented, a much more detailed analysis of its contents and resultant implications would need to be conducted by Pakistan, preferably at the Joint Staff Headquarters level so that a suitable response doctrine/strategy can be evolved to counter the "Cold Start" doctrine.

Pakistan's response to the Cold Start Doctrine has been the development of the latest short range (60 km) ballistic missiles capable of carrying a nuclear warhead. The development and this weapon system by Pakistan has served to virtually negate the Indian Cold Start Doctrine.

Notes

1. The lessons of the 1999 Kargil crisis and the 2001-2002 period of tension that have doctrinal implications have been discussed and elaborated upon in the first article of this series.

2. The author's plan is to comprehensively cover the current doctrinal reawakening that is being witnessed in the Indian military in the following three articles:
   - Factors precipitating the post-1998 doctrinal reawakening among South Asian militaries.
   - Indian Army's "Cold Start" doctrine
   - Indian Navy's Maritime doctrine.

3. The Indian Navy's new doctrine was officially announced on June 23, 2004. With the Pakistan Air Force coming out with its Basic Air Power Doctrine in January this year and the Indian Army pitching in with its "Cold Start" doctrine in April, the year 2004 could well go down in the military history of the sub-continent as the "Year of the Doctrines."

4. According to Faizul Haque writing in "India working on new war doctrine," "This concept was first war-gamed during Exercise Vijay Chakra in the Thar desert by Gen. Oberoi in 2001 and synergised between the three forces during Exercise Brahmastra later that year." http://www.nation.com.pk/daily/Mar-2004/7/main/top1.asp.

5. The Indian Army's three dedicated Strike Corps include I Corps that is headquartered at Mathura, II Corps that is located at Ambala and XXI Corps which has its peacetime headquarters in Bhopal.

6. Dr. Subhash Kapila, "Indian Army's new 'cold start' war doctrine strategically reviewed-Part II (Additional Imperatives)." Accessible on the internet at http://www.saag.org/papers11/paper1013.html. Part-I of this series of two articles by Dr. Subash Kapila can be accessed on the internet at http://www.saag.org/papers10/paper991.html.

7. *Daily Times Monitor*, April 16, 2004, "Indian Army commanders discuss 'cold start.'" http://www.dailytimes.com.pk/default.asp?page=story_16-4-2004_pg1_3.

8. Dr. Subhash Kapila, "Indian Army's new 'cold start' war doctrine strategically reviewed." Part I of two articles. Accessible on the internet at http://www.saag.org/papers10/paper991.html.

9. Ibid. Dr. Kapila further elaborates on this theme by writing, "The offensive military power available with defensive corps in the form of independent armoured brigades and mechanised brigades, by virtue of their forward locations would no longer remain idle waiting to launch counterattacks. They would be employed at the first go and mobilised within hours."

10. Firdaus Ahmed, "The calculus of 'Cold start,'" May 2004. http://www.indiatogether.org/cgi-bin/tools/pfriend.cgi.

11. Pinaki Bhattacharya, "Army chief floats 'new war doctrine.'" http://www.hardnewsmedia.com/may2004/army.php.

12. *Daily Times*, May 8, 2004. Op-Ed written by Brigadier (retired) Shaukat Qadir. Text can be accessed at http://www.dailytimes.com.pk/default.asp?page=story_8-5-2004_pg3_3.

13. *Daily Times*, July 1, 2004, "Indian Army May Create Nuclear Unit." http://actnow.saferworld.org/ctt.asp?u=1434524&l=43318.

15 Indian Navy's "Maritime" Doctrine

Introduction

Following in the footsteps of the Indian Army which announced its "Cold Start" doctrine on April 28, 2004, reports appeared in the press around the same time regarding the Indian Navy's attempts at formulating a doctrine for itself. After a gap of almost two months, the Indian Navy unveiled its "Maritime Doctrine" on June 23, 2004.

This is a significant development on two accounts; firstly because it is the first ever naval doctrine that the Indian Navy has formulated and secondly, because it envisions a significantly greater role for the Indian Navy than was currently envisioned. Specifically, it delves into the realm of extra-regional or "blue-water" operations and also contends that as an established leg of the nuclear triad envisioned in the Indian Draft Nuclear Doctrine, the Indian Navy must be provided the capability of carrying and employing nuclear weapons in order to provide India with a credible "second strike" capability. The aim of this article is to assess the salient aspects of the Indian Navy's Maritime Doctrine.[1]

Factors Influencing the Formulation of the Indian Maritime Doctrine

While the generic reasons for the recently seen doctrinal reawakening amongst South Asian militaries have been elaborated in Chapter 13, those that have specifically contributed to or caused the enunciation of the Indian naval doctrine are listed below:

- In view of the growing debate in India over the role that each military Service is aspiring for in the nuclearised milieu of South Asia, both the Indian Army and the IAF had already gained a foothold while the Indian Navy had not.
- Maritime reach and force projection are considered to be essential attributes of any major global power and as such, India's quest to transform itself from a subregional country to a power possessing regional or higher status requires the availability of a strong navy.
- In order for the Indian Navy to maintain its relevance, it was considered vital that it be assigned a significant strategic military role and function.
- Since the increasingly educated middle class in India could be expected to influence the country's political leadership significantly, it is necessary for the Services that consider themselves to have been overlooked, to take their respective cases to the public. The enunciation of a doctrinal document and offering it for public debate is one of the most effective means of achieving this.
- With India's vastly improving economy and rapidly increasing budgetary allocations for defence, the Services have to strengthen their bid for a greater share of the financial resources and having a viable doctrine

affords a suitable starting point for these efforts. This is because a doctrinal document not only addresses the aspect of development plans but also presents them in a justifiable manner.

- The emergence of geo-economics as the main determinant of interstate relations necessitates the availability of adequate naval potential to ensure that the sea lines of communication (SLOCs) are secured against any type of interference or interdiction by hostile navies. This is especially relevant for India which is predicted to encounter enormous energy shortfalls in the coming years, and cannot afford that her maritime link with the Persian Gulf be obstructed or tampered with in any manner.

- Post-9/11 involvement of the Indian Navy in joint naval patrols with the US and other navies has highlighted the increased role that it can play in regulating the oceans around Indian shores and in the adjacent waters. The creation of the Far Eastern Naval Command (FENC) at Port Blair in the Andaman and Nicobar Islands has afforded India the ability to also monitor the strategic Straits of Malacca.

- Although not entirely correct, the Indian Navy has also harped on the theme of the increased threat that it faces from the navies of Pakistan and China as a justification for force structure enhancements and additions.

- The high degree of freedom with which the US and Coalition navies have maintained their presence in the Indian Ocean has also served to highlight to the Indian Navy, the enormous clout and influence that it could enjoy were it to be provided with the requisite wherewithal and capabilities.

Salient Aspects of the Indian Maritime Doctrine

The foremost aspect of the Indian Maritime Doctrine is to justify a strategic nuclear role for the Indian Navy. In this context, the new doctrine makes several important assertions:

- The Navy is the most potent force to launch an attack with nuclear weapons whenever the situation demands. Moreover, it is convinced that a launch pad in the high seas is preferable since it minimises collateral damage as compared to land-based nuclear delivery systems.[2]

- Even at sea, the nuclear delivery potential should be embodied in the submarines rather than in the surface vessels of the naval fleet. One Indian journalist qualifies this by writing, "The Indian government is in covert talks with the Russians to lease two Akula class nuclear submarines (that have both longer undersea duration and ability to fire nuclear weapons) and has, for nearly two decades, been engaged in making its own nuclear submarine coded Advanced Technical Vehicle."[3]

- Capable of remaining submerged, the nuclear-capable submarines would be the most difficult of the nuclear delivery platforms to detect and engage.

This enhances their relevance as a credible "second strike" capability.

- The freedom of manoeuvre and positioning that is available to nuclear capable submarines significantly enhances the spectrum of targets that can be engaged with nuclear weapons by the Indian military forces.
- Interestingly, in line with India's self-perpetuated vision of herself as a regional power of significance, the new doctrine moves away from the inward-looking focus of earlier naval doctrinal thoughts and specifies developing capabilities to deal with "conflict with an extra-regional power" and, even more ambitiously, "protecting persons of Indian Origin and Indian interests abroad."[4]
- In view of the foregoing, the Indian Navy's doctrine stipulates the primary mission for itself as the provision of conventional and strategic nuclear deterrence against regional states. Interestingly, it also talks of being able to raise the cost of intervention by extra-regional powers and deter them from acting against India's security interests.
- The maritime doctrine also calls for exercising sea control in designated areas of the Arabian Sea and the Bay of Bengal in order to safeguard country's mercantile, marine and sea-borne trade and also to provide security to India's coastline, island territories and offshore assets.
- According to the new doctrine, the main strategy of the Indian Navy would remain "sea control" along with an increased resort to "sea denial" for the hostile navies that it encounters.[5]
- In line with its enhanced presence and "blue-water" aspirations, the doctrine also envisions increasing cooperation with other navies to combat emerging international common concerns like terrorism, transportation of weapons of mass destruction, sea piracy and drug trafficking.6
- In accordance with its vision of an enhanced role, the doctrine also calls for the development of adequate amphibious capability that would enable the Indian Navy to mount sizeable amphibious assaults against Pakistan.

Analysis of the Indian Navy's "Maritime Doctrine"

The most serious shortfall in the new doctrine is the disconnect that exists between the assets that it currently possesses and the capabilities that the new doctrine envisages. According to one source, "There is a considerable gap between the vision of the doctrine and its assets on the ground. With only one new aircraft carrier on the horizon and a shortfall of new ships due to production delays,[7] India's defence planners must consider nurturing an indigenous private defence production industry in general and naval shipyards in particular."[8]

In the past, the slogan that the "Indian Ocean belongs to India" has given rise to suspicions among other regional states regarding Indian "hegemonic" designs. If not explained and articulated correctly, the new doctrine's emphasis on blue water and extra-regional naval operations of the Indian Navy will further accentuate these perceptions.[9]

While the Indian Navy's assertion regarding its claim on a strategic nuclear role is plausible, its assertion that an increasingly powerful Pakistan Navy poses it a major regional threat is ridiculous, to say the least since, while the Indian Navy falls among the top 10 navies of the world, the combat potential of the Pakistan Navy is negligible in comparison with it.[10]

Since the Indian Maritime Doctrine is focused more on power projection in accordance with India's vision of herself as an emerging regional/global power of consequence, the political and diplomatic connotations of the new doctrine appear to be more well-defined than the purely military aspects. The Indian Navy, therefore, expects to be employed more as an instrument of political coercion and military force projection rather than being just another instrument of war like the other two Services.

Summary

The Indian Navy's "Maritime Doctrine" is little more than an attempt at asserting that notwithstanding the lack of importance that has been accorded to it during the recent past, it remains an essential instrument of the Indian military and as such needs to be treated as one. Concerned over having been left out of the strategic nuclear operations by the IAF and the Indian Army, it is out to claim its rightful place in that sphere of operations by highlighting that true "second strike capability" and hence effective deterrence can only be provided by submarine-launched nuclear warhead equipped missiles.

While the overall theme of the doctrine appears to be the quest for more funds in order to fulfil the requirements of becoming a blue-water navy, the new doctrine appears more in line with India's recent aspirations to carve out a more important spot for herself in the international global arena.

As regards the Pakistan Navy, the new Indian Maritime Doctrine definitely merits an in-depth analysis that would help not only in charting out the future development plans of the Pakistan Navy but also in determining its operational doctrine for any future military conflict against India in the foreseeable future.

Conclusion

The year 2004 has been one of doctrinal change as far as the Indian armed forces are concerned, with both the Indian Army and the Indian Navy coming out with their respective doctrines. It has also been reported that the IAF is also giving final touches to its doctrine and would announce it soon. This spurt of doctrinal work among the Indian militaries was what encouraged me to explore this subject further. In Chapters 13 to 17, my endeavour has been to first elaborate on all the factors that have contributed to this doctrinal transformation in the Indian military before venturing on to analysing the Indian Army's "Cold Start" doctrine and the Indian Navy's "Maritime" doctrine in detail. It is hoped that these analyses would encourage Pakistan's doctrinal thinkers towards analysing these new Indian military doctrines at greater length so that the necessary measures that Pakistan needs to take in order to counter these can be put in place before the next military conflict threatens to engulf South Asia.

Notes

1. The author has attempted to comprehensively cover the current doctrinal reawakening that is being witnessed in the Indian armed forces in the following three articles that were published in the Defence Journal as three separate articles and in the US Army's Military Review as one collective piece http://edilly.com/e.p ?u=Oi8vcGliLm5pYy5pbi9hcmNoaWV2ZS9scmVZW5nL2x5cjIwMDMvcmphbjI wMDMvMDQwMTIwMDMvcjA0MDEyMDAzMy5odG1s&b=5&f=norefer:
   - Factors precipitating the post-1998 doctrinal reawakening of Indian Armed Forces.
   - Indian Army's "Cold Start" doctrine
   - Indian Navy's Maritime doctrine
2. Iftikhar Gilani, "Bharat Navy announces 'nuclear doctrine.'" http://www.pakdef. info/forum/showthread.php?p=48250#post48250.
3. Sujan Dutta, "Navy takes plunge for nuclear muscle." http://www.telegraphindia. com/1040624/asp/nation/story_3409050.asp.
4. Saikat Dutta, "Navy charts new course with first doctrine." *The Indian Express*, April 26, 2004.
5. "New naval doctrine stresses on developing nuclear triad," PTI press report available on the internet at http://www.outlookindia.com/pti_news.asp?id=230383.
6. Ibid.
7. http://timesofindia.indiatimes.com/articleshow/63833.cms"t"_ blank">productiondelays.
8. April 27, 2004, The Navy gets a new songbook http://www.paifamily.com/opinion/ archives/2004_ 04.html.
9. C. Raja Mohan "India's new naval doctrine." http://www.hinduonnet.com/thehindu/ thscrip/print.pl?file=2004042904801100.htm&date=2004/04/29/&prd=th&
10. According to "The Military Balance 2013," the Indian Navy has 15 submarines against 8 possessed by the Pakistan Navy and has 21 principal surface combatant vessels as against only 10 held by the Pakistan Navy. These holdings give the Indian Navy a significant 2:1 edge in submarines as well as in major surface combatant vessels. It is also relevant to mention that the Indian Navy's manpower strength of 55,000 is well over twice the Pakistan Navy's personnel strength of 25,000. Additionally, the Indian Navy has the advantage of possessing an aircraft carrier with a potent combat aircraft inventory while another one is on order from Russia. Pakistan Navy, on the other hand, neither possesses an aircraft carrier nor does it operate combat aircraft of its own and is dependent on the Pakistan Air Force for naval air support operations.

16

Indian Air Force's "Aerospace" Doctrine

Introduction

Having been established on October 8, 1932, the Indian Air Force has completed over eighty years of existence and is one of the oldest Air Forces of the world. The latest edition of the IAF's doctrine on which this Chapter is based, was published just in time for the recent Air Force Day that was celebrated in 2012.

One of the most significant aspects of this doctrinal document is the fact that the erstwhile Indian Air Force has now decided to refer to itself as the Indian Aerospace Force—partly in order to highlight its greater role and significance and partly, to indicate the strategic role that the service is now desirous of playing.

While mentioning its ability as well as preference to exploit "Space" as the newest dimension of warfare, the document mentions, "Space is no longer a frontier. The IAF has for long been aware of its importance in modern war fighting. It enables commanders to make decisions in the fog of war and provides the advantage of high ground."

IAF Doctrine Prepares for Star Wars Era

Space will be treated on an equal footing with air, land and sea in India's future defence strategy, according to the Indian Air Force's latest Air Power Doctrine. The initial IAF Doctrine that was based on the lessons drawn from the 1991 Gulf War, was first drawn up in 1995. It has now been modified to add the fourth dimension of space to the traditional three-dimensional air, land and sea conflict. The inclusion of the "Space" dimension has been introduced keeping in consideration future requirements, where the core compentencies of "space power" could encompass the operational domains of intelligence, surveillance, reconnaissance, battle management and weapon guidance.

Besides the pride of place accorded to space, another hallmark of the modified doctrine lies in the new weapons acquisition policy under which future inductions will not be prompted just by what potential adversaries are acquiring, but guided by long-term objectives.

Vision

The IAF's vision is to acquire strategic reach and capabilities across the spectrum of conflict that serve the ends of military diplomacy, nation building and enable force projection within India's strategic area of influence. In this endeavour, *People First, Mission Always* will be the IAF's guiding beacon.

Mission Statement

To be a modern, flexible and professional aerospace power with full spectrum capability to protect and further national interests and objectives.

Core Values

The IAF leadership has identified three core values that must govern whatever it does—in peace or war. These are: *Mission, Integrity & Excellence.*

Process of Development of the IAF Doctrine

The first air power doctrine of the IAF which was issued in October 1995 concentrated on topics such as: the theory of war, characteristics of air power and its relationship with strategy, various air campaigns, combat support operations and aspects related to prosecuting an air war. It provided an exhaustive narrative of the basics of air power employment. Taking into account, the considerable changes in technology and the evolving global security environment, the doctrine was revised with an update and an enhanced two-part publication was published in 2007. In keeping with the evolutionary nature of air power and the need to stay relevant across the spectrum of conflict in an interconnected environment, the need was felt to involve a greater number of national stakeholders other than merely the IAF personnel.

In the Foreword to the 2012 edition of the IAF Doctrine, Air Chief Marshal N. A. K. Browne, the Chief of the Air Staff of the IAF, wrote, "The basic doctrine of the IAF has been declassified and revised. It is reflective of the environment around us, and adopts a holistic approach towards the security paradigm that engulfs us, and is a sincere effort to reach out to a much wider audience which has an equal stake in the security and well-being of India. It is a foundational document which, hopefully, will help the reader understand the nuances of application of air power and lead to better understanding and appreciation of the capabilities of air power. Since a doctrine is not a dogma, it changes and evolves."

General

The IAF reckons that strategy can be effectively employed through the execution of the following three main aerial campaigns:
- Counter Air Operations Campaign
- Counter Surface Force Operations Campaign
- Strategic Campaign

In addition to these three main campaigns, the IAF lays a lot of emphasis on the continuing and omnipresent requirement of Combat Enabling Operations.

The document defines air power in the classic sense as "the total ability of a nation to assert its will through the medium of air" and defined air power doctrine as being a derivative of the fundamental principles that guide the application of air and space power and offers innovative ideas for the optimum exploitation of the medium.

In accordance with its desire for an enhanced role at the national as well as the international level through the inclusion of the "Space" medium, the doctrine asserts that in the modern-day context, "air power has evolved into aerospace power which can be defined as the product of aerospace capability and aerospace doctrine."

Impact of Technology on Aerospace Power

In an effort to stay linked with the historical perspective, the following lessons from the Cold War era are highlighted:

- A multitude of innovative technological enhancements have virtually revolutionised aerial warfare. Some of these innovations include the development of stealth platforms, precision navigation, extended reach, night sensors and significantly enhanced computing power.
- The increased exploitation of the Space medium has necessitated it becoming more closely integrated with warfare since it has now come to be utilised for a variety of functions, such as, Intelligence, Surveillance and Reconnaissance (ISR) functions, secure communications, integrated early warning, weather forecasting and navigation.
- The development of extremely accurate precision weapons that can be employed at very long range has made it possible for air power to cause strategic paralysis on the enemy.
- The development and deployment of Space-based assets has served to significantly enhance the potency of air power by increasing battlefield transparency.

The Changing Nature of Warfare

These monumental technological developments, the doctrinal document contends, have transformed the very nature of modern warfare by the following:

- While short duration wars did not afford enough time space for strategic effects to occur, there was a particular imperative for the creation of swift strategic effect. This was all the more relevant when operating in a nuclear environment and contending with nuclear thresholds.

- The ability of air power to create strategic outcomes without having to traverse or transit through ground terrain made it a primary instrument of choice.
- With technological advancement, air power provided the capabilities that linked tactical actions with strategic outcomes that could prove crucial, especially in short duration wars.
- Air power delivers best when used in synergy with the other components of military power leading to the transformation of linear warfare into non-linear warfare. The increased *focus today is on knowledge and effect* and to apply forces synergistically *to achieve the desired outcome in the shortest period of time, with minimum casualties and collateral damage.*
- From attrition oriented operations, warfare concepts have rapidly moved towards *Effects Based Operations*, with functional paralysis the more desirable end result, rather than the physical destruction of target systems.
- With increasing globalisation, power concepts are moving away from territorial acquisitions to the extracting of political/economic concessions.
- The *Revolution in Military Affairs* has transformed the role of technology and doctrines in fighting wars. The aim now is to isolate the enemy's command and control structures, augment psychological warfare and precision strikes on the critical vulnerabilities deep inside enemy territory. *These changes favour employment of air power more than any other form of military power.* As such, *air power today applies parallel force at all levels of war.*
- The contemporary global environment is characterised by change and the future is expected to be no different.

The Importance of Joint Warfare

Warfare has become a coordinated and integrated tri-service affair in modern times. The IAF does not subscribe to the school of thought that believed that wars could be won entirely by air forces since that is generally based on the experiences of air forces pitted against markedly inferior militaries with little or no air power capabilities. In India's case, it is clear that air power alone cannot win a war, but at the same time, no modern war can be won without it. The IAF doctrine states that joint operations are the only way to achieve political objectives in modern conflict with air power remaining the linchpin of any joint application of combat power in modern warfare.

This assertion is borne out by the fact that in almost every war fought since independence, the IAF has played a significant, and at times a pivotal role. It is also clear that air power can best be exploited not only in synergy with the other two components of the military, but also in tandem with diplomatic efforts and other national civil processes. The spectrum of modern conflict is significantly different and modern wars, whether conventional or sub-conventional (with or without a nuclear overhang) cannot be won singly by any one of the three primary components of military power.

Characteristics of Air Power
- Flexibility & Versatility
- Mobility
- Responsiveness
- Shock Effect
- Reach
- Offensive Action
- Concentration

Limitations of Air Power
- Sustainability
- Base Dependency
- Sensitivity to Technology
- Weather
- Impermanency
- Political Constraints
- Vulnerability

Sources of Air Power
- Air Force
- Air Arm
- Space
- Civil Air Resources

Air Power Doctrine and the IAF
- Military doctrine could be defined as "a set of fundamental principles

by which military forces direct their actions in the quest of national objectives."

- Doctrine is authoritative but its application requires judgment.
- An air force doctrine determines the manner in which air forces organise, train, equip, fight and sustain their forces.
- Air power doctrine enunciates the "fundamental principles that guide the employment of air power elements to achieve national objectives." It is a statement of officially sanctioned beliefs, war fighting principles and terminology that determines and directs the correct use of air forces in military operations.

Structure of Air Power

Air strategy could be termed as the process of coordinating the development, deployment and employment of air power assets to achieve national security objectives.

Air power with its intrinsic characteristics of speed, elevation and reach provides tremendous strategic options. These strategies are then prosecuted by air campaigns which comprise a variety of air operations.

As aerial warfare evolved and the importance of command of the air grew, a distinctive strategic area for application for air power emerged. This involved operations to deter, contain or defeat the enemy's air power, a strategy which came to be termed as "counter-air."

Air forces can also be employed both independently of, and in coordination with, the surface forces to attack vital target systems.

The purpose of an independent strategy was to weaken the enemy's ability to wage war and degrade his will to resist by attacking his sources of power.

Air forces have undertaken to prosecute all the three air strategies simultaneously, although the resources devoted to each have varied considerably. Therefore, air strategy would encompass all these options.

The operations mounted to prosecute the independent strategy came to be known as the "strategic bombing campaign," while those mounted to prosecute the auxiliary strategy were termed "tactical air support," or more recently as a "counter-surface force campaign."

Counter-air, strategic air and counter-surface force operations are the three elements of air strategy.

In contrast, the purpose of the coordinated strategy was to help friendly surface forces contain or defeat the enemy's land and naval forces.

Air Campaigns

Since each of these strategies is meant to achieve a specific aim, and does so by using distinct methods, its prosecution requires a dedicated "campaign." Hence, an air commander may have to wage three distinct but interdependent air campaigns in pursuit of his chosen air strategy.

The sheer flexibility and versatility of modern aerial platforms and weapons allow a commander to conduct parallel operations by prosecuting all campaigns simultaneously.

Normally, control of the air should be the first priority for air forces. This permits own air and surface forces to operate more effectively and denies the same to the enemy. The required degree of control is achieved through counter-air operations.

The strategic air campaign consists of *conventional* and *nuclear* operations.

Air mobility operations that would form part of the combat enabling operations.

The counter air campaign comprises two basic air operations: *Offensive Counter-Air* (OCA) and *Defensive Counter-Air* (DCA).

Air Campaigns and Support Operations

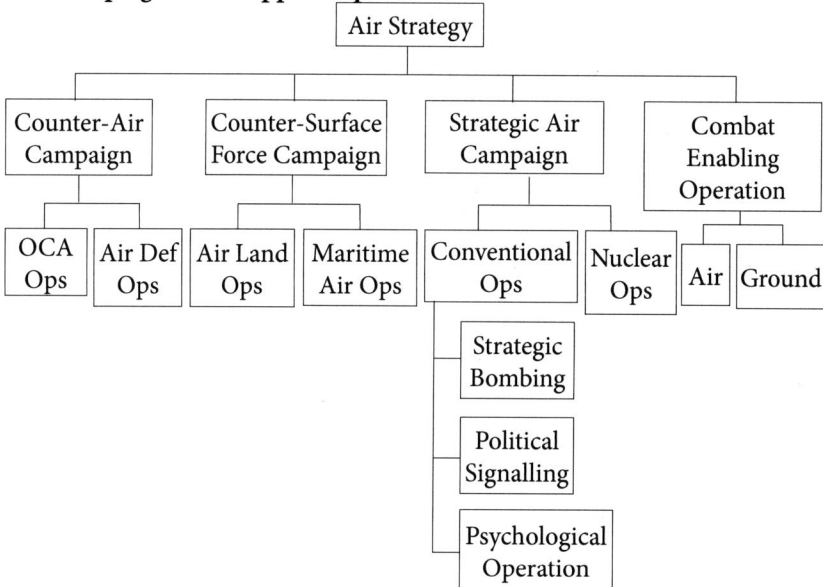

Operational Art

Operational strategy employs the forces earmarked for the military/air campaigns. It can be defined as the art and science of planning, orchestrating and directing military/air campaigns within a theatre to achieve national security objectives.

Whilst the air strategy is developed at the Air HQ, the operational art for employing air power is evolved at IAF Command HQs. For successful execution of operational art a commander must have:

- An understanding of civil military affairs and media management
- An awareness of the national security environment and the political aims
- A clear grasp of the military aim and the strategy
- Technological awareness

Tactics

- Tactics are the art and science of employing forces at the battlefield.
- Tactics are employed on the battlefield while operational strategy brings the forces to the battlefield.
- Tactics must keep pace with advancements in technology and weapons.
- Tactics should be designed to exploit the capabilities of equipment and weapon systems to enhance effectiveness and reduce vulnerabilities. However, in some circumstances, equipment may need to be adapted to fulfil tactical requirements.
- Innovative and unpredictable tactics will always produce positive results.

Inter-Relationships within Air Campaigns

- Each air campaign includes conduct of *specific air operations*, which encompass various tactical level air power functions or "roles."
- For example, the combat roles needed to prosecute OCA include suppression of enemy air defences (SEAD), *airfield attacks, fighter sweeps* and *escorts*.
- To be fully effective these missions need to be enabled by electronic warfare assets, surveillance and reconnaissance information, airborne warning and control systems (AWACS), air-to-air refuelling (AAR) and at times air transport support.
- Combat roles tend to be specific to a particular air operation, combat enabling air roles can apply to many, if not to all, air operations, while

ground support activities apply to all air operations.
- Also necessary are a sound command, control, communications and intelligence system, ground defences, maintenance, logistics and administrative support.
- The air power roles are accomplished through a series of tasks, which involve a number of missions and each mission may involve one or more sorties.

The Structure of Air Power and its Inter-Relationships

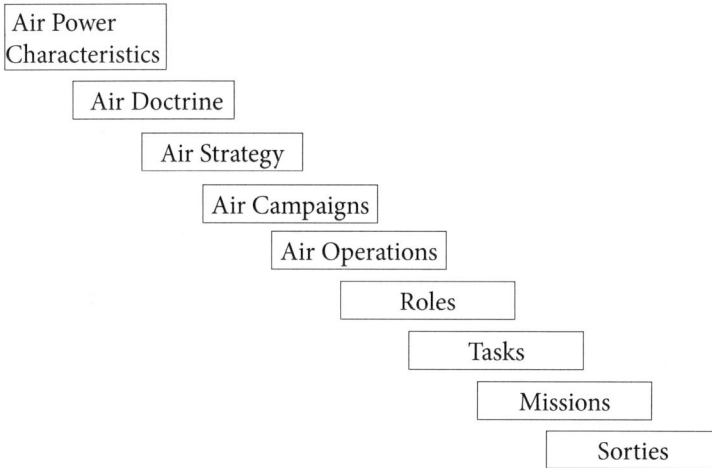

Air Power Characteristics

Air Doctrine

Air Strategy

Air Campaigns

Air Operations

Roles

Tasks

Missions

Sorties

The Structure of Air Power

Air Campaigns and Enabling Functions
- Control of the Air
- Application of Combat Power
- Sustaining Combat
- Enhancing Combat Power

Roles
- During operations, achieve control of the air to the required degree to provide full freedom of action to the air and surface forces.
- Applying direct pressure on the enemy's power of resistance by attacking his crucial centres of gravity.
- Synergising the combat potential of air power with that of the surface

forces to achieve joint military aims and objectives.

- Providing viable second-strike capability in case of a nuclear attack.
- Assisting the government in disaster management or humanitarian relief tasks.
- Executing counterterrorism and counter-insurgency operations.
- Fulfilling international commitments requiring air power assets, consistent with our national policies and interests.
- Deploying and employing forces to protect and project the national interests in any out of country contingency operation.

Summary

The objective of this Chapter was to present a synoptic introduction to the new IAF Aerospace Power doctrine and not to analyse it. Having perused it though, I feel that a more detailed analysis is definitely warranted.

- The IAF aerospace power doctrine does not make any reference whatsoever to several recent air power campaigns.
- It focuses purely on conventional air power operations and does not even allude to strategic operations in the nuclear realm (probably that portion has been included in the classified portion of the IAF aerospace doctrine).
- Insinuates that conventional weapons and platforms could also be employed in the strategic role.
- Mentions several half-truths specifically when referring to Indo-Pak conflicts.
- No mention whatsoever of tactical nuclear weapons.
- Appears to be driven more by technology rather than by concepts.
- Emphasis on helicopter employment for a variety of roles.
- Emphasis on combat enabling operations.
- The realm of Space has apparently been included in this doctrine more to enhance the status of the IAF and to preclude the other Services laying stake to it.

17 Draft Indian Nuclear Doctrine

On August 17, 1999, Indian national security adviser, Brajesh Mishra, released a draft report from the National Security Advisory Board on Indian Nuclear Doctrine. The report, which outlines in broad terms India's rationale and intentions regarding the development of its "minimum nuclear deterrent," has not been formally approved by the caretaker government of Prime Minister Atal Bihari Vajpayee. Below is the full text of the draft doctrine.

Preamble

The use of nuclear weapons in particular as well as other weapons of mass destruction constitutes the gravest threat to humanity and to peace and stability in the international system. Unlike the other two categories of weapons of mass destruction, biological and chemical weapons which have been outlawed by international treaties, nuclear weapons remain instruments for national and collective security, the possession of which on a selective basis has been sought to be legitimised through permanent extension of the Nuclear Non-proliferation Treaty (NPT) in May 1995. Nuclear weapon states have asserted that they will continue to rely on nuclear weapons with some of them adopting policies to use them even in a non-nuclear context. These developments amount to virtual abandonment of nuclear disarmament. This is a serious setback to the struggle of the international community to abolish weapons of mass destruction.

India's primary objective is to achieve economic, political, social, scientific and technological development within a peaceful and democratic framework. This requires an environment of durable peace and insurance against potential risks to peace and stability. It will be India's endeavour to proceed towards this overall objective in cooperation with the global democratic trends and to play a constructive role in advancing the international system toward a just, peaceful and equitable order.

Autonomy of decision making in the developmental process and in strategic matters is an inalienable democratic right of the Indian people. India will strenuously guard this right in a world where nuclear weapons for a select few are sought to be legitimised for an indefinite future, and where there is growing complexity and frequency in the use of force for political purposes.

India's security is an integral component of its development process. India continuously aims at promoting an ever-expanding area of peace and stability around it so that developmental priorities can be pursued without disruption.

However, the very existence of offensive doctrine pertaining to the first use of nuclear weapons and the insistence of some nuclear weapons states on the legitimacy of their use even against non-nuclear weapon countries constitute a threat to peace, stability and sovereignty of states.

This document outlines the broad principles for the development, deployment and employment of India's nuclear forces. Details of policy and strategy concerning force structures, deployment and employment of nuclear forces will flow from this framework and will be laid down separately and kept under constant review.

Objectives

In the absence of global nuclear disarmament India's strategic interests require effective, credible nuclear deterrence and adequate retaliatory capability should deterrence fail. This is consistent with the UN Charter, which sanctions the right of self-defence.

The requirements of deterrence should be carefully weighed in the design of Indian nuclear forces and in the strategy to provide for a level of capability consistent with maximum credibility, survivability, effectiveness, safety and security.

India shall pursue a doctrine of credible minimum nuclear deterrence. In this policy of "retaliation only," the survivability of our arsenal is critical. This is a dynamic concept related to the strategic environment, technological imperatives and the needs of national security. The actual size components, deployment and employment of nuclear forces will be decided in the light of these factors. India's peacetime posture aims at convincing any potential aggressor that:

- any threat of use of nuclear weapons against India shall invoke measures to counter the threat: and
- any nuclear attack on India and its forces shall result in punitive retaliation with nuclear weapons to inflict damage unacceptable to the aggressor.

The fundamental purpose of Indian nuclear weapons is to deter the use and threat of use of nuclear weapons by any State or entity against India and its forces. India will not be the first to initiate a nuclear strike, but will respond with punitive retaliation should deterrence fail.

India will not resort to the use or threat of use of nuclear weapons against States which do not possess nuclear weapons, or are not aligned with nuclear weapon powers.

Deterrence requires that India maintain:

- Sufficient, survivable and operationally prepared nuclear forces,
- a robust command and control system,
- effective intelligence and early warning capabilities, and
- comprehensive planning and training for operations in line with the strategy, and
- the will to employ nuclear forces and weapons.

Highly effective conventional military capabilities shall be maintained to raise the threshold of outbreak both of conventional military conflict as well as that of threat or use of nuclear weapons.

Nuclear Forces

India's nuclear forces will be effective, enduring, diverse, flexible, and responsive to the requirements in accordance with the concept of credible minimum deterrence. These forces will be based on a triad of aircraft, mobile land-based missiles and sea-based assets in keeping with the objectives outlined above. Survivability of the forces will be enhanced by a combination of multiple redundant systems, mobility, dispersion and deception.

The doctrine envisages assured capability to shift from peacetime deployment to fully employable forces in the shortest possible time, and the ability to retaliate effectively even in a case of significant degradation by hostile strikes.

Credibility and Survivability

The following principles are central to India's nuclear deterrent:

Credibility: Any adversary must know that India can and will retaliate with sufficient nuclear weapons to inflict destruction and punishment that the aggressor will find unacceptable if nuclear weapons are used against India and its forces.

Effectiveness: The efficacy of India's nuclear deterrent be maximised through synergy among all elements involving reliability, timeliness, accuracy and weight of the attack.

Survivability:
- India's nuclear forces and their command and control shall be organised for very high survivability against surprise attacks and for rapid punitive response. They shall be designed and deployed to ensure survival against a first strike and to endure repetitive attrition attempts with adequate retaliatory capabilities for a punishing strike which would be unacceptable to the aggressor.
- Procedures for the continuity of nuclear command and control shall ensure a continuing capability to effectively employ nuclear weapons.

Command and Control

Nuclear weapons shall be tightly controlled and released for use at the highest political level. The authority to release nuclear weapons for use resides in the person of the Prime Minister of India, or the designated successor(s).

An effective and survivable command and control system with requisite flexibility and responsiveness shall be in place. An integrated operational plan, or a series of sequential plans, predicated on strategic objectives and a targeting policy shall form part of the system.

For effective employment the unity of command and control of nuclear forces including dual capable delivery systems shall be ensured.

The survivability of the nuclear arsenal and effective command, control, communications, computing, intelligence and information (C4I2) systems shall be assured.

The Indian defence forces shall be in a position to execute operations in an NBC environment with minimal degradation.

Space based and other assets shall be created to provide early warning, communications, damage/detonation assessment.

Security and Safety

Security: Extraordinary precautions shall be taken to ensure that nuclear weapons, their manufacture, transportation and storage are fully guarded against possible theft, loss, sabotage, damage or unauthorised access or use.

Safety is an absolute requirement and tamper proof procedures and systems shall be instituted to ensure that unauthorised or inadvertent activation/use of nuclear weapons does not take place and risks of accident are avoided.

Disaster control: India shall develop an appropriate disaster control system capable of handling the unique requirements of potential incidents involving nuclear weapons and materials.

Research and Development

India should step up efforts in research and development to keep up with technological advances in this field.

While India is committed to maintain the deployment of a deterrent which is both minimum and credible, it will not accept any restraints on building its R&D capability.

Disarmament and Arms Control

Global, verifiable and non-discriminatory nuclear disarmament is a national security objective. India shall continue its efforts to achieve the goal of a nuclear weapon-free world at an early date.

Since no-first use of nuclear weapons is India's basic commitment, every effort shall be made to persuade other States possessing nuclear weapons to join an international treaty banning first use.

Having provided unqualified negative security assurances, India shall work for internationally binding unconditional negative security assurances by nuclear weapon states to non-nuclear weapon states.

Nuclear arms control measures shall be sought as part of national security policy to reduce potential threats and to protect our own capability and its effectiveness.

In view of the very high destructive potential of nuclear weapons, appropriate nuclear risk reduction and confidence building measures shall be sought, negotiated and instituted.

Indian Nuclear Doctrine: January 2003 Statement
- Building and maintaining a credible minimum deterrent;
- A posture of "No First Use": nuclear weapons will only be used in retaliation against a nuclear attack on Indian territory or on Indian forces anywhere;
- Nuclear retaliation to a first strike will be massive and designed to inflict unacceptable damage.
- Nuclear retaliatory attacks can only be authorised by the civilian political leadership through the Nuclear Command Authority.
- Non-use of nuclear weapons against non-nuclear weapon states;
- However, in the event of a major attack against India, or Indian forces anywhere, by biological or chemical weapons, India will retain the option of retaliating with nuclear weapons.[1]

Conclusions[2]
"Credible Minimum Deterrence" is highly elastic.
- Pakistani FU doctrine and procurement goals reflects parochial interests of military and goal displacement.
- Indian nuclear doctrine—strongly influenced by US Doctrine—is moving away from strict NFU.
- Resulting nuclear operations are dangerous.
- Significant room for arms racing, crisis instability, and inadvertent escalation in the future.

Notes
1. "The Cabinet Committee on Security Reviews operationalization of India's Nuclear Doctrine." Ministry of External Affairs, Government of India . January 4, 2003. http://meaindia.nic.in/pressrelease/2003/01/04pr01.htm
2. Scott Sagan, "The Evolution of Indian and Pakistani Nuclear Doctrine" May 7, 2008. http://belfercenter.ksg.harvard.edu/files/uploads/Sagan_MTA_Talk_050708.pdf

18 The Indian Ballistic Missile Programme

Introduction

The Indian missile programme actually predates the Indian space programme by at least four years. The Defence Research and Development Organisation (DRDO) which conducted initial research in missiles was set up in 1958 whereas the Indian National Committee for Space Research (INCOSPAR) was organised in 1962. In 1969, INCOSPAR was reorganised into the Indian Space Research Organisation (ISRO). As such, the Indian space and missile programmes were relatively independent of each other. In fact, in some instances, the managers of these two programmes have actually been competing against each other for allocation of resources.

However, this did not prevent cooperation or even transfer of technology or personnel from one programme to the other. Indeed it is evident that the nuclear missile programme benefited from the civilian space programme and depended on several crucial technologies which had been developed in the civilian space programme.

Linkages between Indian Space and Missile Programmes

The missile programme benefited from the space programme in three ways:
- **Personality**. Dr. Avul Fakir Jainulabdeen Abdul Kalam. (He began his career in DRDO, and moved to ISRO and then back to DRDO.) Widely heralded as the father of the Indian Missile Programme, this eminent scientist has also served for a tenure in the largely ceremonial post of the President of India.
- **Management**. The National "consortium" approach. The Integrated Guided Missile Development Programme (IGMDP) management structure is similar to the one used by ISRO for its original Satellite Launch Vehicle (SLV-3) programme.
- **Technology**. Use of fuel and engines. The first stage of the Agni missile is the same as the first stage of the SLV-3.

Rationale for the Indian Missile Programme

- Prestige rationale
- Political rationale
- Technology rationale
- Military rationale

Prestige Rationale for the Programme

Nuclear capable missiles are prestigious for several reasons:

- Seen as evidence of India's technical prowess and scientific competence (especially when compared to the lower level of technology and development in other sectors, i.e., infrastructure).
- This capability was developed despite efforts to prevent India from acquiring the necessary technology (through a variety of control regimes).
- The missiles are seen as essential to enabling India's admission to the clubs of the select few (such as the UN Security Council) to be taken seriously.
- India also points to the continued dependence on missiles by the middle level powers, such as France and Britain, for purely prestige reasons.

Political Rationale for the Programme
- In the run-up to the election campaign in 1989, Rajiv Gandhi's government ran advertisements showing the first launch of the Agni missile and acclaiming it as one of their major achievements.
- Politicians witnessing the second Agni test on May 29, 1992 (which failed to meet the test parameters) asked the scientists to declare it as a "success" for domestic political consumption.
- International political rationale: seen as a "bargaining chip" to participate in missile related arms control and disarmament agreements which is likely to include only those countries that possess nuclear missiles.

Technological Rationale for the Programme
Success of the nuclear missile programme is seen as critical for the continued funding and patronage of not only the other missiles in the IGMDP but also for the other DRDO projects by the political and bureaucratic establishment.

The success of the nuclear missile programme should not be seen in isolation but in the broader context of the other ambitious DRDO projects, such as the Light Combat Aircraft (LCA) and the Arjun Main Battle Tank (MBT).

One of DRDO's official mandates is "to develop critical components, technologies ... and to reduce the vulnerabilities of major programmes (such as missiles) ... from various sanctions/denial regimes, instituted by advanced countries."

Provided the model to create a "consortium" approach and the related management structure which was replicated for other DRDO projects.

Military Rationale for the Programme

The use of conventionally armed surface-to-surface missiles (SSMs) in conflicts with similar to India's regional setting, such as the Arab-Israel and Iran-Iraq wars, did influence the initial impetus for the IGMDP. Subsequently, the effective military role played by conventionally armed missiles, particularly in Operation Desert Storm in 1991 (where 32 Army Tactical Missile System [ATACMS] projectiles were successfully used against Iraqi logistic sites, bridges as well as artillery and rocket battery positions) and the use of Tomahawk missiles in August 1998 against suspected terrorist camps in Afghanistan also validated the strategic and tactical role of Indian missiles.

The Pakistan Factor. While the Indian programme may have originated on account of a domestic and technical impetus, the appearance of similar programmes on the other side of the border did provide a post-facto rationale.

The China Factor. India's missile programme is also seen as a response to the direct threat posed by China's own missiles as well as the indirect threat posed by the supply of Chinese missiles to Pakistan and Saudi Arabia.

Technological Achievements of the Indian Missile Programme

Consortium Approach. The Indian missile programme brought together sixty-four participating institutions and five types of partners:

- The users—the three Services.
- The defence laboratories—19 of these.
- Other scientific organisations such as ISRO.
- Academic institutes such as the Indian Institutes of Technology (IITs).
- Around 30 different industrial organisations.

One of the objectives of the missile programme was to identify certain "critical technologies" and to ensure self-sufficiency. The following five critical technologies were identified:

- Phase shifters for radars.
- Impact diodes (to be used as high frequency power sources)
- Carbon composites to withstand the heat of re-entry.
- Sensors for guidance systems.
- Computerised fluid dynamic models.

The Prithvi Ballistic SSM System

Type of missile/ service	Status	Nuclear capable/ range/payload	Remarks
SS-150 Prithvi-I (Army)		Yes/150 km/1,000 kg	Inducted into service in 1995 in the newly established 333rd Missile Group that was created in 1993 and stationed at Secunderabad during peacetime. The Indian Army reportedly placed an order for the production of 75 Prithvi-I missiles. More than 15 tests of the Prithvi-I missile system have so far been conducted.
SS-250 Prithvi-II (Air Force)		Yes/250 km/500 kg	Since the Indian Air Force was dissatisfied with the limited range of the Prithvi-I (most PAF targets of relevance are located at ranges greater than 150 kilometres from the likely Prithvi launch sites), it opted for a reduced warhead size of 50% in order to achieve double the range.
SS-350 Prithvi-III (Navy)		Yes/350 km/500 kg	This weapon has also been referred to at various places as the Dhanush and was developed due to the Indian Navy's requirement for a longer range tactical ballistic missile system. The Indian Navy, like the IAF, wanted a longer range version of the Prithvi and was willing to compromise on the warhead size in order to achieve it.

The Prithvi System's Need for Excessive Vehicular Support Apparatus
One of the major and very serious limitations that the Indian Army's SS-150 Prithvi-I ballistic missile suffers from is its requirement for a very huge vehicular support apparatus. A list of the support vehicles that are required to bring the Prithvi-I system to a state of operationalisation, is listed below:

- Missile Transporter
- Warhead Carrier Vehicle
- Missile Launcher
- Mobile Crane
- Missile Handling Trolley
- Launch Control Centre
- Power Supply Vehicle
- Cable Laying Vehicle
- Mosaic
- Safety Vehicle
- Mechanical Workshop Vehicle
- Air Compressor Vehicle
- Air Storage Vehicle
- Oxidiser Transfer Vehicle
- Fuel Transfer Vehicle
- Fuel Carrier Vehicle

Considering the enormous logistic implications and the nightmarish support needs of the Prithvi system, its deployability will be seriously hindered. Moreover, the enormous support wherewithal for a typical Prithvi deployment would make it much easier to being detected and attacked by the enemy.

The Agni Ballistic SSM System

Type	Status	Nuclear Capable or not?	Range/Payload
Agni-I	First tested in May 1989 and technology demonstrator developed	Yes	2,000 km/1,000 kg
Agni-II	First tested in April 1999 and planned to be operationalised	Yes	2,500-3,000 km/1,000 kg
Agni-III	Under development	Yes	3,500 km/1,000 kg

As is apparent from the above data, all the versions of the Agni SSM are capable of carrying nuclear warheads but their range makes them more suitable for employment against distant Chinese mainland targets rather than the Pakistani targets that are located at much shorter ranges and can be effectively engaged by the Prithvi system.

Military Implications

Given India's stated objective of creating a "minimum credible deterrence" and a "no first use" commitment (which also implies a "second strike" capability), do the Agni and the Prithvi missile systems provide this capability?

To some extent, the road mobile Prithvi is a Pakistan specific system (currently based at Secunderabad) and does provide this capability. However, the long preparation time and the need to launch it from pre-designated and prepared sites makes its survivability in a sudden first strike extremely questionable.

The planned railroad deployment of the rail-mobile Agni does provide an element of survivability. However, with its current range the missile can only be fired from a limited number of areas to strike targets in China. This makes both, its credibility and survivability, doubtful.

Therefore, at present the ideal way for India to ensure a minimum credible deterrence and a second-strike capability is not to deploy these missiles in an overt and operational fashion but to retain them in a recessed and covert fashion.

Future of the Indian Missile Programme

India is likely to pursue the development of a classic nuclear triad, with air, land and sea components. However, the shape and size of the triad will not be driven by strategic requirements but by technological capabilities.

India's attempt would be to create longer range missiles; the ideal range would be between 3,500 and 4,500 km and India is unlikely to plan for a weapon system capable of traversing ranges of 5,000 km or more. India is also unlikely at this stage to develop miniaturised or MIRVed warheads. This is partly because such development would require additional testing of not only the warheads but also the re-entry vehicles. Moreover, the current Indian doctrine does not envisage this level of weaponisation.

As per current development plans, India is not expected to achieve a sea-launched MRBM capability in the foreseeable/near future.

Conclusion

The Indian Guided Missile Development Programme (IGMDP) has led to the successful development of the Prithvi and Agni surface-to-surface ballistic missiles systems. While the shorter range Prithvi SSM system is almost entirely Pakistan-specific, the longer-range Agni SSM system could be used against Chinese targets also.

One of the reasons for the Indian success in missile development has been their philosophy of pursuing space and missile research in an integrated manner since this has helped the development of both these specialities simultaneously with one benefiting from the other and vice versa.

Section V

Employment Considerations & Impact

19 Divergence in South Asian Nuclear Doctrinal Thinking

Although nuclear doctrinal thinking in South Asia picked up pace as an organised activity after the May 1998 nuclear tests, it would be incorrect to assume that some sort of rudimentary and basic nuclear doctrinal precepts had not been deliberated upon and finalised by India and Pakistan as they moved towards overt nuclearisation through the weaponisation of their nuclear potential. As such, the basis of their respective nuclear doctrines could be traced back to their motivation for developing nuclear weapons. Notwithstanding the facts that India has publicised a draft document regarding its nuclear doctrine and Pakistan remains quiet on this account, enough material can be gleaned from the statements and writings of scholars and involved individuals which permits the nuclear doctrinal thinking prevailing in the two arch-rivals to be compared.

In this chapter, I intend to analyse the factors that motivated the quest of India and Pakistan for nuclear weapons and use these motivating factors as the basis for highlighting the several significant differences that exist in their respective nuclear doctrinal thinking.

The primary motivational factors that propelled both India and Pakistan in their quest for nuclear weapons capability can be categorised into the Military, Political and Economic considerations and these have been discussed in the subsequent text.

Pakistan's Motivation for the Acquisition of Nuclear Weapons

Military Considerations
- Pakistan's need to balance the enormous conventional military advantage that India has always enjoyed over her. This need was reinforced by the following factors:
  - The conventional military defeat that Pakistan suffered at the hands of the combined Indian Army and Bangladeshi forces in 1971.
  - The availability to India of an unrestricted supply of latest military hardware from Russia with the same being denied to Pakistan by the Western countries.
  - The ability of India's booming progressing economy to sustain significantly higher expenditure on the development plans of its conventional military at a time when Pakistan's significantly weaker economic condition precluded any substantial increase in the her defence spending.

○ The rapidly widening gap between the conventional military potential of the two countries which was continuously tilting more and more in India's favour. Although this disparity has always been there, lately the magnitude of this imbalance has shifted further in favour of India considerably.

○ The possession of a nuclear weapon could deter India from mounting a conventional war and even if this deterrence were to fail, the threat of employment of nuclear weapons could possibly help bring the war to an end before the conditions were reached where the very existence of Pakistan as a state was threatened.

Political Considerations

- The imperative of being able to match Indian nuclear capability which was earlier demonstrated during the Peaceful Nuclear Explosion (PNE) of 1974. In this context, the following aspects need to be highlighted:

  ○ While India had enjoyed an edge in conventional military potential, its advantage fell far short of being of a decisive nature as had been amply proven by the previous conventional wars of 1948 and 1965 that had ended in virtual stalemates.[1]

  ○ With India likely to add nuclear prowess to her military capability, it would achieve a significant superiority over Pakistan which the latter could never hope to balance purely with conventional forces.

  ○ India was well on her way to becoming a major regional and global power with Pakistan simultaneously fading into irrelevance. By going nuclear, Pakistan would be able to reassert herself as a significant, if not a major regional player.

  ○ A nuclear Pakistan would be more comfortably placed for playing a more effective leadership role in the Islamic World.

  ○ The domestic political aspect must also not be lost sight of vis-à-vis Pakistan since the successful weaponisation of nuclear capability would go down extremely favourably with the masses.

Economic Considerations

- Pakistan's flagging and almost stagnant economy could not afford to bear the cost of a conventional arms race with India. Since matching India in the conventional military realm was neither possible nor feasible, recourse to nuclear weapons would be advantageous. Not only would the possession of nuclear weapons reduce the need for any further conventional military build-up but it could possibly result in some savings by reducing the amount that Pakistan was incurring on the maintenance of her conventional military forces.

- The booming Indian economy, however, has permitted the Indian military to embark on an unprecedented budgetary and procurement drive which is already well under way. Some analysts are of the opinion that this expansion drive is aimed at creating a decisive conventional imbalance in India's favour since Pakistan would be unable to match this weapons acquisition spree.

India's Motivation for the Acquisition of Nuclear Weapons

Military Considerations
- The superiority that India had enjoyed since 1947 and continues to enjoy in the conventional military domain was not of a degree where it could be termed as decisive against Pakistan. Considering her enormous size, population and resources, a conventional war ending in a stalemate amounted almost to a defeat while the weaker Pakistan could well justifiably term the same stalemate to be a victory.
- Access to nuclear weapons when combined with her conventional military superiority could make India reach a position of decisive advantage in the military realm against Pakistan.
- Without access to nuclear weapons, India could not hope to match the conventional military might of China.

Political Considerations
- India needed the added prestige of possessing nuclear weapons to strengthen her quest for a significantly greater role not only in the region but also in the world.
- With the enormous might of China immediately to her north, India required nuclear weapons to balance out China's growing influence in the region.
- India's growing right-wing politicians felt it was India's right to possess nuclear weapons in accordance with their vision, warped though it might be, of "Akhand Bharat" or a "Greater Hindustan."

Economic Considerations
- Poised as India was on the verge of a forceful entry into the global

economy, being a nuclear power would strengthen her position amongst the comity of nations.

Divergences in Indo-Pak Nuclear Doctrinal Thought

An analysis of the preceding discourse highlights that notwithstanding the political and economic considerations, Pakistan's prime motivating factors flowed out of its military considerations while those of India emerged from the latter's political and economic considerations. Understandably, therefore, while Pakistan considered her nuclear arsenal as a military weapon, India took hers to be an instrument of political power. Herein lay the basic differences in the nuclear doctrinal thinking of the two countries. I intend to cover the significant divergences in Indian and Pakistani nuclear doctrinal thinking under the following headings:

- Control of Nuclear Arsenal
- Degree of Secrecy/Ambiguity
- Deterrence Philosophy
- Employment Philosophy
- Threat Centricity/Focus
- Developmental Philosophy.

Control of Nuclear Arsenal

Since Pakistan considered her nuclear weapons to be military instruments, the authority to control and supervise these was automatically relegated to her military, specifically her Army, while in India the political leadership was able to retain control of the nuclear arsenal since they considered the nuclear weapons more to be an instrument of political rather than of military power. Although Pakistan did subsequently announce the establishment of a joint civilian-military National Command Authority (NCA),[2] the situation on the ground even today indicates that the Pakistan military, in general, and the Pakistan Army, in particular, are controlling and managing all aspects not only of the country's nuclear weapons programme but also her existing nuclear weapons arsenal.[3]

Degree of Secrecy/Ambiguity

This should be considered as a corollary to the above. Since military aspects are generally shrouded in secrecy and disclosed only on a selective or need-to-know basis, the total control of the Pakistan Army over Pakistan's nuclear weapons led to this programme being shrouded in a thick and impenetrable cloak of secrecy. Although the rationale of "ambiguity favours the weaker nation" has been justifiably put forward as an excuse for the reticence of the Pakistani leadership on the nuclear issue, the fact is that no clear and unambiguous statements have been forthcoming regarding Pakistan's nuclear policy, doctrine and employment philosophy.

The Indian political leadership, on the other hand, after consolidating its control over the nuclear weapons programme, immediately started working on a Nuclear Doctrine and publicised its draft version[4] barely a year after the May 1998 nuclear tests and opened up this crucial area not only for a nation-wide scrutiny but also for a global debate.

While some analysts said that the draft Indian Nuclear Doctrine *presents something of a puzzle,*[5] others contended that it *contained no surprises*[6] while one even termed it as *egregious exercise of bomb-rattling without responsibility.*[7] Notwithstanding these divergent views, however, the document has, over a period of time, been subjected to intense scrutiny and criticism, both positive and negative.

It is significant to mention here that despite almost a decade having passed since this draft was submitted to the Indian Government, it continues to remain just a draft with no official confirmation forthcoming from the Indian Government whatsoever regarding it being approved and accepted as the country's official Nuclear Doctrine.

Deterrence Philosophy

Since the basic motivation for Pakistan in her quest for nuclear weapons capability was the imperative of countering India's conventional military preponderance, Pakistan considers her nuclear weapons to be an instrument of military deterrence that would presumably preclude India's embarking on a conventional military operation against Pakistan. As such, Pakistan's nuclear deterrent is there primarily to ensure that India does not contemplate any conventional military adventure against her. Believers in the efficacy of this stratagem point to the Kargil Conflict of 1999 and the 2001-2002 stand-off between India and Pakistan as examples of situations where a full-scale India-Pakistan war was avoided due to Pakistan's possession of nuclear arsenals and the apparent will of its leadership to employ these.[8]

In the eventuality of India not heeding Pakistan's nuclear deterrent and still waging a limited conventional war against the latter, however, Pakistan's nuclear deterrent changes its character and becomes an instrument of national power that would be employed to ensure national survival by bringing India's conventional military operations to an end before a critical point is reached as regards Pakistan's very existence as an independent and viable state.

The Indian nuclear weapons, on the other hand, are designed to deter the use of nuclear weapons against India by any other country and could, therefore, be categorised as politico-military instruments of national power rather than being purely military instruments.

Employment Philosophy

Since her conventional military inferiority could lead to Pakistan being the first one during any future India-Pakistan military conflict to resort to the use of nuclear weapons, Pakistan has not announced that it would adhere to the employment philosophy of "No First Use." India, on the other hand has unequivocally asserted in her draft Nuclear Doctrine that:

- "India shall pursue a doctrine of credible minimum nuclear deterrence. In this policy of 'retaliation only,' the survivability of our arsenal is critical."[9]
- "India will not be the first to initiate a nuclear strike, but will respond with punitive retaliation should deterrence fail."[10]

If and when the draft Nuclear Doctrine is adopted and approved by the Indian Government, it stands to reason that it would most probably be Pakistan and not India that would be the first to opt for the employment of nuclear weapons in South Asia. This assertion is also borne out by the numerous war-games that the US military has conducted on the scenarios of a nuclear war in South Asia. In almost all these exercises, it surmised that it was Pakistan who is forced to go for the nuclear option before India.

According to Jasjit Singh, "India's nuclear weapons are meant to deter nuclear weapons threat/use. Unlike most other nuclear weapon states, India's nuclear weapons are NOT meant to deter the use and threat of use of conventional weapons, chemical weapons, biological weapons or a generalised formulation of protecting national interests any time anywhere."[11]

The draft Indian Nuclear Doctrine as well as numerous statements of the Pakistani leadership indicate that both the countries have decided to adhere to the tenet of "minimum credible deterrence" as regards their respective nuclear weapon capabilities. This tenet is based on two distinct aspects— the *credibility* of the nuclear deterrent capability possessed by them and its *minimality*. In simplistic terms, these two aspects could also be described as being the defining determinants of the *qualitative* and *quantitative* attributes of their respective nuclear weapons inventories. However, considering the vast divergences that characterise their nuclear doctrinal thought, the decision on what constitutes a "credible minimum" deterrent could also differ significantly for India and Pakistan.

The employment philosophy also influences the state of readiness and preparedness of the nuclear weapons of the two countries. Since Pakistan recognises that she might be the first to resort to the employment of these weapons, it follows that her nuclear weapons might need to be maintained at a significantly higher state of readiness and alert than the Indian nuclear weapons which are planned to be launched only in the retaliatory mode.

Threat Centricity/Focus

Nowhere in the draft Indian Nuclear Doctrine is any potential adversary country identified and the threat has been kept as a generic one. It is safe to conclude, however, that while India is attempting to use her nuclear arsenal to deter not only Pakistan but also possibly China, the Pakistani nuclear weapons are purely India specific and focused.

Another possibility, though remote, that exists is that of another country, e.g., Israel attacking Pakistan's nuclear installations/arsenal and forcing Pakistan to retaliate.

Developmental Philosophy

The nuclear weapons development strategy flows directly from the employment philosophy and the nature of centricity or focus of the country's nuclear doctrine. Since Pakistan's nuclear arsenal is purely India-centric while India has to contend not only with Pakistan but also China, it stands to reason that India needs to pursue a significantly more ambitious nuclear weapons development programme. This is borne out not only by the fact that India is in the process of developing long-range ballistic missiles that could engage targets all over the Chinese landmass but are also intent on developing a triad-based nuclear potential.

Pakistan, on the other hand, is currently limiting the development of its nuclear forces to be dyad-based, i.e., land and air-based/delivered nuclear weapons with effective ranges that can cover the Indian landmass. In future, however, Pakistan could also consider and pursue a sea-based nuclear deterrence potential to further enhance the deterrent potential of her nuclear weapons arsenal. Most observers, however, are of the view that the achievement of a sea-based nuclear weapons capability for India is still far away in the future.[12]

Notwithstanding the fact that nuclear military balance is never gauged or measured in numbers, India's greater threat centricity and focus might also necessitate her producing a larger number of nuclear weapons than those that Pakistan needs to have since the latter only plans to counter one threat, i.e., India.

Another important connotation of the respective employment philosophies of India and Pakistan for their nuclear weapons development programmes lies in the domain of "second strike" potential. While the significance of possessing a viable and credible "second strike" potential does not emerge as being essential for Pakistan, the same is crucial for India because of the retaliatory nature of the latter's nuclear doctrine.

In the realm of nuclear weapons development, it is also vital for Pakistan to not contemplate entering into a nuclear arms race with India since such an endeavour would not only be prohibitively expensive but also unnecessary considering the limited scope, objectives and purpose of the Pakistani nuclear weapons arsenal.

Conclusion

An analysis of the factors that propelled India and Pakistan towards the weaponisation of their respective nuclear capability and analysing the subsequent doctrinal implications of these indicates significant differences that exist in the nuclear doctrinal thinking that persists in India and in Pakistan.

While Indians tend to think of their nuclear weapons as a political instrument of power designed to help their country achieve rightful place and stature amongst the comity of nations, Pakistan's nuclear arsenal is more of a weapon of survival that is designed to ensure that any threats to the very existence of Pakistan as a state are countered and negated by the use, or the threat of use, of these nuclear weapons.

Notes

1.   http://belfercenter.ksg.harvard.edu/files/uploads/Sagan_MTA_Talk_050708.pdf.
      I have purposely excluded the 1971 war from this discussion on "stalemates" because it was more of a civil war than being a true India-Pakistan war in the true sense of the word. Moreover, it was decisive in that it resulted in the creation of Bangladesh as an independent country from what was earlier known as East Pakistan.

2. Pakistan announced the establishment of the National Command Authority (NCA) before the Indians had publicised the details of their nuclear command and control infrastructure. The Pakistan NCA is headed by the Chief Executive (the elected Prime Minister) and includes four members each from the military and the civilian leadership. The four military members are the Chairman Joint Chiefs of Staff Committee (generally a serving 4-star General from either of the three services) and the Chiefs of Staff of the Pakistan Army, the Pakistan Navy and the Pakistan Air Force while the members belonging to the civilian leadership are the four Federal Ministers for Defence, Finance, Foreign Affairs and Interior. President Musharraf modified the NCA such that he, in his capacity as the President of Pakistan, is the Chairman of the NCA rather than this responsibility being handed over to the elected Prime Minister or Chief Executive but President Asif Zardari.

3. Dr. Subhash Kapila, "India and Pakistan Nuclear Doctrine: A Comparative Analysis." Available on the internet at http://www.ipcs.org/India_Pak_articles2. jsp?action=showView&kValue=573&status=article&mod=a.

4. The draft Indian Nuclear Doctrine was prepared by the 27-member National Security Advisory Board (NSAB) and was released by Mr. Brajesh Mishra, India's National Security Adviser on August 17, 1999 in New Delhi. According to the Government of India, this draft proposal was released to encourage public debate and would be considered by the government in due course for a final decision. The text of this document is available from numerous websites but the author downloaded it from http://www.pugwash.org/reports/nw/nw7a.htm.

5. Rajesh M. Basrur, "India's Nuclear Security: Strategic Culture and Doctrine." Available on the internet at http://www.pircenter.org/data/news/basrur.pdf.

6. Zia Mian, "Defended to Death." Available on the internet at http://www.wagingpeace. org/articles/1999/08/24_mian_defended.htm.

7. N. Ram, "Dreaming India's nuclear future." Available on the internet at http://www. frontlineonnet.com/fl1618/16180210.htm.

8. The author was himself closely involved in both these events. During the Kargil conflict, he was the Base Commander of the Pakistan Air Force Base at Skardu which was the only PAF Base in the vicinity of the Kargil theatre of operations while during the period of escalated tensions in 2001-2002, he was serving as the Assistant Chief of Air Staff (Operations) of the Pakistan Air Force. In this assignment, he oversaw the entire process of deployment and response plans of the Pakistan Air Force and even presented the same to then President Pervez Musharraf during his visit to the Command Operations Centre in December 2001.

9. Draft Indian Nuclear Doctrine, paragraph II (iii). The text of this document is available from numerous websites but the author downloaded it from http://www. pugwash.org/reports/nw/nw7a.htm.

10. Ibid., paragraph II (iv).

11. Jasjit Singh, "Indian Draft Nuclear Doctrine: Some Reflections." Available on the internet at http://www.pugwash.org/reports/nw/nw7.htm.

12. Peter Gizewski, "Indian Nuclear Doctrine: A Critical Assessment of the Proposal for a Minimum Nuclear Deterrent." Available on the internet at http://www.dfait.gc.ca/ arms/isrop/research/gizewski_2000/menu-en.asp?#toc.

20 Nuclearisation and South Asian Strategic Stability[1]

Introduction

In my over three decades of service in the Pakistan military, one phrase that I have heard being repeated innumerable times during virtually every military war-game, operational paper-exercise and defence policy presentation that I have been involved in, is the phrase *terminating the war on a favourable note* being cited as one of the objectives of the possible war termination strategies. Despite the fact that I have heard this cliché several times, it is only lately that I have come to question its applicability in the South Asian realm in the post-nuclearisation environment.[2]

Nuclearisation and Strategic Stability in South Asia

One of the biggest questions plaguing the minds of defence and strategic analysts the world over ever since the South Asian nuclear tests of May 1998 is whether the emergence of India and Pakistan as overt nuclear powers on the global scene has enhanced the strategic stability of South Asia or has this event further exacerbated the already unstable situation prevailing in this region.

In military terms, I think this issue could be addressed from two different perspectives by attempting to answer the following basic questions:

- Have the chances of a conventional military conflict increased in South Asia after nuclearisation?
- What are the chances of a nuclear conflict breaking out in South Asia after the overt nuclearisation of India and Pakistan?

Terminating War on a Favourable Note

Seen from the perspective of either of the two countries, one of the foremost objectives for any war that breaks out in the region would be for both the antagonists to attempt *to terminate the war on a favourable note* for their respective sides. Being fairly well acquainted with Indian and Pakistani military thinking on this subject, I feel that this is a generic enough phrase to be used by most militaries, albeit with slightly differing connotations.

What does the usage of this term imply? To me this term and its precise wording has its genesis in the growing realisation amongst the Pakistani military that in case of any future India–Pakistan war, the possibility of either side achieving a clear-cut victory or suffering an abject or total defeat is no more a possibility under the current "nuclearised" circumstances. Though the gross conventional military imbalance initially led to this realisation amongst the Pakistan military, the feeling strengthened much more after the conduct of nuclear tests by India and Pakistan in May 1998. While a clear-cut, decisive or total victory is not conceivable for Pakistan because of the vast differential in conventional military capability between India and Pakistan, the availability of a viable and credible nuclear capability with Pakistan precludes the spectre of an abject Pakistani defeat and thus, a corresponding total victory for India.

Since war termination objectives *define the intended manner of conflict termination and the required military and diplomatic achievements to obtain it,*[3] it follows that the various aspects of war termination have to be built into the planning process that precedes the war. Acceptance of the fact that a clear-cut and decisive victory is not possible for either Pakistan or India to achieve leads one to re-examine the relevance of the phrase "terminating the war on a favourable note." It is obvious from the above that the words *favourable note* denote a set of circumstances which though falling very slightly on the victory side of the pendulum of war, is still well short of a total victory and merely indicates the existence of a position or posture of slight advantage for one side which strengthens its negotiating position during the post-conflict parleys. To me, this gap between *ending war on a favourable note* and *achieving victory in war* or the line separating these two is determined by the *nuclear threshold* of the conventionally weaker adversary since this will be the factor that would ultimately inhibit any escalatory movement from the stage of terminating hostilities on a *favourable note* towards reaching a position of total *victory.*

Does the above imply that the South Asian rivals can never again fight a conventional military war? Michael Krepon's explanation of the Stability-Instability paradox[4] suggests that the overt nuclearisation of the subcontinent has enhanced the strategic stability of the region by rendering conventional conflicts *unwinnable* and as such not worth the enormous effort and losses that they are liable to cause. Nuclearisation, I would assert, has limited the extent of flexibility that either of the major players in South Asia can exercise while contemplating a conventional war against each other and predicting its possible outcome. As such, overt nuclearisation of these two countries could be construed to be an inhibiting factor when considering the possibility of a conventional war between them. It follows, therefore, that while India and/or Pakistan might be tempted to initiate minor military skirmishes or conflicts,[5] the chances of them waging a full-fledged conventional limited war have been rendered increasingly remote by the overt nuclearisation of their militaries. In some ways, the situation in South Asia today is that of a scaled down regional Cold War—similar in many ways to the US-Soviet global Cold War that dominated the geopolitics of the second half of the twentieth century. One must, however, remember that just as in the US-Soviet Cold War, sub-limited confrontations or even limited indirect conflicts do remain a distinct possibility, and the emphasis must be on ensuring that these are not permitted to escalate to a stage where either of the sides to the conflict is forced to contemplate the employment of nuclear or other weapons of mass destruction. In my reckoning, the debate regarding the "Stability-Instability paradox" could well be described as the "Optimist-Pessimist Syndrome" when nuclear deterrence in the South Asian context is studied.

Background

Since my above assertion might appear to be an oversimplification to most readers, allow me to elaborate on my line of thinking. Nations or their leaders usually embark on wars as a means of achieving certain well-defined objectives. While the achievement of the objectives normally indicates a victory, failure to achieve these generally signifies a defeat, or at best, a stalemate. It is against all norms of human rationality and logical behaviour for someone to embark on an endeavour that he knows is bound to a certain failure or a stalemate unless the concerned individual is residing in the realm of irrationality or has his/her back to the wall. Moreover, once war objectives have been stipulated, wars generally continue till these have been achieved. This facet of war was best encapsulated by Abraham Lincoln:

"We accept this war for an object—a worthy object—and the war will end when that object is attained. Under God I hope that it will never end until that time."[6]

This is the situation that now confronts South Asian leaders. While their hyped-up domestic public opinion might go along with their decision to wage a war, the leaders would be required to show some achievement for it when it is all over. In fact, the very survival of the political structure that took the country to war in the first place would depend to quite an extent on the outcome of the war. According to Daniel Cushing:

"Eventually political survival becomes an element in war termination. Unless war aims are achieved at the expected cost, which is rare, then a re-evaluation of objectives must occur, normally while the war is going on. Typically this reassessment involves a calculation of the survivability of the party in power. The increased cost of the war causes a shift in the end game, ultimately driving two parallel aims. Political survival and war termination become so intermixed that the original reasons for conflict are often lost."[7]

In my opinion, the currently prevailing geopolitical and geostrategic situation in the region precludes any conventional military conflict ever leading to even a semblance of a decisive conclusion since the nation that is not doing well in the war would overstep its nuclear threshold before any decisive advantage is gained over it by the adversary. As evidence one could cite the following facts:

- Never since 1945 has any nation resorted to employing nuclear weapons.
- Even at the height of the Cold War and its tensest moments, no mention of the NATO countries nor any member of the erstwhile Warsaw Pact committed any act that could have presumably crossed the other's nuclear threshold.
- Despite the world being a virtual beehive of military conflicts, never have any two nuclear capable nations been involved even in a *direct* conventional military.
- The Kargil conflict and the subsequent period of Indo-Pak military tensions in 2002 are two examples of a conventional stalemate that, in my opinion, did not escalate into even limited conventional wars because of the fear of nuclear escalation.[8] In fact, when one looks back at Operation Gibraltar launched by Pakistan in September 1965, it could well be argued that had India and Pakistan both been nuclear then, Operation Gibraltar could well have fizzled out without escalating into a limited conflict as actually happened.
- From the Indian standpoint, the objectives of any future war with Pakistan must focus on achieving the maximum possible degree of capitulation of Pakistan without violating the latter's nuclear threshold. If this is allowed to happen, massive destruction on both sides would preclude any chances of victory by either, and that fear might avert the war.

Coming back to the phrase *war termination on a favourable note*, I feel that this innocuous looking string of words embodies an entire world of meaning and interpretations inside it that I would now attempt to elaborate:

- Firstly, considering that there are two adversaries involved in a military conflict, it automatically follows that if the war is ending on a favourable note for one then it has to be ending on an unfavourable note for the other. I cannot envisage or imagine a situation where the termination of a war is equally and simultaneously advantageous as well as acceptable for both antagonists.

- Secondly, the use of the words favourable note in one's war objectives by itself denotes the admission of an element of defeat since wars are usually fought for the achievement of defined objectives. As such, it would be generally the militarily weaker of the two sides which could be expected to use this phrase. In the South Asian scenario, this weaker stance and position applies to Pakistan and not to India, since the latter is substantially superior in conventional military capability than the former. As such, while Pakistan's military planners and leadership might be satisfied with terminating a war against a more powerful India on a favourable note, the Indian side would have to plan and aim for a victory, with even a stalemate just not being acceptable to them. As mentioned earlier, however, Indian military planners would have to scale down the nature of this "victory" to a set of advantageous circumstances that can be achieved without overstepping Pakistan's perceived nuclear threshold.

- The phrase *favourable note* has an in-built elasticity within it. While a favourable note might mean "victory" when viewed from the Indian perspective, to the Pakistanis it might signify a situation of just a slight advantage, even at the tactical level. Movement within these two extremes of elasticity would essentially be determined by the comparative conventional military potential of the adversaries. Although this might appear a bit far-fetched to some, I contend that in any future India-Pakistan conventional war, if the Indian gains are not serious enough to make Pakistan cross its nuclear threshold by the time that the war ends, then it could well signify that Pakistan has managed to end the war on a favourable note, since it has been able to force the Indians to a stalemate in the conventional realm without suffering any significant losses. Pakistan's aim in any such war, therefore, would commence with the imperative to force the Indians to a conventional stalemate or a no-win no-loss situation before the nuclear level is reached. Considering the immense global pressure that both India and Pakistan would be under to cease hostilities during any future war, the time available to India to achieve the slight advantage that it seeks before overstepping Pakistan's nuclear threshold will be minimal. This would not only make the conflict very short but could also necessitate India planning to go full bore right from the outset.

- As mentioned earlier, the use of this phrase in routine discussions and presentations by the Pakistan military denotes a certain degree of pessimism that is a fallout of their conventional military inferiority vis-à-vis India. It is this sense of apprehension that has directly motivated the Pakistani pursuit of nuclear military capability and still continues to sustain her ambitious nuclear development plans.

- For a country such as Pakistan that suffers from a significant conventional military disadvantage, the obvious recourse to correcting a gross conventional military imbalance is to rely more and more on its nuclear capability. This is why in the face of the growing Indian conventional might, Pakistan's *nuclear threshold* would be correspondingly reducing while her nuclear arsenal continues to grow in size and capability. Referring back to how I had defined nuclear threshold above, this means that from the Indian perspective, the margin between them terminating a war on a favourable note and them achieving total victory in it is also simultaneously reducing. This would directly impinge on the operational flexibility that Indian military leadership would be able to exercise in any conventional war with Pakistan.

- The most obvious manifestation of this accepted weakness is the fact that Pakistan, unlike India, has reserved the right of *first use* of nuclear weapons.[9] Pakistan's leadership are fully aware that being militarily weaker in the conventional realm, they are far more likely than India to reach their nuclear threshold earlier and as such cannot under any circumstances subscribe to the option of *no first use* as India has stated in her draft nuclear doctrine. Although Pakistan also espouses the desire of possessing a triad-based nuclear force, it currently just has the potential of using either manned aircraft or surface-to-surface ballistic missiles for delivering nuclear warheads, with the third leg of the triad still being developed. It is precisely this realisation that Pakistan would most probably be the first one to resort to employing nuclear weapons, using her two-dimensional nuclear potential, that has motivated India's quest for anti-ballistic missile systems such as the Russian Su-300/Israeli Arrow-210 and the Phalcon AEW[11] that she is desirous of inducting as soon as possible. While the former would serve to provide an element of defence against Pakistan's ballistic nuclear-tipped SSMs, the latter would pose a strong defence against any efforts of the Pakistan Air Force to deliver nuclear weapons, by interdicting the nuclear strike aircraft while these are en route to their targets.[12]

From the foregoing it emerges that it is imperative for Pakistani and Indian military planners to factor in each other's respective nuclear threshold into their operational war plans so as to arrive at an estimation of how far they can afford to go in war as regards the impact on the other. This begs the question—how to determine the adversary's nuclear threshold?

Nuclear Deterrence and South Asia
In simple terms "nuclear threshold" is that point in a military conflict where one of the two antagonists feels that the war is not going well for his side and is forced to contemplate an escalatory transition from the conventional to the nuclear realm. In South Asia, this could be linked with the course or set of circumstances during a war with India that could lead to Pakistan resorting to a "nuclear first use." In my reckoning, a nuclear threshold does not really apply to India since Pakistan does not currently possess the conventional potential to force India's reaching a point where she is forced to employ her nuclear weapons.

Almost all students of military affairs and inter-nation conflicts agree that nuclear weapons are essentially weapons of deterrence. While I entirely endorse this definition of nuclear weapons, I interpret it slightly differently when focusing specifically on the South Asian region. In my reckoning, from the Pakistani perspective, nuclear weapons are not meant to only deter the onset of a war, but rather these are weapons that are also required for deterring and possibly averting an abject defeat.

Deterrence in the South Asian environment has to be viewed as a two-tiered concept, especially from Pakistan's perspective. The massive and almost decisive conventional asymmetry that confronts Pakistan could lead it to view its deterrence policy according to the following requirements:

- First and foremost, the purpose of Pakistan's nuclear arsenal is to preclude the possibility of India embarking on any military adventure against it, even if it is limited to a purely conventional conflict. This is the traditional form of deterrence that this world has witnessed earlier also. By fielding a credible nuclear force, Pakistan wants to deter the initiation of any military operations by India on the basis of her established nuclear capability that is liable to be employed if India does not abstain from embarking on military operations against it. From this perspective, Pakistan's nuclear deterrence could be classified as an instrument for deterring conventional war. Pakistan's military thinking could be summed up by saying that she would project her nuclear arsenal to convince India of the futility of embarking on a full-fledged conventional war against her by insinuating that the availability of nuclear weapons with Pakistan obviates the possibility of the Indian military achieving any significant objectives during a conventional limited war.

- The second tier of Pakistan's deterrence will come into play once hostilities have broken out between the two countries and the war is not going well for Pakistan. In this situation, with its back to the wall, Pakistan could be forced to employ the nuclear weapons as a weapon of last resort to forestall an imminent scenario of abject defeat. The objective here would be for Pakistan to threaten India with its use of the nuclear weapons unless war is brought to an abrupt and complete stop. This would be a really desperate situation from the Pakistani viewpoint that could well justify the employment of nuclear weapons against India. In order to keep the Indians guessing, it can be expected that Pakistan would intentionally maintain an element of ambiguity about her "nuclear threshold" while simultaneously ensuring that it is taken into consideration in the preparation of its war plans.

- Conversely, India's nuclear deterrence, unlike Pakistan's, is not aimed at preventing conventional war. Rather, it is designed to avert the Pakistani usage of nuclear weapons. This indicates that while Pakistan's nuclear wherewithal is aimed at preventing a conventional war, India's is designed to prevent a nuclear exchange. This is a significant difference between the deterrence philosophies of the two South Asian nations that must be taken into account. From this it also flows that while Pakistan's nuclear prowess has more of a "first use" connotation, India's nuclear arsenal is designed more as a second strike or retaliatory option and the draft Indian nuclear doctrine more than amply elucidates these two aspects.[13]

- The fundamental purpose of Indian nuclear weapons is to deter the use, and threat of use, of nuclear weapons by any State or entity against India and its forces.

- India shall pursue a doctrine of credible minimum nuclear deterrence. In this policy of "retaliation only," the survivability of our arsenal is critical.
- This stark difference between the nuclear philosophies of India and Pakistan highlights the point that while Pakistan's nuclear potential is contributing to the maintenance of conventional stability in South Asia, that of India is essentially instrumental in the maintenance of nuclear stability in the region. While the former is aimed at preventing the break-out of a conventional war, the latter serves to dissuade both the countries from going nuclear. This difference in the nuclear philosophies of India and Pakistan would figure very prominently in any future military conflict in South Asia. The comparative nuclear deterrence philosophies of India and Pakistan are illustrated in Table 1 below:

Table 1: Comparative Nuclear Deterrence Philosophies: India and Pakistan

Country	Doctrinal Aim	End-Objective
India	Prevent any nuclear weapons employment against it by threatening severe retaliation	Avert a nuclear exchange
Pakistan	Prevent a conventional war by implying that her low nuclear threshold might warrant an early recourse to the nuclear weapon	Avert a conventional war and if breaks out, force a conclusion of the hostilities before the enemy advantage reaches a decisive stage

Nuclear Weapons Employment in South Asia[14]

An analysis of the nuclear deterrence philosophies of the South Asian nuclear neighbours as depicted above should facilitate our moving forward towards an objective evaluation of the nuclear weapons employment doctrines of Pakistan and India.

Keeping in mind the retaliatory/response undertones of Indian nuclear doctrine and policy, the only situation that could warrant an Indian recourse to nuclear weapons would be a nuclear or strategic strike by Pakistan. In this scenario, the Indian Government would be left with no choice other than to go nuclear. The sequence of events of such a nuclear war scenario in South Asia involving usage of nuclear weapons by both the adversaries could unfold thus:

- Based on Pakistan's continued support to the insurgency inside Indian Occupied Kashmir, India opts to start a low intensity campaign confined geographically to Kashmir with a view to blocking all possible infiltration routes.
- Indian Army operations in the vicinity of the Line of Control bring them in contact with the Pakistan Army and small-scale skirmishes and incidents occur, which blossom over days into a full-fledged firefight between the two armies.
- Pakistan threatens usage of nuclear weapons but Indian troops continue with their operations. International community pressures mount on both India and Pakistan to desist from continuing military operations.
- With the Indian Army poised to overrun a key feature in Pakistan Occupied Kashmir the capture of which could sever Pakistan's link with it, Pakistan opts to go for a nuclear first strike against a major Indian city.
- India is forced to retaliate and responds in kind by launching a nuclear attack against a major Pakistani city.

The comparative nuclear employment philosophies of India and Pakistan are depicted in Table 2 below:

**Table 2: Comparative Nuclear Employment Philosophies:
India and Pakistan**

Country	Scenario	Employment Philosophy	Employment Concept
India	Nuclear weapons employment in response to a Pakistani nuclear/strategic strike	Weapon of *response*	Retaliatory
Pakistan	Threaten to employ nuclear weapons in an attempt to avert break-out of a conventional military conflict	Weapon of *threat* (deterrence)	First Use
	To be employed to avoid a conventional war terminating on very unfavourable terms (defeat)	Weapon of *last resort* (national survival)	First Use

Scary though it might be, the above scenario does depict one of the possible set of circumstances that could lead to the subcontinent being engulfed in a nuclear war. In order to evaluate this train of events, one has to pick out the key events in its progression.

Commencement of a Limited Conventional Campaign by India. The train of events is set in motion by India opting to commence a limited intensity campaign disregarding the threat of a Pakistani first use of her nuclear weapons, possibly on the premise that the limited end-objectives of this campaign would not warrant crossing of Pakistan's nuclear threshold. It is quite possible that India's hand could be forced into doing this by an increased involvement of Pakistan in the Kashmir uprising. Planning for this phase of operations has to be very carefully articulated keeping mind the perceived nuclear threshold of Pakistan, and would have to be integrated with a massive media campaign aimed at convincing not only the domestic populace but also the entire global community that India's hand was forced by the prevailing situation and the adoption of a military option being warranted, India was justified in adopting this extreme course of action. India would also have to ensure that the objectives stipulated by it for the military offensive are so limited in nature and magnitude that these preclude any overstepping of Pakistan's nuclear threshold.

Having been unable to deter India from embarking on a conventional conflict, Pakistan must follow a two-pronged strategy—a diplomatic offensive aimed at heightening the concern of the international community simultaneously with the adoption of a higher state of readiness of its nuclear forces. The second step will signify Pakistan's resolve not only to India but also to the other interested parties of the world.

India's Persistence to Violate Pakistan's Nuclear Threshold[15] and a Nuclear Strike by Pakistan. If India does not get dissuaded by the danger and possibility of a Pakistani nuclear first strike and continues the conventional conflict, this might put Pakistan in a corner with no option but to go nuclear. In this extreme option also, Pakistan must first take the major global powers into confidence and if considered feasible, even warn India of the impending consequences of a nuclear strike against one of her major cities. Apart from conveying the required message to the Indian government and the entire world, this might also allow some of the population of the major Indian cities to move out of their city homes into the neighbouring countryside thus reducing the number of possible casualties. Having taken this decision, the Pakistan Government must also simultaneously start preparing for an Indian retaliatory nuclear strike against one or more of her major metropolitan centres and take all steps to minimise the casualties.

Nature of Pakistan's First strike. Pakistan could adopt the following possible courses of action after having been forced to go nuclear:

- **A Nuclear Warning Shot.** A tactical counter-force strike aimed at exhibiting resolve while ensuring that the collateral casualties and damage are reduced to the minimum. While such a counter-force strike might not be possible in the densely populated plains of Punjab, it could possibly be contemplated in the deserts of Central Punjab and Sindh. The danger to own forces, however, is likely to preclude the adoption of this option. Another military target which could be targeted during such a counter-value strike could be Indian Navy vessels that are at high sea and are located by Pakistan Navy's maritime patrol aircraft or other available means. While any major surface-going Indian Navy warship could be selected for this sort of an attack, the biggest prize would be one of the Indian Navy's aircraft carriers. Being purely aimed at a military target, such a strike could well be explained by Pakistan as a justifiable act of war and might not warrant or precipitate a nuclear retaliation by India. This would constitute the lowest rung of nuclear escalation from the Pakistani viewpoint and would also indicate that the Pakistan Government has not yet reached the limit of its desperation regarding the outcome of the war. As such, this sort of a counter-force first strike could well amount to a demonstration of resolve through a "nuclear warning shot."

- **Massive First Strike against Counter-Value Targets.** Pakistan could be expected to resort to this option if the situation of the war has become really desperate and Pakistan is fearful for its very survival or existence as an independent and sovereign country. The obvious target selection list would include major Indian cities, preferably those that can be reached by Pakistan's nuclear delivery aircraft as well as her surface-to-surface ballistic missiles. This is important since this being the "last shot" that it might ever fire, Pakistan would have to ensure that this effort succeeds. One of the obvious measures to ensure a high degree of success would be to mount a simultaneous aircraft and missile attack so as to allow for the interception and destruction of some of these assets by Indian's defence systems. While some analysts feel that Pakistan would just target one odd Indian city, I feel convinced that due to the "last ditch" nature of this attack and also due to the fear of the massive punitive retaliation that India could, and would resort to, Pakistan could also attack several

Indian cities simultaneously in anticipation of the massive Indian retaliation. The only rationale, warped though it might appear to some, that I can forward for this massive counter-value first strike is based on the following factors:

o   Pakistan would only go nuclear when it is convinced of an abject defeat.

o   Realisation of the fact that India possesses a significant nuclear weapons arsenal along with the requisite delivery capability is enough to convince Pakistani leadership that India would retaliate in a massive manner to any nuclear first strike against her cities.

o   The "nuclear first use" might be the only opportunity available to Pakistan to employ nuclear weapons in order to bring the unfavourable progression of the conventional war to a quick and immediate end. Due to the massive nature of the expected Indian response to it, Pakistan might not have another opportunity of employing her nuclear arsenal to bring the war to an abrupt end.

o   In the face of the expected massive Indian retaliation and the fact that Pakistan would not get another opportunity, her leadership could be induced to increase the quantum and spread of this strike by simultaneously targeting as many Indian cities as possible.

Retaliatory Nuclear Strike by India. Any counter-value nuclear strike by Pakistan against India is bound to force India's hand also to respond in kind and I do not think that it would be possible for any amount of international pressure to dissuade the Indian Government from following suit.

Limitations on the Conduct of Conventional Military Operations

The advent of nuclear weapons has imposed restrictions on the uninhibited use of conventional military force in South Asia. In my opinion, Pakistani and Indian military planners would have to adhere to the following constraints and limitations while planning conventional military operations against each other:

Pakistan

• It would be in Pakistan's national interest to define her nuclear threshold and disseminate that selectively internally within its military while keeping it under a cloud of ambiguity as regards the Indian military.

• Till such a time that the gross conventional disparity existing between the militaries of the two countries is corrected, Pakistan's military should focus on and plan for an effectively defensive military strategy. This means that Pakistan's overall military posture would be one of "Strategic Defence and Tactical Offence."

- The possibility of the Indian Army's offensive formations being positioned close to the international border[16] would impinge on the early warning that the Pakistan Army is normally used to. This would require the defensive formations of the Pakistan Army to be kept at a high enough state of readiness at all times.

- Pakistan could endeavour to create an impression and perception amongst the Indian leadership about its nuclear threshold being low since such a perception would serve to dissuade India from embarking on any conventional military operation against Pakistan. One possible means of sending out a danger signal not only to India but also to the rest of the world could be by raising the level of readiness of Pakistan's strategic nuclear forces.

India

- Indian military planners must consider the perceived nuclear threshold of Pakistan and ensure that this figures prominently in all their war plans.

- The immediate war aims of India should remain within the tactical spectrum as regards the impact on Pakistan.

- Due to intense international pressures to bring the conflict/war to an early end, the Indian military must strive for immediate results.

- The imperative of achieving swift results might necessitate the Indian Army's offensive formations being provided with a high degree of mobility and being stationed in close proximity to the international border even during peacetime.[17]

- It would be in Indian interest to attempt to dispel Pakistan's perception of gross conventional inferiority since this could raise Pakistan's nuclear threshold.

Conclusion

The contents of this paper have essentially been focused on answering the two basic questions that I had set out to answer in the beginning— has nuclearisation enhanced strategic stability is South Asia by rendering conventional wars unwinnable, and what are the chances of a nuclear showdown in the region now that both the main adversary countries are overtly nuclear? My endeavour has been focused on illustrating that not only has nuclearisation enhanced the level of strategic stability that exists in South Asia but it has also significantly reduced the chances of an all-out conventional war between India and Pakistan.

As depicted in the above scenario, the chain of events commences with a limited conventional campaign by India that oversteps Pakistan's nuclear threshold, forces Pakistan's hand at going nuclear and results in a similar India response. This set of circumstances can be divided into four distinct set of events and my objective in this paper has been to indicate that while the first step is a distinct possibility, any progression beyond that lies merely in the realm of imagination since the danger of a nuclear exchange should preclude anyone but the most irrational of leaders from venturing beyond it. It can therefore, be concluded that the overt nuclearisation of India and Pakistan in the volatile South Asian region has ushered in an era of enhanced strategic stability in South Asia by making conventional conflicts unwinnable and as such not worth embarking upon, either by Pakistan or by India. Readers could well classify me as a deterrence optimist, but I am convinced that what we are confronted with in South Asia now is a "Regional Cold War" which is similar in some ways but different in others to the global Cold War that not only characterised but also shaped and dominated the relationship between the United States and the Soviet Union for almost half a century.

Notes

1. Strategic Stability and that too of a region as volatile and unstable as South Asia, is indeed a vast subject with both, internal and external dimensions. For the purpose of this paper, however, only the external dimensions of Pakistan's security environment have been taken into account and not the internal dimensions. The author feels that this could well be another suitable subject on which a paper could be written.

2. The germs of the theme of this article were sown in my mind after listening to Michael Krepon's lecture on the "Stability/Instability Paradox and its applicability to South Asia" at the Pakistan National Defence College in Islamabad. Subsequent work commenced on it after I received a suggestion from Brigadier Feroz Hassan Khan of the United States Naval Post Graduate School in Monterey, California to consider contributing a piece for inclusion in a forthcoming volume on "Strategic Stability in South Asia."

3. Soucy, Shwedo and Haven, "War Termination and Joint Planning," *Joint Forces Quarterly*, Summer 1995, p. 97.

4. While Krepon and other scholars continue to describe this as the "Stability-Instability" Paradox, I tend to see it as the Optimist-Pessimist Syndrome wherein deterrence optimists and deterrence pessimists pit themselves against each other.

5. India and Pakistan have come close to war on two occasions since they went nuclear;

firstly in Kargil in 1999 and secondly during the heightened period of military tensions in 2001-2002. In both the situations, escalation to a full-fledged conventional limited war was precluded, in my reckoning, primarily by the availability of nuclear weapons on both sides and the immense international pressures on the antagonists to de-escalate.

6. Major Daniel E. Cushing, Paper titled "War Termination and Our Cultural Heritage" that can be accessed on the internet at http://www.globalsecurity.org/military/library/report/1992/CDE.htm.

7. Cushing, op. cit.

8. The author was himself closely involved in both these events. During the Kargil conflict, he was the Base Commander of the Pakistan Air Force Base at Skardu while during the period of escalated tensions in 2002, he was serving as the Assistant Chief of Air Staff (Operations) of the Pakistan Air Force. In this assignment, he oversaw the entire process of deployment and response plans of the Pakistan Air Force and even presented the same to President Pervez Musharraf.

9. While the draft Indian Nuclear Doctrine specifies that India would adhere to the concept of "no first use," statements of various Pakistani leaders have indicated that Pakistan will not be adhering to it and will not forgo its right of nuclear first use. To me this appears to be a requirement necessitated by the gross conventional asymmetry that Pakistan is confronted with.

10. Air Commodore Tariq Mahmud Ashraf, "India's quest for a Defence Shield—Acquisition of Green Pine radar and Arrow-2 ABM System" published in *Defence Journal*, Karachi, Pakistan, May 2004.

11. Air Commodore Tariq Mahmud Ashraf, "IAF's Acquisition of Phalcon AEW: A paradigm shift in South Asian air power scenario" published in *Defence Journal*, Karachi, Pakistan, December 2003.

12. India announced an agreement for the purchase of three IL-76 mounted Phalcon AEW radar systems from Israel in October 2003 and the deal worth US$ 1 billion was signed on March 5, 2004 with deliveries expected 44 months after the initial payments are made by the Indian Government. The daily *Dawn* newspaper, Pakistan March 6, 2004, p. 16. As to the Indian quest for the Arrow-2 ABM system, the transfer of this weapon system from Israel to India still awaits US Government approval.

13. Please refer to paragraphs 9 and 10 of the draft Indian Nuclear Doctrine released by the Indian Government.

14. Please see Air Commodore Tariq Mahmud Ashraf, "Nuclearisation, the Changing Nature of Warfare and Future Indo-Pak Wars" published in *Shaheen*—the quarterly journal of the Pakistan Air Force, September 2002.

15. Perhaps the most widely quoted statement of a Pakistani official on the issue of nuclear thresholds surfaced after an interview that Lt. Gen. Kidwai, the Director General of the Strategic Plans Division gave to a group of Italian social scientists. In this statement, General Kidwai was quoted as having said that Pakistani nuclear weapons will be used, according to Gen. Kidwai, only "if the very existence of Pakistan as a state is at stake." This has been detailed by Gen. Kidwai as follows: "Nuclear weapons are aimed solely at India. In case that deterrence fails, they will be used if:

- ◌ India attacks Pakistan and conquers a large part of its territory (*space threshold*)
- ◌ India destroys a large part either of its land or air forces (*military threshold*)
- ◌ India proceeds to the economic strangling of Pakistan (*economic strangling*)
- ◌ India pushes Pakistan into political destabilisation or creates a large scale internal subversion in Pakistan (domestic destabilisation).

16. The possibility of the Indian Army's offensive strike formations being positioned close to the international borders even during peacetime is a distinct possibility in the light of the Indian Army's Cold Start Doctrine. For more details, readers are requested to read the author's article titled "Doctrinal Re-awakening of the Indian Armed Forces" which was published in the US Army's Military Review in Nov-Dec 2004 and can be downloaded from http://usacac.army.mil/cac/milreview/download/English/NovDec04/ashraf.pdf.

17. Ibid.

21 Will Nuclear SSMs ever be
used in South Asia?

Pakistan and India had embarked on ambitious surface-to-surface ballistic missile (SSM) development programmes well before they actually conducted their respective nuclear tests in May 1998. While India was and still continues to centrally administer its Integrated Guided Missile Development Programme through the Defence Research and Development Organisation (DRDO), Pakistan appears to have adopted the parallel route to missile development with several state organisations such as the NDC, NESCOM, PMO, PAEC, KRL, SUPARCO, POF and AWC[1] simultaneously, and at times in competition, working on the development of new SSM systems with improvements in payload size, missile effective range and missile accuracy being the determining criteria for the newer and more improved versions of their respective SSMs.

As has happened with most military developments in South Asia, India and Pakistan have not gotten over their mutual *fatal attraction* for each other despite the lapse of over half a century since the British left India in 1947 and as such, their military development programmes have been focused less on *what their forces actually need* and more on *attempting to negate or neutralise any perceived edge or advantage that the other has achieved.* This sort of a reactive approach has been adopted repeatedly by Pakistan and India not only to convey a strong signal across the border but also to satisfy their respective domestic audiences.

This India-centric phobia of Pakistan and Pakistan-focused approach of India has now created a situation where both the countries have been able to not only develop and test but also to deploy an entire array of SSMs that are capable of carrying nuclear as well as conventional warheads. While both the countries have made tremendous strides in the area of missile technology, I seriously doubt whether the military and political leadership in either of them has considered when and how these fancy weapons will ever be put to use.

The aim of this chapter is to suggest that in the peculiar antagonistic and suspicion filled environment that characterises South Asia's regional dynamics and relationships, SSMs are extremely unlikely to be used, and just as had earlier happened with nuclear weapons, SSMs in South Asia are likely to end up being resorted to and employed more as political hardware and conveying a diplomatic message than becoming actual instruments of the military use that could be employed during war.

Missile Inventories of India and Pakistan
Since the types of SSMs available with India and Pakistan has been already

been covered elsewhere, I will begin this Chapter by looking at the capabilities of these weapon systems.

Capabilities of South Asian SSM Systems

While the maximum reach in terms of distance for the South Asian SSM systems has been included in figure 1, the depiction of this on a map is significantly more revealing. The two maps below depict the comparative coverage of Agni-II with Ghauri-II (Figure 2) and Agni-II with Shaheen-II (Figure 3). Since the maximum ranges of both, the Ghauri-II and the Shaheen-II are the same (2,000 km), the coverages of these missiles are also identical.

Figure 2: Strike Range Comparison: Agni-II vs Ghauri-II[2]

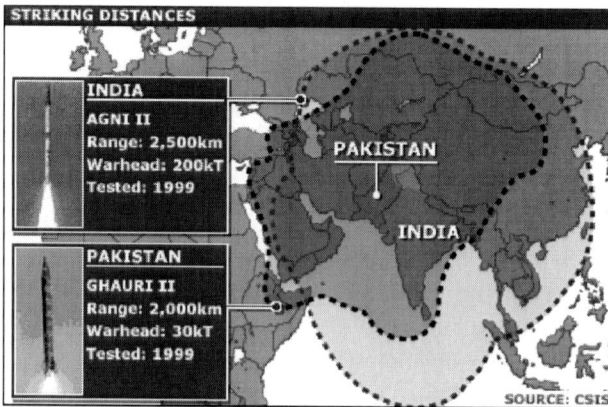

Figure 3: Strike Range Comparison: Agni-II vs Shaheen-II[3]

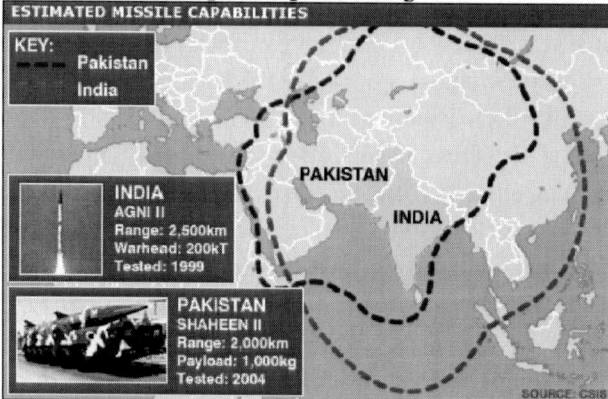

The following interesting aspects emerge from this comparison:

- Both India (with Agni-II) and Pakistan (with either Shaheen-II or Ghauri-II) have the capability of virtually striking anywhere within each other's territorial domain. The only exception to this statement is Pakistan's current inability to strike at the Andaman and Nicobar Islands that now house a major Indian military base.
- While CSIS (the source cited for the information on these maps) indicates that the Agni-II is capable of carrying a 200 kiloton nuclear warhead, the capability of the Shaheen-II/Ghauri-II in this regard is stated to be 30 kilotons).[4]
- India now possesses the strike potential to hit across the entire landmass of China with China's eastern seaboard lying at the fringes of the Agni-II's maximum range.
- Most of Central Asia and the Middle East also fall within the strike radii of Pakistani and Indian SSMs.

Employment of SSMs in South Asia

As it can be seen from the above figures, India with Agni-II and Pakistan with Ghauri-II/Shaheen-II SSMs can conveniently hit anywhere in each other's territory. In fact with its longer range capable missile, India can also cover the entire South East Asian region and also China in the north east.

When considering the aspect of SSMs or, for that matter, nuclear weapons being employed in the South Asian scenario, one must take into account certain peculiarities of the region as well as the type of relations that India and Pakistan have had since they both achieved independence from British colonial rule in 1947.

- **Geographic contiguity**. Unlike the Cold War rivalry where the two main countries were geographically separated and envisaged the war being fought on the territories of their respective European allies, India and Pakistan share a long contiguous border.
- **Pakistan's lack of strategic depth**. Because of its elongated North East–South West orientation, Pakistan's landmass does not provide adequate depth while India's large size allows it to benefit from tremendous strategic depth.[5]
- **Deeply hostile and suspicious relationship**. India–Pakistan relations are based on feelings of mistrust and mutual suspicion that run deep in the psyche of both the nations. In this sort of a relationship even a minor step taken by one could lead to an overreaction by the other.

- **Virtually no Early Warning**. Because of the long contiguous borders, the warning that would be available to either of the two sides would be extremely minimal. This is not only a factor of their contiguity but also because both India and Pakistan do not possess any space-based sensors that could alert them of any missile launch by the other country. The lack of this monitoring capability makes the factor of early warning of vital significance. One must also factor in the possibility, however remote it might be, of an accidental launch by any side or an unannounced missile test by either since both of these could trigger an unwarranted response from the other. In order to avoid any chances of such misunderstandings arising, it is vital that a fail-proof, reliable and robust communication link be maintained between the two countries at all times.

- **Limited reaction time**. As a result of extremely limited early warning being available, the reaction time available to the side against which a missile is launched would be drastically reduced. In simple terms, this reaction time is the time available to the side against which the missile has been launched from the time it detects the missile launch till its impact, during which it has to take all the steps necessary to intercept the missile and destroy it in flight and not allow it to reach the target. Not only do India and Pakistan lack adequate early detection and warning sensors but they also do not currently possess any anti-ballistic missile (ABM) capability.

- **No ABM capability**. Neither India nor Pakistan possess any anti-ballistic missile (ABM) although there have been indications that India is endeavouring to acquire an ABM capability and reports suggest that the US might also bring India on board in its Missile Defence programme. In case the reported Indian request for the Arrow-2 ABM system from Israel is given the green signal by the US Government, this situation could change radically overnight and Pakistan would have to take steps to counter it. Another option that is available to India in this regard is to integrate a suitable Russian SAM system with the already available Green Pine radar and develop an ABM system for protection of its vital strategic targets against Pakistani aircraft/SSM strikes.

- **No means of distinguishing a conventional from a nuclear launch**. Since all Indian and Pakistani SSMs are capable of carrying a conventional or a nuclear warhead and an occasion might arise where either side launches a missile with a conventional warhead, it has to be considered that since there are no means of differentiating between a conventional and a nuclear missile, the side against which the missile has been launched could well respond to its launch assuming a worst-case scenario of a nuclear missile having been launched against it. This is all the more relevant when considered in the environment of mutual suspicion and distrust that permeates the regional dynamics of South Asia.

Conventional/Nuclear SSM Launch

Nuclear weapon targeting is essentially a choice between adopting the "counter-force" or the "counter-value" option. Although not entirely true, it could be argued quite convincingly that whereas the employment of tactical nuclear weapons essentially pertains to the realm of "counter-force" realm, the usage of strategic nuclear weapons would generally fall in the domain of "counter-value" targets.

Though it is not yet known whether India or Pakistan possess any tactical nuclear weapons, there have been some indications that India, at least, has contemplated the tactical employment of its SSMs albeit with a conventional warhead. A specific case in point is the IAF's desire to opt for the Prithvi-II SSM instead of the Prithvi-I wherein it agreed to reduce the warhead size by 500 kg in return for a range increase of 100 km. The 250-km range Prithvi-II SSM now allows the IAF to attack almost all the main operating bases of the PAF with conventional warhead equipped Prithvi-II SSMs.

The range of the Prithvi-II SSM that has been specifically manufactured for the IAF's needs is depicted on the map below with a dark dotted line. As readers would discern, almost all of the PAF's major operational bases located in the provinces of Punjab and Sindh that border on India and the province of NWFP that borders on Afghanistan, lie within the effective strike range of this missile. The only major PAF airfield that appears to be beyond the reach of the IAF's Prithvi-II SSM is the PAF base located in the extreme south-west of the country, adjacent to the border with Iran and Afghanistan, at Samungli near Quetta in the province of Baluchistan.

Figure 4: Strike ranges of Indian SSMs[6]

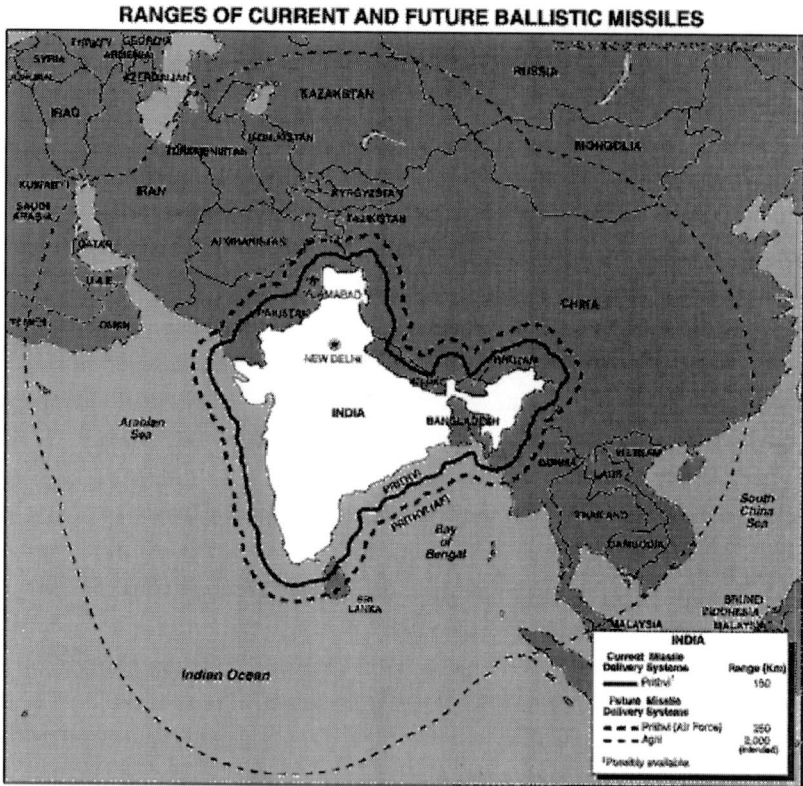

RANGES OF CURRENT AND FUTURE BALLISTIC MISSILES

In South Asia, the employment of tactical nuclear weapons is not considered a high probability because of the following factors:

- Having long contiguous borders and very densely inhabited border areas, both the countries face the danger of hitting a sizeable number of friendly population and assets. If one envisages the northern portion of the Indo-Pak border where Pakistan's most populous province of Punjab shares a frontier with Indian East Punjab, the effects of using even a tactical nuclear weapon would be too devastating for either of the countries to contemplate.

- As highlighted earlier, the two countries do not possess any surveillance or early warning system that could alert them of the launch of a missile in time. Also, even after a missile launch against it has been detected, there are no means available of determining whether the weapon is carrying a conventional warhead or a nuclear one. In this sort of a dilemma, a country like Pakistan that is also confronted with a phenomenal conventional military disadvantage, could well overreact by construing the missile to be having a nuclear warhead and respond in kind.

Conclusion

The theme of the chapter has been to highlight that despite having made tremendous strides in missile development, both India and Pakistan are not likely to employ these in the military sense but would rather continue to maintain these as instruments to be employed for the purposes of diplomatic and political coercion while remaining short of war. This would be primarily based on the realisation that the use of any SSM by any of the two countries would probably be the shortest route to a nuclear exchange which both countries are desirous of avoiding at all costs. The specific reasons why this assertion is being made are summarised below:

- The peculiar geo-dynamics of South Asia preclude any of the antagonists from employing a tactical nuclear weapon.
- In the absence of an effective surveillance and missile-launch detection system, any missile launch by one could easily be construed by the other as a nuclear strike and responded to accordingly.
- The above assertion would equally apply to missiles equipped with conventional warheads that India or Pakistan might contemplate employing.

In essence, therefore, it is the author's contention that since any employment of a missile system in South Asia by either India or Pakistan is expected to provoke a nuclear response from the other, the chances of these weapons ever being physically employed appear to be very slim.

However, considering the deterrent value of these weapons and the political clout that these bestow on the possessor, both India and Pakistan will continue, rather endeavour, to improve their SSM inventories even further. This competitiveness becomes all the more easy to comprehend when one sees that in the case of the almost fifty missile tests that India and Pakistan have conducted till now, most have immediately followed the conduct of a missile test by the other. An article in the April 2003 issue of *Arms Control Today*, mentions, "Since the back-to-back 1998 nuclear tests, a missile test by one state has usually prompted the other to respond with its own test in a face-off of missile strength and capability."[7] Whether these responses were meant to acquaint the enemy of own capabilities or whether these were for the consumption of the domestic public opinion or were actually undertaken to verify a technological advance, such tests can be expected to continue as a political statement of the assertion that one's capability is no less than that of the other.

Additionally, because of their relative ease of dispersion as regards deployment, SSMs would continue to remain a main component of the second-strike force rather than becoming a part of the first-strike potential of both the countries, at least till such time that either is able to field a nuclear capable SLBM weapon system. In this regard also, India reportedly has an edge whereas Pakistan is currently lagging behind.

Notes

1. These abbreviations stand for the following military research organisations that are involved in missile development programmes in Pakistan:
    - NDC: National Development Complex
    - NESCOM: National Scientific Complex
    - PMO: Project Management Organisation
    - PAEC: Pakistan Atomic Energy Commission
    - KRL: Khan Research Laboratories
    - SUPARCO: Space and Upper Air Research Commission
    - POF: Pakistan Ordnance Factories
    - AWC: Air Weapons Complex

    Although essentially the functioning of these organisations in the strategic domain is overseen by the military services in general and by the Strategic Plans Division (SPD) of the Joint Staff Headquarters (JSHQ) in particular, some of their projects are either supplementing each others' efforts while the rest are being pursued in competition with each other.

2. Downloaded from http://news.bbc.co.uk/1/hi/world/south_asia/3016775.stm#graphic.

3. Downloaded from http://news.bbc.co.uk/1/hi/world/south_asia/3015085.stm.

4. Readers should compare these output values of these nuclear warheads with the fact that the bomb that was dropped by the US over Hiroshima on August 6, 1945 had an explosive power of 15 kilotons while the one dropped over Nagasaki three days later was a weapon of 21 kilotons. While Pakistan would be able to install a 20 kiloton warhead on its Ghauri-II/Shaheen-II missiles, it is considered unlikely that India would be able to produce a 200 kiloton warhead for the Agni-II in the immediate future. As such, while the capacity of Agni-II missile to carry a larger warhead does exist, the chances of India being able to manufacture a weapon of this size are considered remote. According to data maintained by the US NRDC, none of the nuclear tests conducted by Pakistan or India in May 1998 were more than 12 kilotons. For more details, please refer to the NRDC website at http://www.nrdc.org/nuclear/nudb/datab22.asp. It should also be remembered that the previous Indian Defence Minister, George Fernandes, while speaking after the successful conduct of an Agni-II SSM, specifically mentioned that India now has the capability of developing a 200 kiloton nuclear warhead.

5. It was this very aspect of limited geographic depth that led to the former Chief of Staff of the Pakistan Army, General Mirza Aslam Beg espousing his theory that Pakistan's strategic depth lay in Iran during the days prior to the 1991 Gulf War.

6. This map has been downloaded from http://www.fas.org/nuke/guide/india/missile/index.html. Readers are requested to refer to the dotted dark lines that depict the maximum reach of the Prithvi-II SSM in order to understand that virtually all of the PAF's main air bases fall within its lethal range.

7. http://www.armscontrol.org/act/2003_04/missiletest_apr03.asp.

22 Simulating a South Asian Holocaust

Introduction

The volatility of the South Asian region and the propensity of India and Pakistan to go to war has made South Asia a region of enormous global concern. This concern has gotten further intensified since the May 1998 overt nuclearisation of India and Pakistan.

Analysts worldwide as well as in the US military have been war-gaming the possible outbreak of a military conflict in nuclearised South Asia so as to bring out the possible lessons and the courses of action that would be available to the US and other major players during the next South Asian War.

While it is true that these experimentations have been concerned more with the causes of the future war and less with its outcome, the analysis of these war-games brings out several lessons both for India and Pakistan.

This chapter brings together the salient analyses[1] of the war-games conducted at the US Naval War College and other US military institutions and think tanks in the aftermath of the May 1998 nuclear tests by India and Pakistan, with the objective of highlighting some of the salient conclusions that should serve as eye-openers for senior military leaders and planners in India and Pakistan.

Considering the complexities of simulating a war in a far away region, experts from 15 countries and from the specialities of diplomacy, military, economy and politics were made a part of the entire effort. Interestingly, representatives from India and Pakistan were also involved in the activity and participated in the exercise.

Exercise Scenarios

As the starting point of the exercise, a suitable scenario had to be generated. Not only did this scenario have to be realistic and plausible but it also had to fall well within the realms of probability. Also, the situation created by the scenario had to be serious enough for India and Pakistan contemplating going to a conventional war with all the chances of escalation to the nuclear level. For these war-games, the designers stipulated the following scenarios outlining the prevalent circumstances that precede the war and led to it:

Scenario 1[2]

Set in the year 2003, the scenario commences with the defeat of a resolution calling for international involvement to resolve the Kashmir dispute that was placed before the UN Security Council. This incident sparked a wave of anti-Western and anti-Hindu protests in India and Pakistan and also saw a sharp increase in the freedom struggle in Indian Held Kashmir (IHK). Events take a turn for the worse when an Indian Air Force transport aircraft carrying several senior government dignitaries including the Minister of Defence, the Minister of Interior and the Indian Army's Chief of Staff was shot down by a shoulder-fired surface-to-air missile en route to Srinagar. This tragic incident was immediately blamed by the Indian Government on extremist Islamic groups operating out of Pakistan with the implied connivance of the Government of Pakistan. Notwithstanding the Pakistani announcements of pacification, India responded by launching Operation *Resolute Sword* with air and artillery attacks against targets in Kashmir and northern Pakistan suspected of harbouring and supporting perpetrators of violence in Kashmir and the rest of India. While declaring that its intentions were limited in both scope and objective, the Indian Government issued an ultimatum demanding the immediate delivery of terrorist leaders who were sheltered in Pakistan, the dismantling of known terrorist headquarters and training facilities, and the removal of all Pakistani military forces from Kashmir. Initially, Pakistan offered little resistance to the Indian attacks, which inflicted heavy damage to the infrastructure targets against which they were delivered.

When Indian forces suspended their attack and began to celebrate the initial successes of *Resolute Sword*, Pakistan seized the opportunity for a surprise attack against Indian forces east and south of Lahore. During a two-day battle, Pakistani units managed to push about fifty kilometres into Indian territory, inflicting heavy casualties on Indian civilians, before a counter-offensive brought the Pakistani onslaught to a halt. To counter the Pakistani advances in Indian Punjab, the Indians commenced a rapid offensive movement across the Thar Desert toward the Indus River. Fearing that India was about to cut Pakistan in two, severing Islamabad's strategic lifeline between the north and the south, the Pakistani high command ordered a barrage of tactical missile strikes. Four of these missiles carried nuclear warheads: three twenty-kiloton weapons were delivered against Indian forces to halt their advance toward the border, and the fourth was used against the supporting rail hub in Jodhpur. These strikes stalled the Indian movement, destroyed the Jodhpur rail hub while simultaneously causing widespread destruction among the civilian population of Jodhpur. Experts from the US Defence Threat Reduction Agency (DTRA) estimated the number of dead and seriously injured in the hundreds of thousands.

All this while the matter had been placed before the UN Security Council but its members could not agree on any resolution. India reacted to the

Pakistani nuclear strike by launching nuclear attacks against twelve selected nuclear installations in Pakistan with devastating consequences. Since most of these nuclear facilities were located near populated areas, expert analysis by the US DTRA estimated some fifteen million casualties from the attack, including one to two million dead.

The five permanent members of the UN Security Council now held separate consultations with India and Pakistan and developed a proposal for ending the crisis: immediate cessation of military activities, renunciation and elimination of nuclear activities by both countries, a return to the status quo that existed in Kashmir prior to the war, and international security guarantees for both India and Pakistan.

Scenario 2[3]

In Gardiner's reckoning, it was almost invariably Pakistan that initiated the hostilities and he envisages an initial attack by Pakistan that cuts the Indian link to Kashmir. India responds against this attack by rushing its main forces towards Lahore—Pakistan's second-largest city, and the country's cultural and intellectual centre in a bid to force Pakistan to withdraw/halt its advance.

As Indian units advance toward Lahore, Pakistan realises that the war is reaching a critical point. If the Indians take the city, they will virtually be able to split Pakistan in two and the Pakistani nuclear weapons will be of little or no use. The Indians must be stopped and that too quickly.

As the scenario is played out, it emerges that the only way for Pakistan to do that is by using nuclear weapons on India's forces inside Pakistan. Strange as that sounds, using nuclear weapons on your own territory has some political advantages, and bears some similarities to NATO strategic options that were in place during the Cold War. The world would see it as a defensive measure and India would be seen as the aggressor.

It takes three or four nuclear weapons to stop the massive Indian attack. Pakistani forces also suffer heavy casualties from the blasts and radiation, but the Indian advance is halted.

India is left with a dilemma. Does it retaliate against Pakistan with nuclear weapons? Should it hit Pakistan's cities in its initial strike? That would only further cede the moral high ground to Pakistan. India picks four or five Pakistani military targets for its first use of nuclear weapons, but the attacks also cause significant civilian casualties. In the simulation, Pakistan responds by dropping a nuclear bomb on New Delhi.

The casualties from this exchange vary depending on the exact targets and the winds, but they would be measured in the millions. If Pakistan drops a relatively primitive nuclear weapon of 20 kilotons, 50 per cent of the people living within a one-mile radius of the blast would die immediately. Fires would ignite as far away as two miles, and blast damage would extend to buildings three miles from the point of impact. People 3½ miles away would suffer skin burns and radiation could extend hundreds of miles, depending on the weather.

Scenario 3[4]
Dr. Kapila in his analysis of the US military's war-games focused on South Asia, does not take into consideration the build-up to the hostilities or the circumstances that lead to the outbreak of war. Based on the immense conventional superiority that India enjoys vis-à-vis Pakistan, he contends that not only would Indian conventional military superiority prevail in the event of Indian counterterrorism military operations against Pakistan but that this would be able to sever Pakistan's North-South communication arteries, thereby throttling Pakistan.

He asserts that the eventuality of Pakistan's strategic north-south communication links being cut would force Pakistan to cross the red-line of its nuclear threshold and result in Pakistan employing its first strike nuclear option.[5] In Kapila's analysis, the conflict in South Asia will progress to the nuclear level in three phases:

- In Phase 1, like Gardiner, he envisages Pakistan resorting to a nuclear first strike primarily as a battlefield tactical nuclear strike against India's strike formations with India following suit.
- In the second phase, like Gardiner and Taylor, Dr. Kapila anticipates India and Pakistan resorting to nuclear strikes against each other's major cities and population centres.
- In the third phase he expects India and Pakistan carrying out nuclear strikes against each other's capital cities, i.e., Islamabad and New Delhi.

In Dr. Kapila's reckoning, while Pakistan is expected to suffer comparatively more damage and casualties during the first two phases, the 3rd phase would see India suffering disproportionately larger damage basically because of the large difference between the sizes of the two capital cities. In his analysis, Dr. Kapila indicates the total number of casualties in South Asia to be in the region of 12 million.

Salient Conclusions

Scary though these must seem, such were the scenarios that were typically played out in the South Asian war-games conducted by the US military. Notwithstanding some of the differences that characterise each particular scenario, several of the lessons that emerged from these different scenarios were similar and an analysis of these is considered essential if we are to draw any lessons from these exercises for the South Asian defence planners and military leaders.

Scenario Described by Taylor

- In analysing the scenario, Ambassador Taylor writes that "while some participants in each event commented that the scenario pushed events more relentlessly toward nuclear war than they would expect in a real situation, no one argued that the scenario could not happen."
- The participants identified no significant military role for the US or its allies in a military crisis between India and Pakistan but did highlight the need for the US to create a standing, deployable "consequence management" force that could help in overcoming the after-effects of a nuclear war in South Asia or elsewhere.
- The participants asserted that the economic costs of a nuclear war in South Asia would far exceed the cost of trying to prevent one.
- While concluding that the US had limited influence in the matter, the participants did question whether the international community was indeed doing enough to help resolve the Kashmir dispute and ensure that it does not lead to a nuclear showdown between India and Pakistan. This was indicative of a realisation among the participants that the international community in general and the major powers in particular had not done enough to resolve the causes of dispute that continue to plague relations between India and Pakistan despite these two hostile countries having become unrecognised nuclear powers.

Scenario Described by Gardiner

- Notwithstanding the disastrous consequences of the nuclear exchange, the fundamental issues bedevilling relations between India and Pakistan remained unresolved even after the war.
- In all the simulations that were played out, it was always some incident that provoked the two countries into bringing their forces to a higher than normal state of readiness, deploying them to the border and contemplating the initiation of military hostilities.

- While Indian conventional military might is far superior to that of Pakistan, Gardiner feels that the decisive elements of the military wherewithal would be the armour and the mechanised formations where the disparity is not as great between the Indian and the Pakistani armies.

- Pakistan could compensate for its disadvantages by the wise use of its units and the desire to act quickly and surprise the enemy would warrant an initiation of hostilities against India. In Gardiners's reckoning, "When it became apparent in the simulations that conflict was inevitable, one of the sides—usually Pakistan—always initiated combat."[6]

- According to Gardiner's assessment, the events of the previous Indo-Pak wars as well as the simulations that he participated in indicate that the "important fighting doesn't take place in that contested area (Kashmir)." He feels that since the mountainous terrain of Kashmir does not offer a suitable battleground for any decisive manoeuvre, "both sides look to other parts of the 2,000-mile border that divides them."

- In Gardiner's assessment, "the critical terrain for both sides is the Punjab valley, where key north-south roads lie. On the Indian side of the border, these roads are the link to Kashmir. On the Pakistani side, they link the southern part of that country with Lahore and Islamabad. These are strategic lifelines for both nations."

- The nuclearisation of South Asia changed the situation drastically. Whereas in previous wars the two countries going nuclear was generally predictable, the advent of nuclear weapons altered the scenario to an extent where "conventional forces were used differently, and the wars certainly ended differently." Gardiner feels that Pakistan's military strategy has been influenced more by nuclearisation than has India's.[7]

- Gardiner envisages the Pakistani success in cutting off Kashmir from India leading to an Indian offensive against Lahore which ends up overstepping Pakistan's nuclear threshold.

- In order to bring the Indian onslaught against Lahore to a standstill, Pakistan employs nuclear weapons against the Indian Army columns advancing towards this important city.[8] The use of 4-5 nuclear weapons by Pakistan does cause enormous casualties to its own forces but succeeds in bringing the Indian offensive against Lahore to a complete halt. The impact of such a nuclear strike by Pakistan is depicted on the following diagram.[9]

- Interestingly, unlike the other analysts, Gardiner anticipates the US coming into the conflict on the side of Pakistan since it is the weaker of the two belligerents.[10]

Situation: Pakistan uses nuclear device against attacking Indian troops.

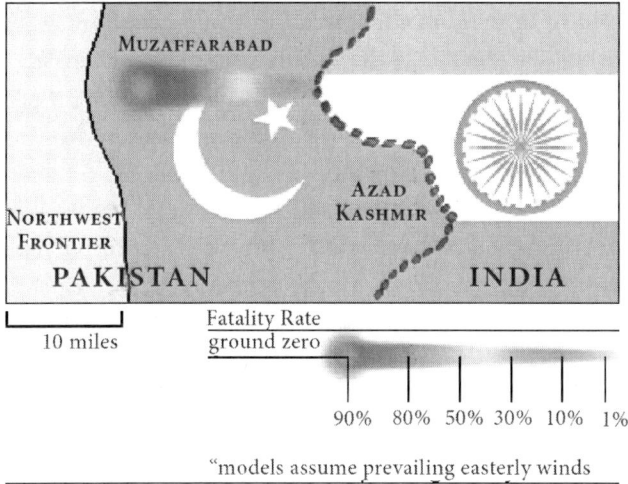

10 miles

Fatality Rate
ground zero

90% 80% 50% 30% 10% 1%

"models assume prevailing easterly winds

Nuclear Device:
10 kiloton fission bomb

Range of initial blast
1.2 miles

Range of lethal fallout:
5.6 miles

Estimated immediate civilian deaths:
3,500

- The eventuality of Pakistan going nuclear leaves Indian leadership confronted with a dilemma; should it retaliate against Pakistan with nuclear weapons and should its initial nuclear reprisal strikes target Pakistani cities? An important consideration while making this decision would be that such an action would amount to further ceding the moral high ground to Pakistan.
- Gardiner envisages India selecting 4-5 Pakistani military targets for a retaliatory nuclear strike but since these are located near large population centres, the enormous loss of life forces Pakistan to respond with a nuclear attack against New Delhi with the total casualties being counted in the millions.

Scenario Described by Dr. Kapila

- Although Dr. Kapila does not mention where the hostilities would commence, he is of the opinion that the war-games indicate Pakistan's nuclear threshold being reached when the Indian Army is in a position to threaten a breach in Pakistan's north-south communication arteries. This being the objective of the Indian Army, it can be expected that its offensive would materialise in South Western Punjab in the proximity of Reti and Rahim Yar Khan. This is the same conclusion that Colonel Sam Gardiner has arrived at in his analysis.

- Like Gardiner, he also reckons that Pakistan would use nuclear weapons over the battlefield to stop the Indian Army's advance but, unlike Gardiner, envisages the Indian response to be a nuclear retaliatory strike against Pakistani cities and population centres. The diagram below illustrates the consequences of India and Pakistan attacking each other's border cities of Amritsar and Lahore with nuclear weapons.[11] Needless to say, the enormous size of Lahore as compared to Amritsar would result in the attack against the former leading to higher loss of life and property.

- In a continuation of the nuclear exchange, he expects the next targets to be the capital cities of Islamabad and New Delhi. The devastation expected to be caused after Islamabad is targeted with a nuclear weapon is depicted on the following diagram:[12]

Situation: Pakistan and India trade nuclear attacks on border cities.

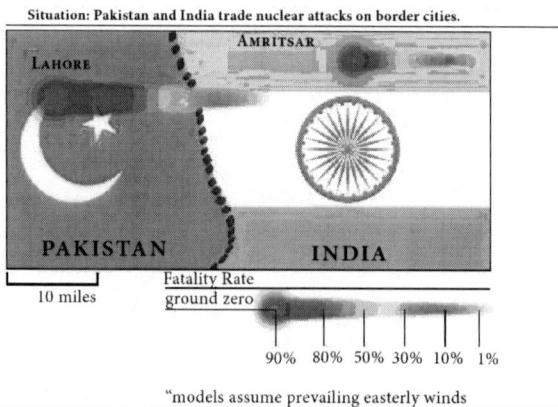

10 miles	Fatality Rate ground zero

90% 80% 50% 30% 10% 1%

"models assume prevailing easterly winds

DIRECT HIT IN LAHORE, PAKISTAN: Nuclear Device: **12 kiloton fission bomb**	DIRECT HIT IN AMRITSAR, INDIA Nuclear Device: **10 kilotlon fission bomb**
Range of initial blast: **1.75 miles**	Range of initial blast: **1.68miles**
Range of lethal fallout:	Range of lethal fallout: **6.3 miles**
Estimated immediate civilion deaths in Lahore: **122,000**	Estimated immediate civilion deaths Amritsar: **112,000**

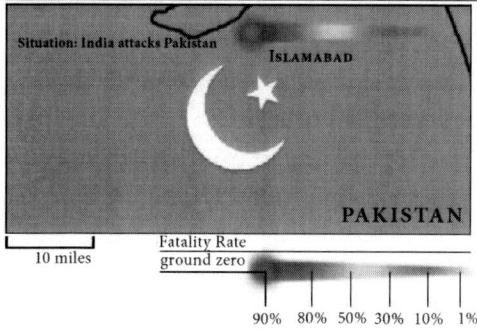

Situation: India attacks Pakistan

10 miles

Fatality Rate
ground zero

90% 80% 50% 30% 10% 1%

"models assume prevailing easterly winds

DIRECT HIT IN ISLAMABAD, PAKISTAN:
Nuclear Device:
12 kiloton fission bomb

Range of initial blast:
1.75 miles

Range of lethal fallout:
6.3 miles

Estimated immediate civilian deaths by blast: **115,000**

Estimated civilian deaths by fallout: **195,000**

- Considering the difference in the size between Islamabad and New Delhi, a similar nuclear strike by Pakistan against the Indian capital would result in substantially larger casualties as depicted on the following diagram:

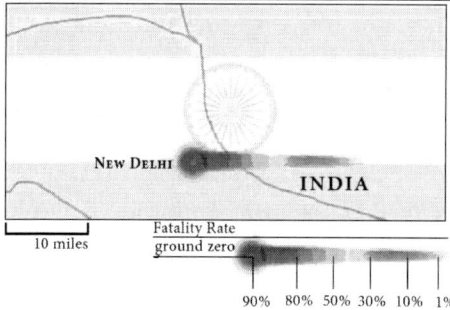

Situation: Pakistan attacks New Delhi

10 miles

Fatality Rate
ground zero

90% 80% 50% 30% 10% 1%

"models assume prevailing easterly winds

DIRECT HIT IN NEW DELHI
Nuclear Device:
12 kiloton fission bomb

Range of initial blast:
1.68 miles

Range of lethal fallout:
6.3 miles

Estimated immediate civilian deaths by blast: **125,000**

Estimated civilian deaths by fallout: **365,000**

- In disagreement with the other two analysts who have been cited in this article, Dr. Kapila asserts that the eventuality of Pakistan exercising the Nuclear First-Use option would only materialise because of the US adopting a permissive attitude that could embolden Pakistan's embattled leadership to go down the nuclear path. In his opinion, not only is the US capable of coming to know of any Pakistani preparations for a nuclear strike but it is also capable of impounding Pakistan's entire nuclear arsenal.

- Unlike the other two analysts, Dr. Kapila does not see the US and the rest of the world sitting idly and permitting the escalation of the conflict to the nuclear level. He contends that: firstly, while its army is engaged with the Indian strike elements, Pakistan is incapable of going nuclear and secondly, it is strategically implausible that the US and the other major powers would permit Pakistan to "proceed with nuclear escalation."[13]

- In order to cater to the threat of a Pakistani nuclear first-use, however, Dr. Kapila suggests that the clause of "No First Use" that is mentioned in the draft Indian Nuclear Doctrine be amended to read "No First Use against non-nuclear states."[14]

- Dr. Kapila concludes by suggesting that the United States should refrain from adopting a permissive attitude that could encourage Pakistani nuclear brinkmanship and should also consider taking pre-emptive steps against Pakistan's nuclear assets if it continues to defy US advice.[15]

Analysis conducted by Brad Hayes. In a detailed analysis of the war-game that was conducted at the US Naval War College in early 1999, Brad Hayes highlights that the deliberations amongst the participants of the war-game brought out the following salient observations:[16]

- International organisations are likely to be ineffective in addressing a nuclear crisis in South Asia, primarily because their deliberations take too long. However, a forum like the UN will still be required for the conduct of critical multilateral negotiations, whether or not the organisation itself gets involved in intervention.

- For the foreseeable future, "managed tension" will remain the norm between India and Pakistan.

- Historic ties shape the perceptions and actions of belligerents as well as those responding to a crisis. Although this may sound like a blinding flash of the obvious, the extent to which historic ties impacted the game was revealing.

- Conventional force confidence-building measures between India and Pakistan need to be complemented by nuclear CBMs.

- Nuclear weapons provide states with enhanced negotiating leverage. Nuclear weapons provide countries with a wild card that they would not otherwise possess.
- Conflicting views concerning the importance of nuclear weapons will continue. India, in particular, sees possession of nuclear weapons as the key to great power status.
- Post-nuclear exchange options are extremely limited.
- As regards the policy options that would be available to the US in the event of a future Indo-Pak military conflict, Hayes lists the following salient ones:[17]
- The US must pursue more sources of leverage that could be used to prevent a crisis from escalating and understand how to employ them aggressively.
- Pre-crisis sanctions and embargo generally weaken, rather than strengthen, the international community's bargaining position.
- Policymakers must recognise that leverage weakens as a crisis escalates.
- Terrorism can precipitate interstate conflict.
- The international community needs to be more proactive in dealing with festering tensions among nuclear powers. The challenge in South Asia remains Kashmir.
- Unilateral options are unlikely to work. US actions were accepted only as long as they were developed in partnership with others.
- Non-proliferation and comprehensive test ban treaties are more likely to delay than to halt the spread of nuclear weapons. Countries currently pursuing nuclear programmes are not likely to renounce them.

Conclusion

The three scenarios described in this chapter, as well as the others that were simulated after the May 1998 nuclear tests conducted by India and Pakistan, invariably culminated in a nuclear exchange. Significantly, none of the scenarios played in these war-games led to direct international intervention in time to prevent the nuclear holocaust. Also, it emerged that even at the global level, disaster relief capabilities to cater for such an eventuality were woefully inadequate to cater to the millions of casualties and the enormous damage to property.

The objective of this chapter was to highlight how probable a nuclear exchange could be in any future conflict in India and Pakistan and to consolidate, in one place, the various analyses that have been conducted of US military war-games focused on a future conflict in South Asia. The purpose has not been to paint a picture of an impending disaster but to bring to the fore some of the possibilities that the political and military leaderships of India and Pakistan must consider while planning the future road-map of their mutual relations.

Notes

1. The following analytical writings on the subject have formed the basis of this article and have been referred to at various places in the text. Fortunately all of these analyses are available on the internet:

   - Sam Gardiner, "It Doesn't Start in Kashmir, and It Never Ends Well." *Washington Post*, January 20, 2002. Accessible on the internet at http://www. washingtonpost.com/ac2/wp-dyn?pagename=article&contentId=A6820-2002Jan19&notFound=true. Sam Gardiner is a retired USAF Colonel who has participated in over 20 War-Games focusing on South Asia that have been conducted by the US military over the past decade.

   - Dexter Ingram, "Possible Nuclear Conflict Scenarios: Pakistan Uses A Nuclear Device on Attacking Indian Army." Web Memo No. 104, June 4, 2002. Accessible on the internet at http://www.heritage.org/Research/NationalSecurity/WM104. cfm.

   - Bradd C. Hayes, "International Game '99: Crisis in South Asia: 28-30 January 1999," sponsored by the United States Naval War College. This detailed analysis of the 1999 War Game conducted at the US Naval War College can be accessed on the internet at http://66.102.7.104/search?q=cache:GnKr4jSDoAsJ:www. nwc.navy.mil/apsg/India--Pakistan%2520International%2520Game%2520Rep ort%2520(Jan%252099).doc+india+pakistan+war+games&hl=en.

   - Chidanand Rajghatta, "N-War games: India pulps Pakistan after taking initial hits." *The Times of India*, New Delhi, May 8, 2001. http://biiss.org/nuclear/May 2001/57.htm.

   - Dr. Subhash Kapila, "United States War-Gaming on South Asia—An Analysis." SAAG Paper No. 476. June 14, 2002. http://www.saag.org/papers5/paper476.html.

   - Paul D. Taylor, "India and Pakistan: Thinking about the Unthinkable—war game scenario involving nuclear weapons." *Naval War College Review*, Summer, 2001. http://www.findarticles.com/p/articles/mi_m0JIW/is_3_54/ ai_80786332/pg_1. This article is continued over four web pages each of which has to be individually accessed in sequence.

2. The salient aspects of the exercise scenario have been extracted from Paul D. Taylor, "India and Pakistan: Thinking about the Unthinkable—War game scenario involving nuclear weapons." *Naval War College Review*, Summer, 2001. http://www.findarticles. com/p/articles/mi_m0JIW/is_3_54/ai_80786332/pg_1. This article is continued over four web pages, each of which has to be individually accessed in sequence.

3. The salient aspects of the exercise scenario have been extracted from Sam Gardiner, "It Doesn't Start in Kashmir, and It Never Ends Well." *Washington Post*, January 20,

2002. Sam Gardiner is a retired USAF Colonel who has participated in over 20 War-Games focusing on South Asia that have been conducted by the US military over the past decade. Accessible on the internet at http://www.washingtonpost.com/ac2/wp-dyn?pagename=article&contentId=A6820-2002Jan19&notFound=true.

4. The salient aspects of the exercise scenario have been extracted from Dr. Subhash Kapila, "United States War-Gaming on South Asia—An Analysis." South Asian Analysis Group (SAAG) Paper No. 476 dated June 14, 2002. http://www.saag.org/papers5/paper476.html.

5. For a detailed analysis of Pakistan's Nuclear First-Use Option, please refer to the author's article titled "Assessing Pakistan's Nuclear First-Use Option" that appeared in the September 2004 issue of the *Defence Journal*, pp. 12-15.

6. Sam Gardiner, op. cit.

7. This could be an outcome of the huge conventional disparity that Pakistan is confronted with. In the situation that Pakistan finds itself, it is logical for it to try and compensate for its conventional disadvantage by relying more on nuclear weapons.

8. Gardiner highlights that this eventuality of dropping nuclear weapons on enemy forces that have ventured inside friendly territory is not new since NATO had planned for similar contingencies during the height of the Cold War. He goes on to elaborate by saying that the world would see it (Pakistan's resort to the nuclear first-use) as a defensive measure with India being seen as the aggressor.

9. This diagram has been taken from Dexter Ingram, "Possible Nuclear Conflict Scenarios: Pakistan Uses A Nuclear Device on Attacking Indian Army." Web Memo No. 104, June 4, 2002. This paper is available on the internet at http://www.heritage.org/Research/NationalSecurity/WM104.cfm. Interestingly, Ingram's analysis of the devastation likely to be caused by nuclear attacks during a South Asian nuclear exchange presupposes that the explosive power of the weapons that India or Pakistan could be expected to deploy would range between 10 and 12 kilotons.

10. In Gardiner's opinion, "Any use of US forces would mean taking sides; three-sided wars are not possible. The United States would have to side with the weaker party, meaning Pakistan. But that still might not prevent a cataclysmic outcome."

11. Dexter Ingram, op. cit.

12. Dexter Ingram, op. cit.

13. Dr. Subash Kapila, op. cit.

14. Ibid. While making the suggestion for the draft Indian nuclear doctrine being modified to read "No first-use against non-nuclear states" instead of the existing clause that reads "No First-Use," Dr. Kapila contends that "It should be made clear to Pakistan that against it, India would not hesitate to use the 'first-strike' nuclear option."

15. Ibid.

16. Brad Hayes, op. cit. His analysis is based on the same scenario that has been dealt with by Ambassador Taylor as elaborated in the earlier text of this paper.

17. Ibid.

23 Air Power Imbalance: Pakistan's Achilles Heel

The overt nuclearisation of India and Pakistan in May 1998 drastically altered the military landscape of South Asia. From being earlier confined to thinking, planning and operating purely in terms of limited wars and conventional weaponry, military planners on both sides now had to grapple and contend with the additional strategic doctrinal dilemmas and considerations of deterrence, nuclear first-use, nuclear first strike, counter-force versus counter-value targeting and nuclear thresholds, etc.

Conventional imbalance in the military domain has been a constant defining characteristic of South Asian defence dynamics ever since India and Pakistan achieved independence in 1947. Understandably, the greater size, population and resources of India have not only necessitated but also enabled her military to stay ahead in conventional military might, with Pakistan continuing to play the "catch-up" game. Needless to say, other than the resources available with them, the quantum of military potential of both the countries has also been shaped significantly by what their respective superpower allies or other friendly countries have been willing to provide them in terms of military wherewithal.[1]

One irrefutable legacy that the Indian and Pakistani militaries got from the British colonials was their rigid adherence and unshakeable belief in the somewhat outdated tenets of continental warfare. This led both the countries to adopt army-centric military doctrines and resulted in more resources being diverted towards their respective Armies with the Navies and the Air Forces being neglected. This was more true in the case of Pakistan where the Army has ruled the country for almost half its total period of existence.

The chronic inferiority in the conventional military realm that Pakistan has continued to be confronted with and still continues to face led to the adoption of a doctrine of *Strategic Defence and Tactical Offence*[2] by the Pakistan Army. While there is no doubt that Pakistan has remained militarily inferior to India, it must be kept in mind that the Indian conventional military superiority has also never reached a stage where it would be classified or categorised as bestowing a "decisive edge" over the Pakistani military. The truth of the indecisive nature of this conventional military imbalance was borne out by the indecisive stalemates that occurred during the 1948 and the 1965 wars.[3]

The situation that I have depicted in the preceding paragraphs remained valid till the conduct of nuclear tests by India and Pakistan in May 1998 since this epochal event altered the South Asian military scenario drastically.

First of all, one needs to understand the essential motivation that drove India and Pakistan to go nuclear. In my reckoning, Pakistan's basic objective in its quest to acquire nuclear military capability has always been the desire to be able to counter the Indian conventional superiority, while India has been driven, among other things, by her desire to emerge as a regional/global power, her need to balance China and, of course, the wish to gain a decisive military advantage over Pakistan which she had failed to achieve in the conventional realm. From this it flows that while Pakistan's nuclear arsenal is designed primarily to deter the launching of a conventional attack by India, the Indian nuclear weapons are likely to be employed for political power projection and to obviate the chances of any country employing nuclear weapons against India. While elaborating on Pakistan's nuclear posture, Ramussino and Martollini write that "nuclear weapons are perceived in Pakistan as an instrument to countervail a manifest conventional inferiority."[4] Explaining this further, they describe how the Pakistani nuclear posture is strikingly similar to the NATO doctrine of extended deterrence during the cold war period which also made constant reference to the possible use of nuclear weapons to countervail conventional inferiority vis-à-vis the Warsaw Pact military forces and refused to issue any no first use declaration.[5] In fact, NATO has not issued any such declaration till this day and continues to maintain ambiguity on this issue just like Pakistan has opted to do.

In any military conflict between two nuclear armed adversaries such as India and Pakistan, it would be safe to conclude that the chances are much higher of the conventionally weaker country, i.e., Pakistan opting to use nuclear weapons first. This is precisely why while India has disavowed nuclear first-use in her draft nuclear doctrine, Pakistan continues to maintain a semblance of ambiguity regarding its nuclear first-use posture while simultaneously continuing to imply that such employment remains a possibility.

Since any future South Asian conflict would start in the conventional realm before escalating to nuclear dimensions and because Pakistan is the more likely of the two adversaries to opt for the use of nuclear weapons first, it is vital for us to study the possible course of events that could make Pakistan move up the conflict escalation ladder by opting to go nuclear. This decision point which is commonly referred to as the *nuclear threshold* could, in my opinion, be better described as the *nuclear escalation threshold*.

Pakistan has maintained an element of ambiguity regarding its nuclear posture and still continues to do so. As such, key issues such as what does Pakistan's "nuclear escalation threshold" actually translate into have not been talked about much. One significant exception to the silence of the Pakistani leadership on this issue occurred when a group of Italian journalists interviewed Lieutenant General Khalid Kidwai, the Director General of Pakistan's Strategic Plans Division (SPD). In a marked departure from earlier statements and interviews which were silent on this vital issue, the DG SPD outlined the limits of Pakistan's *nuclear escalation threshold* in the following words that have been extracted verbatim from the report published by the journalists after their return to Italy:[6]

It is well known that Pakistan does not have a *No First Use Policy*. Pakistani nuclear weapons will be used, according to Gen. Kidwai, only "if the very existence of Pakistan as a state is at stake." This has been detailed by Gen. Kidwai as follows:[7]

"Nuclear weapons are aimed solely at India. In case that deterrence fails, they will be used if

- India attacks Pakistan and conquers a large part of its territory (space threshold)
- India destroys a large part either of its land or air forces (military threshold)
- India proceeds to the economic strangling of Pakistan (economic strangling)
- India pushes Pakistan into political destabilisation or creates a large scale internal subversion in Pakistan (domestic destabilisation)."

Since domestic destabilisation and economic strangulation are not relevant to the theme of this chapter, I will focus on the first two, i.e., territorial or space threshold and the military threshold.

As regards the territorial or space threshold, I had earlier written the following:[8]

"In conventional terms, the occurrence of any of the following events could warrant Pakistan resorting to the nuclear option:

- Penetration of the Indian forces beyond a certain defined line of communication or river.
- Imminent capture of an important Pakistani city like Lahore or Sialkot.

- Indian crossing of the Line of Control in Kashmir to an extent that it threatens Pakistan's control over Pakistan Held Kashmir."

While the denial of Pakistani territory to the Indian military would jointly fall into the domain of the Pakistan Army and the Pakistan Air Force, the former would bear the primary responsibility for it with the latter operating essentially in a supportive role.

At this stage, it would be pertinent for us to have a brief comparative overview of the respective Armies and Air Forces of India and Pakistan since it is these two military arms that would play a major role in determining the outcome of any conventional India-Pakistan war.

As regards the two Armies, one can see that the Indian Army has a 2:1 advantage in personnel and a slightly better one in armour and artillery. It has always been an accepted fact amongst military strategists and practitioners that in order to ensure success, a land force on the offensive must have a 3:1 advantage in numbers over the defending force since the latter is operating from well dug-in and reinforced positions located generally in terrain that the personnel are very familiar with. As the figures indicate, the Indian Army does not by itself possess this decisive advantage over the Pakistan Army. When considered jointly with the might of the Indian Air Force, however, the balance does definitely tilt in favour of the Indians.

The salient comparative aspects of the Indian and the Pakistan Air Forces are depicted on Table 1 below with an explanation of the same in the subsequent text:

Table 1: Comparison of IAF and PAF combat assets and potential[9]

	IAF	PAF	Analysis
Manpower	127,200	70,000	1.81:1
Combat aircraft	872	423	1.84:1[10]
Transport aircraft	238	20	11.9:1[11] IAF has overwhelming edge
Air-to-air refuelling capability	Yes	Yes	Evenly matched
AWACS	Yes	Yes	Evenly matched
BVR air-to-air missiles	Yes	Limited number	IAF superior since PAF capability is restricted to usage only on newer/modified F-16s

UAV	Yes	Yes	IAF enjoys significant superiority
High-tech combat aircraft[12]	244	63	3.78:1 IAF enjoys overwhelming edge

- The IAF enjoys almost a 2:1 advantage purely in numerical terms but its superiority is further accentuated by its possession of BVR weapons in large numbers and their compatibility with most of its combat aircraft along with potent UAV fleet. Purely in terms of numbers, the ratio is not as advantageous to the IAF as it used to be earlier but this comparative reduction in numbers has more than adequately been made up by qualitative improvement.

- The IAF's technological edge is also evidenced by the disproportionately large number of high-technology combat aircraft that it possesses vis-à-vis the PAF. This qualitative edge has shifted to the IAF because it has been able to have unrestricted access to Russian and Israeli technology while Pakistan has been denied any additional aviation assets other than a handful of upgraded F-16 aircraft from USA. China, which has been Pakistan's main military aircraft provider, does not currently produce any combat aircraft that would be comparable to the Western high-technology combat aircraft. Although this ratio might improve slightly after the initially ordered batch of 24 F-16 C/D aircraft enter service (the first two have been delivered), the IAF will again gain the edge with the induction of the additional 126 Rafale combat aircraft that it is in the process of acquiring from France.

- The IAF has a significantly larger transport aircraft fleet that bestows significant military airlift capability on it. The disadvantage of almost 12:1 in this area permits the IAF an almost strategic level of airlift capability while that of the PAF could best be described as one having sub-tactical potential. This enormous air transport potential when looked at from the perspective of the IAF's substantially greater trained manpower pool, adds significantly to the flexibility of operations mobility in terms of rapid deployments/redeployments. The induction of the C-17 and the latest version of C-130 will further accentuate this imbalance in the IAF's favour.

- Other than the areas where the IAF enjoys exclusiveness or will soon do so, the most significant disparity lies in the number of high-technology combat platforms that the two air forces possess.

Although the IAF has a 2.6:1 advantage in overall numbers, its edge in high-tech aircraft exceeds a factor of 3.78:1 and is expected to continue growing as more Su-30 MKI aircraft and the additional 126 Rafale advanced combat aircraft are inducted into the IAF and enter operational service.

Having illustrated the gross imbalance that exists between the two Air Forces, I will now move on to the implications that imbalance would have during any future conventional war between India and Pakistan:

Modern land warfare, to a great extent, is dependent on the achievement of a favourable air situation over the battlefield. This entails the friendly air force being able to support its own army fully while simultaneously preventing the adversary Air Force from interfering with its operations. The IAF vs. PAF comparison indicates that the IAF is much more capable of achieving a favourable air situation over the area of the land battle and as such, it can contribute significantly to the success of the Indian Army's land offensive. Moreover, the strong IAF with its superior beyond visual range missiles (BVR)[13] will be able to neutralise the PAF by mounting a concerted counter-air operations campaign against the latter. Once the PAF has been adequately neutralised, the path to an Indian victory on the ground would be absolutely open and the offensive formations of the Indian Army would be virtually unstoppable. This could well mean the creation of a state of affairs where, as General Kidwai put it, *the very existence of Pakistan as a state is at stake.*[14]

Conclusion

An analysis of the comparative strengths of the Indian and Pakistani military clearly indicates that the weakest link in Pakistan's military is her Air Force—especially when compared directly with the much more powerful and better equipped IAF. The significance of this weakest link must not be underestimated since the destruction of the PAF emerges to be the quickest way to make Pakistan contemplate and undertake the undesirable escalatory step of turning a conventional limited war into a nuclear holocaust.

This conclusion has lessons not only for the Pakistan Government but also for the major global powers. While the Pakistani Government must embark on a crash programme to suitably re-equip its Air Force urgently, the major global powers must also understand the fact that in order to enhance the level of stability in South Asia, it is vital that Pakistan's nuclear escalation threshold be raised and not allowed to drop any further. As this chapter has indicated, the means for raising Pakistan's nuclear escalation threshold lie in strengthening its Air Force since this is currently the weakest link in Pakistan's military chain.

As was shown by the Kargil conflict, the advent of nuclear weapons in South Asia has not rendered limited conventional wars in the region impossible. In fact, as Michael Krepon argues in his discussion of the Stability-Instability paradox, small-scale limited conventional conflicts might even become more frequent in South Asia.[15] The focus of all measures—international as well as regional—that are aimed at promoting and achieving nuclear stability in South Asia must be to ensure that the nuclear escalation threshold of the militarily weaker country, i.e., Pakistan is not allowed to drop. In order to ensure this, the global community must remain alert to any weaknesses emerging in Pakistan's conventional military wherewithal vis-à-vis India and address these immediately lest a limited conventional conflict in South Asia turn into a nuclear holocaust with terrifying consequences not only for the region but also for the entire world.

The aspect to specifically focus on in this context is the serious imbalance between the Air Forces of the two countries since the weak Air Force that Pakistan is currently able to field might well prove to be Pakistan's Achilles heel by becoming the prime reason for it to escalate a limited conflict to the nuclear dimension. Paradoxically, therefore, it appears to be in India's national interest to downplay the increasing strength and potential of her Air Force so as to preclude a further lowering of Pakistan's perceived nuclear escalation threshold.

Notes

1. I am thankful and indebted to Dr. Rodney Jones, President, Policy Architects International, Virginia, USA, for his invaluable support and help in collecting the data for this Policy Brief.
2. Interestingly, this very doctrinal precept that the Pakistan Army has traditionally adhered to is designed to prevent a conventional conflict escalating into a nuclear war but I doubt if the Army ever looked at it in this dimension. What they were more focused on was to end the war on a favourable note.
3. I have intentionally not included the 1971 war here since that was more of a civil war for the Pakistani military and while it did result in the fall of East Pakistan, the situation on the Western borders at the end of the war was once again that of a

stalemate with no significant gains being made by either of the sides.

4. Paolo Cotta-Ramusino and Maurizio Martellini, "Nuclear safety, nuclear stability and nuclear strategy in Pakistan." *A concise report of a visit by Landau Network-Centro Volta.* Available on the internet at http://www.mi.infn.it/~landnet/Doc/pakistan.pdf.

5. Ibid. See explanation for footnote 11.

6. Ibid. Readers should note that Lt. Gen. Kidwai only makes a mention of the destruction of Pakistan Army and Air Force in the realm of military threshold and makes no mention of the Pakistan Navy.

7. Paolo Cotta-Ramusino and Maurizio Martellini, "Nuclear safety, nuclear stability and nuclear strategy in Pakistan." *A concise report of a visit by Landau Network-Centro Volta.* Available on the internet at http://www.mi.infn.it/~landnet/Doc/pakistan.pdf.

8. Air Commodore Tariq Mahmud Ashraf, "Aerospace Power: The Emerging Strategic Dimension." Published by the PAF Book Club, Peshawar Pakistan, June 2003, pp. 147-48.

9. Op. cit.

10. In terms of pure numbers, the advantage that the IAF has enjoyed over the PAF has gradually been narrowing. According to the *The Story of the Pakistan Air Force—A saga of Courage and Honour,"* the IAF enjoyed an almost 5:1 superiority in strength over the PAF during the 1971 war with the PAF only being 22% of the IAF's strength, page 469. The figures for the total number of combat aircraft of the IAF and the PAF have been extracted from Anthony Cordesman and Martin Kleiber, *The Asian Conventional Military Balance in 2006: The South Asian Military Balance* published by the Centre for Strategic and International Studies (CSIS), June 26, 2006.

11. Ibid.

12. The combat aircraft of the two air forces that have been included in the category of high-tech aircraft include the IAF's Su-30 and Mirage 2000 aircraft while the only PAF platform that merits inclusion in this category is the F-16. The figures for the numbers of these types of aircraft possessed by the two air forces as well as the other data has been extracted from "The Military Balance 2013."

13. While IAF's exclusiveness in the AEW domain would remain till such time that the PAF inducts a similar platform, the advantage of the BVR missiles being available only with the IAF might not remain once the PAF inducts the additional batch of 24 F-16 C/D aircraft since these aircraft are reportedly AMRAAM capable and the missiles will also be delivered as a part of the total package.

14. Paolo Cotta-Ramusino and Maurizio Martellini, op. cit.

15. Michael Krepon, Rodney W. Jones, and Ziad Haider, eds. *Escalation Control and the Nuclear Option in South Asia*, Stimson Institute, Washington, DC, November 2004. Please refer to Chapter 1 of this book titled "The Stability-Instability Paradox, Misperception, and Escalation Control in South Asia" authored by Michael Krepon.

24 Nuclear CBMs in South Asia

During any discussion of South Asian affairs, specifically with reference to India and Pakistan, two "pacts" or "treaties" that invariably crop up in the discussion are "Tashkent" and "Simla." So familiar have these two agreements become that most people get stuck on one or the other and refuse to look beyond these.

The Institute of Regional Studies in Islamabad recently hosted an international conference on "Peace and Stability in South Asia."[1] Having attended some of the sessions of this well-attended conference, I was struck by the frequent mention of the Lahore Declaration that was signed jointly by Mr. Atal Bihari Vajpayee and Mr. Muhammad Nawaz Sharif, as a document that could help us in charting the future course ahead of India–Pakistan Nuclear CBMs.[2]

Subsequently, I went into the detailed text of the following three documents in order to collect the material for this analysis:[3]

- Text of the Lahore Declaration.[4]
- Text of the Joint Statement.[5]
- Text of the Memorandum of Understanding (MoU).[6]

The Lahore Declaration[7]

The text of the Lahore Declaration which embodies the formal agreement that was signed by both the Prime Ministers highlighted three significant aspects of the nuclear issue

- The Prime Ministers of India and Pakistan, *recognising that the nuclear dimension of the security environment of the two countries adds to their responsibility for avoidance of conflict between the two countries;*

The realisation that having become nuclear powers was an event of enormous significance, and the tremendous destructive potential of these weapons necessitated that steps be taken to ensure that military conflicts between the two countries are avoided, is fairly evident here. Acknowledging the fact that both India and Pakistan, under the nuclear dimension, have to contend with an enhanced scope of responsible behaviour, both the countries accepted that their respective responsibilities now encompass the avoidance of any military conflict between them since the danger of such a conflict building up into an undesirable and immensely destructive nuclear exchange was something that both countries were desirous of avoiding at all costs.

- and *committed to the objective of universal nuclear disarmament and non-proliferation;*

Both India and Pakistan reaffirmed their commitment to the utopian dream of global/universal nuclear disarmament. While India has been harping on this theme as a sort of justification for continuing with her quest for nuclear weapons, this probably is the first instance where Pakistan has also spoken in the same language. In my opinion, these words should be taken as mere rhetoric since both India and Pakistan fully realise that they are asking for a virtual impossibility. In a manner, I feel that in asking for such an improbable event, both India and Pakistan are attempting to justify their own emergence as nuclear weapon States. The encouraging note here is that it appears that both India and Pakistan can come together when they have a commonality/convergence of interests.

- An agreement that the Governments of India and Pakistan *shall take immediate steps for reducing the risk of accidental or unauthorised use of nuclear weapons and discuss concepts and doctrines with a view to elaborating measures for confidence building in the nuclear and conventional fields, aimed at prevention of conflict.*

The third extract from the Lahore Declaration is perhaps the most important from the perspective of nuclear CBMs in South Asia since it actually delves into some of the actual steps that need to be taken by India and Pakistan. The text of the declaration mentions the following in this regard:

- Take immediate steps to reduce the chances of any inadvertent or accidental use of nuclear weapons.
- Hold discussions on nuclear concepts and doctrines so as to determine areas and steps that could engender mutual confidence in the military domain—both nuclear as well as conventional.[8]
- It stipulates that the prime purpose and objective of these military CBMs would be the prevention of a military conflict between India and Pakistan.

If looked at objectively, the three measures listed above could well form a road-map for the establishment of an environment of confidence in South Asia.

Joint Statement[9]
Recognising the fact that any negotiations on the nuclear issue would indeed be long-drawn-out and would need an element of regularity and persistence,

both the countries agreed in the joint statement that their respective Foreign Ministers would *meet periodically to discuss all matters of mutual concern including nuclear related issues.*

This aspect of the joint statement definitely indicated that the two countries were serious in their resolve to ease the prevalent mistrust through the institution of a regular forum at the highest governmental level.

Memorandum of Understanding[10]

The Foreign Secretaries of India and Pakistan, pursuant to the directive given by their respective Prime Ministers in Lahore, to adopt measures for promoting a stable environment of peace, and security between the two countries; have on this day, agreed to the following:

- *The two sides shall engage in bilateral consultations on security concepts, and nuclear doctrines, with a view to developing measures for confidence building in the nuclear and conventional fields, aimed at avoidance of conflict.*

This paragraph from the MoU indicates the requirement for the two countries to maintain an element of transparency and openness as regards the formulation of their nuclear doctrines and also alludes to mutual consultations being held for enhancing mutual confidence also in the conventional arena.

- *The two sides undertake to provide each other with advance notification in respect of ballistic missile flight tests, and shall conclude a bilateral agreement in this regard.*

One of the few tangible action items that was included in the MoU related to advance warning being provided by the two countries to each other on any planned test launches of their respective ballistic missiles. This clause of the MoU was not really pursued at the official level thereafter and it was only during the recent meetings on nuclear CBMs in 2004 that this understanding has been formalised.

- The two sides are fully committed to undertaking national measures to reducing the risks of accidental or unauthorised use of nuclear weapons under their respective control.
- The two sides further undertake to notify each other immediately in the event of any accidental, unauthorised or unexplained incident that could create the risk of a fallout with adverse consequences for both sides, or

an outbreak of a nuclear war between the two countries, as well as to adopt measures aimed at diminishing the possibility of such actions, or such incidents being misinterpreted by the other.
- The two sides shall identify/establish the appropriate communication mechanism for this purpose.

The above three clauses of the MoU essentially relate to accidents and inadvertent incidents related to nuclear materials and while binding both the countries to take all safeguards to avoid these, also stipulate that they would inform each other in the event of any such mishap through a communication link that would specifically be established for this purpose.
- The two sides shall continue to abide by their respective unilateral moratorium on conducting further nuclear test explosions unless either side, in exercise of its national sovereignty decides that extraordinary events have jeopardised its supreme interests.

In the immediate aftermath of the 1998 nuclear tests, both India and Pakistan affirmed that they would be imposing moratorium on further nuclear tests and this clause is just a reassertion of this aspect.
- The two sides shall conclude an agreement on prevention of incidents at sea in order to ensure safety of navigation by naval vessels, and aircraft belonging to the two sides.

This clause reminds one of the ill-fated incident where an unarmed Pakistan Navy Atlantic maritime surveillance aircraft was shot down by India and was probably included to avoid the recurrence of similar incidents in the future as regards aerial and maritime traffic of both the countries.
- The two sides shall periodically review the implementation of existing Confidence Building Measures (CBMs) and where necessary, set up appropriate consultative mechanisms to monitor and ensure effective implementation of these CBMs.

This clause indicates the desire of the two countries to use the agreed-to CBMs as a foundation and stepping stone to move forward towards lasting peace. It is a measure of their seriousness and earnestness that they even considered the possibility to periodically review the progress on all CBMs that had been agreed to so as to remove any bottlenecks that were hindering their implementation.

- The two sides shall undertake a review of the existing communication links (e.g., between the respective Directors General, Military Operations) with a view to upgrading and improving these links, and to provide for fail-safe and secure communications.

It was agreed to by both the parties that the existing hotline between the Directors General of Military Operations of the two countries that had been established in the immediate aftermath of the 1965 war should not only be maintained but should also be made more elaborate with the incorporation of modern fail-safe technology. It was also felt that this vital communication link must be made secure and tamper proof in all respects.

- *The two sides shall engage in bilateral consultations on security, disarmament and non-proliferation issues within the context of negotiations on these issues in multilateral fora.*

This is probably one of the more interesting clauses of the MoU since it branches out from the bilateral into the multilateral realm by stipulating that both Pakistan and India would continue to conduct their bilateral negotiations on matters pertaining to security, disarmament and non-proliferation issues within the overall context of the negotiations on these issues that take place in multilateral organisations and meetings.

- *Where required, the technical details of the above measures will be worked out by experts of the two sides in meetings to be held on mutually agreed dates, before mid 1999, with a view to reaching bilateral agreements.*

Although this clause of the MoU was an evidence of the speed with which both the countries wanted to move forward, the specified date of mid-1999 for further consultations could not materialise because of the outbreak of the Kargil conflict around that time frame.

Conclusion

A detailed analysis of the Lahore Declaration, the Joint Statement issued on the occasion and the Memorandum of Understanding that was signed during the meetings held on that occasion indicates that these were indeed very significant steps and had created a sound edifice on which India-Pakistan CBMs could have been built up and expanded. Unfortunately, the events of Kargil in 1999 and the India mobilisation and adoption of an exaggerated forward military posture derailed the entire process even before it could have taken off.

Another very significant aspect of these agreements and understanding was that India and Pakistan had been able to venture into the realm of effective nuclear CBMs less than a year after they both had become overt nuclear powers. This compares extremely favourably with the fact that during the Cold War, it took the US and the erstwhile USSR more than two decades before they could agree to any meaningful nuclear weapons related CBMs.

The Lahore parleys were, therefore, not only a sign of the maturity of the political leadership of India and Pakistan but these also indicated the earnest desire of both the countries to embark on a process of building bridges towards the creation of a more harmonious and tension free environment in South Asia.

Since the advantages afforded by the Lahore Declaration could not bear fruit because of the unfortunate events that ensued subsequently, the least that Pakistan and India can do is to pick up the threads from where these were left after Lahore and move forward towards the mutual goal of peace and harmony for this tense and volatile region of the world, and its teeming masses of humanity. We have the basic foundations already in place and just need to build up the superstructure. To repeat an oft repeated cliché, "Let it not be said that we did not prove equal to this task!"

Notes

1. This conference was held in Hotel Marriott, Islamabad between June 7 and 9, 2004.
2. A list of the military/security related CBMs that exist between India and Pakistan is given below:
   - Hotline between Military Operations Directorates (1965).
   - Agreement on the Prohibition of Attack against Nuclear Plants and Facilities (December 1988). This was ratified and implemented in 1992. This agreement also requires both the countries to exchange a list of their nuclear installations and facilities on January 1 every year. This exchange of lists of nuclear installations and facilities has been a regular annual feature since the ratification of this agreement. (Please refer to Reference "A" for complete text.)
   - Establishment of hotline between Prime Minister Rajiv Gandhi and Prime Minister Benazir Bhutto (1989).
   - Agreement on Advance notice on Military Exercises, Troop movements and Manoeuvres (1991).
   - Measures to prevent Air Space violations and overflights/landings by military aircraft (1992).
   - The above list has been taken from South Asia Monitor, No. 49 dated August 1, 2002 that was published by CSIS. The complete paper is available at http://www.csis.org/saprog/sam49.pdf.

3. The complete text of all these three documents is available on the internet on various websites and can be accessed at http://www.usip.org/library/pa/ip/ip_ lahore19990221.html.

4. This was the formal agreement that was signed by the Prime Minister, Mr. A. B. Vajpayee of India and the Pakistan Prime Minister, Mr. Nawaz Sharif, in Lahore on Sunday, February 19, 2004.

5. This joint statement was issued by the two countries on February 21, 2004 at the end of Prime Minister Vajpayee's visit to Lahore.

6. This Memorandum of Understanding was signed by the Foreign Secretaries of India and Pakistan on February 21, 2004 in the presence of the Prime Ministers of both the countries.

7. The complete text of the Lahore Declaration is reproduced as an Reference "B" at the end of this article.

8. Interestingly, the wording of this paragraph of text was changed slightly. While the text included in the Lahore Declaration stated that "shall take immediate steps for reducing the risk of accidental or unauthorised use of nuclear weapons and *discuss concepts and doctrines* with a view to elaborating measures for confidence building in the nuclear and conventional fields, aimed at prevention of conflict" the text inserted into the MoU read, "The two sides shall engage in bilateral *consultations on security concepts, and nuclear doctrines*, with a view to developing measures for confidence building in the nuclear and conventional fields, aimed at avoidance of conflict. This appears to be an attempt to expand the scope of the CBMs to encompass both, conventional as well as nuclear conflict and as such, is all-encompassing. It needs to be recalled that during the Cold War similar stabilisation measures took more than 15-20 years to be attained. The hotline between the US and the USSR was established in 1963, 15 years after the commencement of the Cold War, the Nuclear Accidents Agreement was signed in 1971 and Nuclear Risk Reduction Centres set up only in 1987. All this while the two countries were engaged in an arms race with expanding nuclear capabilities combined with doctrines of first strike and launch on warning postures.

9. The complete text of the Joint statement is reproduced as Reference "C" at the end of this article.

10. The complete text of the Memorandum of Understanding (MoU) is reproduced as Reference "D" at the end of this article.

25 Accepting South Asian Nuclearisation

Introduction

Multilateral organisations and forums are a necessity in today's globalised environment for a multitude of reasons; they bring countries with a similar outlook on issues together, they unite countries that have a convergence of interests and also permit member countries to exercise a degree of collective clout that they would not be able to employ were they to act singly.

The motivations for establishing a multilateral forum could be several; economic, political, security or just plain simple national interest. It is these motivating factors as well as the reasons cited above, that have fostered the creation of several multinational organisations, including the UN which is by far the largest global forum that currently exists.

Understandably, a significant number of the multilateral organisations have a regional basis since it is far more appropriate for countries that are situated in a particular part of the world to come together. Not only do these countries face the same challenges but also find that the opportunities that are available to them are generally similar. Facing the same set of challenges and opportunities works as a catalyst for bringing such regional countries together on one platform. The most prominent examples of such regional organisations which initially started off as pure economic institutions but are gradually evolving into political and security platforms, are the European Union[1] and the ASEAN.[2] Understandably, with geo-economics tending to upstage geostrategic and geopolitical considerations as the primary determinant of interstate relations, the world is seeing more and more economic alliances albeit on a regional basis. Some of the examples in this regard are the NAFTA,[3] SAFTA[4] and ECO.[5]

Other than these purely economic institutions, the world is also seeing alliances of countries that have reached a certain level of development or are endeavouring to reach it. Examples of such groups are the G-8[6] group of Developed States and the D-8[7] group of Developing Muslim States. In the basis for the creation of these two organisations lies the raison d'être for this article which is aimed at suggesting that just as the G-8 and the D-8 organisations have brought together countries with similar levels of economic development, should there not be an N-8 forum also that comprises the eight known (declared or undeclared) nuclear weapons capable countries.

Unlike the International Atomic Energy Agency (IAEA) which oversees nuclear activities world-wide without any differentiation between the nuclear weapons states and the non-nuclear weapon states, the proposed N-8 would bring together only those eight countries that are known to possess nuclear weapons. As such, the N-8 would be a far more exclusive club than some of the other similar organisations that exist in the world today.

The Need for the N-8 Forum and Its Advantages
Acknowledgement of the Nuclear Status of India, Pakistan and Israel. Of the three main categories of Weapons of Mass Destruction (WMD), the one type that stands out prominently is that of Nuclear Weapons and as things stand today, eight countries of the world are known to possess these weapons. Other than the five permanent members of the United National Security Council (UNSC), i.e., United States, Russia, United Kingdom, France and the People's Republic of China, the three remaining countries are India, Pakistan and Israel.

Since nuclear weapons have emerged as the deadliest military invention in the history of mankind, their unregulated spread poses a very serious threat to global security. The possession of these weapons, however, does definitely confer a certain "clout" and it is no mere coincidence that the five permanent members of the UNSC who can also exercise the right of "Veto" are all recognised nuclear powers.

Going by the same logic, it could be argued that the three other nuclear countries should also be accommodated as permanent members of the UNSC, and there have been moves or expressions of desire from at least one—India—regarding this aspect. While the admission of India, Pakistan and Israel into the permanent forum of the UNSC is neither practical nor feasible because of the impact on the other non-nuclear aspirants who have not travelled down the nuclear path by choice, an unofficial recognition of the fact that India, Pakistan and Israel are in fact nuclear states, could remove the uncertainties that continue to prevail.

Specifically in the case of India and Pakistan, their admission into a forum such as the N-8 would mean an unofficial acceptance of their nuclear power status and this would have a positive impact on their domestic polity also. In the case of India, this could well have a face-saving effect since India's quest for a permanent UNSC seat is not likely to see fruition at least in the foreseeable future.

Strengthening of the Non-proliferation Effort. While several of the developed countries like Japan, Canada and major European countries like Germany and Italy do possess the technical skills and the know-how to become nuclear weapon states because of their advanced technological base, the prime threat to nuclear proliferation might still emanate from one of the eight nuclear weapons capable states since these are the ones that have physically been able to weaponise their respective nuclear potential. Bringing these eight countries together in one forum could thus strengthen the non-proliferation efforts significantly.

Revival of the Non-proliferation Regimes. In exchange for the creation of the N-8 and the acceptance of Israel, India and Pakistan into it, the global community in general, and the P-5[8] in particular could demand that India, Pakistan and Israel sign not only the NPT[9] but also the CTBT,[10] FMCT,[11] MTCR[12] and other such global regimes that are aimed at nuclear/missile non-proliferation. This would also provide a significant boost to the global nuclear non-proliferation campaign while simultaneously promoting the cause of global stability.

Limiting the Benefits of Nuclearisation. By according India, Israel and Pakistan an unofficial status outside the permanent membership of the UNSC, the establishment of the N-8 could serve to dissuade other aspiring nuclear weapon states by indicating to them that while they could possibly be accepted unofficial equals as nuclear weapon states, "some (meaning the P-5) would always remain more equal than others."

Cooperation on Nuclear Safety. Since the N-8 countries are the prime candidates from where would-be terrorists or non-state actors could possibly lay their hands on to nuclear material and expertise, bringing these together on one platform would enable the global community to chart out and implement a comprehensive strategy for safeguarding nuclear technology, material and expertise. Such cooperation would especially be relevant for countries like Pakistan and India that do not otherwise discuss these issues on a bilateral basis. The more advanced nuclear countries could also transfer some of their technologies and experiences to the newer nuclear powers for bringing the nuclear command and control structures of the latter on to a more acceptable, reliable and secure footing.

Stability in South Asia. Bringing together India and Pakistan at one forum where all the major global powers are also present could also be expected to bring stability to the volatile South Asian region since, with their newly assumed importance, both the countries could be enticed to mend their fences. This could even be made a precondition for granting them membership of the N-8.

Disadvantages of Establishing the N-8 Forum

The foremost disadvantage of the creation of the N-8 forum would be the impact of this de facto legitimisation of the clandestinely pursued and developed nuclear weapons programmes of India, Pakistan and Israel on other countries that are aspiring to become nuclear weapon states. There is an understandable apprehension such a legitimisation might encourage other countries aspiring to develop nuclear weapons to follow suit. Although there is some logic in this apprehension, we must not lose sight of the fact that despite knowing that they would never be included in the same league as the P-5, neither India, nor Pakistan nor Israel could be dissuaded from developing nuclear weapons.

Conclusion

The theme of this chapter is to suggest that like the fairly effective models of multilateral organisations, such as the G-8 and the D-8, a need can definitely be identified for an organisation of the eight nuclear weapons capable states which could be called the N-8 or Nuclear-8 group. In the opinion of the writer, this would be a welcome move and its numerous advantages would well overweigh the disadvantages or negative impact that its creation could have.

By bringing on board the unrecognised nuclear weapon states, India, Pakistan and Israel, the global community will be able to further the cause of nuclear non-proliferation while simultaneously according a semblance of recognition to these states. Most importantly, the world could possibly rejuvenate the dormant non-proliferation regimes by requiring these three states to join and ratify them as a precondition for the creation of the N-8. At the global level, in forums such as the UNSC, a decision not to admit these countries would further the cause of global stability by maintaining things in the shape that they are today.

The basic theme of establishing the N-8 is to have one forum where all nuclear weapon states can come together and discuss issues pertaining to nuclear proliferation, nuclear terrorism, nuclear security and safety and other similar issues as and when required. Since it would bring together all nuclear capable nations, it can be expected that the efforts of global non-proliferation would get a significant boost and a shot in the arm that would revive and make them more effective.

Notes

1. The European Union now consists of 25 countries (Austria, Belgium, Czech Republic, Cyprus, Denmark, Estonia, Germany, Greece, Finland, France, Hungary,

Ireland, Italy, Latvia, Lithuania, Luxembourg, Malta, Poland, Portugal, Slovenia, Slovakia, Spain, Sweden, the Netherlands and the United Kingdom.

2. Association of South East Asian Nations. This consists of Indonesia, Singapore, Malaysia, Laos, Thailand, Cambodia, Myanmar, Brunei, Vietnam and the Philippines.

3. North American Free Trade Agreement. This agreement brings together the United States of America, Canada and Mexico.

4. South Asia Free Trade Area. This proposed economic arrangement would include the seven member states of SAARC (South Asian Association for Regional Cooperation) i.e., India, Pakistan, Bangladesh, Maldives, Sri Lanka, Nepal and Bhutan.

5. Economic Cooperation Organisation. This is the successor to the previous Regional Cooperation for Development (RCD) organisation formed earlier by Pakistan, Iran and Turkey. It has now been expanded to also include Afghanistan, Azerbaijan, Kazakhstan, Kyrgyzstan, Tajikistan, Turkmenistan and Uzbekistan.

6. The G-8 or Group of Eight Industrialised countries brings together the eight most developed countries of the world and includes the United States of America, the United Kingdom, Germany, Russia, Canada, France, Japan, Canada, the European Community and Italy.

7. The D-8 or Group of Eight developing Islamic countries comprises Pakistan, Nigeria, Indonesia, Turkey, Malaysia, Iran, Egypt and Bangladesh.

8. The term P-5 refers to the five acknowledged nuclear weapon states that are also referred to as the Nuclear Weapon States or NWS. These also happen to be the five permanent members of the United Nations Security Council and can exercise the right of Veto in the United Nations.

9. Non-Proliferation Treaty.

10. Comprehensive Test Ban Treaty.

11. Fissile Material Cut-Off Treaty.

12. Missile Technology Control Regime.

26 The Nuclear Transparency Ladder

Introduction

In the immediate aftermath of the Cuban missile crisis, both the US and the erstwhile USSR realised the importance of holding mutual negotiations and deliberations on the nuclear issue. This gradually encouraged the establishment of arrangements which not only promoted mutual confidence but also contributed to a sort of "regulation" of the nuclear weapons inventories of both the superpowers that reigned supreme in the then bipolar world.

With the emergence of Pakistan and India as nuclear weapons capable countries after the May 1998 tests, a lot of thinking is going into ascertaining means to apply the lessons learnt from the Cold War nuclear CBMs process to South Asia. As a precursor, most analysts agree that transparency to a certain degree is an essential prerequisite for building any CBM regime as regards nuclear capability. In order to apply the lessons of the Cold War nuclear transparency campaign to South Asia, one must first delve into the various manifestations and stages of nuclear transparency.

All nuclear weapons development programmes have essentially been initiated and developed in an environment of complete opacity. This is understandable since most countries wanted to pursue these programmes in utmost secrecy without letting the rest of the world know the degree of progress that they had achieved in their efforts to acquire nuclear weapons. This opacity was considered necessary because of the following reasons:

- Countries embarking on nuclear weapons development programmes were fearful of the backlash from the major global powers and realised that any knowledge about such developmental programmes could subject them to severe diplomatic and economic sanctions that they could ill afford.
- In a regional sense, countries were desirous of keeping a lid on their nuclear development programmes so as to deny this vital information being available to potential adversaries.
- Secrecy was also desirable to prevent any of the hostile regional countries from taking steps to disrupt the nuclear weapons development process. An example of such an action was the Israeli raid against the Iraqi nuclear reactor.
- Disclosures regarding a country having embarked upon a nuclear weapons development programme could lead to it being denied access to technologies and equipment that it would need to take its programme ahead.

As would be apparent from the above, this atmosphere of opacity had to be maintained till the nuclear weapons programme had progressed to a stage where the country was in a position to overtly demonstrate its nuclear expertise and potential by conducting nuclear tests. This, however, is not an inviolable requirement as has been proven by the case of Israel which, though known to possess nuclear weapons capability, has always shied away from testing it and letting its nuclear prowess be known to the world. An analysis of Israel's case, however, indicates that this is more of an exception rather than being the rule since, other than Israel, all of the known nuclear weapons states did not shy away from conducting nuclear tests to let their nuclear potential be known to all.

While an analysis of why Israel opted to remain opaque, while all other countries such as India and Pakistan chose to become transparent regarding their respective nuclear prowess by conducting nuclear tests, goes beyond the theme of this chapter, a detailed look at this aspect is definitely warranted.

Firstly, let us look at what are the factors that could lead a country to conduct nuclear tests and remove the cloak of secrecy that had earlier cloaked its clandestine nuclear weapons development activities. In my view, this is essentially a political and not altogether a military decision, and some of the factors that could lead a country to conduct nuclear tests are:

- Having reached a level of competence in the nuclear weapons realm, the country actually desires to try out and validate its nuclear weapons development capability from a scientific and technological perspective.
- Since the possession of nuclear weapons has led to the creation of an elite and powerful group of five countries, the newly nuclear country could deem the conduct of nuclear tests as an essential prerequisite in order to get its image and stature in the comity of nations elevated.
- A country that is faced with a much larger and more powerful conventional military adversary could be led down the path of nuclear tests in an effort to demonstrate this prowess and possibly deter the more powerful foe from contemplating any conventional military action against it.
- A weak or pliable internal political regime could resort to conducting nuclear tests in an effort to boost its sagging fortunes and gain the favour of the electorate by demonstrating the country's nuclear prowess.

Regardless of the motivations that lead a country to become an overt nuclear weapons capable state by bringing its concealed nuclear weapons programme out of the closet, the conduct of such tests is the first and one of the most crucial steps that the country has to take along the path of nuclear transparency. In fact it could be said that the road to eventual transparency passes through the door of declaration of one's nuclear potential in an overt fashion, as exhibited by the conduct of nuclear tests.

In South Asia, both India and Pakistan have emerged from the regime of wilful opacity that they were earlier implementing and are now endeavouring progressively towards transparency. With their nuclear tests being taken as their first step on the ladder of nuclear transparency, they now are confronted with surmounting the remaining rungs of the ladder that are discussed in the subsequent text.

Transparency of Potential
Demonstrated by the conduct of nuclear tests and indications of the potential to weaponise this capability. Prior to this, the nuclear weapons programme is essentially based on "Opacity" (e.g., Israel). As highlighted above, India and Pakistan have both reached this rung after their nuclear tests in May 1998 and as such, both the countries can now move ahead on the road to transparency.

Transparency of Capability
Conduct of trials (missile tests) that demonstrate the capability of delivering nuclear weapons.

Pursuing weapon development, enhancement and procurement programmes that are often cited as technological breakthroughs in the nuclear weapons field also form an element of the transparency of capability (e.g., continuing India/Pakistani missile tests and reports of India wanting to acquire strategic bomber aircraft from Russia).

Transparency of Intent
Publicised through the announcement of nuclear doctrine and nuclear policy indicating how, why, when and under what circumstances is a country likely to resort to using nuclear weapons (e.g., India's draft Nuclear Doctrine).

The nuclear intent of a country is essentially publicised by the leadership in a controlled manner that is able to convey the desired message to the concerned countries and international community. One of the primary means available for achieving this is the enunciation of a declared Nuclear Doctrine. In this regard, India has taken a lead by opening up her draft nuclear doctrine for comments whereas Pakistan has still to follow suit.

Notwithstanding the fact that Pakistan has not announced its nuclear doctrine or presented it for scrutiny as a wholesome document, adequate material regarding Pakistan's expected nuclear doctrine can be gleaned from the various statements that have been emanating from its leadership circles since 1998. If put together, these statements do provide a meaningful insight into the likely contents of Pakistan's nuclear doctrine.

Nuclear intent could also be publicised by the military leaders as an ingredient of respective service doctrines (e.g., Indian Navy's recently announced Maritime Doctrine). In this regard also, India has taken a lead with the Indian Navy clearly enunciating the imperative for a nuclear triad in India's nuclear arsenal. It could, however, be argued that the Indian Navy's assertion of a nuclear role for itself is possibly an endeavour on its part to address the growing inter-service rivalry that has crept into the Indian military over the command and control of her nuclear capability.

None of the three military services of Pakistan have released any similar document that addresses the issue of nuclear weapons development or employment and even the second edition of the Pakistan Air Force's Basic Air Power tends to skirt around this issue and does not directly address it. The Pakistan Navy and the Army have not come out with any doctrinal pronouncements that deal with nuclear weapons development and employment and, as such, their thoughts on this subject still remain unknown.

Transparency of Resolve

The intent of any country as regards nuclear weapons employment is meaningless unless accompanied by the essential factor of resolve to use nuclear weapons.

During peacetime, this could entail aggressive statements by national leaders regarding the will to employ nuclear weapons (e.g., President Musharraf's various statements to this effect during the 2001-2002 Indo-Pak military stand-off that is referred to by India as Operation Parakaram, as also some of the statements of the former Indian Defence Minister, Mr. George Fernandes).

During wartime, this could take the shape of nuclear forces being brought to a higher state of readiness and alert (Israel during the Arab-Israel war of 1973). Although there have been some unconfirmed reports that Pakistan had brought her nuclear forces to a higher level of readiness towards the later part of the Kargil conflict of 1999, these could never be substantiated and remain objects of conjecture.

How South Asia Weighs up on the Nuclear Transparency Ladder

As highlighted earlier, both India and Pakistan are now on the path of nuclear transparency and considering its importance as an instrument for establishing an environment of bilateral confidence, it is vital that this move towards greater nuclear transparency be facilitated and promoted as much as possible. Depicted below is a chart showing where South Asia today stands vis-à-vis the Nuclear Transparency Ladder.

	India	Pakistan
Transparency of Potential	Transparent	Transparent
Transparency of Capability	Partially Opaque and selectively transparent[1]	Partially Opaque and selectively transparent
Transparency of Intent	Mostly transparent	Mostly opaque though selectively transparent
Transparency of Resolve	Mostly transparent	Generally Vague but periodically transparent[2]

Conclusion

While discussing the various rungs of the nuclear transparency ladder, it needs to be clearly brought out that climbing the various rungs of this ladder is not an end in itself but rather, more of a means to an end. While the conduct of nuclear tests allows a country to emerge from the environment of total opacity, reaching the subsequent rungs of the ladder is necessary to bring the involved countries to a position from where onwards they can embark on a programme of achieving the desired level of nuclear transparency. As such, the various rungs highlighted in this Chapter are essentially the necessary via media the completion of which would enable countries to start contemplating the cultivation of a desirable environment of balanced nuclear opacity and transparency in real earnest.

Both the countries in South Asia, and specifically Pakistan in some aspects, still have to complete the requirements for the various rungs and till such time that these deficiencies are overcome, the establishment of a desirable environment of balanced nuclear opacity and transparency would remain unachievable. Some of the urgent steps that Pakistan needs to take in this regard are the announcement of a clear nuclear doctrine and policy and the inclusion of the nuclear weapons employment consideration in the doctrines of the three military services, as and when these are issued.

Notes

1. While both India and Pakistan have developed nuclear weapons (bombs) that their respective ground attack aircraft could deliver against each other's targets, the developments in the region of missile warheads are still classified with not much being known whether the two countries have developed tactical nuclear warheads.

2. India has fairly clearly specified in her draft nuclear doctrine that her nuclear arsenal would primarily be used as a punitive weapon and means of inflicting unacceptable damage on any potential aggressor, Pakistan generally has stayed away from making any clear declaration in this regard. During periods of tension, however, there have been several statements from Pakistani leaders, specifically from President Pervez Musharraf that the nuclear option remained open for Pakistan if needed.

27 The South Asian Nuclear Military Balance

Introduction

South Asia has emerged as one of the most critical flashpoints on the global map in recent years, more so since the overt nuclearisation of both India and Pakistan in 1998. The lingering dispute over Kashmir, the Indian allegations of Pakistan's overt and covert support to the ongoing insurgency in Indian Held Kashmir (IHK) and the issue of distribution of water resources between the two countries are just some of the main irritants that continue to bedevil the relations between India and Pakistan.

Notwithstanding the significance of South Asia because of its geography and demography, its relevance has been further highlighted in global affairs due to the US-led War on Terror that has been ongoing in Afghanistan since October 2001—barely a month after the tragic incidents of September 11 rocked the entire world and put in place a set of events that are expected to change and alter the existing global order in a significant manner.

Having already fought three conventional wars in 1948, 1965 and 1971, India and Pakistan have been on the verge of war at several other occasions—the most recent being the stand-off between the amassed might of the two countries that took place during 2001-2002.

In view of the emerging significance of the South Asian region because it houses almost one-fifth of humanity, India's emergence as an economic giant and the fact that South Asia offers the shortest and probably the most convenient outlet for the land-locked mineral riches of Central Asia to reach the warm waters, an analysis of the military strengths of the two main military powers of the region is in order. This analysis, however, rather than elaborating on the geopolitics of the region, is aimed more at presenting a comparison of the nuclear military potential and capabilities of both. While *The Military Balance 2013* from which some of the figures have been extracted, essentially confines itself to a listing of the conventional military wherewithal of the two countries, this article is aimed at conducting an appraisal of the nuclear weapons potential as well as the nuclear weapons delivery capability of both.

Comparison of Military Nuclear Capabilities of India and Pakistan

The nuclear tests conducted by India and Pakistan in May 1998 were an event of enormous significance for the region since these upped the ante of future military conflicts in the region by introducing the nuclear dimension. Although both India and Pakistan declared unilateral moratorium on future testing immediately afterwards and are not known to have physically fielded nuclear weapons, it is common knowledge that both the countries are able to deliver nuclear weapons against selected targets against each others' countries.

Weaponisation of their respective nuclear potential was the obvious sequel to the nuclear tests conducted by India and Pakistan and the first medium of delivering nuclear weapons chosen by both was air-delivered nuclear bombs reminiscent of "Enola Gay" and the US nuclear attacks against Hiroshima and Nagasaki in 1945. This was due to a variety of factors:

- Since the nuclear capability of both the countries was essentially rudimentary, it was not possible for them to develop miniaturised warheads that could be encapsulated within small containers such as the tip of a ballistic missile. Putting together an air-delivered nuclear bomb, however, was an easier course of action since it did not impose similar constraints of weight and size on the nuclear warhead.

- Though both India and Pakistan lacked true and specific to the purpose strategic bombers as had been fielded by the US and the erstwhile USSR during the Cold War, the air forces of the two countries did have significant fleets of tactical ground attack aircraft that could be entrusted with the nuclear weapons delivery role.

- In the immediate aftermath of the nuclear tests and the impositions of economic sanctions by the developed world, India and Pakistan would have further antagonised the first world if either of them had actively pursued the development of a new nuclear weapons delivery mechanism. Modifying existing aircraft that already formed a part of the inventories of their respective air forces, therefore, offered a much more acceptable option that could be adopted.

As regards the air delivery of nuclear weapons, the number and reach of the ground attack aircraft that both the air forces possess which lend themselves to being modified for the delivery of nuclear weapons, are tabulated below:

Table 1: Comparative South Asian Holding of Nuclear Weapons Delivery Capable Combat Aircraft[1]

Indian Aerospace Force			
Type	Qty	Load kg	Range
Mirage 2000H	50	3,000	1,205 km
Su-30 MKI	194	5,000	3,000 km
Jaguar	106	4,775	850 km
Total	350		

Pakistan Air Force			
Type	Qty	Load kg	Range
F-16 A/B	63	5,450	925 km
Mirage 5	40	2,000	1,300 km
Total	103		

The following significant conclusions can be derived from the above data:

- The Indian Air Force (IAF) enjoys a significant superiority over the Pakistan Air Force (PAF) since it has a superiority of almost 3.4:1 over the latter in terms of number of attack aircraft that could be modified for the nuclear weapons delivery role.

- With the induction of the Su-30 MKI, the IAF now possesses an aircraft that has a strategic reach—far more than what any of the PAF attack aircraft can boast off. This advantage permits the IAF to reach virtually every nook and corner of Pakistan's territory while the PAF does not possess this capability because of the limited radii of action of its tactical attack aircraft fleet.

The initial efforts of India and Pakistan to develop air-delivered nuclear bombs and modify their existing tactical bomber fleets for carriage and employment of these weapons were supplemented by an almost simultaneous drive to develop surface-to-surface ballistic missiles (SSMs) and miniaturised nuclear warheads that could be housed in them. The basic push behind the development of nuclear-capable SSMs was the Army in both the countries which saw the strategic role shifting from them to the Air Force and wanted to reassert not only their respective relevance in the nuclear milieu but also get a share of the strategic build-up cake.

Aircraft vs. SSMs Employment for Nuclear Delivery

The employment of the aircraft and SSMs in the nuclear role offer certain advantages and also suffer from some disadvantages that are enumerated below.

Advantages

- SSMs have significantly more reach than most of the aircraft possessed by the two air forces. This was specifically true in the case of Pakistan which did not and still does not possess any attack aircraft with a strategic reach.

- Capable of being mounted on mobile transporters and launch platforms, SSMs offer a much greater degree of deployment flexibility than attack aircraft since the latter have to be operated from well-established and permanent air bases, the location of which is almost always known to the enemy. This affords SSMs an additional degree of security against hostile attacks and makes them more suitable for deployment as second-strike forces.
- Being significantly smaller than attack aircraft and having extremely small radar cross-sectional area, SSMs are very difficult to detect through conventional air defence radar systems that are employed for detecting enemy aerial activity. The delayed pick-up of the weapons also reduces the reaction time available to the enemy for taking any effective countermeasures against this weapon.
- The small size of SSMs and the difficulty of detecting them also poses problems as regards their interception. While attack aircraft can be engaged by most surface-to-air weapons systems, SSMs are generally impervious to these means of interception.

Disadvantages

- While attack aircraft can be conveniently recalled or asked to abort the mission, the same does not apply to SSMs. At best, some of the SSMs might be diverted to an uninhabited area or made to self-destruct during flight.
- In the absence of a human being at the controls, SSMs are totally reliant on on-board navigation systems for their guidance to the target. This could induce inaccuracies in their impact point. Manned attack aircraft, on the other hand, with a trained operator sitting at the controls, are less vulnerable to such navigational errors. This element is indicative of the fact that while nuclear warhead equipped SSMs are more suited against area or large targets, attack aircraft offer a better proposition against pinpoint targets requiring high accuracy in engagement.

Another important dynamic of the post-nuclear tests military environment in South Asia was the emergence of the air forces in both the countries as the prime strategic military component. This resultantly led to a reduction in the significance of the land forces which hitherto had enjoyed virtually absolute dominance in all military affairs. The availability of nuclear-tipped SSMs permitted the armies of India and Pakistan to gain an element of strategic relevance which they pounced upon, and in both the countries, the SSMs were placed under the control of the land forces, presumably as a long-range extension of the field artillery component of the two armies.

Comparison of Indian and Pakistani SSM Capabilities

While India possesses a significant air-delivery of nuclear weapons potential, Pakistan's lack in this area stimulated Pakistan's quest for better SSMs with more reach potential. This precipitated a race for the development of nuclear capable SSMs that has resulted in almost 50 missile tests being conducted by the two countries. The SSM potential of the two countries is depicted on the following chart:

Table 2: Comparative South Asian Nuclear warhead capable SSMs[2]

India		Pakistan		
Type	**Range**	**Type**		**Range**
Prithvi-I	150 km	Hatf-I		80-100 km
Prithvi-II	250 km	Hatf-II	Abdali	180 km
Prithvi-III	350 km	Hatf-III	Ghaznavi	290 km
Agni-I	700-900 km	Hatf-IV	Shaheen-I	600-700 km
Agni-II	2-3,000 km	Hatf-V	Ghauri-I	1,300-1,500 km
Agni-III	3,500-4,000 km	Hatf-V	Ghauri-II	2,000 km
		Hatf-VI	Shaheen-II	2,000-2,500 km

The following conclusions can be arrived at from an analysis of the data included in the above table:

- Pakistan, in an obvious effort to compensate for her inferiority/ inadequacy in air delivery of nuclear weapons, has followed a concerted programme to develop nuclear capable SSMs in an attempt to correct the imbalance.
- While Pakistan's SSM programme, as evidenced by the strike reach of these weapons, is purely India-specific and regional, that of India has an extra-regional dimension and could possibly be catering also for China.
- Both India and Pakistan have developed SSMs with tactical as well as strategic reach. This does indicate the possibility of the two countries employing tactical nuclear weapons in the counter-force arena but I personally consider this option impracticable for both and am

convinced that any employment of nuclear weapons in South Asia would remain confined to the strategic realm with a focus on counter-value targeting.

Indian and Pakistani Nuclear Weapons Stocks
Having undertaken an appraisal of the nuclear weapons delivery capability of both the countries, an assessment of the amount of radioactive material that each possesses and the number of weapons that these stocks translate into will now be undertaken.

While Pakistan adopted the difficult route of Uranium enrichment in her quest for nuclear capability, India stayed on the more conventional Plutonium route. Recent reports, however, indicate that while India is desirous of exploring the Enriched Uranium approach, Pakistan is considering the Plutonium route.

The estimation of the nuclear materials stock of any country is an extremely complicated process. The first step has to be an assessment of the functioning of the various nuclear power plants that the country possesses from which an idea about the amount of nuclear material (Plutonium/Uranium) being made available for the weapons can be made. This then has to be converted into Nuclear Weapons Equivalence (NWE) or the number of nuclear devices that this material can be utilised to produce. Since most of this data is hard to come by and suffers from certain inherent deficiencies, the best estimate of a country's nuclear potential would amount to being little more than an educated guess or a "guesstimate."

The charts below provide an estimate of the amount of nuclear material and the number of weapons that this could translate to, for India as well as Pakistan.

Table 3: Fissile Material Stocks and Nuclear Weapons Equivalent[3]

Level of Estimation[4]	India			Pakistan		
	H	M	L	H	M	L
WGP[5] (kg)	600	400	280	45	15	5
WGU[6] (kg)	0	0	0	1,230	1,020	815
NWEs	40-120 weapons			35-95 weapons		

The data depicted in the above table illustrates the following:
- While Pakistan has had success in both the routes (Plutonium and Enriched Uranium) to nuclear weapons development, India has only had success in the Plutonium route.

- Pakistan can almost claim parity with India as regards the total number of nuclear weapons that each country can assemble. This is in sharp contrast to the conventional imbalance that characterises the military equation of South Asia.
- Since nuclear weapons are considered more to be political instruments than weapons of war, both India and Pakistan possess adequate nuclear potential even if they were to freeze their holdings at the current levels from now onwards.

Conclusion

This article has attempted to compare the holding as well as the delivery capability of nuclear weapons of Pakistan and India in order to suggest that unlike the conventional imbalance that plagues the region, a semblance of balance does exist in the nuclear dimension. Some analysts are of the opinion that it is this nuclear parity, and not just the availability of nuclear weapons per se, that is preventing a major conflict from breaking out in South Asia. The following significant points emerge from the analysis conducted in this paper:

- While India enjoys a conclusive edge in air-delivery capability of nuclear weapons, Pakistan has been able to make up for its deficiency in this area by developing a large array of effective SSMs.
- Pakistan's adoption of both, the Plutonium and the enriched Uranium route has contributed to its being able to create a semblance of parity in nuclear capability. As India also actively pursues the enriched Uranium approach, it could be expected to gradually erode this advantage of Pakistan.
- The development of nuclear capable SSMs and their being entrusted to the armies in both the countries has permitted the land forces to maintain an element of strategic military relevance. In the absence of any SLBM capability, their respective inventories of SSMs constitute the second-strike capability for both India and Pakistan.
- Whereas Pakistan's nuclear weapons delivery capability is essentially India-specific and regional in context, that of India also caters for China and as such has some extra-regional connotations.
- Air Power, because of the strategic reach, speed and firepower that are inherent to aircraft, invariably emerges as the nuclear weapons delivery medium of first choice for both India and Pakistan.
- While the possession of nuclear weapons by both antagonists has promoted deterrence, the semblance of nuclear parity that currently exists in the region has served to further strengthen it.

- In a purely India-Pakistan equation, the existing number of weapons that the two countries possess is more than adequate to perpetuate the regime of deterrence stability that currently exists. Any major new development, however, could be expected to upset this fragile state of balance and lead to further instability in the region.[7] Thus even if both the countries were to put a freeze on their nuclear programmes, they would continue to retain adequate nuclear potential to not only deter wars but also to retaliate if struck by nuclear weapons from another country.

- While both India and Pakistan have followed an approach of developing short-range SSMs first and later developing their SSM programmes to also envelop the medium and longer ranges, the impracticability of counter-force targeting in South Asia precludes these weapons being employed in the tactical realm of military operations. Nuclear weapons, therefore, will continue to remain as strategic weapons and those too as military instruments of last resort, in South Asia.

- The tactical ranges of some of the SSMs available to India and Pakistan do lend these to being employed in the tactical role albeit with conventional warheads. A specific case in point is the SS-250 Prithvi-II development of the Indian Prithvi-I SSM that was specifically developed for the IAF which opted for a reduced warhead size in return for the greater reach since this would permit it to engage most PAF bases.[8] Even for this sort of an employment, however, the dangers associated with any missile launch during periods of hostility between India and Pakistan would have to be taken into consideration, since there would be nothing to differentiate between the launch of a conventional warhead tipped SSM and that of a nuclear-tipped one, and this could lead to an overreaction on Pakistan's part, with devastating consequences being the obvious outcome.

Not being able to match India in the conventional military realm with the recent hikes in the Indian defence budget indicating that this gap is going to steadily continue widening, Pakistan has no other option than to continue efforts aimed at maintaining some semblance of parity in the nuclear realm vis-à-vis India. This, however, will have to be done catering to Pakistan's economic constraints since involvement in any arms race is neither affordable nor practical from the Pakistani perspective.

Notes

1. While the aircraft numbers have been taken from "The Military Balance 2013," the figures for the attack radii/ranges have been taken from Dr. Peter Lavoy's talk titled "Managing South Asia's Nuclear Rivalry: Policy Challenges for the United States" that was delivered at an international seminar on "Peace and Stability in South Asia" organised and held under the auspices of the Institute of Regional Studies, Islamabad on June 8, 2004. The payload figures for the aircraft have been extracted from the NRDC website at www.nrdc.org and other internet sources.

2. While the aircraft numbers have been taken from "The Military Balance 2013," the figures for the attack radii/ranges have been taken from Dr. Peter Lavoy's presentation cited above. It is interesting to note that while Pakistan's SSMs, being India specific, do not exceed a range capability of 2,500 km, those of India are capable of much higher ranges, possibly because of the China factor.

3. Dr. Peter Lavoy, op. cit.

4. The figures for the amount of weapons grade Uranium and Plutonium available with India and Pakistan have been categorised into three levels of estimation: High (H), Medium (M) and Low (L).

5. Weapons Grade Plutonium.

6. Weapons Grade Uranium (enriched).

7. Some of these escalatory developments that could occur include the Indian development of submarine launched ballistic nuclear missiles (SLBMs) and the further enhancement of the maximum ranges of Indian SSMs to intercontinental proportions. The latter, though of not much significance to Pakistan, would have serious international implications.

8. While the original Prithvi-I SSM was capable of carrying a warhead of 500 kg to a range of 150 kilometres, the IAF opted for the second variant that can carry a warhead of 250 kg but to a range of 250 kilometres. Thus, a 100 km range increase was achieved at the cost of reducing the warhead size to one-half of the original and brought most of the operational airfields of the PAF within the effective strike range of this weapon system.

28 Nuclear Terrorism and Pakistan

What we have to do is stop the ultimate nightmare: the bringing together of weapons of mass destruction and the terrorist.[1]

Being in the military, I have always considered nuclear weapons to be an instrument of warfare, primarily to be used as a deterrent to avoid war or inhibit the escalation of an ongoing military conflict to an unacceptable level. In line with this myopic and single-tracked thinking process, I had always written on nuclear doctrinal and policy issues with a focus on the elaborate command and control systems that the possession of a nuclear arsenal necessitates. I had truly never seriously considered the "terrorism" dimension of nuclear weapons till Dr. Bruce Blair of the Centre for Defence Information (CDI) indicated to me in an email that he was working on this subject and asked whether I would be willing to cooperate with him on the project.

Over the next few days, I devoted most of my time to researching this aspect of nuclear weapons and was truly amazed at the enormous amount of work that numerous researchers had already done on this subject. My initial impression, therefore, was that I could not possibly add anything new to what most of these experts had written. Subsequently, however, I got to thinking that while I may not be qualified enough to address this issue at the global level, I was ideally placed to discuss the issue with a particular focus on Pakistan and India specifically, and on South Asia at large. Firstly, being a Pakistani, I am more familiar with the situation that persists in this part of the world and secondly, in my reckoning, the senior leadership in Pakistan has already devoted adequate attention and importance to this aspect. This in brief explains the raison d'être for this Chapter.

My effort in addressing the issue of "Nuclear Terrorism in Pakistan" would, apart from focusing on Pakistan, also highlight certain generic issues which could possibly be applied elsewhere in the world. My endeavour here would be to start off by elaborating on what my understanding of nuclear terrorism is, what are the means that are available to a nuclear terrorist, how nuclear terrorism could be conducted and for what purpose and, obviously, how Pakistan figures out in all these areas.

Defining Nuclear Terrorism
Defining nuclear terrorism should not be difficult if an acceptable definition for terrorism can be first arrived at. Essentially *nuclear terrorism involves the actual or potential use of nuclear materials to generate fear, in pursuit of*

political goals.[2] As regards a generic definition for terrorism, however, a clear and accepted definition has yet to be arrived at. One of the most definitive illustrations of the meaning of the term that I have come across has been offered by the Institute for Strategic Studies, London, which defines terrorism as being, *the use of violence, often against people not directly involved in a conflict, by groups operating clandestinely, which generally claim to have high political or religious purposes, and believe that creating a climate of terror will assist attainment of their objectives.*[3]

Dimensions of Nuclear Terrorism

The danger of nuclear terrorism has always been present since human beings first mastered the enormous energy of the atom. There has always been a threat that some renegade nuclear scientist would divulge the secrets of the weaponisation of nuclear capability to some unwanted persons or undesirable group of persons but this aspect gained tremendous significance in the aftermath of the tragic incidents of September 11, 2001. One of the first fallouts of this tragic episode was the realisation that the attacks against the World Trade Centre had made it "far more likely" that terrorists would target nuclear facilities, and that states had to cooperate to stop them because "radiation knows no frontiers."[4] A number of factors have contributed to enhancing the threat of nuclear weapons being employed as instruments of terrorism. These include the following:

Spread of Nuclear Weapons and Technology. From the earlier acknowledged five nuclear powers, the number has now increased to eight with the inclusion of India, Pakistan and Israel. Also, several other states, including North Korea and Iran, are actively pursuing the development of this capability. While this greater availability of nuclear weapons is in itself a source of worry, what bothers me even more is the fact that while the earlier five nuclear states embodied developed societies and stable political regimes, some of the new entrants into the nuclear arena are significantly less stable and much less developed.

Unlike the five acknowledged Nuclear Weapons States (NWS) where the nuclear safety regimes have been developed over the past half a century or even more with the requisite safeguards being put in place, the situation in some of the new nuclear states, specifically India and Pakistan, is far from satisfactory. The reasons for this unsatisfactory state of affairs are many, but some of the salient ones are listed below:

- The militaries of these new entrants to the nuclear club have never earlier had a WMD of such proportions available in their inventories and, as such, protecting their weapon arsenals from internal threats is a fairly new phenomenon for them for which they are neither suitably structured nor trained.

- India to a slightly lesser extent and Pakistan almost completely, are focused towards an external threat from each other and this threat assessment has served to divert their thinking from considering the seriousness and magnitude of the internal threat that they are facing. While India is still more conscious because of the serious internal security problems that she is confronted with in Kashmir and elsewhere for several decades, Pakistan's exposure to internal terrorism is fairly recent, albeit equally or even more serious.

- Some of the new nuclear weapons capable states such as Pakistan are also plagued by serious internal differences and factionalism which provides a fertile breeding ground for undesirable elements attempting to gain control over the country's nuclear weapons in their quest to achieve their political ends by holding the existing government and establishment hostage.

- The ever-increasing number of civilian nuclear establishments such as nuclear power plants and research centres poses another danger since these institutions, unlike the military nuclear infrastructure, are seldom well protected or secured against pilferage or outright occupation by undesirable elements. As per one estimate, Pakistan Atomic Energy Commission (PAEC) is managing eleven different medical centres, agricultural research institutes and food processing facilities in various cities of the country.[5] In addition to these facilities, there are also several hospitals in Pakistan that have equipment with radioactive elements.

- The understandable requirement of locating nuclear research establishments far away from major population centres and military bases causes these to be located in remote and sparsely inhabited areas where they are relatively isolated from other supporting security agencies. As such, not only does the imperative of protecting these involve a major task but these centres are also more prone to being targeted by undesirable elements because of their remote and secluded locations.

- The rapidly increasing use of nuclear and radioactive materials in the medical and industrial establishments also presents an opportunity for potential nuclear terrorists to lay their hands on such material. Apart from the fact that these institutions are significantly more vulnerable to unauthorised entry and infiltration, they also do not have any strict system of accounting and record of all the radioactive materials that they consume during their routine functioning.

Understanding the Nature of the Threat

Pakistan, located in the heart of the volatile South Asian region with an implacable enemy right next door, has understandably opted to implement and adhere to an unswerving policy of India-centricity, both in her conventional military development as well as her nuclear weapons programme. Based on the chequered history of their relationship with India over the past 66 years, Pakistan's public as well as her leadership has been brought up on the theme of India being the enemy Number One. This infatuation with the threat that India poses to the very survival of Pakistan as an independent state is manifested in each and every facet of Pakistan's national policies including her National Security Policy. So strongly is this element of external threat emanating from India ingrained into the psyche of Pakistan's security planners that, at times, one finds them neglecting to pay adequate attention to the internal dimensions of the threat faced by them.

The centrality of India in the threat paradigm is obvious when one considers Pakistan's nuclear installations. As a direct fallout of their focus on the Indian threat, most of Pakistan's nuclear installations have been allocated a variety of air defence systems so that any Indian pre-emptive attacks against these could be deterred. This is apparent when one sees the massive array of air defence infrastructure that has been deployed to protect the Kahuta Nuclear Complex—the so-called heart of Pakistan's Uranium enrichment facility, that is located close to the capital city of Islamabad and is being protected by air defence weapons from both air force and army air defence units.

As alluded to earlier, what is more worrying is the spectre of a group of individuals exploiting the laxity that prevails in the safeguarding of nuclear installations in India and Pakistan in order to lay their hands on nuclear or radioactive materials. From the standpoint of nuclear terrorism, it is only this facet of the threat which at best could be described as a "sub-national" or "internal national threat," that must be countered. What needs to be understood by the Pakistani defence planners and those involved with the security of her nuclear installations is the fact that the external threat from India as envisaged by them and the internal threat posed to them by subversive and terrorist groups are two sides of the threat coin, and both these threat dimensions have to be simultaneously addressed to and catered for. This can only happen if they comprehend that apart from the External Regional Dimension of the threat posed to their nuclear installations and assets by India, there is an equally, if not more serious Internal/subregional Dimension of the threat that is presented by the internal dissident groups and individuals. In fact, from the perspective of nuclear terrorism, this "Internal or subregional dimension" of the threat is what actually has to be catered for and addressed to and not the external threat that both the countries perceive is emanating from each other. The difference between the dimensions and implications of the external threat and the internal threat will prove vital in both the countries being able to counter nuclear terrorism and preclude such incidents from occurring in their respective countries.

Instruments of Nuclear Terrorism

Most writers on the subject of nuclear terrorism have prepared veritable lists of the means available to potential nuclear terrorists but most of these can be ruled out in the case of South Asia. This is primarily because of the low scientific and technological base of the populace of both India and Pakistan. Whereas in the West one could possibly expect to come across civilians with the requisite skills, this is not considered possible in South Asia. Moreover, in the West, numerous laboratories and advanced technology workshops exist that could help in developing the necessary components which go to making up a nuclear weapon while these are virtually non-existent in South Asia.

In a report presented to the IAEA Board of Governors on November 30, 2001, the following three main areas of concern as regards the possible means that nuclear terrorists could resort to, were highlighted:[6]

• Theft of a nuclear weapon
• Acquisition of nuclear material
• Nuclear facilities

The relevance of each of these instruments that nuclear terrorists could resort to, specifically from the South Asian perspective, will be addressed in the subsequent text.

Motivation of Nuclear Terrorists. Having attempted to highlight that the only aspect of nuclear terrorism that should worry all is the internal or the subregional/sub-national dimension of this threat, I will now proceed with an elaboration on how and in what manner this internal threat could materialise in South Asia.

As mentioned earlier, basic nuclear technology and expertise has spread so much that laying hands on it should not be considered an impossibility for a determined band of potential terrorists. Having gained access, these undesirable elements could presumably use these in building a so-called "dirty bomb" that would be a terrorist's dream, not only from the point of view of the huge damage that he could cause but also from the perspective of the huge benefits and concessions that he could gain from a scared and unprepared government.

Most terrorists are driven by their convictions and are apt to be believers that the achievement of their goals and ends more than justifies the employment of any means that they could employ. Considering the magnitude of the threat that nuclear terrorism could imply, the involved terrorists could virtually ask for the moon and probably get it. The enormous benefits that could accrue to their perceived "cause" therefore present a sound incentive and reason for terrorists to embark on this path of quest for nuclear weapons and materials. Brahma Chellaney and Paul Leventhal have described this phenomenon of the lure of nuclear weapons for terrorists thus:

Indeed if risk can be calculated as probability times consequence and the low probability of nuclear terrorism is multiplied by the astronomical consequence of a successful act—the risk of nuclear terrorism must be considered to be high, and to be growing in proportion to increases in nuclear weapons, materials and facilities and to the rise of terrorism worldwide.[7]

While it stands to reason that terrorists would be desirous of gaining access to nuclear technology and materials, a study of terrorists and their methodology reveals that seldom if ever have they indulged in acts of terrorism that have led to a large number of casualties. Most extremist groups operate on the edge of "rationality" and as such are generally averse to arousing strong public opinion and outburst against them since this is likely to make the acceptability of their perceived "cause" extremely difficult. From this most analysts infer that the closest that terrorists would ever come to employing nuclear weapons would remain limited to the threat of their use rather than their actual use. Even while subscribing to this line of thinking, one has to accept that in order to make their threat credible and real, nuclear terrorists would have to have demonstrable evidence of their nuclear prowess. This would entail either the physical possession of actual nuclear weapons or control over sensitive nuclear infrastructure that could be blown up with phenomenal nuclear radiation fallout being the main consequence.

Employment of Actual Nuclear Devices by Terrorists. The first possibility of nuclear terrorism that comes to mind is the danger of potential nuclear terrorists obtaining a functional nuclear device along with the expertise to employ it. This, however, is possibly, and fortunately, one of the most remote possibilities that could occur in South Asia for reasons that have been alluded to in the preceding text and will be elaborated upon in the subsequent text.

Notwithstanding the enormous clout that possession of nuclear weapons would bestow on terrorist groups, it will be extremely difficult for them to actually employ these weapons because of the enormous, and at times unpredictable, consequences that could accompany any employment of a nuclear device. It would be far preferable, therefore, for terrorists, even nuclear-capable ones, to play on the fear created by the threat of the use of a nuclear device rather than actually using one. Although the possibility of potential terrorists actually possessing a nuclear weapon is very remote in South Asia, the possibility cannot be ruled out entirely. In my analysis, the following factors impede the terrorist elements laying their hands on functional nuclear warheads:

- In both India and Pakistan, nuclear warheads are essentially maintained in the custody of the armed forces. As such, these are fairly well-protected and difficult to obtain. In Pakistan, the *military controls the nuclear weapons and has instituted a range of measures to tighten controls over the nuclear weapons complex ... and the military is the least corrupt and the most professional part of the Pakistani society.*[8]

- It is believed that India and Pakistan both maintain a major portion of their nuclear warheads in a disassembled or partially built-up state with some of the components even being stored at different locations. This would make it extremely difficult for a terrorist group to obtain a complete and functional nuclear device.[9]

- Indian and Pakistani populations and societies are technologically not as advanced as some of the Western societies where the manufacture of crude and rudimentary nuclear devices is a distinct possibility. In South Asia, any such attempt or endeavour would have to be undertaken with the assistance of trained nuclear physicists who have access to the requisite equipment and tools. The recent reports of some dissident

Pakistani nuclear scientists having contributed to the clandestine Iranian and Libyan nuclear weapons development programmes further highlight how even trained and professional scientific manpower could be lured into revealing nuclear secrets to external individuals or governments without their own Government even coming to know. What this highlights is the high degree of security clearances that all key personnel involved in nuclear development programmes must possess and how strictly their day-to-day life and their dealings must be monitored on a continuous basis.

In view of the foregoing, it is considered highly improbable that potential nuclear terrorists in South Asia will adopt the course of trying to obtain possession of actual nuclear devices.

Acquisition of Nuclear Materials. Since potential nuclear terrorists in South Asia would be aware of the difficulties that they are going to be confronted with in their efforts at acquiring actual nuclear warheads, the next option available to them is to acquire quantities of nuclear materials that they could subsequently develop into a weapon for use as a component in a "dirty bomb." In this context, the answers to the following three essential questions have to be studied and analysed in detail:

- What are the specific radioactive materials that the terrorists are likely to seek to acquire? The prime target of the potential terrorists would be stocks or quantities of weapons-grade radioactive material—either Plutonium or Highly Enriched Uranium (HEU) since both of these could be used in developing a rudimentary nuclear device provided the requisite scientific and technological expertise is available. Normal terrorists, however, are not expected to possess the technological expertise to fabricate even a rudimentary nuclear device without the active support and involvement of nuclear scientists.
- Where are the radioactive materials desired by the terrorists likely to be available?
- How could the terrorists go about their quest to lay hands on the desired radioactive materials?

Occupation/Destruction of Nuclear Institutions/Infrastructure. This is thought to be the second course of action that offers itself to adoption by potential nuclear terrorists. In the South Asian scenario, this emerges to be a much more likely situation for a number of reasons:

- Both India and Pakistan have a multitude of nuclear installations spread all over their respective territories. Some of these installations are sited in very remote areas and are vulnerable to unauthorised intrusion and occupation.
- Nuclear installations in South Asia are protected more against external threat from across the border than against the internal or sub-national threat emanating from within the country. While India apparently is more prepared to deal with this eventuality, Pakistan did not figure out very well in this regard because of the immense magnitude of the threat that it faces from potential terrorists.
- In view of the lax or limited security measures that have been implemented for the defence of nuclear installations, these emerge as prime targets for terrorists with the promise of enormous blackmail potential.

The above factors all highlight that occupation and subsequent destruction of a nuclear facility such as a power plant or a reactor to achieve devastating results such as the ones experienced at Chernobyl is probably one of the most likely routes that potential nuclear terrorists in South Asia could adopt.

The possibility of terrorists occupying nuclear power plants/reactors/ facilities has been a source of concern internationally but not enough importance has been accorded to this aspect of nuclear security. Some analysts have even gone to the extent of suggesting that nuclear power plants are liable to be used as weapons by undesirable elements and if the inherent vulnerabilities of these installations cannot be removed, these plants might as well be closed down:

An enemy sufficiently resourceful and determined could convert today's nuclear power plants to weapons. Perhaps that vulnerability can be corrected. If not, the plants—which are replaceable, though at some cost— should close.[10]

The seriousness of the threat was highlighted by none other than Muhammad Al-Baradei, the Director General of the International Atomic Energy Agency. Expanding on the threat that nuclear terrorism posed to nuclear installations worldwide, he said, "We need to urgently identify the most vulnerable locations and see they get the necessary security upgrades." In the long term, we need to ensure all countries have a stringent nuclear security framework in place—with high standards to abide by, state-of-the art equipment, and people trained in security."[11]

Manpower for Potential Nuclear Terrorist Groups. While India and Pakistan may not possess populace that is scientifically and technologically advanced enough to indulge in the fabrication of crude and rudimentary nuclear devices, one thing that both the countries are not short of is motivated and dedicated individuals who belong to radical cliques and are willing to go to any length to trouble the government. While India has the members of the Kashmiri liberation movements, the insurgents in Mizoram and other parts of North East India, fanatic Hindu adherents of the militant extremist organs, Pakistan has to contend with the numerous remnants of the Taliban who have filtered across the porous Pakistan–Afghanistan border as well as the adherents of the fanatic sectarian militant organisations including the TTP (Tehrik-e-Taleban Pakistan).

- In addition to the presence of these trouble-creating elements, both India and Pakistan are veritable hotbeds of dissatisfied and disgruntled citizens who have been driven to the extremes of desperation and, as such, can be expected to behave in an irrational and explosive manner. Herein lies the biggest threat of nuclear terrorism in South Asia. Both India and Pakistan have literally scores of people who could be driven to the extreme and this, more than anything else, raises the possibility of nuclear terrorism very high in the region.

- While South Asia may be lacking significantly in the capability to produce nuclear weapons for the potential terrorists, there is not expected to be any shortage of misdirected and misguided individuals who would be willing even to lose their precious lives in such foolhardy endeavours for the advancement of their perceived "cause." From this one could conclude that while the capability might not be there, the intent would definitely be there for unscrupulous elements to attempt to resort to the ultimate weapon of terrorism—the nuclear weapon.

In the case of Pakistan, the saving grace is that the nuclear assets are under the direct control of the regular armed forces and this institution is considered relatively free of any extremist elements that could become potential nuclear terrorists.

Strategy to Prevent Nuclear Terrorism in South Asia

In parallel with the recognition of the seriousness of the threat of nuclear terrorism, several think tanks and concerned analysts have worked on the aspect of avoidance of nuclear terrorism. While presenting its agenda for the prevention of nuclear terrorism, the Saferworld Organisation[12] suggested the following steps that needed to be taken on priority:

- Secure nuclear weapons and materials
- Improve biological defences
- Secure and destroy chemical weapons stockpiles

Based on these essential guidelines and an assessment of the peculiar environment that exists in South Asia, the following are some of the steps that are considered necessary so that the occurrence of incidents of nuclear terrorism in this volatile and unstable region can not only be pre-empted but also avoided:

- Both India and Pakistan must enhance the already substantial security under which nuclear arsenals are maintained so as to make it absolutely foolproof and fail-safe through the incorporation of checks in the system that cannot be evaded or tampered with.
- Nuclear weapons must be kept in an unassembled form by both the countries and, wherever possible, the components of these devices must also be kept at different, albeit nearby locations.
- Shifting her focus from the India-centric outlook, Pakistan must recognise the magnitude of the internal and sub-national threat to her nuclear arsenal. This would require her to stay very watchful of the activities of all dissident and radical organisations and groups such as the remnants of the erstwhile Taliban clique.
- All nuclear reactors, power plants and used fuel storage facilities must be well-protected and defended. In the case of Pakistan, the dedicated Nuclear Security Force (NSF) of over 10,000 troops that has been raised under the aegis of the Strategic Plans Division is a good step in this direction. This force, though raised and trained by the Pakistan Army, is distinct from all existing security elements and formations including the armed forces of Pakistan since it falls directly under the SPD.
- A strict check needs to be maintained on the members and the activities of all potential terrorist organisations that exist in both the countries. To further strengthen these endeavours, India and Pakistan could even join hands in exchanging information about such individuals and organisations who could possibly be contemplating nuclear terrorism.
- All personnel employed in the nuclear programmes of the two countries must be thoroughly screened through stringent and comprehensive background checks. Rather than clearing a person only once, these

checks must be repeated on a regular basis and any individual exhibiting tendencies of aligning himself with radical organisations and outfits must be weeded out without the slightest hesitation.

- India and Pakistan need to induct the necessary detection equipment for ensuring that no unwarranted and illegal transportation of nuclear material can take place within the country or across its frontiers.

- A system of strict checks and accounting for all radioactive materials needs to be instituted on a countrywide basis by both the countries so that even a small amount of material becoming unaccountable can be detected and pursued well in time. Other than the nuclear installations, these checks must also encompass all those laboratories, industries and establishments that use radioactive materials for educational, medicinal or industrial purposes.

- Anti-nuclear emergency response teams such as the NEST[13] that exists in the US need to be created in both the countries in order to improve their capability of reacting to unexpected nuclear incidents in a timely manner. These organisations would essentially deal with Nuclear Disaster Management and must be suitably equipped, trained and manned by specialists for this purpose.

- The movement of nuclear materials including radioactive waste in the respective countries must be made as secure as possible so as to preclude any possibility of these being intercepted or taken over by undesirable elements. In the case of Pakistan, it is suggested that the proposed NSF be also assigned the duty of protecting any radioactive materials that are in transit.

- In order to ensure that a comprehensive campaign against nuclear terrorism can be mounted, it must be made necessary for all agencies, institutions and organisations involved in nuclear related work to coordinate their activities in an integrated manner. One option could be for a single central agency to oversee all aspects of this coordination without overstepping its domain and interfering in any way with the functioning of those whose activities it is coordinating. In the case of Pakistan, this task of coordination could be handled by the Strategic Plans Division (SPD).

Conclusion

Nuclear terrorism, like nuclear weapons, is here to stay. The horrendous spectre of the possible consequence that nuclear terrorism could wreak makes it vital for all possible preventive measures being taken to preclude its occurrence. As highlighted in this Chapter, South Asia is different from the industrialised West in that while its inhabitants might not possess the capabilities, they do include a large number of discontented individuals who could possibly join the ranks of nuclear terrorists. This is precisely what makes South Asia such an important region when viewed from the standpoint of controlling nuclear terrorism.

The major area of concern in South Asia is not that the potential terrorists will be able to obtain a nuclear weapon, but the possibility of these elements occupying, destroying or threatening to destroy a nuclear reactor, power plant or research institute with devastating consequences. All the steps required to avoid such an incident must therefore be taken by both Pakistan and India in this regard.

Since the purpose of this Chapter was just to scratch the surface of the subject of nuclear terrorism and its relevance to South Asia, some areas have either been intentionally not covered in detail or have even been omitted. What emerges even from this brief review is the imperative for a much more detailed and elaborate study being undertaken, separately for both the countries so that this issue can be addressed in totality and in a comprehensive manner. From this perspective, the best that this Chapter can be taken as is as a blueprint or an outline of a much more detailed research study that needs to be undertaken.

Considering the wider regional and territorial implications of an act of nuclear terrorism being committed anywhere, it also stands to reason that all the countries that fear the possibility of nuclear terrorism must act to prevent it in a united manner. This activity could be integrated under the purview of either the United Nations or the International Atomic Energy Agency (IAEA) with formalised agreements being arrived at and finalised so that nuclear terrorism can be tackled with a single purpose of mind and with the combined resources of all those who feel threatened by this menace.

In South Asia, this imperative of inter-country coordination and cooperation necessitates the two major countries of the region coming together and adopting an integrated anti-nuclear terrorism strategy. If India and Pakistan manage to arrive at an amicable arrangement that works to the advantage of both, such an agreement would also serve as yet another significant confidence building measure (CBM) that would help to reduce the all-pervasive tension that characterises this volatile and unstable region of the world which has been made all the more dangerous since both India and Pakistan have become nuclear power states.

Notes

1. Emyr Jones Parry, British Ambassador to the United Nations, promoting a US-British draft Security Council resolution on weapons of mass destruction. Thursday, March 25, 2004, Global Security News. http://www.nti.org/d_newswire/issues/2004_3_25.html#F8C783A8.

2. Rajesh Basrur and Hasan Askari Rizvi, "Nuclear Terrorism and South Asia." Cooperative Monitoring Centre (CMC) Occasional Paper No. 25, February 2003, p. 15.

3. "Defining Terrorism: Focusing on Targets." Strategic Comments, 7, 9 (2001) available on the internet at http//:www.iiss.org.stratcomsubarchive. php?scID=193 and also quoted in Basrur and Rizvi, op. cit., p. 17.

4. "Calculating the New Global Atom Threat," Press Release of the International Atomic Energy Agency (IAEA), November 1, 2001. Can be accessed on the Press Releases page of the IAEA website.

5. Basrur and Rizvi, op. cit., p. 53.

6. In addition to identifying these three main instruments of nuclear terrorism, the report also highlighted the importance of the availability of "Emergency Response Teams" during times of incidents of nuclear terrorism. The entire text of the cited IAEA report can be accessed on the internet at the IAEA website.

7. Brahma Chellaney and Leventhal Paul, "Nuclear Terrorism: Threat, Perception and Response in South Asia." Paper prepared under the auspices of the Nuclear Control Institute's Nuclear Terrorism Prevention Project for presentation to the Institute for Defence Studies and Analysis, New Delhi, October 10, 1988. What is interesting about this paper is the fact that it was prepared and presented almost ten years prior to both India and Pakistan emerging from the nuclear closet.

8. David Albright, "Securing Pakistan's Nuclear Weapons Complex." This paper was commissioned and sponsored by the Stanley Foundation for the 42nd Strategy for Peace Conference, held at Warrenton, Virginia from October 25 to 27, 2001.

9. Basrur and Rizvi, op. cit., p. 13.

10. Peter Bradford, former Commissioner to the US Nuclear Regulatory Commission, Professor of Energy Policy at the Yale School of Forestry and Environmental Studies, On Earth Magazine, Winter 2001. Quoted in Mycle Schneider, Director WISE Paris, The threat of nuclear terrorism—from analysis to preventive measures," National Assembly, December 10, 2001.

11. IAEA Press Release 2001/26, "IAEA Outlines Measures to Enhance Protection Against Nuclear Terrorism." The entire text of the press report can be accessed on the IAEA website in the Press Releases section.

12. These priority measures have been extracted from a brochure titled "Act Now for a Safer World" published by Saferworld.org and available on the internet at www.saferworld.org. This project is an effort of the Nuclear Threat Initiative (NTI). www.nti.org.

13. NEST stands for Nuclear Emergency Search Team, a group of nuclear specialists that has been established by the US Government for rapid reaction to any incident of nuclear accident or terrorism. For details, please refer to Chapter titled "The Nuclear Emergency Search Team," by Mahlon E. Gates available at www.nci.org/pdf/nt-book.pdf pp. 394-402.

29   Security of Pakistan's Nuclear Arsenal

Pakistan's nuclear weapons have never been accepted by the world at large, and by India and Israel, in particular. The international propaganda campaign against Pakistan's nuclear weapons arsenal that commenced with her nuclear weapons being wrongly branded as "Islamic Bombs," has continued unabated ever since in one form or the other. The several threats being posed to Pakistan's nuclear weapons, some imaginary and the other real, are varied, multifaceted and different. Lately, the Western print and electronic media has started focusing increasingly on the danger of the Pakistani nuclear weapons falling into the hands of the Islamic fundamentalist elements. In fact, the vested interests in the West simply used Pakistan's bomb to make Islam and aggression synonymous.

When India exploded its first nuclear device at Pokharan in 1974, the Western powers only reacted with the customary "show of concern" and never gave it a second thought. On the other hand, Pakistan's nuclear programme, which was initiated in response to the Indian acquisition of nuclear weapons, evoked immediate and "serious concern" from the same Western powers. This discriminatory attitude has persisted since then and Pakistan has remained under pressure from the US-led lobby to scrap its programme while the Indians remained relatively and comparatively uncensored. This became apparent when India and the US signed a bilateral nuclear cooperation deal at a time when Pakistan's nuclear system still remained under sanctions.

On one hand, the Western print and electronic media have started continuously and increasingly highlighting the danger of the Pakistani nuclear weapons falling into the hands of the Islamic fundamentalist elements, and have even cited some alleged incidents of this nature that have already occurred, while on the other, there is a growing apprehension regarding the possibility of the US mounting an attack to forcibly attempt to de-nuclearise Pakistan. According to a US analyst, a senior Pakistani military officer confided that he and many of his colleagues believed that the US would move against (Pakistan's) nuclear facilities shortly after the American combat role in Afghanistan ends.

Threats to Pakistan's Nuclear Arsenal
In summary, the threat posed to Pakistan's nuclear weapons could be divided into external and internal threats, which can be further categorised into the following possible scenarios:

External Threat Scenarios	
Scenario A	A joint Indian/Israeli air attack with US intelligence support but with or without active US assistance.
Scenario B	A US Special Forces raid similar to the operation conducted to capture Osama bin Laden.
Scenario C	Counter-force employment by Indian Army.
Domestic Threat Scenarios	
Scenario D	Attack by Taliban/TTP.
Scenario E	Operation by Rogue Elements of the Pakistani military.

Strengths of Pakistan's Nuclear Weapons Control System

The Pakistan military realises fully that its nuclear weapons face a host of threats and as such, ensures that all possible measures are taken to protect them. Since these measures contribute to enhancing the "protectability" of the nuclear arsenal, they could also be categorised as the "strengths" of the system. Of the several steps and measures taken in this regard, the following need to be mentioned:

- **Secret locations**. All the nuclear weapons are kept at extremely secret and secure locations. These locations are never disclosed to unauthorised personnel and are also changed frequently and without prior warning.
- **Staggered locations**. Nuclear weapons are always maintained in a de-mated or semi-assembled stage with the various component elements being also stored at different locations. This makes the job of the attackers very difficult since they would not only have to know exactly where each component is located but will also need to launch a coordinated attack simultaneously at all these targets.
- **Dedicated Defence Force**. The Strategic Plans Division (SPD) maintains a dedicated security force of almost 10,000 trained troops who are entrusted with providing security to the nuclear weapons. These troops are imparted training with the regular infantry training establishments such as the Regimental Centres of the Infantry Regiments.
- **Security Screening of Personnel**. All personnel deployed on duty with SPD or any other organisation dealing directly with nuclear weapons have to regularly undergo periodic, albeit thorough, security screening. The security clearance of these personnel is repeated at short intervals.
- **Permissive Action Links (PALs)**. Although initially established with the help and assistance of the US military, this mechanism has been extensively modified and improved to meet the indigenous needs and requirements.

Frequent Changes in Officer Level Manpower. Manpower at the officer level is changed frequently after short tenures with the SPD (Joint Staff Headquarters), ASFC (Pakistan Army Strategic Forces Command at GHQ) and AFSC (Pakistan Air Force Strategic Command at the Air Headquarters in Islamabad).

Deficiencies in Pakistan's Nuclear Weapons Control System (NWCS)

Domination by the Army

Traditionally, the Pakistan Army has dominated the Pakistan nuclear programme starting from its origin to its development and subsequent employment. For a very short period initially when the only nuclear weapons available to Pakistan were air-delivered nuclear weapons, the PAF did figure prominently in the country's nuclear weapons programme. With the development of the strategic nuclear capable missiles in substantial numbers, however, the Pakistan Army regained its prominence which it has maintained ever since. The pre-eminence of the Pakistan Army in nuclear affairs is evidenced by the following:

- The Pakistan Strategic Plans Division (SPD) has always been headed by a serving or retired Lieutenant General from the Pakistan Army, and while the SPD is nominally placed under the JSHQ, it continues to maintain very strong ties and links with the Pakistan Army and its senior leadership. Neither the Pakistan Navy nor the Air Force have ever been permitted to nominate one of their officers for this key slot.
- There is no representation of either the political leadership, the civilian bureaucracy or the nuclear scientist community in the working level of the SPD. In fact the complete SPD organisation is manned entirely by uniformed personnel, a very high number of which belongs to the Pakistan Army.
- During times of Martial Law when Pakistan is traditionally ruled by the Chief of the Army Staff who acts as the Chief Martial Law Administrator/President, virtually the entire nuclear weapons apparatus is controlled solely by the Army. During such a situation, all the three tiers of the country's nuclear weapons programme would be controlled by the Army, thus creating a serious and strategic imbalance in the system.
- Other than the DG of the SPD, the Army also nominates another Lieutenant General as the head of the Army's Strategic Force Command (ASFC) who sits in the GHQ and actually controls the entire arsenal of strategic ballistic missiles.

Increasing Trend towards Religiosity in the Military

There is a visible and discernible shift towards increasing religiosity in the ranks of the Pakistan military. This shift, the origins of which could be traced back to the time of General Zia-ul Haq's tenure, or even earlier, poses a serious challenge to the hitherto secular posture and nature of the Pakistan military. This is specially worrisome considering the increasing trend towards Islamic fundamentalism which is sweeping the entire country.

Increasing Corruption in the Military

Being an integral part of the national social fabric, personnel in the military are as prone to being tempted away from the path of righteousness as any other citizen. This has become visible as several acts of corruption have started being reported in the national media, something that was virtually unimaginable and unexpected barely a few years ago. Although this might never happen, the possibility of a corrupt group of military officers getting compromised certainly exists and must be guarded against, specially in the realm of nuclear weapons handling.

Exclusion of the Civilian Government Officials from SPD

The entire SPD set-up is manned completely by uniformed military personnel with even areas such as Disarmament Negotiations, which are generally best handled by senior diplomats, and Weapons Development issues, which would be best handled by nuclear scientists, also assigned to regular military officers. These steps further serve to increase the hold of the military on the country's nuclear weapons programme.

While undertaking these improvements by inducting civilians and reducing the excessive presence of Army officers in the NWCS and vital organs of the SPD, more officers from the Navy and the Air Force need to be inducted.

Shifting SPD under Ministry of Defence

The SPD is currently a part of the Joint Staff Headquarters which itself is dominated by the Army. In order to reduce the influence of the Army in nuclear affairs, the following steps should be taken:

- SPD be formally placed under the Ministry of Defence
- Equal percentage of officers from all three armed services should be included in the SPD
- This should be done on rotational basis

Analysis of the Possible Scenarios

Scenario "A": Joint Indian/Israeli/US air attack on Pakistan's NWCS

Their success in neutralising the Iraqi nuclear reactor in 1981 probably encouraged the Israelis to contemplate a similar attack against Pakistan's nuclear facilities near Kahuta. Accordingly, joint Indo-Israeli planning for this operation was initiated in early 1980s with the help of using intelligence information that was provided by the US/CIA. The Israeli pilots, some of whom had participated in the attack on the Iraqi reactor, reportedly built a full-scale mock-up of Kahuta facility in the southern Negev Desert and Israeli pilots went through mock attack exercises.

According to the story published in London by *The Asian Age* citing revelations by journalists Adrian Levy and Catherine Scott-Clark in their book *Deception: Pakistan, the US and the Global Weapons Conspiracy*, the Israeli Air Force planned to launch an air attack on Kahuta in mid 1980s from Jamnagar airfield in Gujarat (India) and land and refuel at a base in northern India. The book claims that "in March 1984, PM Indira Gandhi formally accorded her assent to the Israeli-led operation ... ."

Another report claims that Israel had planned to launch an air strike directly out of Israel. After midway and mid-air refueling, Israeli warplanes were to shoot down a commercial airline's flight over the Indian Ocean that routinely flew into Islamabad early morning. The Israelis would have flown in a tight formation to appear as one large aircraft on radar screens preventing detection. Using the drowned airliner's call sign they would have entered Islamabad's air space, knocked out Kahuta and flown on to land in Jammu in Indian Held Kashmir to refuel and make an exit.

Reliable reports say that in mid 1980s this mission was actually launched one night. But the Israelis were in for a big surprise. They discovered that Pakistan Air Force had already sounded an alert and had taken to the skies in anticipation of this attack. The Indo-Israeli mission had to be hurriedly called off. Pakistan reminded the Israelis that Pakistan was no Iraq and that Pakistan Air Force was no Iraqi Air Force. Using indirect channels, Pakistan is reported to have conveyed that an attack on Kahuta would force Pakistan to lay waste to Dimona, Israel's nuclear reactor in the Negev Desert. Pakistan drew up contingency plans for retaliatory strike on Dimona in case of any future Israeli misadventure. India was also warned that Islamabad would attack Trombay if its facilities in Kahuta were hit. The above quoted book claims that "Prime Minister Indira Gandhi eventually aborted the operation despite protests from military planners in New Delhi and Jerusalem."

In the aftermath of the Indian nuclear tests, Pakistan felt that there was an increased possibility of a joint Indo-Israeli strike against her nuclear installations, with the PAF being required to play a vital role in countering any such attack. The tensions were so high that a PAF F-16 flying low near the nuclear test site on the eve of the Pakistani nuclear tests was, for a moment, mistaken by the personnel on the ground, to be an Israeli warplane and almost caused a serious diplomatic incident between the two countries.

The Pakistan Ambassador to the UN, Ahmed Kamal, told CNN that Pakistan had reliable information about Indian intentions to launch air strikes against Pakistan's nuclear test facilities. He warned that if India strikes, Pakistan's response would be "massive" and would "bode ill for peace." Ambassador Kamal went on to say, "We're involved in this threat and in making sure that it does not arise because if it does, the world must understand that Pakistan is ready, that it will react, that the reaction will be massive and dissuasive, and that it would lead us into a situation which would bode ill for peace and security, not only in the region, but beyond."

In another similar development right on the eve of Pakistan's nuclear tests, Ambassador Munir Akram while speaking at the UN Conference on Disarmament on May 29, 1998, informed the delegates that in the wake of India's recent nuclear tests, Pakistan had been receiving information of the possibility of attacks on its nuclear installations to prevent the country from taking appropriate decisions in its supreme national interest to respond to Indian actions. He said that the Pakistani Foreign Ministry had just issued a statement saying that last night, Pakistan had received credible information that an attack was to be mounted before dawn. The Indian High Commissioner in Islamabad had, therefore, been summoned to the Foreign Ministry early today and asked to convey to New Delhi that Pakistan expected the Indian Government to desist from any irresponsible act. Ambassador Akram said the Indian High Commissioner in Islamabad had been clearly told that any attack on Pakistan's nuclear facilities would be in violation of an existing agreement between the two countries. Any such act would warrant a swift and massive retaliation with unforeseen consequences. Simultaneously, Pakistan had also sent immediate messages to the permanent members of the Security Council, and it had asked the United Nations Secretary-General to counsel restraint on New Delhi. Interestingly, both these senior Pakistani diplomats did not mention regarding an Israeli involvement in the anticipated attack against Pakistan's nuclear installations.

Scenario "B": A US special Forces raid similar to the one conducted to capture Osama bin Laden.

The raid by US special operation forces into the Pakistani garrison town of Abbottabad in May of 2011 to kill Osama bin Laden has been taken as a warning signal by Chief of Army Staff General Ashfaq Kayani of what to expect. The US Government dispatched Senator John Kerry to Pakistan shortly after the raid to explain the American position but did not reduce the general's anxieties when he declined to provide a written guarantee that the US would not attack the Pakistani nuclear storage facilities.

The Pakistan high command believes that the US does not want a Muslim country to possess nuclear weapons and will at some time in the future attempt to seize or destroy its arsenal. Since September 2001, much of the American military action has been directed towards Muslim states. These two facts are enough to convince Pakistan that it is only a matter of time before the US would take on her ally in an attempt aimed at "defanging" the sole Muslim nuclear country of the world.

What makes the matters even worse is the fact that the Americans have a very strong and extremely potent military presence in Afghanistan and till very recently, they had sizeable elements of their military deployed in Tarbela, Shamsi and the FATA. This is why a dedicated Nuclear Defence Force has been established under the Strategic Plans Division (SPD). This force of between 8,000 to 10,000 specially trained troops has been mandated to protect the nuclear storage facilities from an American attempt to seize or destroy the nuclear weapons.

Notwithstanding her strategic desire to de-nuclearise Pakistan, however, I believe that the US cannot contemplate embarking on such a plan till well after a majority of the US forces have been evacuated from Afghanistan. As such, my expectation is that the US military would only contemplate an offensive against the Pakistan NWCS until at least the following conditions are met:

- The majority of the US/ISAF/NATO forces have been evacuated from Afghanistan.
- The Afghanistan National Army has reached adequate manpower strength and training levels.
- The Taliban have been neutralised to a level where they can be adequately handled and countered by the Afghanistan National Army and the Afghan paramilitary forces.
- The Taliban elements who are surviving on the Pakistan side of the Durand Line have been neutralised/weakened to an extent where they cannot interfere with the safe withdrawal of the US forces.

- Pakistan and Afghanistan armies are in a position to sanitise the border belt between both the countries, on both sides of the Durand Line.

It would be evident to the reader that Pakistan's relevance for the US would continue to increase as the time for the withdrawal of the foreign forces from Afghanistan nears. As such, it would be extremely difficult for the US to contemplate taking any offensive action till well after the last US soldier has vacated Afghanistan.

Scenario "C": Counter-force employment by Indian Army

This eventuality could possibly occur during an Indo-Pakistan war where India might react to a Pakistani counter-force strike. The probability of this scenario has increased more since the implementation of the Cold Start Doctrine and the circulation of unconfirmed reports that both India and Pakistan have embarked on the development of tactical nuclear weapons.

With the adoption of the Cold Start doctrine, the Indian Army envisions being able to minimise the mobilisation time as well as the time needed to make sizeable inroads inside Pakistani territory and/or inflict serious damage to Pakistan's military capability. Both of these actions could be expected to make Pakistan cross her nuclear threshold and as such, the adoption of the Cold Start doctrine could well have precipitated the acceleration of the development of tactical nuclear weapons by Pakistan.

Scenario "D": Attack by Taliban/TTP

Writing in the Foreign Policy Journal, Christina Fair says, "the pre-eminent concern among Americans—and increasingly among many Pakistanis too—is that some personnel may support Islamist terrorism in the region and beyond or that perhaps a radical, rogue Islamist column may split off within the Army, endangering Pakistan's stability and the security of its nuclear weapons. Others fear that radical personnel might even give nuclear devices or technology to terrorists. Equally important is that some US observers equate greater Islamisation with deepening anti-Americanism within the Army."

These apprehensions have been galvanised by the numerous terrorist attacks on military and intelligence institutions and personnel that have involved actual or perceived assistance from within the armed forces.

During recent months, the religious militant elements have amply demonstrated their military prowess, capability and potential by conducting attacks/raids against the following military installations/targets:

- General Headquarters of the Pakistan Army
- Pakistan Air Force Base at Kamra (Minhas)

- Pakistan Navy's Mehran Aviation Base in Karachi
- Pakistan Ordnance Factories
- Pakistan Air Force bus plying on the Sargodha-Faisalabad road
- Pakistan Air Force school bus plying on the Kamra-Attock road

The following aspects of these incidents merit special mention:
- None of these incidents was aimed against any nuclear installation.
- The majority of these incidents were aimed at causing maximum human casualties of non-uniformed civilian personnel/children.
- The two incidents that caused serious damage to military equipment were the ones against PAF Base Kamra and against PNS Mehran. While the first led to an AEW aircraft being damaged/destroyed, the second resulted in the destruction of an ASW platform.
- The two incidents against military vehicles were both conducted while these vehicles were plying on mail intercity roads and did not target any military facility or infrastructure.

Scenario "E": Operation by rogue Pakistani military elements
Extremist elements in Pakistan have been encouraged by the growing anti-Americanism that is sweeping across the country and have exploited the growing wave of conservatism to attract more recruits from amongst the military.

Reportedly, at least 12 other officers, mostly from junior ranks but including one Brigadier serving in the GHQ, were arrested on suspicion of extremist links. The senior most officer, Brigadier Ali Khan was subsequently tried by Court Martial, convicted and imprisoned.

Assessment of Possible Scenarios
Having conducted an analysis of all the five possible scenarios, I would like to conclude by conducting an assessment of these by evaluating them against each of the following eight parameters:
- Likelihood of occurrence
- Expected Chances of success
- Degree of success achievable
- Danger of Escalation
- Expected time frame
- De-nuclearisation of Pakistan
- Damage to life and property
- National/International implications

Assessment of Scenario "A"

Joint Indo-Israeli air attack with US intelligence support but with or without active US involvement	
Likelihood of occurrence	Fairly high
Chances of success	Fairly high
Degree of success achievable	Significant
Danger of Escalation	Extremely high
Expected time frame	After US evacuation from Afghanistan
De-nuclearisation of Pakistan	Not achievable
Damage to life and property	Limited
National/International implications	International

Assessment of Scenario "B"

US Special Forces raid similar to the operation conducted to capture Osama bin Laden in Abbottabad	
Likelihood of occurrence	Fairly high
Expected Chances of success	Fairly high
Degree of success achievable	Significant
Danger of Escalation	Very high
Expected time frame	Prior to the US evacuation from Afghanistan
De-nuclearisation of Pakistan	Not achievable
Damage to life and property	Limited
National/International implications	International

Assessment of Scenario "C"

Counter-force Employment by the Indian Military	
Likelihood of occurrence	Very Low
Expected Chances of success	High
Degree of success achievable	Significant
Danger of Escalation	Extremely high
Expected time frame	Indeterminable
De-nuclearisation of Pakistan	Not achievable
Damage to life and property	Fairly High
National/International implications	International

Assessment of Scenario "D"

Attack by Taliban/TTP	
Likelihood of occurrence	Medium
Expected Chances of success	Low
Degree of success achievable	Partial
Danger of Escalation	None
Expected time frame	After US evacuation from Afghanistan
De-nuclearisation of Pakistan	Not achievable
Damage to life and property	Limited
National/International implications	National

Assessment of Scenario "E"

Operation by Rogue Elements of the Pakistani Military	
Likelihood of occurrence	Very Low
Chances of success	Very Low
Degree of success achievable	Limited
Danger of Escalation	None
Expected time frame	Indeterminable
De-nuclearisation of Pakistan	Not achievable
Damage to life and property	Limited
National/International implications	National

Conclusion

The following salient aspects have emerged from the analysis and assessment of the five possible scenarios:

- All three international scenarios would be influenced by the events in Afghanistan and the continued presence of the US forces in that country.
- The three international scenarios emerge as the most dangerous ones.
- The total de-nuclearisation of Pakistan is not a possibility that emerges as an outcome of any of these scenarios.
- The two domestic scenarios both have very low probability of occurrence as well as low chances of success.
- The three international scenarios have the maximum threat of conflict escalation while the domestic ones pose the least.
- Since the one hundred or so nuclear weapons that are expected to be there in Pakistan's nuclear arsenal are all widely spread all around the country, it is virtually impossible for an attacker to plan to take all of these out in one move.

Commencing with an evaluation of the vast variety of threats that the Pakistan NWCS is faced with and has to contend with, this paper then delved at length on the strengths and weaknesses of the System before venturing into a detailed analysis of the five possible scenarios and finally concluded with an assessment of the possible scenarios.

The conclusions of this paper might not appear to be aiming at presenting a complete solution to the issue of ensuring adequate protection to NWCS. Instead, these attempt to offer a set of detailed, considered and deliberated guidelines that could be used to shape the future nuclear policy for Pakistan from the standpoint of being able to ensure its security.

Annexes and References

Agreement between India & Pakistan on Prohibition of Attack Against Nuclear Installations and Facilities

December 31, 1988

The Government of the Islamic Republic of Pakistan and the Government of the Republic of India, hereinafter referred to as the Contracting Parties, reaffirming their commitment to durable peace and the development of friendly and harmonious bilateral relations; conscious of the role of confidence building measures in promoting such bilateral relations based on mutual trust and goodwill; have agreed as follows:

1.
    i.   Each party shall refrain from undertaking, encouraging or participating in, directly or indirectly, any action aimed at causing the destruction of, or damage to, any nuclear installation or facility in the other country.

    ii.   The term "nuclear installation or facility" includes nuclear power and research reactors, fuel fabrication, uranium enrichment, isotopes separation and reprocessing facilities as well as any other installations with fresh or irradiated nuclear fuel and materials in any form and establishments storing significant quantities of radioactive materials.

2.   Each Contracting Party shall inform the other on 1st January of each calendar year of the latitude and longitude of its nuclear installations and facilities and whenever there is any change.

3.   This Agreement is subject to ratification. It shall come into force with effect from the date on which the Instruments of Ratification are exchanged.

Done at Islamabad on this Thirty-first day of December 1988, in two copies each in Urdu, Hindi and English, the English text being authentic in case of any difference or dispute of interpretation.

Reference B

The Lahore Declaration

The following is the text of the Lahore Declaration signed by the Prime Minister, Mr. A. B. Vajpayee, and the Pakistan Prime Minister, Mr. Nawaz Sharif, in Lahore on Sunday:

The Prime Ministers of the Republic of India and the Islamic Republic of Pakistan:

- Sharing a vision of peace and stability between their countries, and of progress and prosperity for their peoples;
- Convinced that durable peace and development of harmonious relations and friendly cooperation will serve the vital interests of the peoples of the two countries, enabling them to devote their energies for a better future;
- Recognising that the nuclear dimension of the security environment of the two countries adds to their responsibility for avoidance of conflict between the two countries;
- Committed to the principles and purposes of the Charter of the United Nations, and the universally accepted principles of peaceful coexistence;
- Reiterating the determination of both countries to implementing the Simla Agreement in letter and spirit;
- Committed to the objective of universal nuclear disarmament and non-proliferation;
- Convinced of the importance of mutually agreed confidence building measures for improving the security environment;
- Recalling their agreement of 23rd September 1998, that an environment of peace and security is in the supreme national interest of both sides and that the resolution of all outstanding issues, including Jammu and Kashmir, is essential for this purpose;
- Have agreed that their respective Governments:
  - shall intensify their efforts to resolve all issues, including the issue of Jammu and Kashmir.
  - shall refrain from intervention and interference in each other's internal affairs.
  - shall intensify their composite and integrated dialogue process for an early and positive outcome of the agreed bilateral agenda.
  - shall take immediate steps for reducing the risk of accidental or unauthorised use of nuclear weapons and discuss concepts and doctrines with a view to elaborating measures for confidence building in the nuclear and conventional fields, aimed at prevention of conflict.
  - reaffirm their commitment to the goals and objectives of SAARC and to concert their efforts towards the realisation of the SAARC vision for the year 2000 and beyond with a view to promoting the welfare of the peoples of South Asia and to improve their quality of life through

accelerated economic growth, social progress and cultural development.
○   reaffirm their condemnation of terrorism in all its forms and manifestations and their determination to combat this menace.
○   shall promote and protect all human rights and fundamental freedoms.

Signed at Lahore on the 21st day of February 1999.
Atal Bihari Vajpayee—Prime Minister of the Republic of India
Muhammad Nawaz Sharif—Prime Minister of the Islamic Republic of Pakistan

Reference C

Joint statement

The following is the text of the Joint Statement issued at the end of the Prime Minister, Mr. A. B. Vajpayee's visit to Lahore:

In response to an invitation by the Prime Minister of Pakistan, Mr. Muhammad Nawaz Sharif, the Prime Minister of India, Shri Atal Bihari Vajpayee, visited Pakistan from 20-21 February 1999, on the inaugural run of the Delhi-Lahore bus service.

2. The Prime Minister of Pakistan received the Indian Prime Minister at the Wagah border on 20th February 1999. A banquet in honour of the Indian Prime Minister and his delegation was hosted by the Prime Minister of Pakistan at Lahore Fort, on the same evening. Prime Minister, Atal Behari Vajpayee, visited Minar-e-Pakistan, Mausoleum of Allama Iqabal, Gurudawara Dera Sahib and Samadhi of Maharaja Ranjeet Singh. On 21st February, a civic reception was held in honour of the visiting Prime Minister at the Governor's House.

3. The two leaders held discussions on the entire range of bilateral relations, regional cooperation within SAARC, and issues of international concern. They decided that:

    (a) The two Foreign Ministers will meet periodically to discuss all issues of mutual concern, including nuclear related issues.

    (b) The two sides shall undertake consultations on WTO related issues with a view to coordinating their respective positions.

    (c) The two sides shall determine areas of cooperation in Information Technology, in particular for tackling the problems of Y2K.

    (d) The two sides will hold consultations with a view to further liberalising the visa and travel regime.

    (e) The two sides shall appoint a two member committee at ministerial level to examine humanitarian issues relating to Civilian detainees and missing POWs.

4. They expressed satisfaction on the commencement of a Bus Service between Lahore and New Delhi, the release of fishermen and civilian detainees and the renewal of contacts in the field of sports.

5. Pursuant to the directive given by the two Prime Ministers, the Foreign Secretaries of Pakistan and India signed a Memorandum of Understanding on 21st February 1999, identifying measures aimed at promoting an environment of peace and security between the two countries.

6. The two Prime Ministers signed the Lahore Declaration embodying their shared vision of peace and stability between their countries and of progress and prosperity for their peoples.

7. Prime Minister, Atal Bihari Vajpayee extended an invitation to Prime Minister, Muhammad Nawaz Sharif, to visit India on mutually convenient dates.

8. Prime Minister, Atal Bihari Vajpayee, thanked Prime Minister, Muhammad Nawaz Sharif, for the warm welcome and gracious hospitality extended to him and members of his delegation and for the excellent arrangements made for his visit.

Lahore,
February 21, 1999

Reference D

Memorandum of Understanding

The following is the text of the Memorandum of Understanding signed by the Foreign Secretary, Mr. K. Raghunath, and the Pakistan Foreign Secretary, Mr. Shamshad Ahmad, in Lahore on Sunday:

The Foreign Secretaries of India and Pakistan:

Reaffirming the continued commitment of their respective governments to the principles and purposes of the UN Charter:

- Reiterating the determination of both countries to implementing the Shimla Agreement in letter and spirit;
- Guided by the agreement between their Prime Ministers of 23rd September 1998 that an environment of peace and security is in the supreme national interest of both sides and that resolution of all outstanding issues, including Jammu and Kashmir, is essential for this purpose;
- Pursuant to the directive given by their respective Prime Ministers in Lahore, to adopt measures for promoting a stable environment of peace, and security between the two countries;

Have on this day, agreed to the following:

1. The two sides shall engage in bilateral consultations on security concepts, and nuclear doctrines, with a view to developing measures for confidence building in the nuclear and coventional fields, aimed at avoidance of conflict.

2. The two sides undertake to provide each other with advance notification in respect of ballistic missile flight tests, and shall conclude a bilateral agreement in this regard.

3. The two sides are fully committed to undertaking national measures to reducing the risks of accidental or unauthorised use of nuclear weapons under their respective control. The two sides further undertake to notify each other immediately in the event of any accidental, unauthorised or unexplained incident that could create the risk of a fallout with adverse consequences for both sides, or an outbreak of a nuclear war between the two countries, as well as to adopt measures aimed at diminishing the possibility of such actions, or such incidents being misinterpreted by the other. The two side, shall identify/establish the appropriate communication mechanism for this purpose.

4. The two sides shall continue to abide by their respective unilateral moratorium on conducting further nuclear test explosions unless either side, in exercise of its national sovereignty decides that extraordinary events have jeopardised its supreme interests.

5. The two sides shall conclude an agreement on prevention of incidents at sea in order to ensure safety of navigation by naval vessels, and aircraft belonging to the two sides.

6. The two sides shall periodically review the implementation of existing Confidence Building Measures (CBMs) and where necessary, set up appropriate consultative mechanisms to monitor and ensure effective implementation of these CBMs.

7. The two sides shall undertake a review of the existing communication links (e.g. between the respective Directors-General, Military Operations) with a view to upgrading and improving these links, and to provide for fail-safe and secure communications.

8. The two sides shall engage in bilateral consultations on security, disarmament and non-proliferation issues within the context of negotiations on these issues in multilateral fora. Where required, the technical details of the above measures will be worked out by experts of the two sides in meetings to be held on mutually agreed dates, before mid 1999, with a view to reaching bilateral agreements.

Done at Lahore on 21st February 1999 in the presence of Prime Minister of India, Mr. Atal Bihari Vajpayee, and Prime Minister of Pakistan, Mr. Muhammad Nawaz Sharif.

Reference E

Statement issued after meeting of Pakistan NSC on 05 September, 2013

A statement of the NCA was held under the chairmanship of the Prime Minister Mian Muhammad Nawaz Sharif on September 05. The meeting was attended all the members of the NCA, Federal Ministers of Finance and Interior, the Adviser to the PM on National Security and Foreign Affairs, Special Assistant the PM on Foreign Affairs, the Chairman Joint Chiefs of Staff Committee and the three Service Chiefs.

The NCA reaffirmed the *centrality of Pakistan's nuclear programme for the defence of the country*. The NCA reposed full confidence in Pakistan's robust Command and Control structure and all the security controls related to the strategic assets of the country. The NCA paid rich tributes to the various scientists as well as the security and policy level officials and diplomats who are associated with Pakistan's strategic programme.

The NCA *reviewed developments at the regional level and reiterated that as a responsible nuclear weapon state, Pakistan would continue to adhere to the policy of Credible Minimum Deterrence, without entering into an arms race with any other country.* Pakistan, however, would not remain oblivious to the evolving security dynamics in South Asia and would *maintain full spectrum deterrence capability to deter all forms of aggression.*

The NCA also *reviewed the developments at the international level and took note of the discriminatory trends and policies* that could have serious implications for Pakistan's national security and the global non-proliferation regime. The NCA reiterated that while maintaining its principled position on various arms control and non-proliferation issues, Pakistan would continue to oppose any arrangement that is detrimental to its security and strategic interests. As for the Fissile Material Cut-off Treaty FM(C)T, Pakistan's position will be determined by its national interests and the objectives of strategic stability in South Asia.

The meeting underscored Pakistan's commitment to play its due part as a mainstream partner in the global non-proliferation regime, and renewed Pakistan's keen interest in joining the multilateral export control regimes on a non-discriminatory basis. Pakistan has the requisite credentials for full access to civilian nuclear technology for peaceful purposes to meet its growing need energy needs for continued economic growth. The meeting noted the importance of Pakistan's positive outreach and enhanced engagement with all the multilateral export control regimes including membership of the Nuclear Suppliers Group (NSG).

The NCA emphasised that Pakistan will continue to participate constructively in the Nuclear Security Summit (NSS) process. As a responsible nuclear weapon state with advanced technology and four-decade long experience in safe and secure operation of nuclear power plants, Pakistan is ready to share its expertise with other interested states by providing fuel cycle services under IAEA safeguards and by providing placements at its Centres of Excellence on Nuclear Security.

Reference F

Amended draft Indian Nuclear Doctrine 2003

1. The Cabinet Committee on Security (CCS) met today to review the progress in operationalising of India's nuclear doctrine. The Committee decided that the following information, regarding the nuclear doctrine and operational arrangements governing India's nuclear assets, should be shared with the public.

2. India's nuclear doctrine can be summarised as follows:
   i.   Building and maintaining a credible minimum deterrent;
   ii. A posture of "No First Use" nuclear weapons will only be used in retaliation against a nuclear attack on Indian territory or on Indian forces anywhere;
   iii. Nuclear retaliation to a first strike will be massive and designed to inflict unacceptable damage.
   iv. Nuclear retaliatory attacks can only be authorised by the civilian political leadership through the Nuclear Command Authority.
   v.   Non-use of nuclear weapons against non-nuclear weapon states;
   vi. However, in the event of a major attack against India, or Indian forces anywhere, by biological or chemical weapons, India will retain the option of retaliating with nuclear weapons;
   vii. A continuance of strict controls on export of nuclear and missile related materials and technologies, participation in the Fissile Material Cut-off Treaty negotiations, and continued observance of the moratorium on nuclear tests.
   viii. Continued commitment to the goal of a nuclear weapon free world, through global, verifiable and non-discriminatory nuclear disarmament.

3. The Nuclear Command Authority comprises a Political Council and an Executive Council. The Political Council is chaired by the Prime Minister. It is the sole body which can authorise the use of nuclear weapons.

4. The Executive Council is chaired by the National Security Advisor. It provides inputs for decision making by the Nuclear Command Authority and executes the directives given to it by the Political Council.

5. The CCS reviewed the existing command and control structures, the state of readiness, the targeting strategy for a retaliatory attack, and operating procedures for various stages of alert and launch. The Committee expressed satisfaction with the overall preparedness. The CCS approved the appointment of a Commander-in-Chief, Strategic Forces Command, to manage and administer all Strategic Forces.

6. The CCS also reviewed and approved the arrangements for alternate chains of command for retaliatory nuclear strikes in all eventualities.

Issued by Cabinet Committee on Security
04 January, 2003